Promoting Health, Preventing Disease

The Economic Case

The European Observatory on Health Systems and Policies supports and promotes evidence-based health policy-making through comprehensive and rigorous analysis of health systems in Europe. It brings together a wide range of policy-makers, academics and practitioners to analyse trends in health reform, drawing on experience from across Europe to illuminate policy issues.

The European Observatory on Health Systems and Policies is a partnership between the World Health Organization Regional Office for Europe, the Governments of Austria, Belgium, Finland, Ireland, Norway, Slovenia, Sweden, the United Kingdom, and the Veneto Region of Italy, the European Commission, the World Bank, UNCAM (French National Union of Health Insurance Funds), the London School of Economics and Political Science, and the London School of Hygiene & Tropical Medicine.

World Health Organization
REGIONAL OFFICE FOR Europe

OECD
BETTER POLICIES FOR BETTER LIVES

European
Observatory
on Health Systems and Policies
a partnership hosted by WHO

Promoting Health, Preventing Disease

The Economic Case

Edited by

David McDaid, Franco Sassi and Sherry Merkur

Mc
Graw
Hill
Education

Open University Press

Open University Press
McGraw-Hill Education
McGraw-Hill House
Shoppenhangers Road
Maidenhead
Berkshire
England
SL6 2QL

email: enquiries@openup.co.uk
world wide web: www.openup.co.uk

and Two Penn Plaza, New York, NY 10121-2289, USA

First published 2015

A catalogue record of this book is available from the British Library

ISBN-13: 978-0-335-26226-7
ISBN-10: 0-335-26226-0
eISBN: 978-0-335-26227-4

Library of Congress Cataloging-in-Publication Data
CIP data applied for

Typeset by RefineCatch Limited, Bungay, Suffolk

European Observatory on Health Systems and Policies Series

The European Observatory on Health Systems and Policies is a unique project that builds on the commitment of all its partners to improving health systems:

- World Health Organization Regional Office for Europe
- Government of Austria
- Government of Belgium
- Government of Finland
- Government of Ireland
- Government of Norway
- Government of Slovenia
- Government of Sweden
- Government of the United Kingdom
- Veneto Region of Italy
- European Commission
- World Bank
- UNCAM
- London School of Economics and Political Science
- London School of Hygiene & Tropical Medicine

The series

The volumes in this series focus on key issues for health policymaking in Europe. Each study explores the conceptual background, outcomes and lessons learned about the development of more equitable, more efficient and more effective health systems in Europe. With this focus, the series seeks to contribute to the evolution of a more evidence-based approach to policy formulation in the health sector.

These studies will be important to all those involved in formulating or evaluating national health policies and, in particular, will be of use to health policymakers and advisers, who are under increasing pressure to rationalize the structure and funding of their health system. Academics and students in the field of health policy will also find this series valuable in seeking to better understand the complex choices that confront the health systems of Europe. The Observatory supports and promotes evidence-based health policymaking through comprehensive and rigorous analysis of the dynamics of health care systems in Europe.

Series Editors

Josep Figueras is the Director of the European Observatory on Health Systems and Policies, and Head of the European Centre for Health Policy, World Health Organization Regional Office for Europe.

Martin McKee is Director of Research Policy and Head of the London Hub of the European Observatory on Health Systems and Policies. He is Professor of European Public Health at the London School of Hygiene & Tropical Medicine, as well as a Co-director of the School's European Centre on Health of Societies in Transition.

Elias Mossialos is a Co-director of the European Observatory on Health Systems and Policies. He is Brian Abel-Smith Professor in Health Policy, Department of Social Policy, London School of Economics and Political Science and Director of LSE Health.

Richard B. Saltman is Associate Head of Research Policy and Head of the Atlanta Hub of the European Observatory on Health Systems and Policies. He is Professor of Health Policy and Management at the Rollins School of Public Health, Emory University in Atlanta, Georgia.

Reinhard Busse is Associate Head of Research Policy and Head of the Berlin Hub of the European Observatory on Health Systems and Policies. He is Professor of Health Care Management at the Berlin University of Technology.

European Observatory on Health Systems and Policies Series

Series Editors: Josep Figueras, Martin McKee, Elias Mossialos, Richard B. Saltman and Reinhard Busse

Published titles

Health policy and European Union enlargement
Martin McKee, Laura MacLehose and Ellen Nolte (eds)

Regulating pharmaceuticals in Europe: striving for efficiency, equity and quality
Elias Mossialos, Monique Mrazek and Tom Walley (eds)

Social health insurance systems in western Europe
Richard B. Saltman, Reinhard Busse and Josep Figueras (eds)

Purchasing to improve health systems performance
Josep Figueras, Ray Robinson and Elke Jakubowski (eds)

Human resources for health in Europe
Carl-Ardy Dubois, Martin McKee and Ellen Nolte (eds)

Primary care in the driver's seat
Richard B. Saltman, Ana Rico and Wienke Boerma (eds)

Mental health policy and practice across Europe: the future direction of mental health care
Martin Knapp, David McDaid, Elias Mossialos and Graham Thornicroft (eds)

Decentralization in health care
Richard B. Saltman, Vaida Bankauskaite and Karsten Vrangbak (eds)

Health systems and the challenge of communicable diseases: experiences from Europe and Latin America
Richard Coker, Rifat Atun and Martin McKee (eds)

Caring for people with chronic conditions: a health system perspective
Ellen Nolte and Martin McKee (eds)

Nordic health care systems: recent reforms and current policy challenges
Jon Magnussen, Karsten Vrangbak and Richard B. Saltman (eds)

Diagnosis-related groups in Europe: moving towards transparency, efficiency and quality in hospitals
Reinhard Busse, Alexander Geissler, Wilm Quentin and Miriam Wiley (eds)

Migration and health in the European Union
Bernd Rechel, Philipa Mladovsky, Walter Deville, Barbara Rijks, Roumyana Petrova-Benedict and Martin McKee (eds)

Success and failures of health policy in Europe: four decades of divergent trends and converging challenges
Johan P. Mackenbach and Martin McKee (eds)

European child health services and systems: lessons without borders
Ingrid Wolfe and Martin McKee (eds)

Implications for health system performance and accountability
Cheryl Cashin, Y-Ling Chi, Peter C. Smith, Michael Borowitz and Sarah Thomson (eds)

Health System Performance Comparison: An Agenda for Policy, Information and Research
Irene Papanicolas and Peter Smith (eds)

Facets of Public Health in Europe
Bernd Rechel and Martin McKee (eds)

Paying For Performance in Healthcare: Implications for Health System Performance and Accountability
Cheryl Cashin, Y-Ling Chi, Peter Smith, Michael Borowitz and Sarah Thomson (eds)

Contents

List of contributors

Marie-Jeanne Aarts is Post-doctoral Researcher, School for Public Health and Primary Care, Maastricht University, the Netherlands.

Adrienne Alayli-Goebbels is Researcher in Health Economics, Maastricht University, the Netherlands.

Peter Anderson is Professor of Substance Use, Policy and Practice, Institute of Health and Society, Newcastle University, UK and Extraordinary Professor of Alcohol and Health in the Faculty of Health, Medicine and Life Sciences, Maastricht University, the Netherlands.

Rob Anderson is Professor of Health Economics and Evaluation, University of Exeter Medical School, United Kingdom.

Natalie Bartle is Business Development Manager, Derby Hospitals NHS Trust, Derby, United Kingdom.

Zachary S. Brown is Environmental and Resource Economist, North Carolina State University, Raleigh, North Carolina, USA and Assistant Professor, Department of Agricultural and Resource Economics, Cluster Faculty in the Genetic Engineering and Society Program, USA. He was previously Environmental and Resource Economist, OECD, Paris, France.

Fiona Bull is Professor/Director, Centre for the Built Environment and Health, School of Population Health, University of Western Australia, Crawley, Australia.

Michele Cecchini is a Health Economist and Policy Analyst, Health Division, Directorate for Employment, Labour and Social Affairs, OECD, Paris, France.

Pim Cuijpers is Professor of Clinical Psychology, VU University Medical Centre, Amsterdam, the Netherlands.

Silvia Evers is Professor of Public Health Technology Assessment, Department of Health Services Research, Maastricht University, the Netherlands.

Corinna Hawkes is Head of Policy and Public Affairs at World Cancer Research International.

Cristina Hernandez-Quevedo is a Health Economist and Policy Analyst, European Observatory on Health Systems and Policies, London School of Economics and Political Science, United Kingdom.

Michael P. Kelly is former Director of the Centre of Public Health Excellence, National Institute of Health and Care Excellence, London, United Kingdom.

Don Kenkel is Professor of Economics, College of Human Ecology, Cornell University, USA.

David McDaid is Senior Research Fellow in Health Economics and Health Policy, Personal Social Services Research Unit and European Observatory on Health Systems and Policies, London School of Economics and Political Science, United Kingdom.

Sherry Merkur is Research Fellow and Health Policy Analyst, European Observatory on Health Systems and Policies, London School of Economics and Political Science, United Kingdom.

A-La Park is Research Fellow and Health Economist, Personal Social Services Research Unit, London School of Economics and Political Science, United Kingdom.

Ionela Petrea is Head of the Department of International Mental Health Development, Trimbos Institute, Utrecht, the Netherlands.

Franco Sassi is Senior Health Economist, Health Division, Directorate for Employment, Labour and Social Affairs, OECD, Paris, France.

Filip Smit is Professor of Evidence-based Public Mental Health, Department of Epidemiology and Biostatistics, VU University Medical Centre, Amsterdam, the Netherlands and Director of Science at the Centre of Prevention and Early

Intervention, Trimbos Institute (Netherlands Institute of Mental Health and Addiction), Utrecht, the Netherlands.

Marc Suhrcke is Professor of Global Health Economics, Centre for Health Economics, University of York, United Kingdom.

Joy Townsend is Emeritus Professor of Health Economics, Epidemiology and Health Services Research, London School of Hygiene and Tropical Medicine, United Kingdom.

Leonardo Trasande is Associate Professor, Department of Population Health, Environmental Medicine and Paediatrics, New York University, New York, USA.

Helen Weatherly is Senior Research Fellow, Centre for Health Economics, University of York, United Kingdom.

Matthias Wismar is Health Policy Analyst, European Observatory on Health Systems and Policies, WHO Regional Office for Europe, Brussels, Belgium.

List of tables, figures and boxes

Tables

Figures

Boxes

Foreword

Today, the economic case for investing in health promotion and non-communicable disease prevention is stronger than it has ever been. Chronic noncommunicable diseases are the main cause of death and disability. Yet the main risk factors associated with chronic diseases are largely preventable, and this book provides compelling evidence that addressing those risk factors is an efficient use of governments' money. In particular, the book presents the case for investing upstream, prior to the onset of illness and before health care services are required.

Actions to improve people's health by making their behaviours and consumption choices healthier are starting to receive more attention in European countries' public health policies. Countries are increasingly reluctant to accept the detrimental consequences of tobacco smoking, harmful use of alcohol, unhealthy diets and sedentary lifestyles, among other risk factors. This book shows that governments can have a major impact on these behaviours by raising the price of unhealthy choices, and making them less affordable, by regulating business conduct in ways that would limit commercial influences on individual choices and ensure that healthier products are placed on the market, and by informing and educating people about healthier lifestyles. The following are some examples from the work presented in this book:

- Raising cigarette prices across Europe to the European Union (EU) average of $5.50 would save hundreds of thousands of lives each year – 100,000, in the Russian Federation alone.
- Over 10,000 years of life in good health could be gained in western Europe each year, and even more in central and eastern Europe, at a negligible cost,

by limiting children's exposure to advertising of foods and beverages high in salt, sugar and fat.

- Cutting salt intake through regulation and food product reformulation led to a gain of 44,000 life-years in good health in England, with savings in health care expenditures largely offsetting implementation costs.
- Road traffic accidents cost European countries as much as 3 per cent of GDP; measures to cut this burden pay for themselves within 5 to 10 years.
- The value of the health and economic benefits generated by regulating chemical hazards for children and adults is ten times larger than the costs of implementing regulatory measures.

All this can be achieved in partnership with a wide range of state and non-state partners, while it is essential that verifiable targets are set, and progress towards key health objectives is closely monitored and evaluated.

This book is the result of a collaborative effort between the European Observatory on Health Systems and Policies, the Organisation for Economic Co-operation and Development, and the World Health Organization (WHO) Regional Office for Europe. The economics of health promotion and noncommunicable disease prevention features prominently in our two organizations' agendas. We have been working together, in a cross-disciplinary way, to present the best available evidence on what countries should be doing to prevent unhealthy behaviour.

The evidence of this study has informed the development of the new WHO European region policy framework and strategy for health and well-being – *Health 2020*. The OECD's Economics of Prevention Programme has made a major contribution to the evidence base for tackling leading risk factors for chronic diseases. The Programme aims at enhancing public health and creating the conditions for economic growth and development. By shaping environments conducive to healthier consumption choices, people's health and life expectancy will be improved, health care systems will be relieved of a meaningful share of the burden of treating chronic diseases, the economy will benefit from a healthier and more productive workforce, and society will enjoy greater welfare and fairer health outcomes.

Developing the evidence base on what works to promote better health and well-being, in different contexts, and at what cost, is a key element in achieving progress towards national health policy goals. *Health 2020* is value- and evidence-informed, and aims at improving the health and well-being of populations, reducing health inequalities, strengthening public health and ensuring sustainable people-centred health systems. It envisages actions and outcomes well beyond the boundaries of the health sector and beyond the remit of health ministries.

This book has benefited from wide consultations with Member States and experts that have taken place over the last two years. It shows that promoting health and preventing chronic diseases through interventions aimed at modifying lifestyle risk factors is possible and cost-effective. However, this often requires fundamental changes in individual and collective behaviours. As this joint work by the OECD, the WHO European Region and the European Observatory on Health Systems and Policies shows, such changes can only be triggered by wide-ranging promotion and prevention strategies addressing multiple determinants of health across social groups.

Zsuzsanna Jakab, *WHO Regional Director for Europe*
Angel Gurria, *Secretary General, Organisation for Economic Co-operation and Development*

Executive summary

Health promotion and disease prevention have a major role to play in health policy worldwide, yet they are underused, partly because evidence to support a strong case for action is difficult to gather. Aimed at a broad audience of policymakers, practitioners and academics, this book is designed to provide an economic perspective on the challenges to better health promotion and chronic disease prevention. Chronic noncommunicable diseases, including cardiovascular conditions, cancers, mental disorders, chronic respiratory conditions and diabetes, are the main cause of disability and death worldwide. Some of the disease burden associated with these diseases can be avoided through health promotion and disease prevention. A key question is whether or not there is an economic case for action, rather than treating poor health when it arises.

The first chapters of the volume look at how economics can contribute to our understanding of the pathways through which chronic diseases are generated, and of the choices and behaviours involved in those pathways. They include a discussion of basic concepts and theories, including the economic rationale for action, as well as a practical illustration of the methods, and measures of cost and outcome, that are typically used in economic analysis.

One key conclusion is that many different market failures create a compelling economic rationale for government intervention in health promotion and disease prevention, as a way of improving social welfare. Behaviours conducive to poor health may entail costs that are not borne by those who engage in such behaviours. Externalities associated with their adverse impacts go beyond the individual. They affect families and can put a strain on public services. Examples include the harms caused by passive smoking, violent and disorderly behaviour associated with alcohol abuse, and road traffic injuries resulting from reckless driving. Prices are unlikely to reflect these impacts in a free market.

There may be a lack of information for consumers to make rational and efficient choices, often compounded by uncertainty or miscommunication on the health benefits and harms of different lifestyle choices. And, people do not always act rationally when making choices, sometimes because their behaviours may be addictive, or habit-forming, as with smoking and gambling, sometimes because they can be myopic, choosing to 'enjoy' an unhealthy lifestyle today, either dismissing future risk or intending but failing to change future behaviour. Choices are also influenced by the way in which products are advertised or displayed in shops, and by peer pressures.

The core of the book contains reviews of the economic evidence for tackling specific behavioural risk factors, including tobacco smoking, harmful alcohol use, physical inactivity and unhealthy diets, as well as selected risk factors related to the environment, roads and mental health and well-being. Cross-cutting themes, including interventions on selected social determinants of health, with a focus, in particular, on education and early life interventions, the distributional implications of policy interventions and key implementation issues are then considered in subsequent chapters.

A central message is that there is strong evidence of the cost-effectiveness of at least some actions in all of the thematic areas examined. In many of these areas, a combination of measures involving fiscal policies, regulation and improved access to health-relevant information are more cost-effective than any one measure in isolation. In the case of tobacco control, for instance, taxation is the single most cost-effective action; but even greater health benefits can be obtained by combining this with legislation on smoke-free environments, banning advertising, making use of warning labels and running mass media campaigns, still with favourable cost-effectiveness.

Efficient alcohol policies include restricting access to retailed alcohol, enforcing bans on alcohol advertising, including on social media, raising taxes and instituting a minimum price per gram of alcohol. More expensive, but still cost-effective measures include enforcing drink-driving laws through breath testing, delivering brief advice for higher risk drinking, and providing treatment for alcohol-related disorders. Media campaigns, on their own, and school-based health promotion programmes, do not appear to be cost-effective. A strategy that combines interventions is likely to generate additional health benefits, while still remaining cost-effective.

There is also evidence for actions that improve the quality of people's diets. Taxes on foods high in salt, sugar and fat are consistently cost saving, but tend to be regressive. They may need to be designed carefully to avoid undesirable substitution effects – for instance, by coupling them with subsidies targeting healthy food and drinks, or disadvantaged consumers. Policies aimed at reducing salt content in processed foods have favourable cost-effectiveness in several studies, but evidence on other reformulation (e.g. to reduce trans-fat content) is very limited. Policies aimed at making fruit and vegetables more available in schools can have a positive, albeit modest effect. Food labelling schemes can be cost-effective, but they have only been assessed in a handful of studies. A few studies support restrictions on food advertising to children, which are found to work better, and to be more efficient, when implemented on a mandatory basis rather than through self-regulation.

The promotion of physical activity through mass media campaigns is cost-effective and relatively inexpensive. However, returns in terms of health outcomes may be lower than those provided by more targeted interventions – for instance, those set in the workplace. Changes in the transport system and increased access to opportunities for physical activity in the wider environment, such as the provision of bicycle trails, also have potential benefits, but require careful evaluation to ascertain affordability and feasibility. Actions targeting the adult population and individuals at higher risk tend to produce larger effects in a shorter time frame than actions targeted at children and young people.

The economic case for mental health promotion and disorder prevention is encouraging. Evidence suggests a favourable return on investment from many actions across the life course, starting from early actions in childhood to strengthen social and emotional learning, coping skills and improved bonds between parents and children. There are also economic arguments supporting investment in workplace initiatives to promote better psychological health, with much of the benefits falling on employers. Cost-effective prevention programmes can also be targeted at high-risk groups of the population, including isolated older people and new mothers.

Actions to prevent road traffic accidents, including road design modification, urban traffic calming and camera and radar speed enforcement programmes, are supported by sound economic evidence, especially when applied in higher-risk areas. Active enforcement of legislation to promote good road safety behaviours, including measures to reduce drink-driving, can also be highly cost-effective.

Favourable economic studies support action to tackle environmental chemical hazards. Examples include the comprehensive reform of the 2007 Regulation on Registration, Evaluation, Authorisation and Restriction of Chemicals (REACH) in Europe; the removal of lead-based paint hazards; the abatement of mercury pollution from coal-fired power plants and reduced vehicle emissions in high-traffic areas, e.g., through congestion charging schemes. These measures can reduce health care and other costs associated with childhood asthma, bronchiolitis and other early life respiratory illnesses.

A further key message is that adequate implementation and monitoring are essential to realize the cost-effectiveness potential of many interventions reviewed. Steps need to be taken to help facilitate implementation of actions that must be delivered outside of the health sector. These could include voluntary or mandatory partnerships across sectors, possibly with the sharing of financial risks and rewards of investment to overcome narrow sector-specific interests.

Finally, it is crucial that expectations concerning the benefits of health promotion and disease prevention remain realistic. Reducing health expenditure should not be regarded as the sole goal of prevention. An economic case should be made in the same way as for other health interventions. This volume indicates that prevention and health promotion can help improve health and well-being, with a cost-effectiveness that is as good as, or better than, that of many accepted forms of health care.

Acknowledgements

This book is the result of collaboration between the European Observatory on Health Systems and Policies and the Organisation for Economic Co-operation and Development. We are especially grateful to all the authors for their valuable contributions.

We are also very grateful to the reviewers of this volume: Kenneth Warner, University of Michigan; Falk Mueller-Riemenschneider, Charite University; Bruce Traill, Reading University; Dan Chisholm, WHO Headquarters; Timothy Taylor, University of Exeter School; Rune Elvik, Transport Institute; Anne Ludbrooke, University of Aberdeen; and Richard Cookson, University of York for their very helpful comments and suggestions.

Finally, this book would not have appeared without the hard work of the production team led by Jonathan North, with the able assistance of Caroline White.

List of abbreviations

$Int	international dollars (currency)
A$/AUD	Australian dollars (currency)
ACI	activated carbon injection
ACSM	American College of Sports Medicine
BBBF	Better Beginnings, Better Futures
BCSP	Bowel Cancer Screening Programme
BDI	Becks Depression Inventory
BHPS	British Household Panel Survey
BLLs	blood lead levels
BMI	body mass index
C$	Canadian dollars (currency)
CAAA	Clean Air Act Amendments
CAP	Common Agricultural Policy
CBA	cost-benefit analysis
CBT	cognitive behavioural therapy
CCA	cost-consequence analysis
CDI	Children's Depression Inventory
CE	cost-effectiveness
CEA	cost-effectiveness analysis
CIS	Commonwealth of Independent States
CMA	cost-minimization analysis
COI	cost of illness
CSDH	Commission on Social Determinants of Health
CUA	cost-utility analysis

CV	contingent valuation
CVD	cardiovascular diseases
DALYs	disability-adjusted life-years
DCE	discrete choice experiment
DKK	Danish krone (currency)
DRNCDs	diet-related chronic noncommunicable diseases
ECD	early childhood development
EPA	Environmental Protection Agency
EU	European Union
EUPASS	European Physical Activity Surveillance System
EuroNCAP	European New Car Assessment Programme
FCTC	Framework Convention on Tobacco Control
FOBT	faecal occult blood test
FSU	former Soviet Union
FYRR	first year rates of return
GDA	guideline daily allowance/amount
GDP	gross domestic product
GP	general practitioner
GPAQ	global physical activity questionnaire
HDA	Health Development Agency
HDL	high-density lipoprotein
HEHA	Healthy Eating, Healthy Action
HEPA	Health-Enhancing Physical Activity [Network]
HPV	high production volume
ICAP	International Centre for Alcohol Policies
ICECAP	ICEpop CAPability measure
ICER	incremental cost-effectiveness ratio
IPAQ	international physical activity questionnaire
IQ	intelligence quotient
ISA	Intelligent Speed Adaptation
IY	[Webster-Stratton] Incredible Years
MATS	Mercury and Air Toxics Standards
NGOs	non-governmental organizations
NCDs	noncommunicable diseases
NHS	National Health Service
NICE	National Institute for Health and Care Excellence
NIS	newly independent states
NOPA	European Database on Nutrition, Obesity and Physical Activity
NRT	nicotine replacement therapy
OECD	Organisation for Economic Co-operation and Development
PA	physical activity
PLN	Polish zloty (currency)
PPP	purchasing power parity
PUFA	polyunsaturated fats
QALYs	quality-adjusted life-years
RCT	randomized controlled trial
REACH	Regulation on Registration, Evaluation, Authorisation and Restriction of Chemicals

ROI	return on investment
RUR	Russian rouble (currency)
RWJF	Robert Wood Johnson Foundation
SAPM	Sheffield Alcohol Policy Model
SDH	social determinants of health
SDR	standardized death rate
SEG	socioeconomic group
SEK	Swedish krona (currency)
SES	socioeconomic status
TSCA	Toxic Substances Control Act
TTCs	transnational tobacco companies
UKK	Urho Kaleka Kekkonen walking test
UN	United Nations
UNEP	United Nations Environment Programme
WIC	Women, Infants and Children [Fruit and Vegetable Voucher Campaign]
WEMWBS	Warwick–Edinburgh Mental Well-being Scale
WHO	World Health Organization
WTO	World Trade Organisation
VAS	visual analogue scale
VAT	valued-added tax
YLL	years of life lost
YLD	years lived with disability

Part I

Introduction

Introduction

chapter one

Introduction to the economics of health promotion and disease prevention

Franco Sassi, Sherry Merkur and
David McDaid

Economics, health promotion and disease prevention

This book is designed to provide an economic perspective on health promotion and chronic disease prevention. The book includes a framework for analysing the consequences of prevention strategies, which draws from disciplines such as psychology, sociology, epidemiology, and public health, in addition to economics. It also provides a compendium of evidence of the economic impacts of a range of policy interventions in a number of core areas of public health action. The approach builds on the hypothesis that countering the epidemic of chronic diseases that countries in Europe and elsewhere are experiencing with appropriate prevention strategies would provide the means for better increasing social welfare and/or enhancing health equity, compared with not taking preventive actions and simply treating chronic diseases once they emerge.

An economic perspective is about more than counting the costs associated with diseases, whether medical care costs or productivity losses. And, it involves more than assessing the cost-effectiveness of preventive interventions, although the latter is an important role for health economics. The potential for an economic approach to shape and inform the debate on prevention stretches beyond those aspects. Economics contributes to our understanding of the pathways through which chronic diseases are generated and of the choices and behaviours involved in those pathways. It provides the tools for developing effective and efficient policy strategies and addressing potential trade-offs between the goals of increasing social welfare and improving the distribution of health across individuals and population groups.

This book is designed for a broad audience of health policy makers, national and local, in countries at all levels of income; for public health practitioners and advocates; and for scholars in a number of relevant disciplines, ranging from health economics to sociology, political science, medicine and public health. It is meant to provide those audiences with a comprehensive view of the current evidence base in support of a broad range of public health interventions, addressing not only their effectiveness in improving population health, but also their implementation costs, impacts on health expenditures, and other economic consequences. Individual chapters provide critical reviews of the evidence base in specific areas, with a view to assessing the validity of the evidence and its generalizability to different settings. The geographical perspective of this book is that of the World Health Organization's (WHO's) European Region, but its scope stretches more widely, as evidence is reported and reviewed from studies undertaken in many countries, within and outside Europe.

The scope of the book

The field of health promotion and disease prevention is potentially vast, and in no way could this book have covered it comprehensively. A number of choices had to be made on the scope covered. The first one was about the health promotion and prevention interventions to be assessed. The book deals with interventions for the prevention of chronic noncommunicable diseases (NCDs), and certain types of injuries, while it does not cover the prevention of infectious diseases or their chronic sequelae. The choice was driven by the prominence that NCDs have acquired in many countries, due to their large and increasing disease burden, discussed later in this chapter. Correspondingly, the relative weight of infectious diseases has progressively decreased.

Much of the prevention of chronic NCDs is based on tackling behavioural risk factors, which are key determinants of those diseases. These include, in particular, tobacco smoking, harmful alcohol use, unhealthy diets, lack of physical activity, and other health-related behaviours. Several chapters later in the book address specific risk factor areas, focusing on the interventions available to prevent diseases by eliminating, or containing the impacts of, those risk factors.

Health-related behaviours are the dominant, albeit not exclusive, focus. This implies that the types of interventions reviewed are mostly those designed for healthy people with risk factors, and aimed at steering their behaviours towards healthier patterns. These interventions are often delivered outside the health care system, using resources from different areas of government spending. Less attention is devoted to the many forms of prevention that are typically delivered within the health care system, such as screening programmes, or pharmacological prevention (e.g. with statins, or anti-hypertensive medications), which of course are no less important than more upstream actions, but have been studied much more extensively than the latter.

Finally, the book takes primarily a government policy perspective, based on the argument developed later in this chapter that prevention is a legitimate area for government intervention because of market and rationality failures that would otherwise prevent individuals from maximizing their own welfare, and because of an undesirable distribution of health. However, the book also addresses interventions that are not solely, or not at all, part of the government policy toolkit. Interventions led by private sector – business or civil society – organizations are discussed in several chapters, and evidence of their impacts is reviewed alongside that available for government interventions.

Chronic noncommunicable diseases and their prevention

Chronic NCDs are currently the main cause of both disability and death worldwide. This heterogeneous group of diseases, including, among others, cardiovascular conditions, cancers, chronic respiratory conditions and diabetes, affect people of all ages and social classes (WHO 2002). The latest global burden of disease estimates indicate that NCDs account for 85 per cent, 80 per cent and 75 per cent of the global burden of disease, respectively, in Western, Central and Eastern Europe. Similarly injuries, particularly on the roads or as a result of self-harm, account for a further 10 per cent, 11 per cent or 18 per cent of total disease burden (IHME 2013).

Globally, of the 58 million deaths occurring in 2005, approximately 35 million, or 60 per cent, were due to chronic causes. Most of them were due to cardiovascular disorders and diabetes (32 per cent), cancers (13 per cent), and chronic respiratory diseases (7 per cent) (Abegunde et al. 2007). This burden is predicted to worsen in the coming years. A WHO study projected an increase of global deaths by a further 17 per cent in the period 2005–15, meaning that of the 64 million estimated deaths in 2015, 41 million people will die of a chronic disease (WHO 2005), and NCD deaths would further increase to over 51 million in 2030, with three out of four NCD deaths expected in low- and lower-middle-income countries.

Chronic diseases and the increased mortality associated with them are not distributed evenly across social groups. Those in the most disadvantaged socioeconomic conditions typically display higher prevalence and mortality rates than those at the opposite end of the social spectrum, with a continuous gradient among groups positioned between the two extremes. In countries such as Finland, Norway, Denmark, Belgium, Austria and England researchers demonstrated a widening of inequalities in premature mortality from cardiovascular diseases and many cancers between socioeconomic groups (Mackenbach 2006).

The action plan devised by WHO as part of the global strategy for the prevention and control of NCDs (WHO 2008) focused on four chronic diseases accounting for 60 per cent of deaths worldwide: cardiovascular disease, cancer, diabetes, and respiratory disorders. Prominent, yet largely preventable, behavioural risk factors associated with these diseases – either directly or indirectly via risk factors such as increased blood pressure or cholesterol concentrations – include tobacco, harmful alcohol use, unhealthy diets, physical inactivity, and obesity. Smoking alone is estimated to be responsible for 22 per cent of cardiovascular diseases in industrialized countries, and for the vast majority of some cancers and chronic respiratory diseases (WHO 2002), and is responsible for the loss of 157 million disability-adjusted life-years (DALYs) globally (Lim et al. 2012). Alcohol use is associated with a loss of 75 million DALYs in men and 23 million in women. Overweight and obesity account for the loss of 94 million DALYs, lack of physical activity for 70 million, and high cholesterol for 41 million (Lim et al. 2012).

An economic approach

Health: social determinants or individual responsibility?

The question whether health and health-related behaviours are the result of individual choice or external determinants and influences has been at the centre of the public health debate for a long time. Opposing views have formed on the subject, often linked with different ideological stances.

If health-related behaviours are viewed purely as the result of free choice, the case for 'collective intervention' is weakened. This may also lead to a culture of 'victim-blaming' (Evans and Stoddart 1994). If, on the other hand, behaviours are viewed as individual responses to environmental influences, the focus of policy will shifts towards the environmental factors that determine individual behaviours. A balanced approach would, of course, recognize that elements of free choice coexist and interact with social determinants and influences in shaping individual health-related behaviours. Cutler and Glaeser (2005) observe that individual characteristics alone are unlikely to explain the uptake of health-related behaviours. They found that the correlation of risky behaviours in individuals appears to be very low: smokers are unlikely to be also heavy drinkers (correlation 12.9 per cent); obesity has virtually no correlation with smoking or heavy drinking; the uptake of medical preventive services like flu shots or screening is negatively, but very weakly, correlated with risky behaviours such as smoking, excess drinking, or having a high body mass index (BMI). Cutler and Glaeser also found empirical support for the hypothesis that certain 'situational influences' are likely to trigger specific lifestyle choices in those who are exposed to such influences, with an intensity of response that may be modulated by individual characteristics. One such situational influence that the same authors explore in some depth is change in food production technology. This has been partly responsible for dietary changes and for the rise of obesity rates, particularly in individuals and families whose time available for meal preparation and cooking has become increasingly limited (Cutler et al. 2003). This work lends support to the hypothesis that health-related behaviours are primarily determined by interactions between individual characteristics and specific environmental influences, rather than by the former alone.

If lifestyle choices are the result of environmental influences interacting with individual characteristics, then the socioeconomic gradient in lifestyles and related health outcomes is likely to reflect differences between individuals in the degree of control they have over their own environment. Research conducted in the United Kingdom since the 1970s on the relationship between socioeconomic position and health (Marmot 2004) underscores the importance of the ability of individuals to gain control over their own environment as a crucial determinant of the same individuals' health and health-related behaviours. Evidence is becoming available of the role of work-related stress in the relationship between socioeconomic position and health. Stress was shown to be causally associated, for instance, with unhealthy lifestyles, the metabolic syndrome and coronary heart disease (Chandola et al. 2008). However, the direction of the causal relationship remains uncertain. Are individuals predisposed (genetically or by other means) to achieving a better control over their own environment also able to reach more privileged socioeconomic positions as well as a better health status through healthier lifestyle choices, or does a privileged socioeconomic position confer better control and healthier lifestyles?

An early and popular model of the determinants of health and health inequalities was centred on the individual and on his/her biological characteristics, with various 'layers of influence' on health (Dahlgren and Whitehead 1991). The latter include: individual lifestyle factors; social and community influences; living and working conditions; general socioeconomic, cultural and environmental conditions. Each of these layers has a direct influence on individual health, but interactions between layers contribute significantly to shaping the impact of each group of determinants. For instance, ample evidence suggests that lifestyle factors, or health-related behaviours, are in turn determined by social and community influences, as well as by general socioeconomic, cultural and environmental conditions. The existence of a socioeconomic gradient in all layers of determinants supports the view that these are closely interconnected. Understanding the relationships between layers of influence is as important as understanding the direct impact of each layer on individual health. The model was adopted as a conceptual basis for a review of health inequalities in the United Kingdom in the late 1990s (UK Department of Health 1998).

WHO established a Commission on the Social Determinants of Health in 2005 to emphasize the role of socioeconomic influences in shaping recent dramatic changes in population health patterns and trends at the global level. Wilkinson and Marmot (2003) identified ten areas in which solid evidence exists of the role of aspects of the social environment on health, elsewhere developed into a more extensive inventory of social determinants of health and evidence of their impact (Marmot and Wilkinson 2006). The conceptual framework developed for the work of the Commission attempts to build an overall model of the influences of two main groups of determinants: structural determinants, such as the socioeconomic and the political contexts, social structures and socioeconomic position; and intermediary determinants, which mediate the effect of the former, including biological and behavioural factors, living and working conditions, psychosocial factors and health system determinants (Solar and Irwin 2007).

The rationale for government intervention in health promotion

An economic approach to prevention involves interpreting health-related behaviours as the result of market dynamics leading to the consumption of commodities such as tobacco, alcohol, food and physical activity or leisure time. Individual choices are subject to many external influences and constraints, and are driven by opportunity, costs and other incentives. The dynamics, or mechanisms, that help shape our choices about our health-related behaviours are viewed by economists in the same way as market forces that influence other choices we make, for instance about the purchase of goods and services. This is regardless of whether or not any money changes hands. The health determinants that influence our lifestyles are in turn the result of similar dynamics.

Sometimes markets fail to operate efficiently. If those failures could be avoided, social welfare would be increased. Information failures may contribute to the adoption of unhealthy behaviours and lifestyles through an inadequate knowledge or understanding of the long-term consequences of such behaviours. The negative consequences of the unhealthy behaviours and poor lifestyles of any one individual can often have adverse impacts on many other people. The harm to public health from excessive alcohol consumption (which can increase the risk of domestic abuse and road traffic accidents) is one example of these additional impacts, which are referred to by economists as 'externalities'. Externalities may lead to the social costs and benefits of certain forms of consumption not being fully reflected in their private costs and benefits to individual consumers. For instance, the cost of a bottle of beer may not be high enough to fully reflect all the adverse impacts to society of excessive alcohol consumption. A biased perception of the importance of future risks may also prevent individuals from making choices in their own best interest now.

From an economic perspective, government intervention is justified in the presence of significant failures that limit people's ability to maximize their welfare through the market interactions in which they engage. This is largely what makes the economic perspective different from the public health perspective. In the absence of such significant failures, government intervention would be less justified, or not at all. Where market failures exist and have a significant impact, the benefits potentially deriving from tackling the inefficiencies they cause may sometimes justify some form of corrective action, either by governments or other actors, provided such actions are viable and effective. Several economists have reviewed potential market failures in relation to chronic diseases and prevention (e.g. Kenkel 2000; Cawley 2004; Suhrcke et al. 2006; Brunello et al. 2008). A summary of the main failures observed in connection with health-related behaviours is provided in the following sections.

Classical market failures: externalities and poor information

Health-related behaviours may entail costs that are not borne by those who engage in such behaviours. These spillover effects, or externalities, are a typical cause of market failure. Passive smoking is a common example, as it has been shown to cause negative health effects on individuals other than the smoker. Such effects would not be reflected in the price of cigarettes if this were set in a free market between the smoker and the tobacco manufacturer. This means that people are more likely to engage in poor behaviours than would be socially desirable, given the costs imposed on others. In many cases, these externalities can be 'internalized' so that the uptake of the behaviours that generate them may be brought in line with their actual social costs and benefits, rather than with the private costs and benefit experienced by the individual consumers themselves. Such measures are generally financial transfers, such as taxes or subsidies, which may be imposed on, or offered to, the consumers or the suppliers of the commodity that generates the externality.

The use of taxes and subsidies in the presence of externalities may improve the efficiency of market exchanges, but they will also produce distributional changes (Sassi et al. 2013). For instance, if a government imposes a tax on a form of consumption that generates negative externalities, it may or may not be possible, or desirable, for the government in question to redistribute the tax revenues raised to those who suffer the consequences of the negative externality (which will be diminished by the tax, but not eliminated altogether). Similarly, if a commodity that produces positive externalities is subsidized, it may not be possible to fund the subsidy by charging those who enjoy the positive external effects. From a mere efficiency standpoint, what matters is just that welfare gains exceed any losses, but societies are not indifferent to the distribution of those gains and losses, therefore governments will have to take this into account in assessing the desirability of a policy to address externalities.

Externalities may derive from health-related behaviours such as, for instance, tobacco use – through second-hand smoking, violent and disorderly behaviour associated with alcohol abuse, or traffic accidents resulting from reckless driving. There are also deferred externalities, when people develop risk factors and chronic diseases that make them less productive, increase their use of medical and social services, which may be publicly funded, or require care to be provided by family and friends. Conversely, a reduced life expectancy may mean a less prolonged use of publicly funded medical and social services at the end of life. In addition to health expenditure and productivity, further externalities potentially associated with health-related behaviours can be found in the areas of consumption and savings (e.g. reduced consumption associated with disease), and education and human capital accumulation (e.g. reduced education of family members) (Suhrcke et al. 2006).

A second classical market failure is associated with the lack, or limited availability, of sound and reliable information on the costs and benefits of health-related behaviours. Information is a critical factor for markets to operate efficiently. In order to make rational and efficient choices, consumers have to be fully informed about the characteristics and quality of the goods they consume, about the benefits (utility) they will derive from consumption, and about the opportunity costs they will incur. In the case of health-related consumption behaviours, information is often lacking on the nature and the magnitude of the associated health risks. Information may be lacking because it does not exist (e.g. information on the long-term health effects of the consumption of genetically modified crops); because it is concealed or communicated in a misleading form by parties that have a vested interest (e.g. information on the health effects of smoking withheld by the tobacco industry in the recent past); or because it is complex and not easily accessible to the lay person (e.g. information on the health risks involved in the consumption of different types of fats).

The importance of information in forming health-related beliefs, a first step towards influencing lifestyle choices, is shown, for instance, by Cutler and Glaeser (2006) in their analysis of the determinants of higher smoking rates in Europe compared to the United States of America. The authors reach the conclusion that beliefs were changed in the United States when 'substantial information about the harms of smoking' was made available to the public, while the same information appears to have been communicated less effectively in Europe.

The direct provision of information by governments (e.g. health education campaigns to influence individual behaviours) or the regulation of information (e.g. limits on advertising, guidelines on food labelling) are usually justified by limited or imperfect information on the part of the consumer. When information failures cannot be fixed, for instance because communication of information is difficult, governments may still attempt to compensate for the effects of imperfect information by influencing behaviours through appropriate incentives (e.g. fiscal incentives like taxes and subsidies).

Behavioural failures

A fast growing body of behavioural economics research has shown that the assumption of rationality of the agents involved in market transactions does not always reflect the actual behaviours of those agents. Failures of rationality may affect the way choices are made, the information upon which choices are based, or the preferences that guide those choices. The first aspect includes, for instance, the use of heuristics, or rules of thumb, in decision-making. The second includes a biased perception of the information available, because the way information is presented (framing) influences choices and because of cognitive errors in the interpretation of information. The third aspect includes inconsistent preferences for outcomes expected at different points in time, or for gains and losses.

Detailed studies of heuristics and framing effects are providing valuable insights into certain health-related behaviours for designing policies that are effective in making those behaviours more conducive to good health. Behavioural insights, in particular, have paved the way for new policy approaches, including changing default options, increasing the salience of the information provided to consumers, and are also helping to refine more traditional policy approaches such as regulation (mainly to prevent suppliers of health-related commodities from exploiting heuristics and framing effects to their own advantage) and taxation (by refining our knowledge of how different types of consumers are likely to react to price changes).

Time preferences also play a critical role in health-related behaviours. Understanding the way in which people discount future costs and benefits in making their lifestyle choices is critical to the design of effective policies to counter the possible long-term ill health effects of particular behaviours. A large body of empirical literature about time preferences in relation to a variety of outcomes, including health (reviewed by Lipscomb et al. 1996), suggests that there are no particular reasons for the future health risks associated with certain lifestyle choices to be discounted at particularly high, or particularly low rates. Some characteristics of those choices, such as the relatively small size of the perceived health risks involved, will make people discount more heavily those future risks. But other characteristics of the same choices will have the opposite effect.

Substantial empirical evidence shows that individual health-related behaviours often reflect hyperbolic discounting. This refers to an accelerated form of discounting, which heavily penalizes future outcomes in present judgements in a way that makes time preferences inconsistent. This is essentially a self-control problem. Take, for instance, an obese person who is perfectly aware of the long-term health risks associated with her condition. She may decide that such risks are offset by the pleasure she derives from her dietary habits and sedentary lifestyle at present, therefore she will choose to postpone quitting her habits. Procrastination is a key feature of hyperbolic discounting. She perceives this as a postponement because she feels that after some time (say, in one year) she will no longer value pleasure from her current lifestyle more highly than the long-term health risks associated with it. She is convinced that a year later she will be prepared to change some of her dietary and activity behaviours. However, after one year she will find herself discounting future health risks more heavily than she previously thought she would do, and she will still feel that the pleasures of her lifestyle offsets future health risks. Inconsistency in time preferences is reflected by the discrepancy between the way the individual originally thought she would discount future outcomes and the way she actually discounted them one year later. The result is a likely indefinite postponement of the decision to quit current habits. At least some evidence of hyperbolic discounting has been found in relation to obesity, one study reported that 'time inconsistent preferences regarding weight is a very common problem among teenagers, since the majority of them end up failing to reduce their BMI after having declared to be trying to lose weight' (Brunello et al. 2008).

Paternalistic government intervention to counter self-control problems would require 'tricky social welfare decisions', or a judgement of whether individuals' future self, or long-term preferences, should be given priority over their present self, or short-term preferences (Glaeser 2006). Such problems, in Glaeser's view, are best addressed by increasing the availability of 'technologies or contracts that facilitate private self-control'. An example could be the fiscal deductibility of private expenditures on devices that may facilitate self-control (e.g. nutrition advice, organized physical activities, etc.), or coverage of nicotine replacement therapies to aid smoking cessation. The latter measures, which essentially broaden individual choice, are often viewed as non-paternalistic interventions, as discussed in the section, 'Chronic noncommunicable diseases and their prevention', although in fact they do interfere with individual choice, and they may involve a significant cost, to be shared among all social groups when interventions are publicly funded.

Government intervention may also be justified when health-related behaviours are addictive, or habit-forming. This may happen because the commodities involved may generate forms of chemical dependence that make it difficult for individuals to quit consuming them, as is the case with many drugs, or because of psychological mechanisms that encourage the reiteration of consumption. The term 'habit' is generally used in relation to the latter, while the term 'addiction' is applied more widely, both in relation to drugs or tobacco smoking (which involves a certain degree of dependence on nicotine) and in relation to consumption that does not involve chemical dependence (e.g.

gambling addiction). It is the non-independence of these acts of consumption, as they may be influenced by previous consumption experiences, which may cause concern about individuals' ability to maximize their welfare. The presence of a chemical dependence may strengthen the justification for intervention, but some forms of psychological addiction may also be extremely powerful and potentially damaging. Forms of consumption involving interdependent choices over time are sometimes interpreted in economics as rational addictions, based on models originally proposed by Becker and Murphy (1988), strongly supported by empirical evidence (e.g. Chaloupka and Warner 1999).

Habit-forming behaviour is consolidated behaviour in which individuals engage over a prolonged period of time and from which they find it difficult to wean themselves. Habits typically involve a reduced motivation to seek and use information that may lead to a better understanding of the consequences of the behaviour in question, and to a tendency to discount the value of new information that is received, particularly when it highlights risks associated with the habitual behaviour. In addition, people who engage in habitual behaviour act on the implicit assumption that if they found the behaviour desirable when they first adopted it, it must also be desirable for them to continue to engage in the same behaviour (Maio et al. 2007). Consumers take up habits because they find it convenient to do so, but habits may prevent them from maximizing their own welfare.

Equity and health

A further factor that may contribute to justifying government intervention is an undesirable distribution of social welfare, of which health is an important component. Evidence of significant disparities in health status and longevity has been available for several decades in many countries, and governments have made commitments to reduce major disparities in health on equity grounds. Concepts of equity adopted by national governments and international organizations in relation to health often focus on health care and tend to be centred on notions of equality with respect to some relevant dimension, a common example being equal access for equal need. However, even when the focus is narrowly placed on health care, policy decisions are sometimes inconsistent with regard to their distributional effects and the balance they achieve between the goals of equity and efficiency (Donaldson and Gerard 1993; Sassi et al. 2001). Approaches to promoting equity with regard to health status have been more cautious, generally avoiding direct references to notions of equality, and rather focusing on the reduction of variations across population groups.

There is generally recognition that health disparities are likely to persist as long as social structures allow some degree of inequality. It has been argued that health inequalities, at least to a certain extent, are acceptable, or even desirable (Collison 1988), because of trade-offs between equity and efficiency, non-modifiable risk factors (for example, genetic heritage) and individual choice (driving, at least to some degree, health-related behaviours). The question for governments is what health inequalities should be tackled, and how much effort should be put into redressing them.

Prevention is bound to have distributional impacts. Different individuals and groups have different probabilities of developing chronic diseases, and have different outcomes once such diseases occur. Different individuals and groups also respond differently to preventive interventions. Potential distributional effects cannot be ignored in the design of preventive interventions. Not only should they be accounted for, but they can be openly pursued, in line with the distributional objectives of health and broader government policy. Prevention offers excellent opportunities for redistribution of health and longevity. Prevention strategies are not subject to the same moral imperative of health care, and may be more easily targeted to those individuals and groups who are deemed to need and deserve them the most. Chapter 12 provides an analysis of how alternative health promotion and disease prevention policies may impact on the distribution of health and social welfare.

Forms of government intervention in health promotion

Government interventions in health promotion and disease prevention have a significant potential for improving health, but will also interfere, at least to some degree, with individual choices and behaviours.

The least intrusive interventions are those aimed at widening choice by expanding the range of options individuals can choose from, or those aimed at making certain existing options more affordable. Persuasion and other non-price devices such as default rules are often advocated as minimally intrusive interventions which do not significantly affect rational consumers. However, governments may not always deliver persuasion effectively and in the best interest of individuals, and it is difficult to monitor whether they do so. Taxes and consumption bans are more transparent and contestable, although they may lead to welfare losses when consumers display varying degrees of rationality. Taxation models targeting the least rational consumers may be possible, but their development is still at a very early stage. Outright bans of selected choice options involve the highest degree of interference with individual choice. They may be difficult to enforce, particularly when demand is strong or consumption is addictive.

Heavier interference with individual choices may be justified when departures from rational decision-making and from an ideal efficient market model for lifestyle choices are significant, or when the consequences of those departures are particularly severe. The political costs of prevention, in the form of interference with individual choice, often follow an inverse pattern relative to the economic costs. Interventions that involve lower degrees of interference tend to have higher economic costs, and vice versa.

Actions that widen choice or make certain options more accessible are generally well accepted, despite the objections of some critics and their mild interference with free market interactions. These actions include support to access technologies that help private self-control. Opportunities for adopting actions of these types find their main limits in their financial costs, their efficiency and distributional implications. The use of actions involving higher levels of interference with individual choice may be met with increasing degrees of hostility, especially when only certain forms of consumption of a commodity are unhealthy and consumers differ in terms of the nature of their consumption. These actions become more appropriate when the consumption of a commodity is invariably unhealthy and bears a large potential for self-harm; in the presence of important classical market failures, particularly externalities; when actions may be targeted to population groups at the upper extreme of the bounded rationality spectrum (e.g. children, whose early life experiences and behaviours appear to contribute significantly to the formation of their long-term tastes and preference for food and drink, as well as their participation in physical activity) or groups that are particularly exposed to external influences that may trigger unhealthy behaviours (e.g. disadvantaged socioeconomic groups).

Whole-of-government and whole-of-society approaches

Health promotion and disease prevention policies are by no means confined to the health care sector. A large number of polices typically developed in other areas of government action may have an impact on health-related behaviours and, ultimately, on the health of a population. For instance, agricultural policies adopted in most countries, often based on taxes and subsidies, may change the relative prices of healthy foods, such as fruit and vegetables, as well as less healthy foods, such as those high in fat and sugar. Town planning, the design of the built environment and traffic regulation may provide incentives or disincentives for active transport (such as walking and cycling) as opposed to inactive (vehicular) transport. More generally, there is growing evidence that commodities like education, often delivered through public programmes, or at least publicly financed, may be positively associated with health, partly through their effects on lifestyle choices.

This book takes a whole-of-government approach, recognizing that public health policies must be developed across different sectors of government intervention, and that a sound and effective health promotion strategy must address policies in most areas of government intervention, which have potential consequences on population health. This approach, and the challenges it involves, are discussed in detail in Chapter 14.

Health promotion and disease prevention, however, are not an exclusive domain of government action either. Certain types of actions, particularly those aimed at widening choice, lowering the prices of certain choice options, influencing choices through persuasion, and even some regulatory actions, may be promoted or undertaken by actors other than governments, acting alone or in cooperation with governments. These actors may be as diverse as groups of individuals organized for the pursuit of special or general interests (e.g. community action groups, patient organizations, trade unions); professional and business organizations; research organizations and think tanks; civil society organizations; or the mass media. The importance of non-governmental action is underscored, for instance, by a comparative analysis of trends in smoking rates in the United States and Europe, discussed previously under the heading, 'Classical market failures: externalities and poor information', which shows that information was conveyed more effectively in the United States thanks to the entrepreneurial action of anti-smoking interest groups (Cutler and Glaeser 2006).

Disparate motives may lead non-government actors to engage in actions aimed at influencing individual consumption choices in the best interest of consumers. Organized groups of individuals (e.g. consumer groups) may be particularly motivated to take action in situations of asymmetric market power, i.e. markets in which supply may be relatively concentrated, or in which information may be asymmetrically distributed between consumers and suppliers. In the absence of government intervention, because governments do not wish to interfere or intervention would be inefficient, consumers, or other individuals who care for their interests, may attempt to strengthen their position through organized actions. Professional organizations are a special case of such groups, particularly when professionals act as agents of consumers in the protection of their health, as with public health or medical professionals. Businesses may engage in the production and commercialization of healthy commodities whenever market opportunities emerge, but they will also engage in the production and commercialization of unhealthy, or potentially unhealthy, commodities when a market for these can be established. In the latter case, business organizations may be motivated to seek deviations from market dynamics in the best interest of consumers under the threat of tougher actions by other subjects, especially governments, which may affect the interests of their own members. For instance, business organizations may decide to adopt voluntary self-regulation schemes to pre-empt more cogent regulatory actions by government. Employers may, individually or collectively, promote lifestyle interventions for their own employees with a view to improving the overall health of the workforce and increasing productivity, or as part of a 'social contract' with workers. Health insurance organizations, again individually or collectively, may find that lifestyle change and prevention may provide the means for containing health expenditures by raising average levels of health in the pool of insurees. Research organizations, think tanks and the mass media often act as watchdogs on market dynamics and other social phenomena, and in this capacity they may be motivated to take action in the interest of consumers. Actions like those envisaged so far may purportedly be in the best interest of consumers, but even when in good faith, the actors who promote those actions may be prone to influences, biases, and other limitations of rationality that may cause the outcomes of such actions to deviate from their original goals.

The roles played by non-government actors are potentially very important in determining the success of complex preventive interventions. Unilateral actions by governments or others may often prove ineffective or impossible if other actors are not fully engaged in the design and implementation of such actions. In most cases, health promotion and disease prevention require sacrifices on the part of some of the actors involved, which may well be offset by the health benefits of prevention, but nevertheless must be understood and accepted by those who will have to bear them. Direct participation in the development of preventive interventions by all those who have a stake in the process is increasingly regarded as a pre-condition for successful prevention policies.

The structure of the book and remaining chapters

The first chapters of the book (2 and 3) are meant to provide a detailed view of the economic approaches available for the evaluation of policy interventions in the areas of health promotion and disease prevention. These include both a discussion of basic concepts and theories, and a practical illustration of methods and measures of cost and outcome that are typically used in such evaluations. Chapters 2 and 3 are intended to provide readers with the tools to interpret the evidence reviewed in the rest of the book, and also to offer guidance to those who intend to contribute to the economic evidence base on health promotion and chronic disease prevention.

The next set of chapters (4 to 10) represents the core of the book, and contains detailed reviews and analyses of the economic evidence available in specific risk factor areas. In particular, chapters 4 to 7 address behavioural risk factors (tobacco smoking, harmful alcohol use, physical inactivity and unhealthy diets), while Chapter 8 covers selected environmental risk factors, Chapter 9 road traffic injuries, and Chapter 10 mental health risk factors and conditions. The main findings of these chapters are also presented in a Policy Summary jointly published by the European Observatory and the Organisation for Economic Co-operation and Development (OECD) in December 2013.

The next four chapters address cross-cutting themes, including intervention on selected social determinants of health, with a focus, in particular, on education and early life interventions (Chapter 11); the distributional implications of policy actions in health promotion and disease prevention (Chapter 12); key implementation issues (Chapter 13) and cross-sectoral challenges (Chapter 14). Chapter 15 provides overall conclusions from the evidence presented in the rest of the book. A series of summary tables provides a critical appraisal of the evidence available on specific types of interventions, summarizing the key contents of chapters 4 to 10. These tables can be found in the Policy Summary (Merkur et al. 2013: 48-72).

References

Abegunde, D. O., Mathers, C. D., Adam, T., Ortegon, M. and Strong, K. (2007) The burden and costs of chronic diseases in low-income and middle-income countries, *The Lancet*, 370(9603): 1929–38.

Becker, G. S. and Murphy, K. M. (1988) A theory of rational addiction, *The Journal of Political Economy*, 96(4): 675–700.

Brunello, G., Michaud, P. C. and Sanz-de-Galdeano, A. (2008) *The Rise in Obesity Across the Atlantic: An Economic Perspective*. IZA Discussion Paper No. 3529. Bonn: IZA.

Cawley, J. (2004) An economic framework for understanding physical activity and eating behaviors, *American Journal of Preventive Medicine*, 27(3S): 117–25.

Chaloupka, F. J. and Warner, K. E. (1999) The economics of smoking, in J. Newhouse and A. Culyer (eds.) *The Handbook of Health Economics*, Volume 1B. New York: North Holland, pp. 1539–627.

Chandola, T., Britton, A., Brunner, E. et al. (2008) Work stress and coronary heart disease: What are the mechanisms?, *European Heart Journal*, doi:10.1093/eurheartj/ehm584.

Collison, P. (1988) Equality and its bounds, in D. Green (ed.) *Acceptable Inequalities*. London: IEA Health Unit.

Cutler, D. and Glaeser, E. (2005) *What Explains Differences in Smoking, Drinking and Other Health-Related Behaviors?* NBER Working Papers No. 11100. Cambridge, MA: NBER.

Cutler, D. M. and Glaeser, E. L. (2006) *Why Do Europeans Smoke more than Americans?* NBER Working Paper No. 12124. Cambridge, MA: National Bureau of Economic Research.

Cutler, D. M., Glaeser, E. L. and Shapiro, J. M. (2003) Why have Americans become more obese?, *Journal of Economic Perspectives*, 17(3): 93–118.

Dahlgren, G. and Whitehead, M. (1991) *Policies and Strategies to Promote Social Equity in Health*. Stockholm: Institute for Futures Studies.

Donaldson C. and Gerard, K. (1993) *Economics of Health Care Financing: The Visible Hand*. New York: St Martin's Press.

Evans R. G. and Stoddart, G. L. (1994) Producing health, consuming health care, in R. G. Evans, M. L. Barer and T. R. Marmor (eds) *Why are Some People Healthy and Others Not? The Determinants of Health of Populations*. New York: Aldine de Gruyter, pp. 27–63.

Glaeser, E. (2006) Paternalism and psychology, *University of Chicago Law Review*, 73: 133–56.

IHME (Institute of Health Metrics and Evaluation) (2013) *Global Burden of Disease Database*. Seattle: Institute of Health Metrics.

Kenkel, D. S. (2000) Prevention, in A. J. Culyer and J. P. Newhouse (eds) *Handbook of Health Economics*, Volume 1B. New York: North Holland, pp. 1675–720.

Lim, S. S., Vos, T., Flaxman, A. D. et al. (2012) A comparative risk assessment of burden of disease and injury attributable to 67 risk factors and risk factor clusters in 21 regions, 1990–2010: A systematic analysis for the Global Burden of Disease Study 2010, *The Lancet*, 380: 2224–60.

Lipscomb, J., Weinstein, M. C. and Torrance, G. W. (1996) Time preference, in M. R. Gold, J. E. Siegel, L. B. Russell and M. C. Weinstein (eds) *Cost Effectiveness in Health and Medicine*. New York: Oxford University Press, pp. 214–46.

Mackenbach, J. P. (2006) *Health Inequalities: Europe in Profile*. Brussels: European Commission.

Maio, G. R., Manstead, S. R., Verplanken, B. et al. (2007) *Tackling Obesities: Future Choices – Lifestyle Change – Evidence Review*. London: Foresight, Department of Innovation Universities and Skills.

Marmot, M. (2004) *The Status Syndrome*. New York: Henry Holt.

Marmot, M. and Wilkinson, R.G. (eds) (2006) *Social Determinants of Health*, 2nd edn. Oxford: Oxford University Press.

Merkur, S., Sassi, F. and McDaid, D. (2013) *Promoting Health, Preventing Disease: Is there an Economic Case?* Copenhagen: WHO Regional Office for Europe. Available at http://www.euro.who.int/__data/assets/pdf_file/0004/235966/e96956.pdf?ua=1 [Accessed September 2014].

Sassi, F., Archard, L. and Le Grand, J. (2001) Equity and the economic evaluation of healthcare, *Health Technology Assessment*, 5(3): 1–138.

Sassi, F., Belloni, A., and Capobianco, C. (2013) The Role of Fiscal Policies in Health Promotion, OECD Health Working Papers, No. 66, OECD Publishing.

Solar, O. and Irwin, A. (2007) *A Conceptual Framework for Action on the Social Determinants of Health*. Discussion Paper. Geneva: World Health Organization, Commission on Social Determinants of Health.

Suhrcke, M., Nugent, R. A., Stuckler, D. and Rocco, L. (2006) *Chronic Disease: An Economic Perspective*. London: Oxford Health Alliance.

UK Department of Health (1998) *Independent Inquiry into Inequalities in Health – Report*. London: HMSO.

Wilkinson, R. G. and Marmot, M. (2003) *Social Determinants of Health: The Solid Facts*, 2nd edition. Copenhagen: WHO Regional Office for Europe.

World Health Organization (WHO) (2002) *The World Health Report 2002*. Geneva: World Health Organization.

World Health Organization (WHO) (2005) *Preventing Chronic Diseases: A Vital Investment*. Geneva: World Health Organization.

World Health Organization (WHO) (2008) *2008–2013 Action Plan for the Global Strategy for the Prevention and Control of Noncommunicable Diseases*. Geneva: World Health Organization.

chapter two

Supporting effective and efficient policies: the role of economic analysis

*David McDaid, Franco Sassi
and Sherry Merkur*

Chapter 1 has set out the scope, conceptual framework and structure of this book. This chapter and the next provide a detailed overview of how economic approaches are used for the evaluation of policy interventions in the areas of health promotion and disease prevention. Here, in Chapter 2, we provide an introduction to how economic analyses can be used as a tool to help inform decision-making processes on different potential investment choices for the promotion of better population health and well-being. Chapter 3 then goes on to look in detail at how outcomes and costs are assessed in economic evaluation. Both of these chapters are intended to provide readers with an understanding of the role of economic tools to help interpret the evidence reviewed in the rest of the book, and also to offer guidance to those who intend to contribute to the economic evidence base on health promotion and chronic disease prevention.

Chapter 1 highlighted the considerable challenges that policymakers face in promoting and protecting health around the globe. New estimates of the global burden of disease for noncommunicable diseases, including heart disease and stroke, diabetes, cancer, chronic lung diseases, low back pain and poor mental health, indicate that they account for more than 80 per cent of the burden of disease in Europe (Institute of Health Metrics 2013). Moreover, while average life expectancy at birth has been increasing, reaching 76.7 years in 2011, there are substantial disparities across countries. In 2011, life expectancy in the 15 countries that were European Union (EU) members before May 2004 was 81.3 versus 76.0 in the 13 countries joining the EU since 2004, and just 69.8 for countries in the Commonwealth of Independent States (WHO Regional Office for Europe 2014).

The importance of addressing these challenges is recognized in the new health policy framework and strategy of the WHO European Region, *Health 2020* (WHO Regional Office for Europe 2013). This is focused on improving the health and well-being of populations, reducing health inequalities, strengthening public health and ensuring the sustainability of health systems. This builds on an ever mounting body of literature emphasizing the importance of tackling the social determinants of health over which individuals may have little or no control (Commission on Social Determinants of Health 2008; Braveman et al. 2011). It takes a whole-of-government and whole-of-society perspective, emphasizing the importance of actions which go well beyond the traditional boundaries of the health sector and ministries of health.

Chapter 1 has also set out the economic rationale for investing in health promotion and disease prevention; a lack of intervention by government is likely to lead to a sub-optimal allocation of resources to these activities. It may also serve to widen inequalities in health. The challenge then is to determine just how to intervene, with the core question for policymakers in Europe and elsewhere being the extent to which investments in both upstream interventions that target the circumstances that produce adverse health behaviours, and downstream actions that aim to change adverse behaviours, represent a good use of the limited resources at our disposal.

From an economic perspective, how do different interventions stack up when compared with each other or against investment in the treatment of health problems? For example, are there potential gains to be made by reducing or delaying the need for the consumption of future health care resources? Are they more cost-effective for some population groups than others and, if so, will this widen inequalities in health? Might they limit some of the wider costs of poor health to society, such as absenteeism from work, poorer levels of educational attainment, higher rates of violence and crime and early retirement from the labour force due to sickness and disability?

To answer these questions, information is needed on both the effectiveness and cost-effectiveness of different actions in different contexts, taking into account some of the challenges associated with effective implementation. Economic analysis can help address many of these questions and as we shall go on to indicate it is now being increasingly used to look at the case for health promotion and disease prevention.

Resource scarcity and the role of economic analysis

If resources were limitless it would be relatively straightforward to argue for investment in disease prevention and health promotion actions of proven effectiveness. Resources are, however, scarce and careful choices have to be made. These decisions may be even more important in any downward phase in an economic cycle in countries, where public finances including health, social care and education budgets are under even greater pressure. Evidence on effectiveness alone is insufficient for decision-making; in addition to knowing what works and in what context, information on the economic impacts of these choices is required. Such economic evidence is increasingly a formal element of decision-making processes, and can be compelling in putting forward a case for policy change.

There are at least four key economic questions that can be helpful to decision-makers in the difficult task of allocating resources (Knapp and McDaid 2009) (see Box 2.1). In this chapter we will focus in particular on the third question, that

Box 2.1 Economic questions to inform policymaking and practice

The costs of inaction: What are the economic consequences of not taking action to promote and protect the health of the population?

The costs of action: What would it cost to intervene by providing a promotion or preventive measure?

The cost-effectiveness of action: What is the balance between what it costs to intervene and what would be achieved in terms of better outcomes – e.g. emotional well-being, physical health, improved quality of life, educational performance?

The levers for change: What economic incentives can encourage more use of those interventions that are thought to be cost-effective and less use of those interventions which are not?

of classical economic evaluation – that is, establishing the cost-effectiveness of alternative policy options for health promotion and disease prevention. We now will briefly look at these four questions, then describe different approaches to economic evaluation, including how economic modelling tools can be used. We will then look at how the economic evidence base on health promotion and disease prevention has evolved.

The cost of not taking action

Economic methods can be used to assess the costs of *not taking action*. In the case of health promotion and disease prevention, this would include not only quantifying the resources needs and costs of delivering health and other services to treat what would have been preventable health problems, but also quantifying the broader impacts of risky behaviours and poor health. In the case of alcohol-related harm, for instance, this would include costs to the criminal justice system of alcohol-related crimes and the costs of alcohol-related road traffic accidents and workplace injuries (Anderson et al. 2013). At an even broader level this could also include estimating the costs of stigma and discrimination associated with some avoidable health problems such as HIV/AIDS (Brent 2013) or behavioural problems in children (Scott et al. 2001; Colman et al. 2009; McDaid et al. 2014).

Estimating the costs of intervention

A second question that economics can address is to determine the costs of intervention. This can include all the initial implementation costs associated with putting in place the necessary infrastructure for a health promotion programme, as well as the ongoing maintenance costs for that programme. This can go beyond costs to government or other programme funders; there may be further costs to society as a whole, for instance out-of-pocket costs that must be incurred by members of the population if they wish to make use of a health promotion programme or activity. One example of this, for instance, is the cost to families of purchasing bicycle helmets following the introduction of legislation on their mandatory use (Taylor and Scuffham 2002; Hendrie et al. 2004).

Informing the allocation of resources

Answering these first two questions provides valuable information to decision-makers, but it does not provide guidance on how best to allocate resources to promote and protect health. This is something that can be addressed by the third question which implies the use of economic evaluation techniques. Widely used in the health care, environmental and transport sectors, economic evaluation can be considered 'the comparative analysis of alternative course of action in terms of both their costs and consequences' (Drummond et al. 2005). It acknowledges that scarcity is an endemic feature of all societies and implies that investment in one specific public project will mean a lost opportunity to use these resources for another purpose. Even in the absence of long-term effectiveness data, as we shall discuss later, economic evaluation can use modelling techniques to assess the long-term costs and effects and/or identify the level of effectiveness a strategy would have to achieve to be considered cost-effective.

Economic evaluation techniques compare incremental changes in costs with incremental changes in outcomes for two or more policy options. If, using economic evaluation techniques, a new intervention is both less costly and more effective than the existing situation, then the decision is usually straightforward – invest in the new intervention. If it has poorer outcomes and costs more, it will also be rejected. But if an intervention is both more effective and more costly (or in theory less effective and less costly), then policymakers must make a value judgement as to whether it is worthwhile.

Care has to be taken in interpreting the results of economic evaluation. The resources and infrastructure available will influence that what may be deemed cost-effective in Ireland or France may not be in Tajikistan or Georgia. Something that is cost-effective when only looking at the impact to the health system may appear cost-ineffective when costs to the economy as a whole are considered. Furthermore, an intervention that does not appear cost-effective over a 12-month period may appear highly cost-effective if a longer time horizon is considered. Guidelines on the ways in which economic studies should be reported have been published (Husereau et al. 2013) and there are some databases, most notably, the NHS Economic Evaluation Database at the University of York, that provides independent critical appraisals of the quality of these studies.[1]

For all of these reasons the results of economic evaluations should not be used in isolation, and other factors will need to be taken into consideration as part of any decision-making process. Investment in the most cost-effective intervention might conflict with other policy goals, such as reducing inequality in health or non-health outcomes between social groups. Other economic inputs taken into deliberation may include the budgetary impact of implementing an intervention, the need to address any inequalities in outcomes between population sub-groups, issues of fairness in access to services and support, and the economic impacts on the wider local economy of a population health measure, such as banning smoking in pubs and restaurants and local political concerns.

Using economic incentives to influence behaviour

The fourth question in Box 2.1 is concerned with how different economic incentives can be used as levers to encourage more use of those interventions that are demonstrated to be cost-effective, and less use of those interventions which are not. This might, for instance, involve looking at how the level of flexibility in the ways in which budgets are allocated influences the development of partnerships to deliver health promotion services across sectors (Johansson and Tillgren 2011; McDaid 2012). This is an issue that is discussed in detail in Chapter 14. It might also look at how different payment mechanisms and financial incentives in service contracts can influence the success of health promotion and disease prevention activities. The role of financial and other incentives to encourage a target population group to participate and/or sustain health promoting activities is another area of research that may be examined (Thomson et al. 2012). This fourth question also covers the long history of research looking at the links between taxation policy within one country or even across international boundaries and risky behaviours (Johansson et al. 2009; Doran et al. 2013; Johansson et al. 2014). In recent years, there has also been a growing interest in looking at how tools from behavioural science can be used to influence individual behaviours; one example of this is work looking at whether commitment contracts which financially reward individuals for achieving a health behaviour goal, such as losing weight or quitting smoking, really do lead to long-term sustained change (John et al. 2011; Relton et al. 2011; Allan et al. 2012; Loewenstein et al. 2012; White et al. 2013).

Approaches to economic evaluation

Having briefly looked at each of the four questions in Box 2.1, we now focus on approaches to economic evaluation. A number of authors have looked at the strengths and weaknesses of different economic evaluation methods for health promotion and disease (Kelly et al. 2005; Cookson et al. 2009; McDaid and Needle 2009; Weatherly et al. 2009; Lorgelly et al. 2010; Marsh et al. 2012; McDaid and Suhrcke 2012). Chapter 3 discusses these issues in detail. Here we briefly introduce the main types of economic evaluation. They have much in common – for instance, they share a common approach to the conceptualization, definition and measurement of costs, but there are important differences in how they define and assess outcomes, primarily because they seek to answer slightly different questions.

If the question to be addressed by an economic evaluation is essentially about improving some specific aspect of health, information will be needed on the comparative costs of the different health promotion actions available (and also on the cost of a no-action option). The comparative outcomes may be measured using some specific measure of health status. This would be known as cost-effectiveness analysis. While it is easy to understand it can be of limited use as the outcome measures used would vary from study to study, meaning that little could be said at a macro level about how best to use resources in a health promotion budget.

An alternative approach would be to measure all health-related outcomes using a common metric such as the quality-adjusted life-year (QALY) (see Chapter 3 for more on this). This approach is known as cost-utility analysis. Using a common metric, health system decision-makers can compare cost per QALY gained for very different health promotion and health care interventions. They can then take this information into account when making decisions on how to allocate their budgets.

However, throughout this volume many of the interventions that are described are likely to be delivered outside of the health system, for instance by ministries responsible for food standards, transport or education. In these cases, using even broader measures of impact that are relevant across all of these public policy areas can be helpful. The usual approach for such a broad impact measure is to value all outcomes in terms of money, leading to a form of evaluation called cost-benefit analysis.

These choices on economic evaluation technique do not have to be mutually exclusive: a single study can support more than one approach if the right combination of evaluative tools is used. However, guidelines from health technology assessment bodies tend to recommend the use of cost-utility analysis. In England, public health guidance developed by the National Institute for Health and Care Excellence (NICE) allows the use of cost-consequences analysis as an addendum to cost-utility analysis (Kelly et al. 2010). This approach can present cost per change in a range of natural health and non-health outcomes, such as heart attacks avoided or a reduction in crime rates. It is then up to policymakers to assess which outcome (if any) may be most important. Public health guidance from NICE also enables a broader perspective on costs than the conventional consideration of costs to the health and social care system seen in many health technology assessment systems elsewhere. It can, for instance, also examine the effects of workplace health promotion programmes on the costs to business of absenteeism and reduced productivity levels.

Cost-benefit analysis is widely used in the assessment of the economic case for health promoting actions in the fields of transportation and the environment, but is unusual in the health sector. The challenges of eliciting accurate monetary values for outcomes and negative public perceptions of valuing health in monetary terms, as illustrated in Chapter 3, may have limited the use and acceptability of cost-benefit analysis in the health sector (Rush et al. 2004; Kelly et al. 2005; McDaid and Needle 2009).

How can economic modelling help?

Economic modelling techniques are widely used in making the case for health promotion and disease prevention interventions. There are many different reasons for making use of economic models (Box 2.2). Paramount is the need to reduce any uncertainty about the strength of evidence on the effectiveness and costs of different interventions. Such uncertainty increases the likelihood of making a sub-optimal policy decision. One key cause of uncertainty is that many of the impacts of health promoting actions go well beyond the time frame covered by conventional evaluative studies. Modelling is often the only way of estimating the impacts of an intervention over the long term. For instance, many of the health-related benefits of avoiding the onset of obesity will not be manifest for several decades (Sassi 2010).

As subsequent chapters in this volume will show, economic models are very widely used to estimate benefits over many decades for disease prevention and health promotion (e.g. Wang et al. 2002; Wang et al. 2003; Chisholm et al. 2004; Cobiac et al. 2009; Cecchini et al. 2010; Cobiac et al. 2010). Most trials or longitudinal studies only follow up participants for no more than a few years at best (Hodgson et al. 2007). Readers should also be aware that judging the success of investing in a health promotion programme based solely on the outcomes, say of a 12-month controlled study, may be misleading and very different from a study with the same programme evaluated over much a longer follow-up period (Haji Ali Afzali et al. 2012).

Models can extrapolate information from trials and literature to provide estimates of longer-term cost-effectiveness. They can make different assumptions, for instance on the persistence of effectiveness of any intervention, as well as the need for ongoing or booster sessions. These longer-term models can also be designed to take account of the risk of future negative events and patterns of disease progression. For instance, in the case of chronic mental disorders this may involve looking at the risk of a relapse or how past suicidal behaviour impacts on the risk of further suicidal events (McDaid 2014).

Models are also used to look at the impacts of adapting the evidence on effective interventions to different contexts and settings. Economic models are always prepared to inform deliberations at NICE, in England, on public health guidance (Kelly et al. 2010). These models often take effectiveness and resource use data reported in non-United Kingdom settings and adapt this to a United Kingdom context. Models might also be used to look at the minimum level of engagement and continued use of an intervention that would be needed for one to be considered cost-effective in everyday conditions.

Box 2.2 The role of economic modelling for health promotion and disease prevention

---

- Addressing uncertainty in the results of any one trial.
- Synthesizing data from multiple trials and effectiveness studies on different costs and effects of interventions, often using different head-to-head comparators rather than relying on findings from one study alone.
- Modelling the costs and effectiveness of different interventions for longer time periods than seen in most evaluative studies.
- Modelling potential intervention pathways, and their effectiveness and costs in contexts and settings where local empirical evidence is unavailable.

- Modelling the costs and effectiveness of interventions for specific sub-population groups.
- Modelling the cost-effective implications of differing rates of coverage, uptake and continued engagement with different interventions.

A discussion of the strengths and weakness of different modelling approaches goes beyond the scope of this chapter, but this has been widely discussed in the literature (Barton et al. 2004; McDaid 2014), including in the context of health promoting interventions (Barton et al. 2011). Different modelling approaches involve different levels of complexity and time to develop. Some models can be constructed relatively quickly and do not require investment in expensive computing equipment. At the other end of the spectrum there are complex macro-simulation models that have been used to model some packages of preventive interventions, e.g. for obesity, diet and physical activities (Cecchini et al. 2010). These complex models, while in theory being more precise, can take a team of researchers many months to build. They can also require a large amount of computational power using mainframe computers – something which may not be available.

Growth in the use of economic evaluation to assess health promotion and disease prevention interventions

Many European countries have formally made use of economic evidence when considering whether to reimburse new *health care* interventions and procedures for some years (McDaid and Cookson 2003). Historically, less attention has focused on the strength of the evidence for most health promotion and disease prevention strategies. Although many complex health promotion and public health interventions do not lend themselves easily to evaluation through randomized controlled trials, the real challenge may not lie in scepticism over methodologies of evaluation, but rather in the very limited levels of resources available for evaluating many public health and health promoting interventions that do not have an obvious commercial appeal. This is particularly the case for those interventions focused on the social determinants of health that play a major role in influencing population health.

Without solid evidence on effectiveness it is nigh on impossible to determine the cost-effectiveness of any action. With little private sector motivation to invest in public health, research is largely reliant on funding from government and charitable foundations. Budgets for pubic health research are often modest, and until recently there appear to have been few incentives to undertake economic evaluations of public health and health promoting interventions (Hale 2000; Godfrey 2001; Holland 2004; Kelly et al. 2005; McDaid and Needle 2009).

Therefore health technology assessment agencies and other comparable organizations have focused on the case for reimbursing what are often expensive new pharmaceuticals and technologies. Early assessments of the economic case for preventive actions focused on technologies that may have been more straightforward to evaluate, such as screening and vaccination policies, as well as assessing interventions to tackle already established poor health behaviours such as smoking (McGhan and Smith 1996) and risky sexual practices (Wang et al. 2000). The impacts of changes in pricing policies and taxes on harmful behaviours have been examined for decades (Levy and Sheflin 1983; Ornstein and Levy 1983). Many interventions have also been evaluated within the context of decision-making processes in other sectors, as in the case of the economic appraisal of road safety interventions (Elvik et al. 2009).

In recent years there has been a growth in both the absolute number of economic evaluations that have been undertaken and the types of intervention that they cover (McDaid and Needle 2009; Weatherly et al. 2009; Saha et al. 2010; Sassi 2010; Vos et al. 2010; McDaid and Suhrcke 2012; Owen et al. 2012; Alayli-Goebbels et al. 2013). Chapters 4 to 11 in this volume will go on to look at much of this evidence. There is increasingly a greater focus on complex interventions, including evaluations of combinations of interventions and some evaluation of behaviour change interventions. The increased availability of sophisticated modelling software has also allowed much more intricate analysis to be conducted, taking a very long-term or even lifetime perspective (Cecchini et al. 2010; Ortegon et al. 2012).

There has also been an increase in the use of economic evidence to inform formal decision-making processes at national and regional level, with actions identified in countries such as Australia, Belgium, Canada, Denmark, England, Finland, the Netherlands, New Zealand, Norway, Sweden and the US (McDaid and Suhrcke 2012). In Europe, NICE in England has been a pioneer on the use of economic evidence for decisions on health promotion and public health interventions delivered outside of the health system. It has been assessing the economic case for these interventions since 2005, publishing guidance which has been influenced by mandatory economic modelling work and systematic reviews of economic evidence (Owen et al. 2012). This guidance should be followed by health care system stakeholders and is discretionary for other relevant interested parties such as local government and private sector employers (Kelly et al. 2010).

Moving forward

The economic evidence base for health promotion and disease prevention continues to grow, and the importance of assessing the economic case for prevention is acknowledged in many health policy circles. Potentially, the economic benefits of investing in health promotion and disease prevention could be high, but it is important that well-designed evaluations are undertaken prior to large-scale investment. Adding an economic dimension retrospectively to those areas of public health where evidence on effectiveness is strong may be one pragmatic and relatively rapid way of helping to expand an evidence base which, as we shall see, is still dominated by studies from a handful of countries. Modelling techniques can also be used to help expand the evidence base and look at potential costs and benefits over different time periods, making different assumptions on effectiveness and resource configuration, in different geographical contexts and from the perspective of different budget holders or the economy as a whole.

Many challenges lie ahead, including the ways in which outcomes will be measured. This is discussed fully in Chapter 3, but one issue for economic evaluation is to develop appropriate metrics to be able to compare improvements in health outcomes with improvements in well-being, where this is defined as being over and above the absence of illness. Well-being, for instance, has also been discussed in terms of the capability approach which suggests that well-being should be measured not according to what individuals actually do (functioning), but what they can do (capabilities) (Lorgelly et al. 2010). More can also be done to take on board equity, as well as efficiency concerns, when looking at health promotion and disease prevention; this challenge will be explored in Chapter 12. Another challenge will be to better translate economic evidence messages into implemented actions (Chapter 13), both within and beyond the health system. Chapter 14 will examine what more can be done to overcome barriers to more intersectoral working.

We have indicated in the first two chapters of this volume that there is much interest at a policy level on the potential for adopting health promotion and disease prevention strategies, but this interest does not always appear to be matched by investment. Recent analysis from the Organisation for Economic Co-operation and Development (OECD) found that more than three-quarters of OECD countries reported a cut in real-term spending on prevention programmes in 2011 compared to 2010, and half spent less than in 2008. There were cuts to spending on effective prevention programmes on obesity, harmful use of alcohol and smoking (OECD 2013). This is why it is vital to further strengthen the evidence base and communicate findings effectively. Cuts to health promotion and disease prevention budgets may reduce the pressure on health care finances in the short-term, but the longer-term impacts of poorer health are likely to have a much greater impact on future health care finances.

Note

1   http://www.crd.york.ac.uk/CRDWeb/

References

Alayli-Goebbels, A. F., Evers, S. M., Alexeeva, D. et al. (2013) A review of economic evaluations of behavior change interventions: Setting an agenda for research methods and practice, *Journal of Public Health (Oxford)*, 36(2): 336–44.

Allan, C., Radley, A. and Williams, B. (2012) Paying the price for an incentive: An exploratory study of smokers' reasons for failing to complete an incentive based smoking cessation scheme, *Journal of Health Services Research & Policy*, 17: 212–8.

Anderson, P., Casswell, S., Parry, C. and Rehm, J. (2013) Alcohol, in K. Limmo, E. Ollila, S. Pea, M. Wismar and S. Cook (eds) *Health in all Policies*. Brussels: European Observatory on Health Systems and Policies, pp. 225–55.

Barton, P., Andronis, L., Briggs, A., McPherson, K. and Capewell, S. (2011) Effectiveness and cost-effectiveness of cardiovascular disease prevention in whole populations: Modelling study, *British Medical Journal*, 343: d4044.

Barton, P., Bryan, S. and Robinson, S. (2004) Modelling in the economic evaluation of health care: Selecting the appropriate approach, *Journal of Health Services Research & Policy*, 9: 110–8.

Braveman, P. A., Egerter, S. A. and Mockenhaupt, R. E. (2011) Broadening the focus: The need to address the social determinants of health, *American Journal of Preventive Medicine*, 40: S4–18.

Brent, R. J. (2013) The economic value of reducing the stigma of HIV/AIDS, *Expert Review of Pharmacoeconomics & Outcomes Research*, 13: 561–3.

Cecchini, M., Sassi, F., Lauer, J. A., Lee, Y. Y., Guajardo-Barron, V. and Chisholm, D. (2010) Tackling of unhealthy diets, physical inactivity, and obesity: Health effects and cost-effectiveness, *The Lancet*, 376: 1775–84.

Chisholm, D., Rehm, J., Van Ommeren, M. and Monteiro, M. (2004) Reducing the global burden of hazardous alcohol use: A comparative cost-effectiveness analysis, *Journal of Studies on Alcohol and Drugs*, 65: 782–93.

Cobiac, L., Vos, T., Doran, C. and Wallace, A. (2009) Cost-effectiveness of interventions to prevent alcohol-related disease and injury in Australia, *Addiction*, 104: 1646–55.

Cobiac, L. J., Vos, T. and Veerman, J. L. (2010) Cost-effectiveness of interventions to reduce dietary salt intake, *Heart*, 96: 1920–5.

Colman, I., Murray, J., Abbott, R. A. et al. (2009) Outcomes of conduct problems in adolescence: 40 year follow-up of national cohort, *British Medical Journal*, 338: a2981.

Commission on Social Determinants of Health (2008) *Closing the Gap in a Generation: Health Equity Through Action on the Social Determinants of Health*. Final report of the Commission on Social Determinants of Health. Geneva: World Health Organization.

Cookson, R., Drummond, M. and Weatherly, H. (2009) Explicit incorporation of equity considerations into economic evaluation of public health interventions, *Health Economics, Policy and Law*, 4: 231–45.

Doran, C. M., Byrnes, J. M., Cobiac, L. J., Vandenberg, B. and Vos, T. (2013) Estimated impacts of alternative Australian alcohol taxation structures on consumption, public health and government revenues, *Medical Journal of Australia*, 199: 619–22.

Drummond, M. F., Schulpher, M., Torrance, G. W., O'Brien, B. J. and Stoddart, G. (2005) *Methods for the Economic Evaluation of Health Care Programmes*. Oxford and New York: Oxford University Press.

Elvik, R., Hoye, A., Vaa, T. and Sorenson, M. (eds) (2009) *Handbook of Road Safety Measures*, 2nd edn. Bingley: Emerald Group.

Godfrey, C. (2001) Economic evaluation of health promotion, *WHO Regional Publication European Series*, 149–70.

Haji Ali Afzali, H., Karnon, J. and Gray, J. (2012) A critical review of model-based economic studies of depression: Modelling techniques, model structure and data sources, *Pharmacoeconomics*, 30: 461–82.

Hale, J. (2000) What contribution can health economics make to health promotion?, *Health Promotion International*, 15: 341–8.

Hendrie, D., Miller, T. R., Orlando, M. et al. (2004) Child and family safety device affordability by country income level: An 18 country comparison, *Injury Prevention*, 10: 338–43.

Hodgson, R., Bushe, C. and Hunter, R. (2007) Measurement of long-term outcomes in observational and randomised controlled trials, *British Journal of Psychiatry Supplements*, 50: s78–84.

Holland, W. (2004) Health technology assessment and public health: A commentary, *International Journal of Technology Assessment in Health Care*, 20: 77–80.

Husereau, D., Drummond, M., Petrou, S. et al. (2013) Consolidated Health Economic Evaluation Reporting Standards (CHEERS) statement, *Value Health*, 16: e1–5.

Institute of Health Metrics (2013) *Global Burden of Disease Database.* Seattle, WA: Institute of Health Metrics.

Johansson, C., Burman, L. and Forsberg, B. (2009) The effects of congestions tax on air quality and health, *Atmospheric Environment,* 43: 4843–54.

Johansson, P., Pekkarinen, T. and Verho, J. (2014) Cross-border health and productivity effects of alcohol policies, *Journal of Health Economics,* 36C: 125–36.

Johansson, P. and Tillgren, P. (2011) Financing intersectoral health promotion programmes: Some reasons why collaborators are collaborating as indicated by cost-effectiveness analyses, *Scandinavian Journal of Public Health,* 39: 26–32.

John, L. K., Loewenstein, G., Troxel, A. B., Norton, L., Fassbender, J. E. and Volpp, K. G. (2011) Financial incentives for extended weight loss: A randomized, controlled trial, *Journal of General Internal Medicine,* 26: 621–6.

Kelly, M. P., McDaid, D., Ludbrook, A. and Powell, J. (2005) *Economic Appraisal of Public Health Interventions.* London: National Institute for Health and Clinical Excellence.

Kelly, M., Morgan, A., Ellis, S., Younger, T., Huntley, J. and Swann, C. (2010) Evidence based public health: A review of the experience of the National Institute of Health and Clinical Excellence (NICE) of developing public health guidance in England, *Social Science and Medicine,* 71: 1056–62.

Knapp, M. and McDaid, D. (2009) Making an economic case for prevention and promotion, *International Journal of Mental Health Promotion,* 11: 49–56.

Levy, D. and Sheflin, N. (1983) New evidence on controlling alcohol use through price, *Journal of Studies on Alcohol and Drugs,* 44: 929–37.

Loewenstein, G., Asch, D. A., Friedman, J. Y., Melichar, L. A. and Volpp, K. G. (2012) Can behavioural economics make us healthier?, *British Medical Journal,* 344: e3482.

Lorgelly, P. K., Lawson, K. D., Fenwick, E. A. and Briggs, A. H. (2010) Outcome measurement in economic evaluations of public health interventions: A role for the capability approach?, *International Journal of Environmental Research and Public Health,* 7: 2274–89.

Marsh, K., Phillips, C. J., Fordham, R., Bertranou, E. and Hale, J. (2012) Estimating cost-effectiveness in public health: A summary of modelling and valuation methods, *Health Economics Review,* 2: 17.

McDaid, D. (2012) Joint budgeting: Can it facilitate intersectoral action?, in D. McQueen, M. Wismar, V. Lin, C. Jones and M. Davies (eds) *Intersectoral Governance for Health in All Policies: Structure, Actions and Experiences.* Copenhagen: World Health Organization, pp. 111–28.

McDaid, D. (2014) Economic modelling for global mental health, in G. Thornicroft and V. Patel (eds) *Global Mental Health Trials.* Oxford: Oxford University Press.

McDaid, D. and Cookson, R. (2003) Evaluating health care interventions in the European Union, *Health Policy,* 63: 133–9.

McDaid, D. and Needle, J. (2009) What use has been made of economic evaluation in public health? A systematic review of the literature, in Z. Morris and S. Dawson (eds) *Future Public Health: Burdens, Challenges, and Opportunities.* Basingstoke: Palgrave Macmillan, pp. 248–64.

McDaid, D., Park, A. L., Currie, C. and Zanotti, C. (2014) Investing in the well-being of young people: Making the economic case, in D. McDaid and C. L. Cooper (eds) *Well-being: A Complete Reference Guide. Volume 5: Economics of Well-being.* Oxford: John Wiley, pp. 181–214.

McDaid, D. and Suhrcke, M. (2012) The contribution of public health interventions: An economic perspective, in J. Figueras and M. McKee (eds) *Health Systems, Health, Wealth and Societal Well-being.* Maidenhead: Open University Press, pp. 125–52.

McGhan, W. F. and Smith, M. D. (1996) Pharmacoeconomic analysis of smoking-cessation interventions, *American Journal of Health-System Pharmacy,* 53: 45–52.

Organisation for Economic Co-operation and Development (OECD) (2013) *Health at a Glance 2013*. Paris: OECD Indicators, OECD Publishing.

Ornstein, S. I. and Levy, D. (1983) Price and income elasticities of demand for alcoholic beverages, *Recent Developments in Alcoholism*, 1: 303–45.

Ortegon, M., Lim, S., Chisholm, D. and Mendis, S. (2012) Cost-effectiveness of strategies to combat cardiovascular disease, diabetes, and tobacco use in sub-Saharan Africa and South East Asia: Mathematical modelling study, *British Medical Journal*, 344: e607.

Owen, L., Morgan, A., Fischer, A., Ellis, S., Hoy, A. and Kelly, M. P. (2012) The cost-effectiveness of public health interventions, *Journal of Public Health (Oxford)*, 34: 37–45.

Relton, C., Strong, M. and Li, J. (2011) The 'Pounds for Pounds' weight loss financial incentive scheme: An evaluation of a pilot in NHS Eastern and Coastal Kent, *Journal of Public Health (Oxford)*, 33: 536–42.

Rush, B., Shiell, A. and Hawe, P. (2004) A census of economic evaluations in health promotion, *Health Education Research*, 19: 707–19.

Saha, S., Gerdtham, U. G. and Johansson, P. (2010) Economic evaluation of lifestyle interventions for preventing diabetes and cardiovascular diseases, *International Journal of Environmental Research and Public Health*, 7: 3150–95.

Sassi, F. (2010) *Obesity and the Economics of Prevention: Fit not Fat*. Paris: OECD.

Scott, S., Knapp, M., Henderson, J. and Maughan, B. (2001) Financial cost of social exclusion: Follow-up study of antisocial children into adulthood, *British Medical Journal*, 323: 191.

Taylor, M. and Scuffham, P. (2002) New Zealand bicycle helmet law – do the costs outweigh the benefits?, *Injury Prevention*, 8: 317–20.

Thomson, G., Dykes, F., Hurley, M. A. and Hoddinott, P. (2012) Incentives as connectors: Insights into a breastfeeding incentive intervention in a disadvantaged area of North-West England, *BMC Pregnancy and Childbirth*, 12: 22.

Vos, T., Carter, R., Barendregt, J. et al. (2010) *Assessing Cost-Effectiveness in Prevention (ACE–Prevention)*. Brisbane: University of Queensland.

Wang, L. Y., Burstein, G. R. and Cohen, D. A. (2002) An economic evaluation of a school-based sexually transmitted disease screening program, *Sexually Transmitted Diseases*, 29: 737–45.

Wang, L. Y., Davis, M., Robin, L., Collins, J., Coyle, K. and Baumler, E. (2000) Economic evaluation of Safer Choices: A school-based human immunodeficiency virus, other sexually transmitted diseases, and pregnancy prevention program, *Archives of Pediatrics and Adolescent Medicine*, 154: 1017–24.

Wang, L. Y., Yang, Q., Lowry, R. and Wechsler, H. (2003) Economic analysis of a school-based obesity prevention program, *Obesity Research & Clinical Practice*, 11: 1313–24.

Weatherly, H., Drummond, M., Claxton, K. et al. (2009) Methods for assessing the cost-effectiveness of public health interventions: Key challenges and recommendations, *Health Policy*, 93: 85–92.

White, J. S., Dow, W. H. and Rungruanghiranya, S. (2013) Commitment contracts and team incentives: A randomized controlled trial for smoking cessation in Thailand, *American Journal of Preventive Medicine*, 45: 533–42.

World Health Organization (WHO) Regional Office for Europe (2013) *Health 2020. A European Health Policy Framework and Strategy for the 20th Century*. Copenhagen: WHO Regional Office for Europe.

World Health Organization (WHO) Regional Office for Europe (2014) *European Health for All Database*. Updated April 2014. Copenhagen: WHO Regional Office for Europe.

three

Measurement challenges in the economic evaluation of public health interventions

Silvia Evers, Marie-Jeanne Aarts and Adrienne Alayli-Goebbels

Introduction

Chapter 2 provided an introduction on how economic evaluations are a tool that can help to inform decision-makers and other stakeholders about different potential investment choices for the promotion of better population health and well-being. Most national guidelines on economic evaluation (Jacobs et al. 1995: www.ispor.org/peguidelines/index.asp) recommend that these economic evaluations are performed from a societal perspective, meaning that all relevant costs and outcomes are included, regardless of who bears the costs and receives the outcomes. As a result, broad measurement of health impacts, both in terms of costs and outcomes, is usually an important component of economic evaluations.

This chapter provides a brief primer on how outcomes and costs are assessed, especially related to health and well-being in economic evaluation. It also briefly looks at how resources and their costs consequences are factored into economic evaluation. The aim of this chapter is to help policymakers and other stakeholders, not well versed in economic evaluation, to get a sense of how changes in outcomes and costs can be measured. For further in-depth details on outcome and cost measurement, please see other in-depth overviews (Spilker 1995; Drummond and McGuire 2001; Bowling 2005; Drummond et al. 2005; Brazier et al. 2007; Glick 2007).

This chapter begins by looking at the state of the art with regard to measuring and valuing outcomes and costs. Challenges and solutions in outcome and cost measurement for health promotion and disease prevention are then discussed in the following section. Finally, key recommendations are formulated for policymakers and other stakeholders who may be funding, participating in, or making use of economic evaluations.

Outcome and cost measurement: the current state of the art

Types of economic evaluation

A common way of classifying types of economic evaluation distinguishes between cost-consequence analysis (CCA), cost-effectiveness analysis (CEA), cost-utility analysis (CUA), and cost-benefit analysis (CBA). In fact, the first three may be grouped under the label of CEA, whose theoretical grounding differs from that of CBA. However, what matters here is that the above types of analysis differ in the way that outcomes are measured and valued, while the different types do not vary in the way that resource use and costs are measured. Table 3.1 summarizes the main characteristics, and some of the advantages and disadvantages, of these four types of economic evaluation that have been used to evaluate public health interventions. CCA collects information on two or more outcomes, without defining a primary outcome measure. CEA and CUA both use a single outcome measure. CEA uses a natural unit of measurement, e.g. changes in body mass index; while in the case of CUA, the single outcome measure used is a utility that represents the strength of an individual's preference for a specific health state, typically seen in terms of quality of life or levels of disability. In CBA, both outcomes and costs are valued in monetary terms.

Table 3.1 Types of economic evaluation

	Costs	Outcomes/benefits	Advantages	Disadvantages
CCA	Monetary value (e.g. Euro)	Multiple (two or more) outcomes not aggregated to one overall outcome measure.	Uses outcomes known to the field (disease-specific measures). Representation of multiple outcomes.	No aggregated outcome.
CEA	Monetary value (e.g. Euro)	Natural units (e.g. number of lung cancer patients averted, number of traffic accidents prevented, percentage reduction in children suffering from obesity).	Uses outcomes known to the field (disease-specific measures). Intermediate as well as final outcomes can be included.	Comparison between interventions with different outcomes is difficult.
CUA	Monetary value (e.g. Euro)	Utilities (e.g. QALY, DALY).	Valuation; generic outcome. Enables comparison between interventions addressing different risk factors or diseases.	QALYs and DALYs might not be sensitive enough to pick up (small) changes produced by public health interventions.

CBA	Monetary value (e.g. Euro)	Monetary value (e.g. Euro).	Valuation; generic outcome. Enables comparison between interventions across different policy sectors.	Some outcomes are difficult to value in monetary terms.

A review of economic evaluations in public health indicated that the majority of published studies use simple CEAs and CCAs. CUA and CBA, which are more complex looking at the outcome measurement, are used less frequently and account for only 13 per cent and 5 per cent of the economic evaluation studies in the field of public health, respectively (McDaid and Needle 2009). In addition to these four types, a fifth type of economic evaluation study is often identified: cost-minimization analysis. In a CMA, two or more interventions have been demonstrated to be equally effective, hence the evaluator is focused solely on identifying the intervention with the lowest net costs. However, given the uncertainty that persists on differences in the effectiveness of interventions, the approach is becoming rarer, is often not considered robust, and is regarded as inferior to the other approaches (Briggs and O'Brien 2001).

Important features of outcome measurement

To have a better understanding of how outcomes are measured in economic evaluation, four features are important: 1) the use of incremental cost-effectiveness ratios (ICERs); 2) the description of a health state versus valuation; 3) generic outcomes versus disease-specific outcomes, and 4) process versus outcome measurement. Each will be discussed in turn.

1) The use of ratios in relation to nominal versus cardinal scales

When comparing outcomes for economic evaluations, it is preferable to do this by means of incremental analysis. This means that the comparison focuses on additional benefits of one alternative public health intervention compared to the additional benefits of another alternative public health intervention. In CEA and CUA, which are frequently used methods (McDaid and Needle 2009) in the field of public health, the incremental analysis is done by means of an ICER (see equation). The incremental ratio is based on the differences in costs between the public health intervention and a comparator (for instance, usual care or another public health intervention) divided by the differences in outcomes between the public health intervention and the comparator.

$$ICER = (C1 - C2) / (E1 - E2)$$

Note: C1 and E1 are the cost and effect in the intervention group, and C2 and E2 the cost and effect in the control care group.

2) Description of a health state versus valuation

In CUA and CBA, it is important to recognize that there is a difference between the reporting of a health state and the value that a respondent may attach to this health state. CEA and CCA usually do not involve making any subjective judgement about the value of a health improvement, i.e. the explicit value which respondents have on a scale is regarded as the same for every respondent. In contrast, in CUA and CBA, a relative weight is attached to an improvement in health. This valuation may come from the general population, patients or other stakeholders. For instance, looking at tobacco control, reduction of tobacco use might be seen as an improvement from a clinical point of view and can be used as an outcome measurement in CEA, while individual smokers might place less of a value on this outcome if they have to endure a craving for cigarettes which will influence their quality of life and can be captured as part of outcome measurement in CUA.

Valuation in CUA is given in terms of a utility score, which is often represented as being between 0 and 1, where 0 usually represents death and 1 represents full health. One of the simplest ways of deriving such a value is by asking individuals to indicate this graphically on a visual analogue scale, which is somewhat similar in appearance to a thermometer. Other more sophisticated methods to elicit preferences can take account of uncertainty and risk associated with interventions. Describing these is beyond the scope of this chapter, but they include techniques known as the standard gamble and time trade-off. Detailed information about these methods is available (Brazier et al. 2007).

In CBA, we have noted that outcomes are valued in monetary terms. CBA is well accepted and used for the evaluation of public health interventions in the fields of transport and the environment (Kelly et al. 2005; McDaid and Needle 2009; see also Chapter 9). However, obtaining meaningful values can be challenging, and there are different ways in which values are obtained. One frequently used approach is the contingent valuation (CV) method. In CV, participants are asked for the maximum amount they would be willing to pay to receive a public health intervention and obtain a certain level of outcome, e.g. asking 'How much are you willing to pay per year for the programme you received?' (Bala 1999; Jacobs et al. 2011). The CV method has the advantage that it does not impose restrictions on the types and number of outcomes that can be valued (Olsen and Smith 2001). However, CV studies valuing broader benefits of public health interventions are, to date, very limited (Borghi and Jan 2008) and are usually conducted as freestanding willingness-to-pay studies, which means that they are not performed within an economic evaluation framework (Weatherly et al. 2009). One of the reasons for the limited use of CV within economic evaluation may be that there are concerns regarding the validity of the method. There are, for instance, several examples in the literature, showing that respondents express the same willingness to pay for interventions with different health gains. This suggests that respondents are not considering the scope of the outcome (Gyrd-Hansen et al. 2012).

Discrete choice experiments (DCEs) have been suggested as an alternative method for monetary valuation of public health interventions. As opposed to

CV, which is generally used to elicit willingness to pay for a total programme, DCEs require respondents to make trade-offs between different attributes or characteristics of a programme (Lanscar and Louviere 2008). When making these trade-offs they are asked to consider differences in the scope of outcomes or other programme attributes. Hence, sensitivity to scope is to some extent forced in DCE studies (Hanley et al. 2001). DCEs can be used for calculating the total monetary value of a programme for use in cost-benefit analysis, but also for determining utility weights to calculate QALYs for use in cost-utility analysis (Lanscar and Louviere 2008). Both approaches could be very useful for the economic evaluation of public health actions, but there have been few applications (Bekker-Grob et al. 2012) and these have so far been limited to other health care interventions (Ryan et al. 2006; Negrín et al. 2008).

Traditionally, and most commonly, valuations of health states come from those participating in a study as: 1) the health of the participant is of interest to the policy and 2) this is the person who is experiencing the intervention. In the last two decades, especially since the publication of the Washington Panel on Cost-Effectiveness in Health and Medicine (Gold et al. 1996), there has been some discussion (Dolders et al. 2006; Krabbe et al. 2011) that health valuations should be those of the general population, mainly based on the arguments that: 1) the general population is unbiased, i.e. they have no self-interest in any specific health state and 2) that public health is financed by public funding, so it is the preferences of the public as a whole that should be reflected in valuation.

3) Generic outcomes versus disease-specific outcomes

As the ultimate goal of economic evaluation is to indicate which interventions provide good value for money, or to indicate which interventions should be considered as 'best buys', a generic outcome measure that allows comparison of interventions across different domains of health promotion and disease prevention is preferred. Such generic outcomes could be used, for instance, to compare a tobacco prevention intervention with an intervention aimed at stimulating physical activity. In contrast, disease-specific outcomes can only be used within one disease category, such as the Becks Depression Inventory (BDI) (see Chapter 10).

The differentiation between generic outcomes and disease-specific outcomes also relates to advantages and disadvantages of different types of economic evaluations (see Table 3.1). Both the CBA and CUA have the advantage that they always use generic health outcomes, often referred to as generic preference-based instruments. CEA and CCA, in contrast, often use disease-specific measures, although generic measures such as life-years saved can also be used. However, improvements in public health may be too small to detect with generic instruments and may only be detected with very sensitive disease-specific instruments which are already used in the promotion of public health. For instance, the results of a lifestyle intervention aimed at a higher intake of fruit and vegetables may be visible in a specific food intake diary, but will not show in a generic quality of life measure. As a result, in economic evaluation one can often see that evaluators seek to obtain the best of both worlds, using a disease-specific instrument in CEA and a generic instrument in CUA. In that way they can optimally inform professionals in the field (by the CEA) and permit comparison between all types of intervention in and outside of health promotion and public health (by the CUA) (see Chapters 6 and 7); whereas in transport and the environment, CBA is often used to allow cross-sectoral comparison (see Chapters 8 and 9).

4) Process vs outcome measurement

Economic evaluation studies tend to focus on measuring intervention outcomes only. These can be either intermediate outcomes (e.g. measures of behaviour change) or final outcomes (e.g. survival or quality of life). Process outcomes, such as duration, intensity of the intervention or location, are usually ignored. However, the need to consider process outcomes has been discussed extensively in the literature (Mooney 1994; Donaldson and Shackley 1997; Ryan 1999; Watson et al. 2009) and numerous studies have provided empirical support for the importance of process outcomes to consumers of health interventions (Ryan 1999; Kjaer et al. 2006; Kimman et al. 2010; Fiebig et al. 2011). Given that public health and health-promoting interventions often have lengthy time horizons and require continuous investments by participating individuals and institutions (for instance, in terms of behaviour changes and resources), it is likely that the intervention process here plays a more important role than for health care interventions. Studies examining consumer preferences towards public health interventions aiming to improve physical activity and diet suggest, for instance, that the following process factors are relevant: frequency and intensity of physical activity, form of diet, setting (informal vs organized group), type of support, extent of physician involvement, travel time, and whether financial incentives or costs are associated with participation (Roux et al. 2004; Brown et al. 2009; Owen et al. 2010). Despite this, the challenge remains that methods to incorporate such process outcomes in economic evaluation studies are not well developed.

Utilities, QALYs, DALYs and well-being

A frequently used generic instrument, depicted in Figure 3.1, for deriving utilities in health prevention and promotion is the EuroQol questionnaire or the EQ-5D™ (Brooks 1996).

The EQ-5D™ is a standardized instrument for self-completion by respondents, frequently used as a measure of health outcome in the field of health promotion and prevention. It is designed to be applicable to a wide range of health conditions and a large variety of public health interventions. As is shown in Figure 3.1, the left-hand side of the EQ-5D™ consists of a descriptive profile and on the right-hand side, the EQ-5D™ has a single index to value a health status using a thermometer or visual analogue scale (VAS). The descriptive profile of the EQ-5D™ consists of five domains of health-related quality of life, namely mobility, self-care, daily activities, pain/discomfort and depression/anxiety. Each dimension can be rated either on three levels (EQ-5D-3L) or five levels (EQ-5D-5L), varying from no problems to unable to perform a certain activity. The five dimensions can be aggregated to create a health state. Next

Describing your own health today	Valuing your own health today	
By placing a tick in one box in each group below, please indicate which statements best describe your own health state today.	To help people say how good or bad a health state is, we have drawn a scale (rather like a thermometer) on which the best state you can imagine is marked 100 and the worst state you can imagine is marked 0.	Best imaginable health state 100
Mobility I have no problems in walking about I have some problems in walking about I am confined to bed		9.0
Self-care I have no problems with self-care I have some problems washing or dressing myself I am unable to wash or dress myself	We would like you to indicate on this scale how good or bad your own health is today, in your opinion. Please do this by drawing a line from the box below to whichever point on the scale indicates how good or bad your health state is today.	8.0 7.0
Usual activities (e.g. work, study, housework, family or leisure activities) I have no problems with performing my usual activities I have some problems with performing my usual activities I am unable to perform my usual activities		6.0 5.0
Pain/discomfort I have no pain or discomfort I have moderate pain or discomfort I have extreme pain or discomfort	Your own health state today	4.0 3.0
Anxiety/depression I am not anxious or depressed I am moderately anxious or depressed I am extremely anxious or depressed		2.0 1.0 0 Worst imaginable health state

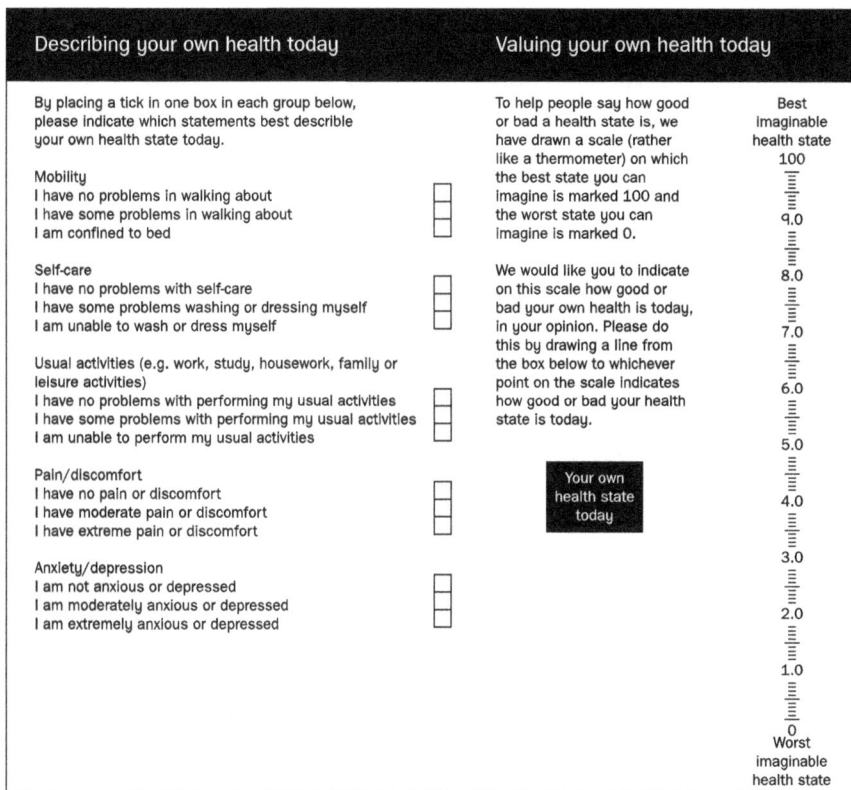

Figure 3.1 EuroQoL questionnaire

UK (English) v.2 © 2009 EuroQol Group.

to valuation using a VAS thermometer, most countries have population values elicited from the general population (Brooks 1996: www.euroqol.org).

Public health interventions are designed to promote health and prevent disease, which may increase life expectancy and quality of life. As mentioned earlier, utilities are generic to value the improvement in quality of life. Outcome measures should ideally incorporate both changes to quality of life and length of life (survival). Both the quality-adjusted life-years (QALY) and the disability-adjusted life-years (DALY) combine quantity (mortality) and quality (morbidity) of life in one outcome measure.

In economic evaluation studies in high income countries, the QALY is the most commonly used generic outcome measure. A QALY can be defined as a measure of health outcome which assigns to each period of survival a utility weight (Brazier et al. 2007). All these weights, which can be calculated by using the EQ-5D™, are aggregated across time periods to form the QALY. As a result, one QALY is equal to one year in optimal health. Another commonly used generic outcome measure that combines both quantity and quality of life is the DALY. The DALY can be considered a variant of the QALY (Murray and Acharya 1997) and is a measure of overall disease burden, expressed as the number of years lost due to ill-health, disability or early death. DALYs are calculated by taking the sum of Years of Life Lost (YLL) plus Years Lived with Disability (YLD). The key distinction between QALY and DALY is that the QALY measures health gains, while the DALY measures health losses (Sassi 2006).

Although the use of a generic outcome measure such as the QALY is widely accepted and employed in economic evaluations, the main criticism is that it only captures health-related quality of life and ignores other aspects that contribute to quality of life, such as education, employability, safety and social connectedness, while a full economic evaluation would incorporate all components of life that potentially contribute to well-being. The discussion refers to the fact that most health-related quality of life measures, such as the EuroQol, solely look at the presence of symptoms and diseases, while there is a growing consensus that health is not merely the absence of illness, but also includes the presence of positive feelings (emotional well-being) as well as positive functioning in individual life (psychological well-being) and community life (social well-being) (Lamers et al. 2011). As a result, a number of well-being scales have been developed, such as the Warwick–Edinburgh Mental Well-being Scale (WEMWBS) (Tennant et al. 2007).

Important features of cost measurement

The cost measurement of economic evaluation in the field of health promotion and disease prevention consists of three phases: cost identification, cost measurement and cost valuation.

1) Identification

In the identification step, the researcher decides which costs will be included in the study. Crucial in the cost identification is that the total impact of the public health intervention is considered. It does not matter for the identification step if these costs are paid or unpaid, reimbursed or not. Which costs are relevant depends on a number of aspects, i.e. the public health problem to tackle, type of public health intervention, the perspective of the study and the time horizon of the study. Regarding the public health problem and the public health intervention, it is crucial to realize that an economic evaluation looks at a broader view of costs than those of the intervention and one or more comparators alone. An economic evaluation study should encompass all relevant costs during the follow-up period of the study which are due to the problem or the intervention, regardless of who bears these costs or in which sector these costs occur. This means that, for each intervention, other costs are relevant. For instance the economic impact of a free needle programme for hard drug abusers will be quite different from the economic impact of a pneumococcal vaccine programme for older people. When looking at hard drug abuse, costs in other sectors might be influenced by the free needle programme, such as the judicial and domestic affairs sectors, the educational sector and the social welfare sector. Related to this, the perspective, that is the viewpoint of the economic evaluation study, is relevant, i.e. from a societal perspective, all costs will be relevant, while from an institutional perspective, a health care perspective, or an insurance perspective, more limited costs are relevant. Associated with the perspective is the time horizon of the study. In general, the broader the perspective of the study, the longer the time horizon of the study has to be in order to contain all relevant costs. In general, economic evaluation studies looking at health-promoting interventions will identify health care costs, unpaid and paid production losses, informal caring costs, and costs in other sectors.

To map costs, two principal classification categorizations are used. In the first, older categorization costs are classified as: a) direct costs which in general relate to health care sector costs; b) indirect costs which relate to productivity losses; and c) intangible costs, which entail costs that cannot be expressed in monetary terms. This classification was interpreted differently by various researchers, leading subsequently to another categorization by Drummond and colleagues (Drummond et al. 2005) where costs are classified as: a) health care sectors costs; b) costs for patients and families; and c) costs in other sectors.

2) Measurement

After identification, costs have to be measured. For this, several techniques can be used varying from retrieving information from patient files, databases from health care institutions and databases from insurance companies, as well as the use of cost questionnaires and cost diaries (Goossens et al. 2000). The two latter techniques are most often used in economic evaluation studies if the study is performed from a societal perspective. With these techniques, questionnaires or diaries about their resource use are completed by the client. This is the most valid method due to the fact that only the clients have a total overview of all the resources used (paid/unpaid, formal/informal, reimbursed/out-of-pocket) related to the public health problem and intervention. As mentioned before, the follow-up period has to be lengthy enough to include the total economic impact of the public health intervention. The periods for which clients are asked about their resource use should not be too lengthy in order to prevent recall biases. Research has shown that a follow-up period of three to six months is the maximum (van den Brink et al. 2005). As a result, in a follow-up period of one year one might ideally have five measurement points, i.e. a baseline measurement for costs and subsequent cost measurements at three months, six months, nine months and twelve months

3) Valuation

In the third step, valuation, volumes of resources use are translated into monetary values. This is simply done by multiplying the volumes with the unit prices for these volumes. Calculating a reliable cost price can be very time-consuming. Therefore, several countries have guidelines in which cost prices for the most common health care interventions are listed, for instance (Oostenbrink et al. 2002; Tan et al. 2012). As noted earlier, health promotion and protection interventions often incur resource use outside the health care sector, and as a result the valuation step, when looking at these interventions, is often more complex.

Challenges with measuring outcomes and costs

This section highlights the challenges with economic evaluations of public health interventions, as well as discussing potential solutions and future directions for addressing these problems.

The randomized controlled trial as a gold standard for economic evaluations?

Traditionally, the randomized controlled trial (RCT) has been the gold standard for collecting effectiveness data for economic evaluations of health care interventions. Due to the randomization of patients into an intervention and control group, this type of evaluation is particularly suitable for demonstrating causality. Randomizing patients or clients into an intervention group that receives the treatment and a control group that receives care as usual, or a placebo, is more difficult when having to deal with complex interventions, including many in the public health sphere. Public health and health-promoting interventions can have several components and may not be easy to randomize when targeted at the general population. A typical goal of such interventions is to stimulate a healthy lifestyle (e.g. healthy diet, physical activity, quitting smoking, or reducing alcohol intake). Lifestyle change happens in a real-life situation, and it is often not possible to control or monitor behaviour as in a laboratory setting.

Dutch research among local health promotion practitioners has revealed that an intervention that works is characterized as something that produces its intended effects after being realized in a local situation (Kok et al. 2012). Hence, the effectiveness of an intervention is dependent on contextual factors in the local setting. These authors suggest that following a 'linear' evidence-based approach, in which evidence of effectiveness is gathered first in a controlled setting before the intervention is implemented in practice, is unrealistic for most health promotion initiatives. Instead, they suggest following an approach that 'depends on the local capacities to design and realize interventions and learn during that process' (Kok et al. 2012).

Although there is no clear-cut alternative to conducting an RCT in public health interventions, these authors do provide the following guidelines that contribute to evidence-based public health interventions, based on interviews with local health promotion professionals:

1. Encourage developers to better anticipate the conditions in which an intervention has to work.
2. Describe in detail the elements that indicate an intervention that works.
3. Assign responsibilities and ownership roles for interventions and their elements.

4. Coordinate activities between all involved organizations at local and national level.
5. Support and respect the stewardship roles of local organizations.
6. Gather lessons from various kinds of learning processes.

External effects and spillovers

Public health interventions aim to improve health for their target group, but can also have beneficial health effects or savings for a broader population. For example, family members, neighbours, classmates, or colleagues, may benefit from the spillover effects of public health interventions. A health-promoting intervention that is aimed at reducing overweight among pre-diabetic patients may, for example, have positive effects on the weight of other family members by changing habits in the family's diet. Furthermore, an increasing number of public health interventions have the community, not the individual, as the focus of the intervention (Shiell and Hawe 1996).

These external effects of public health promotion and broader community effects are not always taken into account in economic evaluations, but ideally they should be estimated by including their impacts on the direct social environment within each economic evaluation. In practice, this means that not only the respondents receiving a public health intervention, but also relevant individuals in their direct social environment should be included in the assessment of the cost-effectiveness of an intervention, for example by filling in a quality of life questionnaire such as the EQ-5D™ before and after the intervention.

Lengthy time horizons

While many treatment interventions, such as medication or surgery, yield health effects within a short time period, public health interventions often take a much longer time to demonstrate effect. Typically, the largest health gain is to be expected when a healthy life style is adapted in (early) childhood and maintained throughout adulthood. Health gains in terms of a reduced number of people living with disease such as diabetes, cancer, or cardiovascular disease can be measured only after a long time span. In developing National Institute for Health and Care Excellence (NICE) guidelines for evidence-based public health in England, the length of the causal chain between interventions and outcomes was described as one of the key challenges for economic evaluations of public health interventions (Kelly et al. 2010).

When used in addition to trial-based economic evaluations, which usually do not exceed a follow-up period of between two and five years at most, modelling studies may provide a solution to overcome the problem of lengthy time horizons. For some interventions it is possible to measure intermediate outcomes or risk factors, such as changes in blood glucose levels or blood pressure, which can be measured after shorter time spans. Eventually, these intermediate outcomes can be used to calculate expected long-term outcomes, such as the number of cases of disease prevented, using a modelling approach. The key challenge is to further map clinical disease pathways to improve the validity of modelling approaches in all relevant areas for public health intervention.

Broader, non-health outcomes and costs

Unlike interventions aimed at treating health problems, in which both the investments and benefits are to be expected to lie mainly within the health sector, the distribution of costs and benefits of public health interventions often crosses policy borders.

On the one hand, public health interventions typically require investments from sectors outside the public health domain. For example, sectors like urban planning, transportation, youth and education, sports, safety and environmental affairs, can all have effects on the determinants of health and in this way contribute to an environment that facilitates or stimulates a healthy lifestyle. The importance of making a cross-sectoral case for investment in public health interventions can be found later in this volume (Chapter 14).

Public health interventions can yield benefits that go beyond health, and fall within other sectors. Examples are the increased employability or educational achievements of the beneficiaries of public health interventions. The non-health benefits of public health interventions may be also relevant for individuals participating in intervention programmes – for example, older people who participate in group-based programmes to prevent falls can also benefit from increased social networks. Moreover, non-health benefits may spillover to significant others like family members – for example, when children achieve better school results when alcohol abuse among their parents can be prevented. Non-health outcomes can even affect the wider population – for example, when crime rates decrease due to prevention of drug abuse, or when air pollution decreases due to an increase in cycling to work as a result of an active living promotion programme.

Although the fact that the costs and benefits of public health interventions have a cross-sectoral character is widely recognized, there is an ongoing debate about how to deal with these cross-sectoral costs and benefits in economic evaluations. One possible strategy is to conduct a CCA and include all relevant outcomes per sector. The disadvantage of such an approach is that interventions with different outcomes cannot be easily compared. Conducting a CBA and expressing all outcomes in monetary terms can overcome this problem, but some outcomes are hard to capture in monetary terms.

One option, as described earlier, is that discrete choice experiments as well as the contingent valuation technique, can be used to elicit monetary values on non-health outcomes. Alternatively, a solution for taking into account cross-sectoral costs and benefits would be to include more domains within the QALY concept or use an alternative instrument to measure broader outcomes alongside, or instead of, traditional QALY measurement in a CUA. An example of an instrument that includes broader outcomes is the ICEpop CAPability measure (ICECAP), which is based on the capability approach originally developed by Sen (Lorgelly et al. 2010). This states that it is not a person's actual functioning, but the opportunities they have to achieve their goals (capabilities) that should be central in outcome measurement. The ICECAP measure includes the domains of: **attachment** (love and friendship), **security** (thinking about the future without concern), **role** (doing things that make you feel valued), **enjoyment** (enjoyment and pleasure) and **control** (independence). Although the ICECAP measurement tool was initially developed for older people, an adapted version for the general adult population is being developed at the moment (www.icecap.bham.ac.uk). An alternative measurement tool that captures one ultimate outcome, such as using a happiness-index – see, for example, the Oxford Happiness Questionnaire (Hills and Argyle 2002) – could replace the traditional QALY concept. It is debatable, however, whether such an overall index is sensitive enough to pick up short-term changes due to health promotion initiatives. Therefore, a critical reflection on the domains currently included in the QALY was necessary, which has resulted in the development of instruments such as the WEMWBS (Tennant et al. 2007).

Equity considerations

Inequalities in health according to socioeconomic position (e.g. education level, occupational class or income) are a persistent problem within the field of public health (see Chapter 12). An international comparative study by Mackenbach and colleagues has shown that in many European countries, rates of death and poorer self-assessments of health were substantially higher in groups of lower socioeconomic status (SES) (Mackenbach et al. 2008). Public health interventions are often specifically aimed at people in deprived or disadvantaged situations to contribute to closing the health gap between low and high SES groups. Hence, from a public health perspective, an intervention that has only modest effects on population health in general, but is able to reduce health inequalities, may be preferred over an intervention that increases average health of the population quite markedly, but exaggerates health inequalities, because the health gains mainly accrue to the higher socioeconomic groups (which in general are already in a better health position).

From an economic perspective, however, the goal is to reach the maximum total health gain by the most efficient allocation of the available budget, without paying attention to the consequences for health inequalities between subgroups of the population. A review by Weatherly and colleagues has shown that equity considerations are rarely mentioned in empirical studies (Weatherly et al. 2009). Including a narrative analysis of the consequences of an intervention for health inequalities could be a first step towards considering health inequalities in economic evaluations of public health interventions. Whenever possible, analyses in different subgroups of low and high SES should be conducted to quantify the cost and effects of an intervention in terms of health inequalities (McDaid and Sassi 2010). Weatherly and colleagues also suggest that more budgets should be allocated to the evaluation of those interventions that are most likely to reduce health inequalities, so that the cost-effectiveness of interventions that reduce health inequalities can be demonstrated (Weatherly

Table 3.2 Challenges and solutions for economic evaluation of public health interventions

Challenge	Possible solution
RCT not suitable	Practice-based evidence
External and spillover effects	Include direct social environment in economic evaluation
Lengthy time horizons	Modelling approach, intermediate outcome measurement
Broader, non-health outcomes	CCA, CBA, capability approach, critical reflection on domains included in current QALY concept
Equity considerations	Include narrative analyses on health inequalities, conduct subgroup analyses

et al. 2009). Other authors (McDaid and Needle 2009) have argued that additional investment is needed to increase uptake in socially disadvantaged groups when looking at public health interventions. In order to limit inequalities, nudging has become of increased interest in public health. Nudging interventions are based on behavioural psychology and economics, and in these interventions individuals are 'gently pushed' towards making more healthy decisions. An example of nudging to stimulate physical activity is to make stairs, not lifts, more prominent and attractive in public buildings (Marteau et al. 2011). More information about the impact of prevention programmes on health inequalities can be found later in this volume (Chapter 12).

The challenges and solutions for outcome measurement in economic evaluations of public health interventions are summarized in Table 3.2

Key recommendations for policymakers

Based on the issues explored above, some recommendations for policymakers can be made on economic evaluations of public health interventions. First, the relevant type of economic evaluation to be used to evaluate health promotion and disease prevention interventions depends on the way intervention outcomes are measured. It is important to keep in mind that each outcome measure has specific advantages and disadvantages. Second, to inform decision-makers who have to deal with the allocation of resources across sectors, as well as decision-makers who have to deal with the allocation of resources within one sector, economic evaluations should ideally combine generic preference-based outcomes (to be used for CUA or CBA) with disease-specific outcomes (to be used in CEA).

Third, a standard RCT may not always be desirable for economic evaluations in the field of public health; instead, more practice-oriented designs (e.g. quasi-experimental designs) should be considered as alternative evidence for use in economic evaluation, as well as modelling. Furthermore, because public health interventions may have external and spillover effects, the direct social environment in which an intervention operates has to be included in economic evaluation in the field of public health to account for these.

With regards to measurement, the traditional QALY concept only measures health-related quality of life and ignores other aspects such as well-being and non-health outcomes. There is an ongoing debate about the possible solutions (CCA, CBA, the capability approach, critical reflection on domains included in current QALY concept) for tackling this problem. Undoubtedly, because public health interventions have a high potential to reduce socioeconomic health inequalities, economic evaluation should pay more attention to the differences in the cost-effectiveness of these interventions between several groups, for instance by conducting narrative analyses on health inequalities or conducting subgroup analyses. Due to the many challenges in measuring outcomes and costs, policymakers are encouraged to critically assess the results of economic evaluations of public health interventions to ensure that these results are relevant for their given context.

References

Bala, M. V., Mauskopf, J. A. and Wood, L. L. (1999) Willingness to pay as a measure of health benefits, *Pharmacoeconomics*, 15: 9–18.

Bekker-Grob, D., Ryan, M. and Gerard, K. (2012) Discrete choice experiments in Health Economics: A review of the literature, *Health Economics*, 21: 101–12.

Borghi, J. and Jan, S. (2008) Measuring the benefits of health promotion programmes: Application of the contingent valuation method, *Health Policy*, 87: 235–48.

Bowling, A. (2005) *Measuring Health: A Review of Quality of Life Measurement Scales*. Maidenhead: Open University Press.

Brazier, J., Ratcliffe, J., Salomon, J. A. and Tsuchiya, A. (2007) *Measuring and Valuing Health Benefits for Economic Evaluation*. Oxford: Oxford University Press.

Briggs, A. H. and O'Brien, B. J. (2001) The death of cost-minimization analysis?, *Health Economics*, 10: 179–84.

Brooks, R. (1996) EuroQol: The current state of play, *Health Policy*, 37: 53–72.

Brown, D. S., Finkelstein, E. A., Brown, D. R., Buchner, D. M. and Johnson, F. R. (2009) Estimating older adults' preferences for walking programs via conjoint analysis, *American Journal of Preventive Medicine*, 36: 201–7.

Dolders, M. G., Zeegers, M. P., Groot, W. and Ament, A. (2006) A meta-analysis demonstrates no significant differences between patient and population preferences, *Journal of Clinical Epidemiology*, 59: 653–64.

Donaldson, C. and Shackley, P. (1997) Does 'Process Utility' exist? A case study of willingness to pay for laparascopic cholecystectomy, *Social Science and Medicine*, 44: 699–707.

Drummond, M. F. and McGuire, A. (2001) *Economic Evaluation in Health Care: Merging Theory with Practice*. Oxford and New York: Oxford University Press.

Drummond, M. F., Schulpher, M., Torrance, G. W., O'Brien, B. J. and Stoddart, G. (2005) *Methods for the Economic Evaluation of Health Care Programmes*. Oxford and New York: Oxford University Press.

Fiebig, D. G., Knox, S., Viney, R., Haas, M. and Street, D. J. (2011) Preferences for new and existing contraceptive products, *Health Economics*, 20: 35–52.

Glick, H. (2007) *Economic Evaluation in Clinical Trials*. Oxford and New York: Oxford University Press.

Gold, M. R., Siegel, J.E., Russell, L. B. and Weinstein, M. C. (1996) *Cost-Effectiveness in Health and Medicine*. Oxford: Oxford University Press.

Goossens, M. E., Rutten-van Molken, M. P., Vlaeyen, J. W. and van der Linden, S. M. (2000) The cost diary: A method to measure direct and indirect costs in cost-effectiveness research, *Journal of Clinical Epidemiology*, 53: 688–95.

Gyrd-Hansen, D., Kjaer, T. and Nielsen, J. S. (2012) Scope insensitivity in contingent valuation studies of health services: Should we ask twice?, *Health Economics*, 21: 101–12.

Hanley, N., Mourato, S. and Wright, R. E. (2001) Choice modelling approaches: A superior alternative for environmental valuation?, *Journal of Economic Surveys*, 15: 435–62.

Hills, P. and Argyle, M. (2002) The Oxford Happiness Questionnaire: A compact scale for the measurement of psychological well-being, *Personality and Individual Differences*, 33: 1073–82.

Jacobs, P., Bachynsky, J. and Baladi, J. F. (1995) A comparative review of pharmacoeconomic guidelines, *Pharmacoeconomics*, 8: 182–9.

Jacobs, N., Drost, R., Ament, A., Evers, S. and Claes, N. (2011) Willingness to pay for a cardiovascular prevention program in highly educated adults: A randomized controlled trial, *International Journal of Technology Assessment in Health Care*, 27: 283–9.

Kelly, M., McDaid, D., Ludbrooke, A. and Powell, J. (2005) *Economic Appraisal of Public Health Interventions*. London: Health Development Agency.

Kelly, M., Morgan, A., Ellis, S., Younger, T., Huntley, J. and Swann, C. (2010) Evidence based public health: A review of the experience of the National Institute of Health and Clinical Excellence (NICE) of developing public health guidance in England, *Social Science & Medicine*, 71: 1056–62.

Kimman, M. L., Dellaert, B. G., Boersma, L. J., Lambin, P. and Dirksen, C. D. (2010) Follow-up treatment for breast cancer: One strategy fits all? An investigation of patient preferences using a discrete choice experiment, *Acta Ocologica*, 49: 328–37.

Kjaer, T., Gyrd-Hansen, D. and Willaing, I. (2006) Investigating patients' preferences for cardiac rehabilitation in Denmark, *International Journal of Technology Assessment in Health Care*, 22: 211–8.

Kok, M. O., Vaandrager, L., Bal, R. and Schuit, J. (2012) Practitioner opinions on health promotion interventions that work: Opening the 'black box' of a linear evidence-based approach, *Social Science & Medicine*, 74: 715–23.

Krabbe, P. F., Tromp, N., Ruers, T. J. and van Riel, P. L. (2011) Are patients' judgments of health status really different from the general population?, *Health and Quality of Life Outcomes*, 9: 31.

Lamers, S. M., Westerhof, G. J., Bohlmeijer, E. T., ten Klooster, P. M. and Keyes, C. L. (2011) Evaluating the psychometric properties of the Mental Health Continuum-Short Form (MHC-SF), *Journal of Clinical Psychology*, 67: 99–110.

Lanscar, E. and Louviere, J. (2008) Conducting discrete choice experiments to inform health care decision making: A user's guide, *Pharmacoeconomics*, 26: 661–77.

Lorgelly, P. K., Lawson, K. D., Fenwick, E. A. and Briggs, A. H. (2010) Outcome measurement in economic evaluations of public health interventions: A role for the capability approach?, *International Journal of Environmental Research and Public Health*, 7: 2274–89.

Mackenbach, J. P., Stirbu, I., Roskam, A. J. et al. (2008) Socioeconomic inequalities in health in 22 European countries, *New England Journal of Medicine*, 358: 2468–81.

Marteau, T. M., Ogilvie, D., Roland, M., Suhrcke, M. and Kelly, M. P. (2011) Judging nudging: Can nudging improve population health?, *British Medical Journal*, 342: d228.

McDaid, D. and Needle, J. (2009) What use has been made of economic evaluation in public health? A systematic review of the literature, in S. Dawson and Z. S. Morris (eds) *Future Public Health: Burdens, Challenges and Opportunities*. Basingstoke: Palgrave Macmillan, pp. 248–64.

McDaid, D. and Sassi, F. (2010) Equity, efficiency and research synthesis, in I. Shemilt, M. Mugford, L. Vale, K. Marsh and C. Donaldson (eds) *Evidence-based Decisions and Economics: Health Care, Social Welfare, Education and Criminal Justice*. Chichester: Wiley, BMJ Books.

Mooney, G. (1994) What else do we want from our health services?, *Social Science and Medicine*, 39: 151–4.

Murray, C. J. and Acharya, A. K. (1997) Understanding DALYs (disability-adjusted life years), *Journal of Health Economics*, 16: 703–30.

Negrín, A. M., Pinilla, J. and León, C. J. (2008) Willingness to pay for alternative policies for patients with Alzheimer's Disease, *Health Economics, Policy and Law*, 3(Pt 3): 257–75.

Olsen, J. A. and Smith, R. D. (2001) Theory versus practice: A review of 'willingness-to-pay' in health and health care, *Health Economics*, 10: 39–52.

Oostenbrink, J. B., Koopmanschap, M. A. and Rutten, F. F. (2002) Standardisation of costs: The Dutch Manual for Costing in economic evaluations, *Pharmacoeconomics*, 20: 443–54.

Owen, K., Pettman, T., Haas, M., Viney, R. and Misan, G. (2010) Individual preferences for diet and exercise programmes: Changes over a lifestyle intervention and their link with outcomes, *Public health nutrition*, 13: 245–52.

Roux, L., Ubach, C., Donaldson, C. and Ryan, M. (2004) Valuing the benefits of weight loss programs: An application of the discrete choice experiment, *Obesity Research*, 12: 1342–51.

Ryan, M. (1999) Using conjoint analysis to take account of patient preferences and go beyond health outcomes: An application to in vitro fertilisation, *Social Science and Medicine*, 48: 535–46.

Ryan, M., Netten, A., Skatun, D. and Smith, R. D. (2006) Using discrete choice experiments to estimate a preference-based measure of outcome: An application to social care for older people, *Journal of Health Economics*, 25: 927–44.

Sassi, F. (2006) Calculating QALYs, comparing QALY and DALY calculations, *Health Policy Plan*, 21: 402–8.

Shiell, A. and Hawe, P. (1996) Health promotion community development and the tyranny of individualism, *Health Economics*, 5: 241–7.

Spilker, B. (1995) *Quality of Life and Pharmacoeconomics in Clinical Trials*. Philadelphia, PA: Lippincott Williams & Wilkins.

Tan, S. S., Bouwmans, C. A., Rutten, F. F. and Hakkaart-van Roijen, L. (2012) Update of the Dutch Manual for Costing in economic evaluations, *International Journal of Technology Assessment in Health Care*, 28: 152–8.

Tennant, R., Hiller, L., Fishwick, R. et al. (2007) The Warwick–Edinburgh Mental Well-being Scale (WEMWBS): Development and UK validation, *Health and Quality of Life Outcomes*, 5: 63.

van den Brink, M., van den Hout, W. B., Stiggelbout, A. M., Putter, H., van de Velde, C. J. and Kievit, J. (2005) Self-reports of health-care utilization: Diary or questionnaire?, *International Journal of Technology Assessment in Health Care*, 21: 298–304.

Watson, V., Ryan, M. and Watson, E. (2009) Valuing experience factors in the provision of chlamydia screening: An application to women attending the family planning clinic, *Value in Health*, 12: 621–3.

Weatherly, H., Drummond, M., Claxton, K. et al. (2009) Methods for assessing the cost-effectiveness of public health interventions: Key challenges and recommendations, *Health Policy*, 93: 85–92.
www.euroqol.org [Accessed 1 March 2012]
www.icecap.bham.ac.uk [Accessed 1 March 2012]
www.ispor.org/peguidelines/index.asp [Accessed 1 March 2012]

Part II

Making the economic case for tackling key risk factors to health

chapter four

Curbing tobacco smoking

Joy Townsend

'We all know that tobacco is one of the greatest disasters in human history and that the cure is government action.' Gro Brundtland, Director WHO 1998–2003

Smoking brings enormous physical harm to its users. There is a huge body of knowledge documenting its manifold risks, its high public costs, and the effective means to control its use. That it is still in use is largely due to the power of the transnational tobacco companies and the addictive nature of the product. It is the cause of one and a quarter million European deaths each year, accounting for 16 per cent of all deaths, including more than 330,000 in the Russian Federation and around 100,000 in each of the United Kingdom, Germany, Ukraine and Italy (WHO 2012b).

The WHO European Region's smoking rates are among the highest in the world, with 41 per cent of men and 22 per cent of women over the age of 15 smoking (WHO 2014). This chapter will show that price is a major factor determining use. The prices of the 'cheapest cigarettes' vary twentyfold between countries, while prices of the 'most sold cigarettes' vary ninefold. Each 10 per cent difference in price is associated with a 2.5 per cent to 5 per cent difference in cigarette consumption in the opposite direction, and price differences account for much of the threefold difference in smoking rates between European countries. Rates are highest in countries where prices are lowest, as well as among lower socioeconomic groups, the unemployed, and lone parents. Smoking is a major cause of inequality in health and mortality. Raising cigarette prices across Europe, even to the average European Union (EU) price of $5.5, would save hundreds of thousands of lives per year, including 100,000 in the Russian Federation alone. While public health advocates continue to appeal for higher tobacco taxes on the basis of social costs, few individuals would deny the justification of a tax increase based on the health benefits.

The chapter will also show that evidence-based tobacco control policies have been shown to be highly cost-effective, and many are cost saving; a 10 per cent price rise via a tax increase being the most cost-effective at $4–$105 ($3–$78 in 1995 prices) per disability-adjusted life-year (DALY) averted and excluding substantial tax revenue benefits, $307–$1,066 ($229–$794 in 1995 prices) per DALY averted for cessation support, and $52–$1,052 ($39–$784 in 1995 prices) for other effective policies in Eastern Europe; the comparative figures in Western Europe are $111–$3,719 ($83–$2771 in 1995 prices), $1,007–$9,672 ($750–$7206 in 1995 prices) and $934–$18,689 ($696–$13,924 in 1995 prices), respectively. Tobacco control is therefore more cost-effective than most current medical and surgical treatments.

The chapter also shows that evidence-based policies to reduce smoking and its harm are in place, especially in the EU, but are hampered in many countries by inadequate government action, and the hostile influence of the transnational tobacco companies, including foreign investment. Addressing these with serious action across the Region will save lives and strengthen economies.

The smoking epidemic

Tobacco brings enormous physical harm to its users. It was first imported to Europe from America over three centuries ago, and was smoked in pipes and later as cigars. Many of the immediate harmful effects on health were recognized even then, and taxes imposed. Smoking tobacco as cigarettes developed through the first half of the twentieth century and proved to be far more dangerous than pipes or cigars, as the smoke was inhaled, cigarettes were socially acceptable and very cheap, and so were smoked not as the occasional one or two, but as 20 or so a day. The introduction and growth of cigarette smoking was followed roughly 30 years later by a parallel shadow of lung cancer (Figure 4.1) (Townsend 1978), and from the 1930s, physicians began to relate lung cancer to tobacco use in case control studies (Doll and Hill 1956; Wynder et al. 1957).

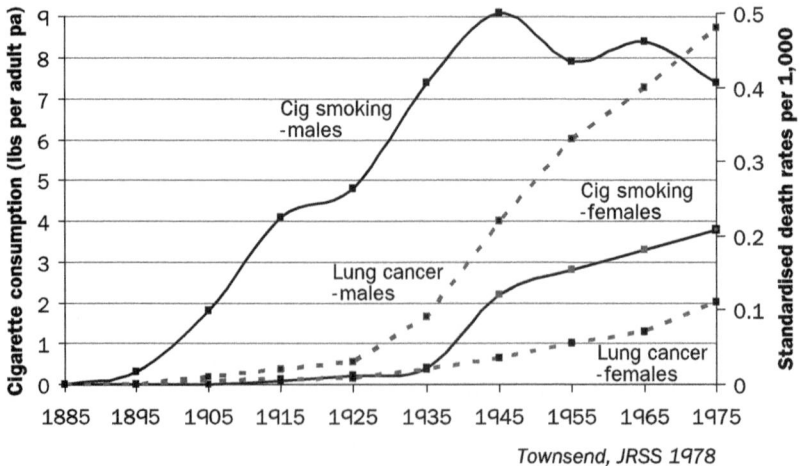

Townsend, JRSS 1978

Figure 4.1 Cigarette consumption and lung cancer (United Kingdom)

But it was the results of the huge definitive longitudinal studies of smokers and non-smokers (Doll and Hill 1964; Hammond 1966; Kahn 1966) that clearly established the relationship, not only with cancer but also with cardiovascular disease, chronic obstructive airways disease, and a host of other diseases.

It is one of the greatest causes of premature death in Europe, causing over one and a quarter million deaths, making up 16 per cent of all deaths every year in the Region (WHO 2014). These include 330,000 in the Russian Federation; 114,000 in the United Kingdom; 111,000 in Germany; 99,000 in Ukraine; and 80,000 in Italy. Over a quarter of all deaths of men in Belgium, Poland, the Netherlands, the Russian Federation, Hungary, the Czech Republic, Croatia and Estonia are attributed to smoking, and many other European countries approach these rates, including for women.

There are wide differences in daily smoking rates across the Region: for men, they range from 22 per cent in Uzbekistan, to 63 per cent in Greece; for women the range is twentyfold, from 2 per cent in Armenia to 45 per cent in Austria. With the exception of Greece, the highest smoking rates for men tend to be in the Former Soviet Union (FSU) countries and in Eastern Europe (Table 4.1).

The long lag between smoking and disease, particularly for lung disease, means there is not always a clear relationship between current smoking prevalence and current death rates; for some countries, including the United Kingdom, high death rates relate to previous very high smoking rates which have since declined. (There is also a data lag as the latest WHO death rates relate to 2000.)

Half of regular smokers are predicted to die prematurely from their smoking and to lose, on average, twenty years of their lives.[2] This is not surprising considering the 4,800 different chemicals in tobacco smoke, including carbon monoxide, hydrogen cyanide, ammonia, butane, formaldehyde, benzene, polonium 210, vinyl chloride and 60 other carcinogens, between them affecting virtually every organ system, and including risk factors for the major causes of deaths in Europe, particularly cardiovascular disease, lung cancer and chronic obstructive pulmonary disease (WHO 2008) (Figure 4.2).

Table 4.1 Prevalence of smoking any tobacco product among adults aged 15+ in selected WHO European Region countries (2009)

Highest Prevalence				*Lowest Prevalence*			
Men		*Women*		*Men*		*Women*	
Greece	63%	Austria	45%	Uzbekistan	22%	Armenia, Kyrgyzstan	2%
Albania	60%	Greece	41%	United Kingdom	25%	Uzbekistan	3%
Russian Federation	59%	Bosnia and Herzegovina	36%	Iceland	27%	Republic of Moldova	5%
Georgia	57%	Hungary	33%	Finland	28%	Georgia	6%
Armenia	51%	Andorra	32%	Israel	29%	Belarus	9%

Source: WHO 2012a.

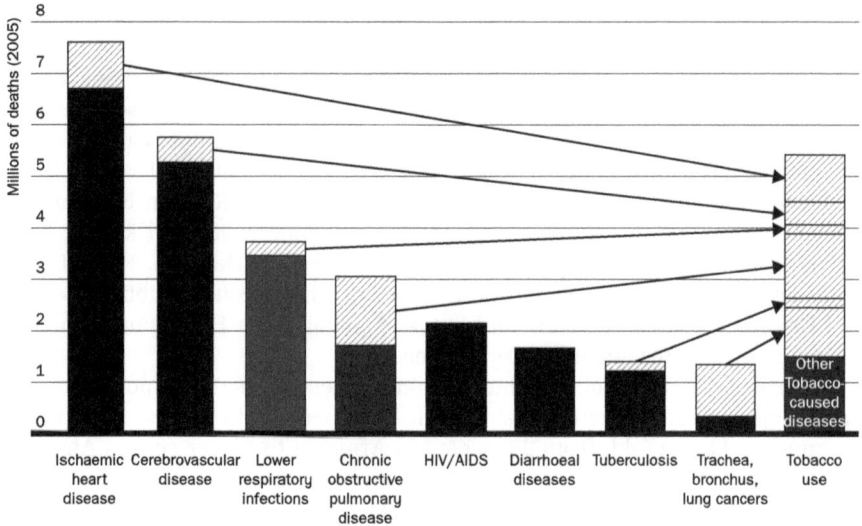

Figure 4.2 Tobacco use is a risk factor for six of the eight leading causes of death

Treatment is of limited effectiveness, or too late, for many of these diseases by the time symptoms are apparent. However, the risk of dying from smoking is reduced dramatically by stopping; smoking cessation at age 30 may regain the full ten years on average (half of smokers die from smoking and lose twenty years each on average; the average smoker therefore loses ten years of life), nine years at 40, six years at 50, and, even at age 60, three years of life may be regained. Stopping smoking benefits health substantially and provides the major benefits of tobacco control, accruing decades earlier than those from reduced smoking uptake (Peto et al. 1992).

In Europe, cigarette smoking is increasingly concentrated in lower income groups, and is rising among young people – especially young women. In the absence of effective interventions, these groups and low- and middle-income populations are forecast to experience major increases in cigarette smoking disease.

The costs of smoking

Economics and tobacco are inextricably linked. Large profits drive the supply side; prices, taxes, tax harmonization or variations, advertising and other pressures modify demand. Externalities relating to extra health care, premature mortality and fires may be borne by non-smoking members of society or members of other societies, and so cause third-party costs and smoking-related mortality.

The authors of a book on the economic evaluation of smoking control policies stated that, to their knowledge, there have been no studies on the costs of smoking (Goel and Nelson 2008). This is not entirely true, but measuring costs is complex and problematic and, for good reason, not often undertaken. In considering costs, the perspective needs to be decided – whether the costs are to society, government, the health service, or the individual; the period of costs needs to be decided, as smoking has a long shadow with lags of decades between smoking initiation and cost, cessation and savings. Costs and savings need to be assessed relative to realistic alternatives – other uses of these resources.

Costs of tobacco to the world economy have been estimated at some $500 billion in lost productivity, health care costs, deforestation, pesticide/fertiliser contamination, fire damage, cleaning costs, and discarded litter; smoking has been estimated to reduce individual national income by as much as 3.6 per cent (Shafey et al. 2009) and smoking-related conditions were estimated to cost the NHS in England $10 billion (£5.2 billion in 2005 prices), equal to 6.5 per cent of the health care budget for England (Godfrey et al. 2011).

But individual smokers and their families pay the most heavily in terms of direct costs, reduced income from smoking diseases, and loss of income for other urgent family needs. In Albania, for example, it is estimated that the average smoker spends two months' wages ($436) per year on cigarettes. Viscusi and Hersch have estimated the private mortality costs of smoking in terms of value of life, to add $237 ($222 in 2006 prices) per packet for men and $100 ($94 in 2006 prices) for women (Viscusi and Hersch 2008).

Tobacco control measures

That there is little research into the costs of smoking is probably because it is not possible to make very useful or meaningful estimates. More useful, because it includes the costs and benefits of change, is to look at the cost-effectiveness of policy instruments. There was surprisingly little policy response around the world following the initial publication of the research which established the lethal effects of smoking. Slowly this changed; initially through the pressure from doctors and pressure groups, including an early banning of cigarette advertising on television in the United Kingdom in 1965.

Evidence of the effects of, and rationale for, different tobacco control measures are discussed below. These were introduced gradually across the world, culminating in the World Health Organization Framework Convention on Tobacco Control (FCTC) which came into force in 2005. By 2014, 178 countries were enforcing the FCTC, including the EU and most of Europe, with the notable exceptions of Switzerland and the United States, committed to a wide range of policies including banning advertising and promotion, smoke-free workplaces, cessation support, warnings on packets, increases of taxation, control of smuggling, and avoidance of influence of the tobacco industry on policies.

Rationale for tobacco control and interventions in the tobacco market

Tobacco control measures such as mass media campaigns, warnings on packs and cessation support, give information and support to smokers and non-smokers regarding a lethal product on the market. Smoke-free policies keep non-smokers and others free of the risks of second-hand smoke. Bans on advertising and promoting tobacco avoid misinformation to the public. For these policies, the rationale is clear and fairly uncontroversial, although all policies are opposed by the tobacco industry. Taxation is sometimes seen as more controversial, particularly by free market economists who consider there should be no interference with the workings of the market and that tax will reduce the welfare of smokers.

Tax revenue efficiency

All governments need to raise tax revenue, and the economic justifications for taxes are to raise revenue, to adjust for externalities, and as a sumptuary tax to reduce the effects of harmful products (Warner et al. 1995; Townsend 1996). Tobacco fulfils all these criteria well. It is also in the unique position of being a popular tax in many countries in Europe (Currie et al. 2012). Tobacco tax is a relatively efficient vehicle for raising tax as it has a high elasticity of total revenue with respect to the tax rate, compared to other products. Also, as the price elasticity of demand for cigarettes is low, the dead weight welfare loss or excess burden (loss of satisfaction to the consumer, less the gain to the government in revenue) is minimized. So, on the grounds of economic efficiency alone, there is a case for shifting taxes from other commodities to tobacco. There is also the serious issue that, in Europe, most smokers begin smoking in their teenage years, become addicted and then the majority regret being smokers, and wish to give up the habit. Tax is often the trigger to make this happen. A meeting of economists from the United States and the United Kingdom concluded that the value of increased taxation in discouraging children from becoming addicted to nicotine was potentially the most powerful argument supporting increased taxes (Warner et al. 1995).

As Hanson and Kysar have put it, 'Our awe ... may sometimes cause us to overlook less desirable aspects of the market system. Put differently, the fact that all manner of fresh fruits and vegetables can be purchased year-round at extremely low prices truly is a marvel. The fact that 3,000 (US) children are convinced every day to purchase and ignite a combination of chemicals that may well addict them, enfeeble them, and ultimately kill them, is a tragedy. And it remains a tragedy even if accomplished efficiently.' (Hanson and Kysar 2001).

Tobacco taxation and price increase

A first principle of economics is that the demand for a normal good is related negatively to its price. The extent of the decrease is assessed by a unit free measure – price elasticity. Many studies from countries around the world, including European and cross-Europe studies, have confirmed the important role of price in determining whether, and how much, people smoke. These studies have demonstrated that a 10 per cent increase in the real price of cigarettes would result in a decrease of about 2.5 per cent to 5 per cent in cigarette consumption, and vice versa (Townsend 1997; Gallus et al. 2003). Half the effect is likely to be from a reduction in smokers, and half from a reduction in the amount smoked by the remaining smokers. These elasticity estimates are mainly from higher-income countries; earlier research has shown higher price response in lower/middle-income countries, but recent evidence is more mixed, showing price response more similar to that in high-income countries (Chaloupka et al. 2011, 2012). As an illustration of smokers' response to price changes, Figure 4.3 shows price in real terms against demand for cigarettes in Italy, from 1970 to 2012.

Tax has been singled out by WHO, the World Bank and others as the most effective means of tobacco control and the most productive and cost-effective means for reducing the demand for tobacco (Jha and Chaloupka 1999; Chisholm et al. 2006; Lai et al. 2007; Vos et al. 2010; Ortegon et al. 2012). It also has a low administrative burden. Ranson and colleagues have estimated that a 10 per cent price increase could have the hugely beneficial effect of 0.6 to 1.8 million fewer premature deaths in Eastern European and Central Asian countries, at a cost of only $4–$105 ($3–$78 in 1995 prices) per DALY in the short run (Ranson et al. 2002). Several studies have estimated that the reduction in demand would be twice as much in the long run as in the short run, requiring a continuous increase in real price to keep pace with inflation. Another study, using Global Adult Tobacco Survey data, found that a 10 per cent increase in tax increased the probability of smoking cessation in Russia, Poland and Ukraine by between 1.6 and 2.3 per cent (Ross et al. 2014).

Most governments impose tobacco taxes purely to raise revenue, and this is insisted on by the International Monetary Fund for certain countries in budget deficit. Increasing tax rates will almost always raise extra government revenue, and as well as being the most effective tobacco control measure per se, is a necessary

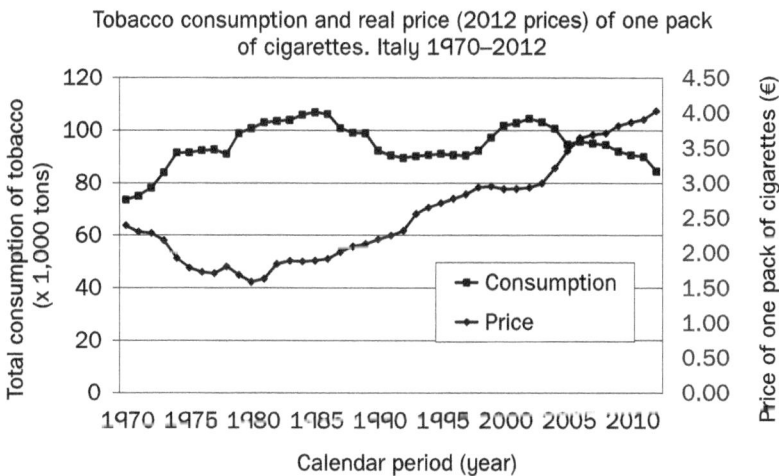

Figure 4.3 Cigarette consumption is sensitive to changes in real price (Italy)

Source: Produced by Silvano Gallus using ISTAT (2013) and World Bank (2014).

adjunct to the effects of other tobacco control measures which, by decreasing demand for tobacco, will also decrease tax revenues. Tobacco companies across Europe and the globe try to convince governments of the fallacy that tobacco tax revenues will fall if taxes are raised and consumption falls.

The tax rate elasticity of tax revenue

The tax rate elasticity for tax revenue is positive and equal to $1+ (T/P) x e$, where T/P is the share of tax in price, and e is the elasticity of demand (Townsend 1997).

Tax revenue will increase with a tax rate increase (tax elasticity > 0)

if T/P x e < –1.0 that is if e < –P/T

As T/P is typically 0.4 to 0.8 (tax is usually 40 per cent to 80 per cent of the price of a packet of cigarettes), P/T will typically be between 1.25 and 2.5, and no estimates of (– e) have been as high as 1.25 (typically 0.25 to 0.5).

Tax revenue will therefore rise with a rise in tax rate and the tax elasticity will be typically 0.68 to 0.86, meaning that a 10 per cent rise in tax rate will result in a 6.8 to 8.6 per cent rise in tax revenue, other things being equal.

Research from many countries reports increases in government tax revenue following tobacco tax rate increases, and also falls following reductions in the real tax rate (Chaloupka et al. 2011, 2012). For example, Figure 4.4

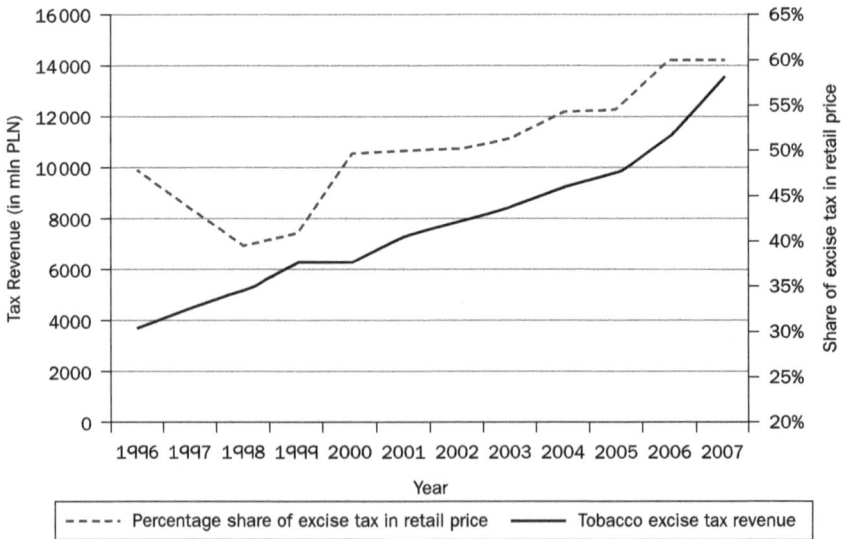

Figure 4.4 Tax and tax revenue (million PLN) Poland, 1996–2007

Source: Polish Ministry of Finance 2008

shows how tobacco revenue increased when tobacco tax rates were increased from 29 per cent to 59 per cent of the retail price in Poland, between 1996 and 2007.

Tobacco industry officials frequently argue that a reduction in tobacco consumption may result in increased unemployment and so have damaging effects on the economy. However, the manufacture of cigarettes is very highly capital intensive and most job losses in the industry have been due to increased capitalization. Few other industries are as capital intensive as tobacco manufacturing (Buck et al. 1995). If the consumption of tobacco products falls, the money previously spent on tobacco will be spent on other products, and create jobs elsewhere (Jha and Chaloupka 1999) from more labour intensive goods or services. A United Kingdom study predicted a net increase of almost 100,000 jobs if income spent on tobacco were shifted to other luxury items (Buck et al. 1995).

Smoking prevalence and price in Europe

Cigarette prices vary hugely across the Region, from $1.05 in Kazakhstan to $9.70 in Ireland for the 'most sold' cigarettes (WHO 2008).[1] This represents a ninefold difference. Even greater variations are evident in the prices of the 'cheapest' cigarettes sold in each country, which vary, more than twentyfold, from $0.41 in Kyrgyzstan to $8.79 in Ireland. In many of the FSU countries the prices are below $2. In the EU, prices tend to be higher as there is the requirement to adhere to the European Commission Directives.

Price is not the only factor influencing the variation in smoking between European countries; however, for men it is a major influence, as can be seen in Figure 4.5. The relationship between cigarette price and prevalence of smoking by men in the countries of the WHO European Region is highly significant, and price alone explains 40 per cent of the variation.[2]

This implies that every $1 lower price between countries in Europe is associated with a 3 per cent higher prevalence of male smoking. The price elasticity of demand across the region is estimated at about –0.35. For the Russian Federation, this would mean that raising the price of cigarettes – even to the average European price of about $5.5 – would reduce smoking by about one-third, and save possibly over 100,000 Russian lives in the long term.

Women and price

For cultural reasons, the price/prevalence relationship is different for women. Smoking prevalence is very low in some countries, particularly in the FSU, even though prices are low in Russia, Ukraine, Kazakhstan, Belarus, Georgia, the Republic of Moldova, Uzbekistan and Kyrgyzstan. 'Within country' time-series analyses suggest that adult women are more sensitive than men to price increases (Townsend et al. 1994; US Department of Health and Human Services 2001). A Canadian study has shown also that women who smoke are at greater

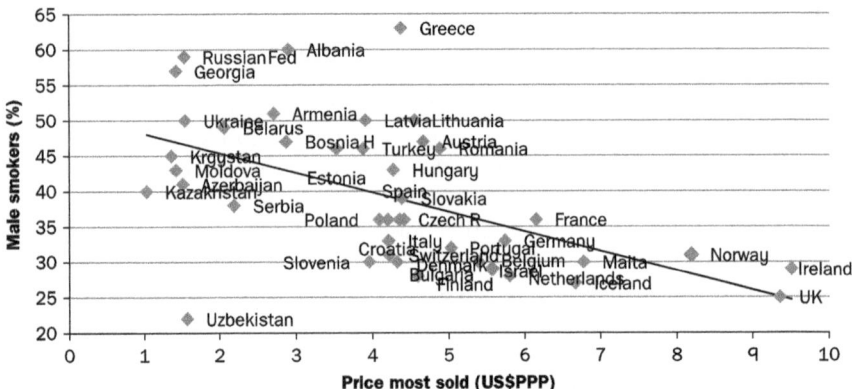

Figure 4.5 Price most sold (US$PPP) by per cent male smokers, data from WHO 2011

risk than men from heart disease, so are likely to benefit even more than men from smoking cessation (Shields and Wilkins 2013).

Tobacco tax structure

The choice of tobacco tax structure affects prices, and is partly responsible for the low tax in FSU countries and the wide differences in cigarette prices between countries. Tobacco companies act to minimize the tax impact whatever the structure, and have most control when the tax is entirely or mainly levied as an ad valorem tax, as keeping the 'before tax' price low yields a low tax and a low price. Ad valorem taxes were common in Southern European countries; they tend to result in a wider range of prices and make it easier for smokers to trade down to cheaper brands. A high specific, or minimum tax, allows the least manipulation from the industry, and is generally considered the best for tobacco control. It requires regular adjustment in line with inflation and income changes. The ideal structure is a high specific or minimum tax with an additional high ad valorem tax, so that higher priced or longer cigarettes also get appropriately taxed.

Fine-cut tobacco used for roll-your-own cigarettes is taxed at a much lower rate than manufactured cigarettes in all European countries; even the EU minimum tariff for fine-cut is much lower than for manufactured cigarettes. This again provides an option for smokers, particularly low income smokers, to trade down to a cheaper product and bypass raised taxes, as can be seen in the case of Hungary over the short period from 2000 to 2005 (Figure 4.6). Due to the increasing divergence in the price of manufactured cigarettes, roll-your-own cigarettes have also become used to a much higher extent in the United Kingdom, France and Finland (Currie et al. 2012). Increasing tobacco prices is particularly effective in encouraging young people in their twenties to give up smoking, but has not been shown to be a significant factor in initiation of smoking by adolescents (Lewit et al. 1981; Grossman and Chaloupka 1997).

Hungary
Total tax on different tobacco products (HUF/20)

Total tax on different tobacco products
Jan 2005 (HUF/20)

Market share of hand-rolled cigarettes
(of total tax paid tobacco sales)

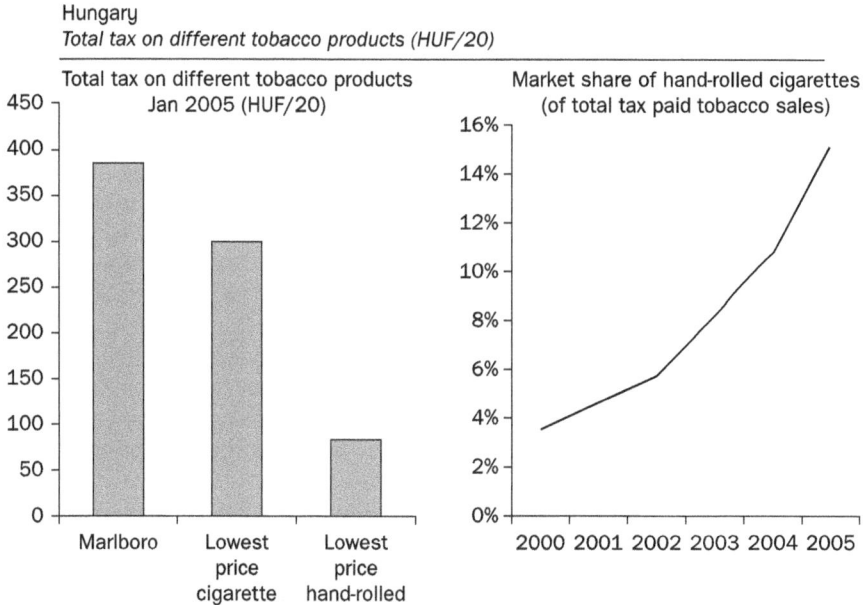

Figure 4.6 Product substitution as a way to avoid tax

Box 4.1 Case study on smoking in the EU 2002–7

Problem: High smoking rates and smoking disease across EU.
Highly diverse tax structures and levels across EU.
Need to harmonize EU–15, and then new EU member states from 2004.

Policies: Directives requiring structural move to harmonization.
Minimum tax rates increased.
Average tax rates increased 33 per cent.

Result: 2002–7
Smoking fell by 12 per cent.
Tax revenue receipts rose 15 per cent.
Fine-cut for roll-your-own increased from low level.
Problem of smuggling from EU Eastern border increased.

Illicit trade

Illicit trade and cross-border smuggling reduce the average price and so increase the demand for tobacco, with subsequent health effects. Cross-border smuggling may increase if tobacco prices are raised in one country, making a significant difference in price across the border, such as the EU Eastern border (see Box 4.1). Harmonizing tobacco tax upwards between countries is therefore in the interest of the health and revenues of all countries.

Price and tax differences are not the main cause of smuggling, and an empirical analysis for European countries estimated that price increases led to increased revenue, even when smuggling was increasing (Merriman et al. 2000). Corruption, organized crime and distribution networks for illicit goods are of greater importance than price, and little relationship has been shown between the extent of tobacco smuggling and its price or tax (Joossens et al. 2000).

Parties to the FCTC negotiated a Protocol for a universal system for counteracting illicit trade in tobacco. The main elements are tracing (the recreation of the route of seized illicit cigarettes) based on unique, secure and non-removable markings on all unit packets and packages and outside packaging of cigarettes within five years (and of other tobacco products within ten years) of entry into force of the Protocol. It also requires licensing of all those involved in manufacturing, distributing and retailing tobacco. Resources will be needed to monitor and enforce the agreement and illicit production of cigarettes, but these should be more than repaid by the increase in tax revenue available to governments from the fall in illicit trade (see the United Kingdom case study in Box 4.2). One study found that eliminating the illicit cigarette trade in the United Kingdom would reduce cigarette consumption by 5.0 to 8.2 per cent, and lower the tobacco death toll by 4,000 to 6,560 premature deaths per year (West et al. 2008). A later study concluded that the revenue lost globally to governments by illicit trade was about US$ 40.5 billion a year, and cost 164,000 premature deaths a year from 2030 onwards; this burden currently falls disproportionately on low- and middle-income countries (Joossens et al. 2010).

Cost-effectiveness of tobacco control measures

Ranson and colleagues have estimated the cost-effectiveness of different tobacco control measures in terms of cost per disability-adjusted year of life saved (Ranson et al. 2002). Their figures are adjusted to 2010 values (in Table 4.2), based on highly conservative assumptions of effectiveness and assuming maximum costs, and are therefore likely to be more cost-effective than their estimates imply. Price increases, including administrative costs but excluding the increases in tax revenue, were found to be the most cost-effective form of tobacco control, particularly for Eastern Europe and Central Asia, where prices are low and consumption is high. In addition, there would be huge additional benefit to governments in terms of extra tax revenue, so that for governments, tax increases are not only cost-effective, but are highly cost saving. For Eastern Europe, the next most cost-effective measure would be a combination of other non-price measures, and then nicotine replacement therapy (NRT) support for smoking cessation (as shown in Table 4.2).

Hurley and Matthews estimated the Australian National Tobacco Campaign to have cost $6.5 million ($A 9 million in 2007 prices) and to have saved $536.5 million ($A 740.6 million in 2007 prices) in net health care costs alone, taking into consideration the later health care costs of survivors who would have died earlier, but not including their pension costs (Hurley and Matthews 2008). It was reported to be highly cost saving, paying for itself

Box 4.2 Case study: United Kingdom plan to reduce smoking prevalence

Problem: Early 1990s, high smoking rates of 28 per cent and high rates of smoking-related disease. Late 1990s, rapid increase in smuggling of cigarettes and fine-cut tobacco into the United Kingdom.

Policies: Raise tax 3 per cent above inflation 1993–6; 5 per cent above inflation in 1997. After smuggling problem, tax increased in line with inflation 2001–8. To reduce smuggling: large increase in staff and scanners; fiscal marks and covert markings introduced, new supply chain legislation, new marketing strategy, memoranda of understanding with tobacco companies. After 2008, when smuggling reduced, tax raised above inflation each year.

Results: Smoking prevalence fell from 28 per cent to 21 per cent for adults, and 13 per cent to 6 per cent for children aged 11–15. Smuggling reduced from 23 per cent to 10 per cent of consumption. Tobacco tax revenue rose and then steadied. The increased tax revenue was ten times the cost of the anti-smuggling operations. At least 1.2 million lives saved from premature death in the long run.

70 times over. There was a subsequent substantial reduction in mortality from heart disease from 1995 to 2006 of 42 per cent, and in cerebral vascular disease of 36 per cent. Another Australian study assessed the impact of televized anti-smoking advertising and other tobacco control policies on adult smoking prevalence over the years 1995 to 2006. They reported a 0.3 per cent reduction in prevalence from weekly televized advertisements, and a similar reduction for each 0.3 per cent increase in price. There was no detectable effect of sales of NRT, or smoke-free restaurant laws (Wakefield et al. 2008).

Table 4.2 Cost for different policies adjusted to 2010 US$ per disability-adjusted life-year (DALY)

Policy options	High-income countries, including most Western and Northern European countries	Eastern Europe and Central Asia	World
Price increase of 10 per cent	111–3,719	4–105	16–420
Publicly provided cessation support with NRT (0.5–2.5 effectiveness)	1,007–9,672	307–1,066	481–2,573
Combination of other (non-price) effective measures (2 to 10 per cent effectiveness)	934–18,689	52–1,052	195–3,887

Source: Adapted from Ranson et al. 2002.

Mass media campaigns

The importance of population-based approaches to smoking cessation using mass media campaigns has been stressed by Lawrence and colleagues, noting that these tend to be neglected, and so important tobacco control opportunities have been missed (Lawrence et al. 2011). Good mass media campaigns raise awareness and change attitudes about the risks of using tobacco and the benefits of quitting (Flay 1987; WHO Regional Office for Europe 2003). They can be effective in preventing young people from starting to smoke, and can increase cessation rates of both youth and adults, especially when combined with other interventions (Hopkins et al. 2001). A youth-targeted anti-tobacco multimedia campaign in Norway reported that non-smoking youth in the intervention counties were less likely to start smoking than those in the control counties (WHO Regional Office for Europe 2003). Forty years ago, it was reported that the broadcasting of anti-smoking advertisements between 1968 and 1970, in the United States, reduced cigarette smoking by 14 per cent per year, and was a much greater deterrent from smoking than advertising was an encouragement, and that this was clearly appreciated by the tobacco companies (Hamilton 1972). Campaigns need to be sustained with appropriately targeted messages for the intended population (Lantz et al. 2000).

Widespread media reporting of research findings showing the harmful effects of tobacco have been particularly effective where knowledge of the health consequences of tobacco use is low, as is often the case in emerging economies (Jha and Chaloupka 1999). Media reporting was very effective in the 1960s in the United States and the United Kingdom (Atkinson and Skegg 1973) and may also be an important strategy for some European countries.

Advertising and promotion bans

Advertising bans were the earliest responses to the need for tobacco control. The effects are not easy to measure due to the time required to achieve the full effect, which may then last for many years. Three main types of analysis have been used: correlation of year-by-year fluctuations; cross-sectional comparisons between countries; and analyses of cigarette consumption before and after banned tobacco advertising. The latter present the most direct measure.

The tobacco advertising ban in New Zealand was estimated to have reduced consumption by 5.5 per cent (New Zealand Department of Health 1989), in Canada by 4 per cent (Department of Health Economics and Operational Research Division 1992), in Finland by 7 per cent (Pekurinen 1989), and in Norway by 16 per cent (Laugesen and Meads 1991). An OECD cross-sectional study of 22 countries reported a significant effect of different levels of advertising restriction, scored from 1 to 10, with each point associated with a 1.5 per cent decrease in consumption (Laugesen and Meads 1991). A time-series study suggested that a ban would reduce consumption by 7.5 per cent (McGuinness and Cowling 1975). On average, it is estimated that bans reduce smoking by some 7 per cent.

Another study reported that partial bans have little or no effect on smoking, as the tobacco industry simply rechannels its marketing to other media (Saffer and Chaloupka 1999). In Switzerland in 1993, an initiative to ban all direct and indirect advertising of tobacco products was voted down by an unusually large majority because the tobacco industry enlisted the support and influence of other stakeholders including media, the sports industry, and cultural activity planners, many of whom relied on tobacco advertising revenue (Cornuz et al. 1996). Other actions to improve consumer information, including labelling, smoking restrictions in public places and advertising bans, often generate savings in health care expenditures which offset any implementation costs. Even when this is not the case, the cost-effectiveness of these interventions is among the best in the entire health sector – less than $1,227 ($1,115 in 2005 prices) per DALY saved or QALY gained – with the potential to avoid a major proportion of the health and economic burden of smoking (Chisholm et al. 2006).

Warning labels

Warning labels on cigarette packs are recommended by the FCTC and are a requirement for EU countries. They have been shown to be effective in some cases. A study in the United States reported that teenagers considered warning labels (not graphic) on cigarette packets, 'uninformative and irrelevant' (Crawford et al. 2002). However, in Canada, 90 per cent of surveyed smokers reported that they had noticed the highly graphic warning labels on cigarette packages, 43 per cent had become more concerned about the health risks, and 44 per cent felt more motivated to quit (Shafey et al. 2009). To increase the potential for effectiveness, it has been recommended that warning labels be prominent, placed on the largest surfaces (front and back) of the packages, and be very distinct graphically from the rest of the package design (Strahan et al. 2002). One systematic review, of 87 studies, concludes that health warning on packages are among the most direct and prominent means of communicating with smokers, a source of health information to both smokers and non-smokers, and that larger warnings with pictures that elicit strong emotional response are the most effective – including among the young – and may prevent initiation (Hammond 2011).

Australia has also passed laws requiring plain packaging of cigarettes, as the pack 'has been used for years to generate luxury, freedom, glamour, status, masculinity, femininity, and false comfort about health effects' (Hastings et al. 2008). In 2014, cases against it were in progress with the World Trade Organisation (WTO) via five countries (Miles 2014). Uruguay is also facing law suits. New Zealand is introducing a bill to Parliament on plain packaging (Turia 2014), while an independent review of the case for plain packaging has recently been undertaken in England.

Smoke-free environments

An early systematic review of interventions for preventing smoking in public places concluded that such restrictions in workplaces reduced the prevalence of smoking by almost 4 per cent (Fichtenberg and Glantz 2002) and may yield reductions of up to 10 per cent (Evans et al. 1999; Yurekli and Zhang 2000).

In a more recent review of 37 studies of smoke-free policies in worksites or communities, 1976 to 2005, 21 reported reduced prevalence of 3.4 per cent (1.4 to 6.3), and a further 11 studies reported increased cessation of 6.4 per cent (1.3 to 7.9) (Hopkins et al. 2010). Four of the studies demonstrated economic benefits. However, a time-series analysis of 21 countries or states, which had implemented comprehensive smoke-free legislation, reported that the legislation had increased the rate at which prevalence was declining in some locations, but in the main had had no measurable impact on existing trends (Bajoga et al. 2011). Other countries have reported reductions in heart disease deaths following smoke-free legislation, and it is generally considered to be highly successful.

Cessation support

Physician advice to patients to quit smoking has long been demonstrated to be cost-effective (Williams 1985) compared to other common interventions for secondary prevention, such as drug therapies for hypertension and high blood cholesterol (Woolacott et al. 2002). Individual counselling by a cessation specialist and group therapy have also been shown to be effective (Silagy and Stead 2001). A comparative cost-effective modelling study estimated the incremental cost per QALY of various cessation interventions over and above the non-intervention control rate of quitting. Brief opportunistic advice from a general practitioner (GP) with telephone or self-help material (A) was the most cost-effective, next was opportunistic advice alone from a GP or hospital nurse (B), and, lastly, opportunistic advice plus NRT (C) was still cost-effective, but at four times the cost of B and eight times the cost of A (Parrott et al. 2006). Other modelling studies also point to the cost-effectiveness of smoking cessation measures (Ranson et al. 2002; Chisholm et al. 2006; Vos et al. 2010). The more effective methods, being expensive, are not the most cost-effective, and there is debate as to whether NRT works at a population level. One United Kingdom study of NRT use for smoking reduction or temporary abstinence concluded that the use of NRT for smoking reduction does not appear to be associated with lower cigarette consumption relative to smoking reduction without NRT (Beard et al. 2011).

A particularly important area for cessation relates to pregnant women. Smoking during pregnancy increases the risk of miscarriage, premature birth, low birth weight, still birth and sudden infant death syndrome (Royal College of Physicians 1992) in addition to the usual smoking risks. It is estimated that it cost the British National Health Service $30 to $130 million (£20 to £87.5 million in 2010 prices) per year to treat mothers and infants under a year old, with problems caused by smoking in pregnancy. Intervention to assess pregnant women and advise and refer for cessation is particularly important. A United Kingdom study estimated that spending $21 to $55 (£14 to £37 in 2010 prices) per pregnant smoker on low-cost smoking cessation interventions would be cost saving (Godfrey et al. 2010). Evidence from a number of studies in high-, middle- and low-income countries indicates that these are cost-effective (Ratcliffe et al. 1997; Secker-Walker et al. 1997; Chisholm et al. 2006; Hurley and Matthews 2008; Ha and Chisholm 2011).

Youth and tobacco control

Smoking by youth is reducing in some countries, but increasing elsewhere. Most smokers start smoking as adolescents, with a peak at age 15 in Europe, and the initiation age is rapidly reducing. It may therefore seem obvious to aim tobacco control measures directly and specifically at them. Policies directed specifically at youth include school education and health promotion and age restrictions and access; school health education has resulted in a high level of awareness of the risks of smoking, has influenced children's attitudes, and undoubtedly is essential.

However, evaluations have failed to show an effect of information on adolescents' decisions to start smoking, although there is some evidence that it may delay uptake. Anti-smoking programmes for youth are consistently evaluated as less effective than programmes to adults, due also to the long-term consequences of smoking, to which youth do not easily relate. It is known that young people are most likely to smoke if their parents smoke or if their parents have a liberal attitude towards their smoking. Many adolescent smokers, in particular, underestimate their risk of addiction to nicotine.

There is evidence that multimedia campaigns can prevent young people from starting, and persuade them and adult smokers to stop (Hopkins et al. 2001). One review looked at the results of 33 studies on behavioural interventions to prevent smoking in children and youth (Müller-Riemenschneider et al. 2008). They reported some evidence for the effect of community-based and multi-sectoral interventions, but not for school-based programmes.

Restrictions on youth access have generally been reported as non-effective and difficult to implement, although a study in England, where there was a rise in the legal age of sale from 16 to 18 years in 2007, reported a relative fall in prevalence of 16/17-year-olds of 4.7 per cent (odds ratio 1.36, p=0.024) (Fidler and West 2010).

A report on 29 European countries, using data for 2005/6, reported that boys but not girls smoked less where there were restrictions on vending machines (odds ratio 0.7, p=0.2) or a price policy (odds ratio 0.97, p=0.05) (Hublet et al. 2009). Many studies have confirmed the effects of price rises in reducing youth smoking; Kostava and colleagues concluded that cigarette prices are very important to adolescent smoking, with a total price elasticity of cigarette demand of –2.11 (Kostova et al. 2011). Research by Emery and colleagues, looking at whether young people's decision to experiment with cigarettes was influenced by price, concluded that it was not, as they were typically 'given' cigarettes at this early experimental stage (Emery et al. 2001). They reported that price was important for more established smoking behaviour, and so may reduce progress to established smoking. The Public Health Research Consortium systematic review of 45 studies of adolescent smoking, reports that price increases do appear to reduce smoking participation, prevalence, level of smoking, increases in quit rates and in smoking initiation (Rice et al. 2009). Figure 4.7 demonstrates from the United States that price does have a clear negative effect on prevalence of smoking among youth. In conclusion, it seems clear that the most effective means of reducing youth smoking is to reduce adult smoking, via the mechanisms of price increases, smoke-free policies, and good, well-directed multimedia programmes.

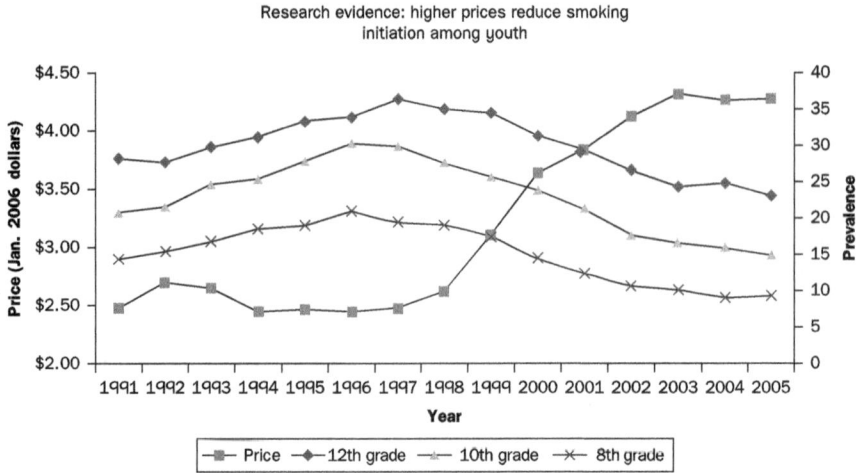

Figure 4.7 Youth smoking prevalence and cigarette price United States, 1991–2005

Source: Tax Burden on Tobacco, 2006, US Monitoring the Future Surveys, and author's calculations.

Smoking and poverty, inequalities and smoking by socioeconomic group

Smoking prevalence tends to be highest among adults of poor socioeconomic circumstances. The decline in smoking in many Western European countries over recent decades has been lowest amongst low-income smokers (Townsend 1995; Peretti-Watel et al. 2009). Smoking is one of the major causes of inequalities in health and mortality in many European countries, being particularly high among those in lower socioeconomic groups (SEGs), the unemployed, and lone parents (Jarvis and Wardle 2005; Jha et al. 2006b).

Adults in families with low incomes have the highest smoking rates, and suffer the highest morbidity and mortality from lung cancer, heart disease and high sickness absence; they also spend a disproportionately large share of their income on tobacco. Smoking therefore not only directly harms their health, but also decreases resources available to them more generally for food, education and health care (Efroymson et al. 2001).

It has been shown in the United Kingdom that, whereas smokers from all SEGs are equally likely to try to quit smoking, those in higher grades A and B (professional and managerial) are twice as likely to be successful as those in the lowest groups E (unskilled manual). The triggers for trying to quit differ, with those in higher grades being concerned about future health, and those of lower SES (socioeconomic status) being concerned about cost and present health problems (Vangeli et al. 2008), suggesting that smoking cessation programmes need to be tailored and targeted differentially. There is evidence that pregnant women are more likely to be smokers if they are of lower SES or of low educational attainment.

There is concern that tobacco tax is regressive, and this is stressed by the tobacco industry. This is a complex issue, as increases in tax are also the most effective means by which poorer people are released from addiction to smoking, and the heavy risk of poor health and premature death. Studies from the United States and the United Kingdom have shown that, on average, tobacco tax increases are in fact progressive as poor smokers are most likely to reduce their smoking or quit in response to price rises (Gallus et al. 2003) and so, on average, reduce their tax spend. However, for those who do continue to smoke and do not cut down, the tax they pay will increase with tax increases. It is important that this is addressed so that poor smokers in particular are offered good cessation support, and targeted social welfare and services, education and health programmes need to be used to offset any regressivity. There is evidence of widespread popular support for tobacco tax revenues to go towards such costs.

Smokers from low SEGs are more likely to use fine-cut tobacco for roll-your-own, and discounted cigarette brands (Joossens et al. 2014). Effective tobacco tax structures and policy, including equal taxation on all tobacco products, can be useful in nudging low-income smokers to quit, and need to be supported by the provision of good cessation support and mass media campaigns to reduce health inequalities.

Tobacco industry

The tobacco industry is the greatest obstacle to tobacco control. It operates to minimize tobacco control measures in every country, wherever – and however – it can. It lobbies strongly to persuade governments to keep tobacco taxes low, and to keep taxation structures in the interest of the companies. It argues against smoke-free policies, advertising bans, and warnings on packs. It also often works through other organizations and even countries, as with the action against Australia's introduction of plain packages, where it has persuaded three countries to object to the World Trade Organisation.

Uruguay has some of the strongest tobacco control laws in the world, including graphic health warnings that cover 80 per cent of cigarette packages, and a policy of one package per brand, which was adopted to deter the tobacco industry's use of packages with colours and other symbols to substitute misleading descriptors such as 'light' and 'low tar' cigarettes. In February 2010, Philip Morris International filed for arbitration at the World Bank's International Centre for Settlement of Investment Disputes, claiming that the use of a single presentation of a brand, as well as graphic health warnings that cover 80 per cent of tobacco packages, poses a risk to its investments. This lawsuit was a legal manoeuvre designed to force the Government of Uruguay to weaken its tobacco control laws, and therefore no longer effectively protect its citizens from the deadly consequences of tobacco use.

The influence of the tobacco industry in Bulgaria, Poland and the Czech Republic has also been investigated (Shirane et al. 2012). With regard to excise level changes resulting from Bulgaria's EU accession, the study provides evidence that transnational tobacco companies (TTCs) primarily lobbied for derogation, were greatly concerned to prevent any significant increase in excise duties with accession, and acted to insure that any such increases would be gradual. TTCs worked collectively to prevent and postpone excise increases, and lobbied successfully for derogation of excise level increases in accession countries. As a result of derogations, and with EU accession also leading to rising incomes, cigarettes actually became slightly more affordable in some accession countries. There are very many similar examples.

The European tobacco industry consists mainly of a few huge TTCs, most of which are based in Europe, and aggressively marketing to the developing world. As the British American Tobacco Chairman wrote in 1990 there are 'strong areas of growth, particularly in Asia and Africa ... it is an exciting prospect' (WHO 2004). This is bad news for developing countries, which are expecting to experience a projected doubling in smoking and smoking-related deaths in the next quarter century. Into these impoverished economies the tobacco industry is expanding and marketing tobacco by association with glamour, sport and modern living – methods they claimed to have given up 30 years ago. Smoking in Africa increased 50 per cent between 1995 and 2000, and is now rising by 4.3 per cent per year, with some 29 per cent of men and 7 per cent of women now smoking. Some rates are much higher; for example, in Uganda, a third of 13–15-year-olds are smokers. Cancers, cardiovascular disease and tuberculosis ensues. Tobacco tax is low in most African countries, often due to tobacco industry advice to governments. The World Bank estimates that a 10 per cent rise in tobacco tax across sub-Saharan Africa would result in three million smokers giving up the habit, and some 1.1 million lives might be saved (Jha et al. 2006a). As many of these tobacco companies are based in Europe, European governments need to take responsibility for their policies. The International Monetary Fund is also responsible, having promoted the lifting of trade restrictions on tobacco and private state-owned tobacco industries as part of its loan conditions. This has led to increased marketing, reductions of excise taxes, falls in prices, and overall increased cigarette consumption.

Foreign investment by tobacco companies has done great harm to tobacco control. The profits leave the country of investment, and they are left with the health effects and household poverty. The Framework Convention on Tobacco Control guidelines contain no provision covering tobacco industry investments, but this is seen by some as a serious gap (Lo 2010).

Conclusions

Smoking takes a huge toll on life and health in the WHO European Region. It also costs economies heavily in terms of health care costs, reduced productivity, and fires caused by smoking. Effective tobacco control measures have reduced tobacco use in some countries, particularly in Western Europe and the rest of the EU, but the overall level of smoking is still high, and the death rate from smoking appalling. Tobacco control measures – especially good tax measures, mass media programmes, smoke-free policies, advertisement and promotion bans, and well-run smoking cessation support – have been shown to be cost-effective and, in many cases, cost saving. Smoking cessation support is central to reduce smoking and for countries to reap the economic benefits. A number of economic studies indicate that combining many of these interventions leads to even greater health benefits, while still being cost-effective (Chisholm et al. 2006; Lai et al. 2007; Ortegon et al. 2012).

The huge price discrepancies between countries, with very low prices and taxation in some countries, particularly in the east of the Region, are the biggest problems. They keep smoking levels and deaths high, and deprive governments of tax revenue, and also cause problems of cross-border cheap trade with other European countries, making them reluctant to raise their taxes. Increasing taxes in the low-tax countries would benefit them threefold, by increasing their tax revenue, decreasing their health care costs, and increasing productivity, as well as expanding other sections of their economies. Few would argue against their benefits to health.

There is an urgent need for taxes to be raised across the Region, at least in line with the European Commission Directive levels, to be predominantly specific, or a high minimum, with equivalent taxes on all products, and these should be increased at least annually in line with inflation and income levels. This policy would provide governments with more tax revenue, reduce smoking and lower health and productivity costs, and also reduce inequalities in health and youth smoking. A portion of the tax revenue should be made available for tobacco-control purposes, particularly cessation support.

There are still huge gaps between countries in the levels of other tobacco control measures; most countries fail to use good mass media campaigns, and many lack adequate bans on advertising, smoke-free policies, warnings on packs, or cessation programmes.

Smoking by youth is decreasing in some countries, particularly in Western Europe, but is increasing elsewhere. There are two important issues here: to protect children from taking up smoking, and to protect them from others' smoke. The evidence is clear: that initiation is most affected by reducing adult smoking, by increasing mass media campaigns, and by reducing advertising and promotions. To protect them from others' smoke, full smoke-free policies are required. In parts of Europe, smoking by women is still very low, but tobacco companies see them and young people as promising potential markets to be exploited; action needs to be taken to prevent these developments.

Tobacco companies, particularly transnational companies, have pernicious influence in presenting misinformation to governments to undermine tobacco control and keep taxes low. There is good evidence that direct foreign investment by TTCs has resulted in increased advertising, low taxes, holding back other tobacco control measures, and serious misinformation to governments, at the cost of the health of the recipient countries.

Recommendations

Smoking is a huge public health problem, and good tobacco-control policies will benefit the economies and health of all countries. There is a wealth of knowledge concerning how the different elements are best implemented;

putting these into practice, and restraining the influence of tobacco companies would be highly beneficial for all countries and highly cost-effective.

However, it is difficult for tobacco control to be fully effective while the influence of the tobacco industry is unrestrained, and governments fail to acknowledge its danger. Corruption is a major issue in some countries, and needs to be seriously addressed and dealt with.

Taxes need to be raised across the Region, at least in line with the European Commission Directive levels, and should be predominantly specific tax, or at a high minimum monetary level. All tobacco products should have equivalent taxes, and these should be increased at least annually above inflation and increases in income levels. This will provide governments with more tax revenue, reduce health costs and low productivity, and also reduce inequalities in health, and youth smoking. A portion of the tax revenue should be made available for tobacco-control purposes, particularly for free access to cessation services for low-income smokers.

In addition, all countries would benefit from the use of well-targeted, ongoing, good mass media campaigns supporting tobacco control, coupled with a ban on the advertising and promotion of tobacco products, including so called 'social responsibility' promotions. Partial bans and voluntary agreements are ineffective. The introduction of comprehensive smoke-free policies in workplaces and public spaces will both reduce the harm from others' smoke, and reduce smoking levels.

There is also scope for increasing the visibility of warning messages. Packs of cigarettes and loose tobacco should have warnings and/or warning pictures that cover at least two-thirds of the pack. Consideration should also be given to the growing evidence of the benefits of plain packaging of cigarettes. Another element would be to provide effective advice and support to smokers to help them give up smoking, as well as harm reduction measures to reduce the harmful health effects of smoking to those who find it very difficult to give up.

All countries should make resources available for serious action against illicit trade and illicit production of cigarettes, and support the FCTC protocols on illicit trade. Country-specific plans of action should be developed covering all of these recommendations, setting out targets to reduce both adult and youth smoking of all tobacco products. Finally, consideration should be given to the responsibility of European governments to limit exporting and promoting the sale of tobacco to low- and middle-income countries, given the focus of the tobacco industry in expanding demand in these markets.

Notes

1   All values in this chapter are in 2010 US$PPP values, but for ease we simply use the $ sign to indicate dollar value.
2   (R2 = 0.40), with Log prevalence = 0.53(0.024) – 0.0314(0.0061) log price(p=0.000007) + error term, (standard errors in parenthesis and author's calculations).

References

Atkinson, A. B. and Skegg, J. L. (1973) Anti-smoking publicity and the demand for tobacco in the UK, *The Manchester School*, 41(3): 265–82.

Bajoga, U., Lewis, S., McNeill, A. and Szatkowski, L. (2011) Does the introduction of comprehensive smoke-free legislation lead to a decrease in population smoking prevalence?, *Addiction*, 106(7): 1346–54.

Beard, E., McNeill, A., Aveyard, P., Fidler, J., Michie, S. and West, R. (2011) Use of nicotine replacement therapy for smoking reduction and during enforced temporary abstinence: A national survey of English smokers, *Addiction*, 106(1): 197–204.

Buck, D., Godfrey, C., Raw, M. and Sutton, M. (1995) *Tobacco and Jobs: The Impact of Reducing Consumption on Employment in the UK*. York: Society for the Study of Addiction and Centre for Health Economics, University of York.

Chaloupka, F. J., Straif, K. and Leon, M. E. (2011) Effectiveness of tax and price policies in tobacco control, *Tobacco Control*, 20(3): 235–8.

Chaloupka, F. J., Yurekli, A. and Fong, G. T. (2012) Tobacco taxes as a tobacco control strategy, *Tobacco Control*, 21(2): 172–80.

Chisholm, D., Doran, C., Shibuya, K. and Rehm, J. (2006) Comparative cost-effectiveness of policy instruments for reducing the global burden of alcohol, tobacco and illicit drug use, *Drug and Alcohol Review*, 25(6): 553–65.

Cornuz, J., Burnand, B., Kawachi, I., Gutzwiller, F. and Paccaud, F. (1996) Why did Swiss citizens refuse to ban tobacco advertising?, *Tobacco Control*, 5(2): 149–53.

Crawford, M. A., Balch, G. I. and Mermelstein, R. (2002) Responses to tobacco control policies among youth, *Tobacco Control*, 11(1): 14–9.

Currie, L., Townsend, J., Leon Roux, M. et al. (2012) *Policy Recommendations for Tobacco Taxation in the European Union: Integrated Research Findings from the PPACTE project*. Dublin: The PPACTE Consortium.

Department of Health Economics and Operational Research Division (1992) *Effect of Tobacco Advertising on Tobacco Consumption*. London: Department of Health.

Doll, R. and Hill, A. B. (1956) Lung cancer and other causes of death in relation to smoking; a second report on the mortality of British doctors, *British Medical Journal*, 2(5001): 1071–81.

Doll, R. and Hill, A. B. (1964) Mortality in relation to smoking: Ten years' observations of British doctors, *British Medical Journal*, 1(5395): 1460–7, Concl.

Efroymson, D., Ahmed, S., Townsend, J. et al. (2001) Hungry for tobacco: An analysis of the economic impact of tobacco consumption on the poor in Bangladesh, *Tobacco Control*, 10(3): 212–7.

Emery, S., White, M. M. and Pierce, J. P. (2001) Does cigarette price influence adolescent experimentation?, *Journal of Health Economics*, 20(2): 261–70.

Evans, W. N., Farrelly, M. C. and Montgomery, E. (1999) Do workplace smoking bans reduce smoking?, *American Economic Review*, 89(4): 728–47.

Fichtenberg, C. M. and Glantz, S. A. (2002) Effect of smoke-free workplaces on smoking behaviour: Systematic review, *British Medical Journal*, 325(7357): 188.

Fidler, J. A. and West, R. (2010) Changes in smoking prevalence in 16–17-year-old versus older adults following a rise in legal age of sale: Findings from an English population study, *Addiction*, 105(11): 1984–8.

Flay, B. R. (1987) Mass media and smoking cessation: A critical review, *American Journal of Public Health*, 77(2): 153–60.

Gallus, S., Fernandez, E., Townsend, J., Schiaffino, A. and La Vecchia, C. (2003) Price and consumption of tobacco in Italy over the last three decades, *European Journal of Cancer Prevention*, 12(4): 333–7.

Godfrey, C., Ali, S., Parrott, S. and Pickett, K. (2011) *Economic Model of Adult Smoking Related Costs and Consequences for England*. York: Public Health Research Consortium, University of York.

Godfrey, C., Pickett, K., Parrott, S., Mdege, N. and Eapen, D. (2010) *Estimating the Costs to the NHS of Smoking in Pregnancy for Pregnant Women and Infants*. York: Public Health Research Consortium, University of York.

Goel, R. K. and Nelson, M. A. (2008) *Smoking in Relation to the Death Rates of One Million Men and Women*. Aldershot: Ashgate.

Grossman, M. and Chaloupka, F. J. (1997) Cigarette taxes. The straw to break the camel's back, *Public Health Reports*, 112(4): 290–7.

Ha, D. A. and Chisholm, D. (2011) Cost-effectiveness analysis of interventions to prevent cardiovascular disease in Vietnam, *Health Policy Plan*, 26: 210–22.

Hamilton, J. L. (1972) The demand for cigarettes: Advertising, the health scare and the cigarette advertising ban, *Review of Economics and Statistics*, 54(4): 401–10.

Hammond, D. (2011) Health warning messages on tobacco products: A review, *Tobacco Control*, 20(5): 327–37.

Hammond, E. C. (1966) Smoking in relation to the death rates of one million men and women, *National Cancer Institute Monograph*, 19: 127–204.

Hanson, J. and Kysar, D. (2001) The joint failure of economic theory and legal regulation, in P. Slovic (ed.) *Smoking: Risk, Perception, and Policy*. Thousand Oaks, CA: Sage Publications, pp. 229–77.

Hastings, G., Gallopel-Morvan, K. and Miguel Rey, J. (2008) The plain truth about tobacco packaging, *Tobacco Control*, 17(6): 361–2.

Hopkins, D. P., Briss, P. A., Ricard, C. J. et al. (2001) Reviews of evidence regarding interventions to reduce tobacco use and exposure to environmental tobacco smoke, *American Journal of Preventive Medicine*, 20(2): 16–66.

Hopkins, D. P., Razi, S., Leeks, K. D., Priya Kalra, G., Chattopadhyay, S. K. and Soler, R. E. (2010) Smokefree policies to reduce tobacco use. A systematic review, *American Journal of Preventive Medicine*, 38(Suppl. 2): S275–89.

Hublet, A., Schmid, H., Clays, E., Godeau, E., Gabhainn, S. N., Joossens, L. and Maes, L. (2009) Association between tobacco control policies and smoking behaviour among adolescents in 29 European countries, *Addiction*, 104(11): 1918–26.

Hurley, S. F. and Matthews, J. P. (2008) Cost-effectiveness of the Australian National Tobacco Campaign, *Tobacco Control*, 17(6): 379–84.

ISTAT (2013) *Tobacco sales data – various years*. Available at: http://www.istat.org [Accessed 22 October 2014].

Jarvis, M. J. and Wardle, J. (2005) Social patterning of individual health behaviours: the case of cigarette smoking, in M. Marmot and R. Wilkinson (eds.) *Social Determinants of Health*, 2nd edn. Oxford: Oxford University Press, pp.224–37.

Jha, P. and Chaloupka, F. (1999) *Curbing the Epidemic: Governments and the Economics of Tobacco Control*. Washington, DC: World Bank.

Jha, P., Chaloupka, F., Moore, J. et al. (2006a) Tobacco Addiction, in D. T. Jamison, J. G. Breman, A. R. Measham et al. (eds) *Disease Control Priorities in Developing Countries*, 2nd edn. Washington, DC: World Bank, pp. 869–86.

Jha, P., Peto, R., Zatonski, W., Boreham, J., Jarvis, M. J. and Lopez, A. D. (2006b) Social inequalities in male mortality, and in male mortality from smoking: Indirect estimation from national death rates in England and Wales, Poland, and North America, *The Lancet*, 368(9533): 367–70.

Joossens, L., Chaloupka, F., Merriman, D. and Yurekli, A. (2000) Issues in the smuggling of tobacco products, in P. Jha and F. Chaloupka (eds) *Tobacco Control in Developing Countries*. Oxford: Oxford University Press, pp. 393–406.

Joossens, L., Lugo, A., La Vecchia, C., Gilmore, A. B., Clancy, L. and Gallus, S. (2014) Illicit cigarettes and hand-rolled tobacco in 18 European countries: A cross-sectional survey, *Tobacco Control*, 23(e1): e17–23.

Joossens, L., Merriman, D., Ross, H. and Raw, M. (2010) The impact of eliminating the global illicit cigarette trade on health and revenue, *Addiction*, 105(9): 1640–9.

Kahn, H. A. (1966) The Dorn study of smoking and mortality among U.S. veterans: Report on eight and one-half years of observation, *National Cancer Institute Monograph*, 19: 1–125.

Kostova, D., Ross, H., Blecher, E. and Markowitz, S. (2011) Is youth smoking responsive to cigarette prices? Evidence from low- and middle-income countries, *Tobacco Control*, 20(6): 419–24.

Lai, T., Habicht, J., Reinap, M., Chisholm, D. and Baltussen, R. (2007) Costs, health effects and cost-effectiveness of alcohol and tobacco control strategies in Estonia, *Health Policy*, 84(1): 75–88.

Lantz, P. M., Jacobson, P. D., Warner, K. E., Wasserman, J., Pollack, H. A., Berson, J. and Ahlstrom, A. (2000) Investing in youth tobacco control: A review of smoking prevention and control strategies, *Tobacco Control*, 9(1): 47–63.

Laugesen, M. and Meads, C. (1991) Tobacco advertising restrictions, price, income and tobacco consumption in OECD countries, 1960–1986, *British Journal of Addiction*, 86(10): 1343–54.

Lawrence, D., Mitrou, F. and Zubrick, S. R. (2011) Global research neglect of population-based approaches to smoking cessation: Time for a more rigorous science of population health interventions, *Addiction*, 106(9): 1549–54.

Lewit, E. M., Coate, D. and Grossman, M. (1981) The effects of government regulation on teenage smoking, *Journal of Law and Economics*, 24(3): 545–69.

Lo, C.-F. (2010) FCTC guidelines on tobacco industry foreign investment would strengthen controls on tobacco supply and close loopholes in the tobacco treaty, *Tobacco Control*, 19(4): 306–10.

McGuinness, T. and Cowling, K. (1975) Advertising and the aggregate demand for cigarettes, *European Economic Review*, 6: 311–28.

Merriman, D., Yurekli, A. and Chaloupka, F. (2000) How big is the worldwide cigarette-smuggling problem?, in P. Jha and F. Chaloupka (eds) *Tobacco Control in Developing Countries*. Oxford: Oxford University Press, pp. 365–92.

Miles, T. (2014) Australia demands opponents stop stalling WTO tobacco case, *Reuters*, 27 March.

Müller-Riemenschneider, F., Bockelbrink, A., Reinhold, T., Rasch, A., Greiner, W. and Willich, S. N. (2008) Long-term effectiveness of behavioural interventions to prevent smoking among children and youth, *Tobacco Control*, 17(5): 301–2.

New Zealand Department of Health (1989) *Health or tobacco? An end to tobacco advertising and promotion*. Wellington: Toxic Substances Board.

Ortegon, M., Lim, S., Chisholm, D. and Mendis, S. (2012) Cost effectiveness of strategies to combat cardiovascular disease, diabetes, and tobacco use in sub-Saharan Africa and South East Asia: Mathematical modelling study, *British Medical Journal*, 344: e607.

Parrott, S., Godfrey, C. and Kind, P. (2006) *Cost-effectiveness of Brief Intervention and Referral for Smoking Cessation*. York: University of York.

Pekurinen, M. (1989) The demand for tobacco products in Finland, *British Journal of Addiction*, 84(10): 1183–92.

Peretti-Watel, P., Constance, J., Seror, V. and Beck, F. (2009) Cigarettes and social differentiation in France: Is tobacco use increasingly concentrated among the poor?, *Addiction*, 104(10): 1718–28.

Peto, R., Lopez, A. D., Boreham, J., Thun, M. and Heath, C., Jr. (1992) Mortality from tobacco in developed countries: Indirect estimation from national vital statistics, *The Lancet*, 339(8804): 1268–78.

Polish Ministry of Finance 2008. *Tobacco Tax and tobacco Tax Revenues*. Warsaw: Ministry of Finance.

Ranson, M. K., Jha, P., Chaloupka, F. J. and Nguyen, S. N. (2002) Global and regional estimates of the effectiveness and cost-effectiveness of price increases and other tobacco control policies, *Nicotine & Tobacco Research*, 4(3): 311–19.

Ratcliffe, J., Cairns, J. and Platt, S. (1997) Cost-effectiveness of a mass media-led anti-smoking campaign in Scotland, *Tobacco Control*, 6: 104–10.

Rice, N., Godfrey, C., Slack, R., Sowden, A. and Worthy, G. (2009) *A Systematic Review of the Effects of Price on the Smoking Behaviour of Young People*. York: Public Health Research Consortium, University of York.

Ross, H., Kostova, D., Stoklosa, M. and Leon, M. (2014) The impact of cigarette excise taxes on smoking cessation rates from 1994 to 2010 in Poland, Russia, and Ukraine, *Nicotine & Tobacco Research*, 16(Suppl. 1): S37–43.

Royal College of Physicians (1992) *Smoking and the Young*. London: Royal College of Physicians.

Saffer, H. and Chaloupka, F. (1999) *Tobacco Advertising: Economic Theory and International Evidence*, working paper 6958. Cambridge, MA: National Bureau of Economic Research.

Secker-Walker, R. H., Worden, J. K., Holland, R. R., Flynn, B. S. and Detsky, A. S. (1997) A mass media programme to prevent smoking among adolescents: Costs and cost-effectiveness, *Tobacco Control*, 6: 207–12.

Shafey, O., Eriksen, M., Ross, H. and Mackay, J. (eds.) (2009) *Tobacco Atlas*, 3rd edn. Atlanta, GA: American Cancer Society.

Shields, M. and Wilkins, K. (2013) Smoking, smoking cessation and heart disease risk: A 16-year follow-up study, *Health Reports*, 24(2): 12–22.

Shirane, R., Smith, K., Ross, H., Silver, K. E., Williams, S. and Gilmore, A. (2012) Tobacco industry manipulation of tobacco excise and tobacco advertising policies in the Czech Republic: An analysis of tobacco industry documents, *PLoS Medicine*, 9(6): e1001248.

Silagy, C. and Stead, L. F. (2001) Physician advice for smoking cessation, *Cochrane Database of Systematic Reviews*, CD000165.

Strahan, E. J., White, K., Fong, G. T., Fabrigar, L. R., Zanna, M. P. and Cameron, R. (2002) Enhancing the effectiveness of tobacco package warning labels: A social psychological perspective, *Tobacco Control*, 11(3): 183–90.

Townsend, J. (1978) Smoking and lung cancer: A cohort data study of men and women in England and Wales 1935–70, *Journal of the Royal Statistical Society*, 141(1): 95–107.

Townsend, J. (1995) The burden of smoking, in M. Benzeval, K. Judge and M. Whitehead (eds) *Tackling Inequalities in Health: An Agenda for Action*. Kings Fund: London.

Townsend, J. (1996) Price and consumption of tobacco, *British Medical Bulletin*, 52(1): 132–42.

Townsend, J. (1997) *Tobacco Price and the Smoking Epidemic*. Copenhagen: Smoke free Europe.

Townsend, J., Roderick, P. and Cooper, J. (1994) Cigarette smoking by socioeconomic group, sex, and age: Effects of price, income, and health publicity, *British Medical Journal*, 309(6959): 923–7.

Turia, T. (2014) *First Reading of the Smoke-free Environments (Tobacco Plain Packaging) Amendment Bill*. Wellington: New Zealand Government.

US Department of Health and Human Services (2001) *Women and Smoking: A Report of the Surgeon General*. Atlanta, GA: US Department of Health and Human Services, Public Health Service, Center for Disease Control, National Center for Chronic Disease Prevention and Health Promotion, Office of Smoking and Health.

Vangeli, E., Sykes, C. and West, R. (2008) A qualitative exploration of smoking relapse: The role of identity, *Psychology & Health*, 23: 265.

Viscusi, W. K. and Hersch, J. (2008) The mortality cost to smokers, *Journal of Health Economics*, 27: 943–58.

Vos, T., Carter, R., Barendregt, J. et al. (2010) *Assessing Cost-Effectiveness in Prevention (ACE–Prevention)*. Brisbane: University of Queensland.

Wakefield, M. A., Durkin, S., Spittal, M. J. et al. (2008) Impact of tobacco control policies and mass media campaigns on monthly adult smoking prevalence, *American Journal of Public Health*, 98(8): 1443–50.

Warner, K. E., Chaloupka, F., Cook, J. et al. (1995) Criteria for determining an optimal cigarette tax: The economist's perspective, *Tobacco Control*, 4(4): 380–6.

West, R., Townsend, J., Joossens, L., Arnott, D. and Lewis, S. (2008) Why combating tobacco smuggling is a priority, *British Medical Journal*, 337: a1933.

Williams, A. (1985) Economics of coronary artery bypass grafting, *British Medical Bulletin*, 291: 326–9.

Woolacott, N. F., Jones, L., Forbes, C. A. et al. (2002) The clinical effectiveness and cost-effectiveness of bupropion and nicotine replacement therapy for smoking cessation: A systematic review and economic evaluation, *Health Technology Assessment*, 6(16): 1–245.

World Bank (2014) Inflation data – various years. Available at: http://www.worldbank.org [Accessed 22 October 2014].

World Health Organization (WHO) (2004) *The Tobacco Industry Documents: What They Are, What They Tell Us and How to Search Them: A Practical Manual*. Geneva: World Health Organization.

World Health Organization (WHO) (2008) *WHO Report on the Global Tobacco Epidemic, 2008: The MPOWER package*. Geneva: World Health Organization.

World Health Organization (WHO) (2012a) *Prevalance of tobacco use among adults and adolescents*. Geneva: World Health Organization. Available at http://gamapserver. who.int/gho/interactive_charts/tobacco/use/atlas.html [Accessed 31 January 2014].

World Health Organization (WHO) (2012b) *WHO Global Report: Mortality Attributable to Tobacco*. Geneva: World Health Organization.

World Health Organization (WHO) (2014) *Tobacco: Data and statistics*. Copenhagen: WHO Regional Office for Europe. Available at http://www.euro.who.int/en/health-topics/disease-prevention/tobacco/data-and-statistics [Accessed December 2013].

World Health Organization (WHO) Regional Office for Europe (2003) *Which are the Most Effective and Cost-effective Interventions for Tobacco Control?* Copenhagen: Health Evidence Network, World Health Organization Regional Office for Europe.

Wynder, E. L., Hultberg, S., Jacobsson, F. and Bross, I. J. (1957) Environmental factors in cancer of the upper alimentary tract; a Swedish study with special reference to Plummer-Vinson (Paterson-Kelly) syndrome, *Cancer*, 10(3): 470–87.

Yurekli, A. A. and Zhang, P. (2000) The impact of clean indoor-air laws and cigarette smuggling on demand for cigarettes: An empirical model, *Health Economics*, 9(2): 159–70.

chapter five

Tackling alcohol-related harms

Peter Anderson

Introduction

That alcohol is an intoxicant and improves the drinker's mood in the short-term is perhaps the main reason why most people drink (Anderson and Baumberg 2006). Alcohol plays a role in everyday social life, marking such events as births, weddings and deaths, as well as marking the transition from work to play and easing social intercourse. However, this intoxicating effect comes with a price, alcohol being a teratogen, a neurotoxin and a carcinogen (Anderson 2014).

There are many reasons for having policies and programmes to reduce the harm done by alcohol. First and foremost, alcohol itself, as well as heavy drinking and the state of being dependent on alcohol, cause enormous damage to the health, well-being and personal security of individuals, families and communities. One way to summarize this is through alcohol's impact on disability-adjusted life-years (DALYs), a summary measure used by the World Health Organization that captures both impairment due to ill-health and premature death. In 2010, it has been estimated that alcohol was the fifth most important risk factor for DALYs worldwide after high blood pressure, tobacco (including second-hand smoke), household air pollution from solid fuels, and a diet low in fruits (Lim et al. 2012).

Economic efficiency can be improved in the alcohol market when the negative externalities due to alcohol consumption can be reduced and where the socially optimum level of alcohol is sold and consumed in society. A socially optimum level can be one where the level of harm is minimized (Doran and Jainullabudeen 2010; Doran and Byrnes 2012). This optimum level requires analysing the interactions between regulating the alcohol market through controls on availability, marketing and price, and individual consumer factors such as willingness to buy alcohol and personal income.

Another reason for alcohol policies stems from injustice and inequalities. Within and between countries, alcohol is both a cause and a consequence of inequalities. At any given level of alcohol consumption, poorer people can be as much as three or four times as likely to die from an alcohol-related condition as richer people (Rehm et al. 2009b). Within the European Union, at least one quarter of the difference in life expectancy between newer and older member states is due to alcohol (Zatonksi 2008). Economic downturns also increase alcohol-related deaths (Stuckler et al. 2009).

In addition, policy can address market failures by deterring children from using alcohol (Anderson et al. 2012b), protecting people other than drinkers from the harm done by alcohol (Laslett et al. 2010), counteracting alcohol's direct impact in cheating the brain to think that it gives more reward than it does regardless of harms, and providing all consumers with information about the effects of alcohol (Anderson 2009b). These market failures could be corrected by regulations that affect price, availability and advertising.

Finally, the concept of stewardship implies that liberal states have a duty to look after the important needs of people individually and collectively. It emphasizes the obligation of states to provide conditions that allow people to be healthy and, in particular, to take measures to reduce health inequalities (Nuffield Council on Bioethics 2007).

Of course, it is not just alcohol policies per se that reduce the harm done by alcohol. There are also a variety of other policies which can reduce or increase alcohol-related problems but which are not normally described as alcohol policies, since they are not implemented specifically to reduce alcohol-related harm as a primary aim. An example is general road safety measures. Reducing speed limits on roads and making roads safer reduces drink-driving fatalities, without any added drink-driving counter measures (Anderson 2007). Workplace health promotion policies that address reward/demand imbalances and work/life imbalances reduce alcohol-related harm, independent of whether or not there are specific work place alcohol policies (Anderson 2012a). Social welfare policies and labour policies that aim to reintegrate the unemployed into the labour market reduce alcohol-related harm, irrespective of any direct alcohol policy (Stuckler et al. 2010).

This chapter will continue by briefly summarizing alcohol's impact on individual and social health, pointing out that in addition to its health impact, alcohol, and, more so, heavy drinking reduce educational attainment, employment, and increase absenteeism from work and presenteesim whilst at work. At the societal level, it will be shown that productivity losses constitute between some one half and two-thirds of all the social costs of alcohol across a range of countries.

The chapter will then continue by noting that alcohol's burden is avoidable through a range of policies. The three 'best buys' for reducing alcohol-related harm, increasing price, reducing availability and bans on advertising, will be briefly described. The chapter will follow by summarizing a simplified cost-benefit analysis of a price increase in England, which demonstrated a cost-benefit ratio of tangible costs of well over 100:1, and of intangible costs (non-financial welfare gains: loss of consumer surplus) of 2:1 (Anderson and Baumberg 2010).

Given the dissonance between alcohol's health burden and the poor policy response throughout the world (Anderson et al. 2013), the chapter finishes with some explanations of why there has been such little progress. Among the reasons, it seems that an all too cosy relationship between governments and the alcohol industry, and lack of proper regulation of the industry, are foremost.

The impact of alcohol on individuals

Both the volume of lifetime alcohol use and a combination of frequency of drinking and the amount drunk per drinking occasion increase the risk of alcohol-related harm, largely in a dose-dependent manner (Anderson 2012c).

Personal security

Alcohol is an intoxicant affecting a wide range of structures and processes in the central nervous system which, interacting with personality characteristics, associated behaviour and sociocultural expectations, is a causal factor for intentional and unintentional injuries and harm to people other than the drinker, including interpersonal violence, suicide, homicide, crime and drink-driving fatalities (Anderson et al. 2009), and a causal factor for risky sexual behaviour, sexually transmitted diseases and HIV infection (Rehm et al. 2009a).

Health

Alcohol is a dependence-producing drug, similar to other substances under international control, through its reinforcing properties and neuroadaptation in the brain (WHO 2004). It is an immunosuppressant, increasing the risk of communicable diseases, including tuberculosis and community acquired pneumonia (Rehm et al. 2010). Alcoholic beverages and the ethanol within them are classified as a carcinogen by the International Agency for Research on Cancer, increasing the risk of cancers of the oral cavity and pharynx, oesophagus, stomach, colon, rectum and female breast in a linear dose–response relationship (IARC 2010).

Alcohol use is related overwhelmingly detrimentally to cardiovascular disease (Anderson 2012c). The exceptions to this are ischaemic diseases, for which, on average, light to moderate drinking has a protective effect on (Roereckc and Rehm 2012). However, a large part of this effect is due to confounders, with low to moderate alcohol use being a proxy for better health and social capital (Hansel et al. 2010). In any case, the protective effect totally disappears when drinkers report at least one heavy drinking occasion per month (Roerecke and Rehm 2010).

It is mostly the middle aged (and men in particular) who die from alcohol (Jones et al. 2009; Rehm et al. 2011). Taking into account a lifecourse view, however, the adolescent brain is particularly susceptible to alcohol, and the longer the onset of consumption is delayed, the less likely that alcohol-related problems and alcohol dependence will emerge in adult life (Norberg et al. 2009). The absolute real risk of dying from an adverse alcohol-related condition increases linearly with the amount of alcohol consumed over a lifetime, with no safe level (National Health and Medical Research Council 2009).

Educational attainment

There is evidence, although not from all studies, that drinking can impair educational attainment (Lye and Hirschberg 2010). Carrell et al. (2011) examined the effect of alcohol consumption on student achievement at the United States Air Force Academy. They were able to take advantage of the strict enforcement of the minimum legal drinking age of 21 years at the Academy, finding that drinking in those students over the legal drinking age caused significant reductions in academic performance, particularly for the highest-performing students.

Jobs and income

Heavy drinking increases the risk of unemployment, absenteeism, and presenteeism (Anderson 2012a). A meta-analysis of eleven studies that had reported a positive impact of alcohol consumption on earnings, a proxy measure of productivity, suggested that the relationship was an artefact, with alcohol consumption proving to be an imperfect proxy for all personality traits that have a positive influence on human capital (Lye and Hirschberg 2010). The workplace, itself, can lead to alcohol-related harm through structural factors, such as stress, and high effort/low reward work (Anderson 2012a).

The impact of alcohol on societies

Health burden

In 2010, the latest year of summarized data, it has been estimated that alcohol was the cause of some 2.7 million deaths, an increase from the 2 million alcohol-caused deaths in 1990 (Lim et al. 2012). The contribution of heavy drinking (40+ g of pure alcohol per day for women and 60+ g for men) and alcohol dependence to alcohol-related mortality has been studied in the European Union. About 80 per cent of all alcohol-related deaths (net of any protective effect) arise in people who are heavy drinkers or alcohol dependent, and about 70 per cent of all alcohol-related deaths arise in people who are alcohol dependent (Shield et al. 2012). In 2010, it has been estimated that alcohol was the fifth most important risk factor for DALYs worldwide, accounting for 121 million life-year DALYs lost, an increase from 87 million in 1990 when alcohol was the eighth most important risk factor (Lim et al. 2012).

At times of economic crisis and increased unemployment, although per capita consumption of alcohol tends to decrease, episodic heavy drinking increases and deaths from alcohol-related disorders increase. An analysis of associations between changes in employment and mortality for 26 European countries between 1970 and 2007 found that a more than 3 per cent increase in unemployment increased suicides at ages younger than 65 years by nearly 5 per cent and deaths from alcohol use disorders by 28 per cent (Stuckler et al. 2009).

Cost burden

A range of studies across the world find that the economic costs from alcohol's impact on health, well-being and productivity reach some $USPPP 300–400 per head of population in any one year, with well over one half to two-thirds of all of these costs due to lost productivity (Rehm et al. 2009b).

Inequalities and alcohol: For the same amount of alcohol consumed, people who live in lower income regions of the world have higher alcohol-related deaths and DALYs than people who live in higher income regions of the world (Rehm et al. 2009a). The same applies within countries; for the same amount of alcohol consumed, people with lower incomes have higher alcohol-related deaths than people with higher incomes (Anderson and Baumberg 2006). Socioeconomic variables act on the collective as well as the individual level (Blomgren et al. 2004), such evidence is consistent with social networks being found to influence the drinking behaviour of the individual (Rosenquist et al. 2010).

Economic development and alcohol: As gross domestic product GDP increases, per capita adult alcohol consumption increases, at least up to a GDP of USPPP$10,000, largely driven by abstainers starting to drink, see Figure 5.1 (Shield et al. 2011). Thus, having effective alcohol policies in place to manage the expected increases in consumption and harm with economic development becomes crucial.

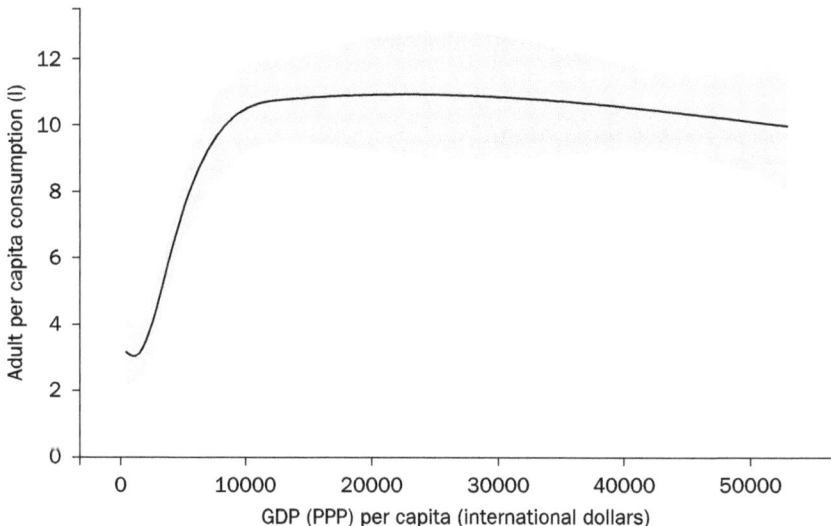

Figure 5.1 Relationship between recorded adult per capita alcohol consumption and GDP for 189 countries across the world

Effective alcohol policies

Alcohol's global harm is preventable. There is a very extensive evidence base to inform the implementation of effective alcohol policy (Anderson et al. 2009; WHO 2009; Babor et al. 2010; Anderson et al. 2012a).

The WHO summarizes this evidence by estimating the impact of policies, their costs and cost-effectiveness (as is summarized in Table 5.1) for three culturally and geographically distinct WHO sub-regions: countries of the Americas with low child and adult mortality, *AmrB*, including Latin American countries such as Brazil and Mexico; countries of the European region with low child mortality but high adult mortality, *EurC*, including countries such as Russia and Ukraine; and countries of the Western Pacific region with low child and adult mortality, *WprB*, including countries such as China and Viet Nam (Anderson et al. 2009).

Specific intervention strategies need not, and indeed do not, get implemented in isolation, but should be combined to maximize possible health gains up to the point where it remains affordable to do so. The optimal mix of interventions at different spending limits will depend on the relative cost and cost-effectiveness of the individual components, as well as the synergies that exist between them. Table 5.1 includes an example of a wide-ranging combination strategy, which shows that while cost-effectiveness is maintained, implementation costs naturally go up.

The Organisation for Economic Co-operation and Development (OECD) has recently undertaken a new analysis of the health and economic impacts of a range of alcohol policies in a selection of its member countries, which supports the conclusions summarized in Table 5.1. OECD analyses, based on a microsimulation model designed to assess population-level impacts over a 40-year time horizon, show that brief advice in primary care and policies to raise alcohol prices are especially effective in improving health outcomes, and the latter can reduce government expenditure. All of the alcohol policies evaluated were found to have favourable cost-effectiveness ratios, albeit at different levels of the cost-effectiveness spectrum (Sassi 2015).

Best buys for alcohol policy

In their joint submission to the 2011 UN high level meeting on noncommunicable diseases, the World Economic Forum and the World Health Organization (2011) listed the three best buys for alcohol policy as price increase, limits on availability and bans on advertising, which will be discussed in turn.

Price increases

Table 5.1 shows that tax increases represent the most cost-effective response in countries with a high prevalence of heavy drinking (each DALY saved costs less than $550 in both the American and Eastern European sub-regions). In lower-prevalence contexts, including the Western Pacific sub-region, where alcohol use by women is relatively infrequent, population-level effects drop off and cost-effectiveness ratios rise accordingly. The effect of alcohol tax

Table 5.1 Cost and cost-effectiveness of interventions relating to different target areas for alcohol public health policy

Target area Specific intervention(s)	Coverage	WHO sub-region (exemplar countries)					
		Americas: AmrB (e.g. Brazil, Mexico)		Europe: EurC (e.g. Russia, Ukraine)		Western Pacific: WprB (e.g. China, Viet Nam)	
		Annual cost per capita ($)[1]	Cost per DALY saved ($)[2]	Annual cost per capita ($)[1]	Cost per DALY saved ($)[2]	Annual cost per capita ($)[1]	Cost per DALY saved ($)[2]
1 Raising awareness and political commitment							
School-based education	80%	0.32	N/A *	0.37	N/A *	0.64	N/A *
2 Health sector response							
Brief interventions for heavy drinkers	30%	1.14	4,258	1.96	2,939	0.51	2,218
3 Community action							
Mass media campaign	80%	0.34	N/A *	0.87	N/A *	0.23	N/A *
4 Drink-driving policies and countermeasures							
Drink-driving legislation and enforcement (via random breath-testing campaigns)	80%	0.48	1,017	0.79	859	0.29	1,388
5 Addressing the availability of alcohol							
Reduced access to retail outlets	80%	0.24	567	0.52	624	0.20	1,438
6 Addressing marketing of alcohol beverages							
Comprehensive advertising ban	95%	0.26	1,024	0.52	1,057	0.20	1,051

(Continued overleaf)

Table 5.1 Cost and cost-effectiveness of interventions relating to different target areas for alcohol public health policy (*continued*)

| | | WHO sub-region (exemplar countries) | | | | | |
| | | Americas: AmrB (e.g. Brazil, Mexico) | | Europe: EurC (e.g. Russia, Ukraine) | | Western Pacific: WprB (e.g. China, Viet Nam) | |
Target area	Coverage	Annual cost per capita ($)[1]	Cost per DALY saved ($)[2]	Annual cost per capita ($)[1]	Cost per DALY saved ($)[2]	Annual cost per capita ($)[1]	Cost per DALY saved ($)[2]
7 Pricing policies							
Increased excise taxation (by 20%)	95%	0.37	305	0.74	418	0.24	1,494
Increased excise taxation (by 50%)	95%	0.37	265	0.74	369	0.24	1,265
Tax enforcement (20% less unrecorded)	95%	0.61	515	0.96	548	0.45	2,864
Tax enforcement (50% less unrecorded)	95%	0.69	524	1.02	528	0.52	3,007
Combination strategy[3]		2.59	760	4.51	830	1.58	1,875

Notes: $ for a full list of member states by WHO sub-region, see http://www.who.int/choice/demography/regions (accessed 14 March 2009).
[1] Implementation cost in 2005 International dollars converted to $USPPP for 2010.
[2] Cost-effectiveness ratio, expressed in international dollars per disability-adjusted life-year saved for the year 2005 converted to $USPPP for 2010.
[3] Brief advice, random breath-testing, reduced access, advertising ban, plus increased tax (by 50 per cent) and its enforcement (50 per cent less unrecorded consumption).
* Not applicable because effect size not significantly different from zero (cost-effectiveness ratio would therefore approach infinity).

increases stands to be mitigated by illegal production, tax evasion and illegal trading. Reducing this unrecorded consumption via concerted tax enforcement strategies by law enforcement and excise officers is estimated to cost more than a tax increase but – in the three sub-regions included in the table at least – produces similar levels of effect. In settings with higher levels of unrecorded production and consumption such as India, increasing the proportion of consumption that is taxed (and therefore more costly to the price-sensitive consumer) may represent a more effective pricing policy than a simple increase in excise tax (which may only encourage further illegal production, smuggling and cross-border purchases).

There are a number of parameters to consider when managing the price of alcohol (Österberg 2012b). First, it is the affordability of alcohol compared with other goods that matters (Rabinovich et al. 2009). So, if price stays the same, but incomes go up, consumption goes up. Or, if price stays the same and the relative price of other goods in the shopping basket goes up, consumption goes up.

Second, specific or targeted taxes do not necessarily work. This is the case, for example, of the German alcopop tax which simply switched consumption of spirits-based mixed beverages to beer-based mixed beverages (Anderson et al. 2012b).

Third, alcohol prices differ between neighbouring jurisdictions, which does lead to consumers crossing nearby borders to purchase cheaper alcohol (Rabinovich et al. 2009). But, this is much less of an issue than imagined. It is also important to note that some responses can make matters worse. In 2004, when Estonia joined the European Union, Finland dropped alcohol taxes by one third to act as a disincentive for consumers to buy cheaper alcohol from Estonia. However, the consequence was that sudden alcohol-caused deaths jumped immediately by 17 per cent (government revenue fell by the same amount) (Koski et al. 2007). And, it was the more deprived who were penalized, with the vast majority of the increase in deaths occurring among poorer, as opposed to richer, consumers (Herttua et al. 2008). The damaging effects came from Finnish, not Estonian, alcohol.

Fourth, because of the addictive nature of alcohol, price elasticities of alcoholic beverages may not be symmetrical. In other words, a decrease of a certain magnitude in alcohol prices may have a greater impact on alcohol consumption than the same magnitude of price increase realized afterwards. This is illustrated by the above Finnish example. Following the 33 per cent reduction in excise duty rates in 2004, total alcohol consumption per capita was 12 per cent higher in 2005 than in 2003. In 2008 and 2009, alcohol excise duty rates were increased three times, by an average of about 10 per cent each time. Between 2007 and 2010, total alcohol consumption fell by 3 per cent. Thus, consumption went up by 12 per cent when taxes fell by 33 per cent, but went down by only 3 per cent when taxes went up about 30 per cent, an example of asymmetry in elasticities (Österberg 2012b).

Fifth, alcohol is not normally taxed per gram, which would be a rational way to reflect that, for health, it is the number of grams of alcohol that matter; in some countries, alcohol is not subject to an excise tax at all. A volumetric tax which taxes alcohol equally across beverage types is less distortive of consumer preferences and more efficient at reducing consumption than where taxes are charged at varying amounts per litre of pure alcohol depending on beverage type (Byrnes et al. 2010).

And, finally, sixth, a tax increase is not normally followed by an equivalent price increase, with producers and retailers responding in different ways (Rabinovich et al. 2012). Sometimes the price goes up more than would be expected. Other times, and more commonly, the price goes up less than expected, meaning that producers and retailers have the capacity to absorb some of the price that would have resulted from a tax increase.

One way to get round some of these issues is to set a minimum price per gram of alcohol sold. This option also has many other advantages, in that, even more than tax increases, which also do the same, introducing a minimum price per gram of alcohol sold targets heavy drinking occasions and heavy drinkers, much more so than lighter drinkers (Purshouse et al. 2010), and appears minimally regressive (Ludbrook et al. 2012). Minimum alcohol prices in British Columbia, Canada, have been adjusted intermittently over the years 1989–2010 (Stockwell et al. 2012). Time-series and longitudinal models of aggregate alcohol consumption with price and other economic data as independent variables found that a 10 per cent increase in the minimum price of an alcoholic beverage reduced its consumption relative to other beverages by 16.1 per cent. Time-series estimates indicated that a 10 per cent increase in minimum prices reduced consumption of spirits and liqueurs by 6.8 per cent, wine by 8.9 per cent, alcoholic sodas and ciders by 13.9 per cent, beer by 1.5 per cent, and all alcoholic drinks by 3.4 per cent. A 10 per cent increase in minimum prices was also found to reduce wholly alcohol attributable deaths by 32 per cent (Zhao et al. 2013).

Limits on availability

Increasing the availability of alcohol sales times by two or more hours increases alcohol-related harm (Hahn et al. 2010). With the international trend towards increased bar opening hours, few studies have examined the impacts of reduced alcohol service hours in bars. However, in Newcastle, Australia, pub closing times were restricted in 2008 following police and public complaints about violence, disorderly behaviour and property damage related to intoxication. The restrictions led to a reduction in recorded assaults of 37 per cent (Kypri et al. 2010). Greater alcohol outlet density is associated with increased alcohol consumption and harms, including injury, violence, crime and medical harm (Bryden et al. 2012; Österberg 2012a). One form of alcohol sales regulation used in many countries is for the government to monopolize ownership of one or more types of retail outlet. In addition to limiting outlet density and the hours and days of sale, such monopolies remove the private profit motive for increasing sales. There is substantial evidence that such monopolies reduce alcohol consumption and alcohol-related harm (Österberg 2012a).

Table 5.1 shows that the impact of reducing access to retail outlets for specified periods of the week has the potential to be a very cost-effective countermeasure, but only if fully enforced (each healthy year of life restored costs between $550–1,450).

Restricting availability increases the time costs and inconvenience in obtaining alcohol, and there are interactions between price and availability measures, with price elasticities tending to be higher with less restrictions on availability, because price then forms a greater component of the cost (for an example, see Zhao et al. 2013).

Bans on advertising

A meta-analysis of 132 econometric studies found a small but significant positive association between alcohol advertising and alcohol consumption, although only for spirits advertising (Gallet 2007). Looking at alcohol advertising expenditure data across the United States, Saffer and Dave (2006) found, when controlling for alcohol price, income and a number of socio-demographic variables, that advertising expenditure had an independent yet modest effect on the monthly number of adolescents drinking and binge-drinking. It was estimated that a 28 per cent reduction in alcohol advertising would reduce the monthly share of adolescent drinkers from 25 per cent to between 24 per cent and 21 per cent. For binge-drinking, the reduction would be from 12 per cent to between 11 per cent and 8 per cent. Controlling for price, income and minimum legal drinking age across the United States, Nelson (2003) found that although total alcohol consumption was negatively related to a ban on the advertising of spirit prices (the ban led to less consumption, coefficient –0.009), it was positively related to a ban on billboards (which accounted for only 8 per cent of total alcohol advertising) which led to more consumption, coefficient 0.054. In a more recent study, the effect of partial bans was reported not to have affected alcohol consumption in 17 countries over 26 years (Nelson 2010). There are methodological difficulties with these econometric studies primarily due to alcohol advertising expenditure being used as approximate measures of the effectiveness of alcohol marketing.

In contrast, evidence from longitudinal observational studies shows that commercial communications, particularly through social media and electronic communication outlets, encourages non-drinkers to start drinking and existing drinkers to drink more (de Bruijn 2012). Even simply watching a one-hour movie with a greater number of drinking scenes, or viewing simple advertisements, can double the amount drunk over the hour's viewing period (Engels et al. 2009). In many jurisdictions, much store is put on self-regulation of commercial communications and withdrawal of communications that are found to breach self-regulatory codes. However, these approaches are irrelevant, since extensive evidence shows that withdrawn commercial communications simply live on, accessible to all, in social media, which are, in any case, heavily financed by global alcohol producers (Anderson et al. 2012b).

Table 5.1 shows that the impact of implementing a comprehensive advertising ban has the potential to be a very cost-effective countermeasure if fully enforced (each healthy year of life restored costs between $1,000–1,100).

Cost-benefit analyses of alcohol policies

The cost-effectiveness analysis, summarized above in Table 5.1, found that all policies have cost per DALY ratios that are likely to be efficient in terms of willingness to pay for a DALY. However, cost-effectiveness analysis does not comprehensively take into account the full range of social benefits and costs of any given policy. This is achieved by a cost-benefit analysis (CBA); although traditionally used for infrastructure investments, economic regulation, and environmental policy, it has also been applied to social policy (Weimer and Vining 2009; Vining and Weimer 2010). The application of CBA to alcohol policies requires prediction of the effects of investments of resources by society and the valuation of these effects in a money-metric. The purpose of CBA is to identify the most efficient policy. Efficiency simply means getting the most value from the resources available.

Anderson and Baumberg (2010) reviewed cost-benefit analyses of alcohol policy and found no complete examples. They concluded that the Sheffield Alcohol Policy Model (SAPM) in England was the closest approach to a CBA (Purshouse et al. 2010). Anderson and Baumberg (2010) undertook their own CBA based on a hypothetical counterfactual of an increase in alcohol excise taxes that would result in an across-the-board 10 per cent increase in alcohol prices in England, with estimates of the impact of such a price increase obtained from the SAPM. The results are summarized in Table 5.2 below.

The cells in the two top rows in the table are real tangible monetary costs, whereas the cells in the bottom row are monetary valuations of non-tangible costs, and thus do not represent real tangible money. The SAPM did not report on implementation costs. However, the WHO CHOICE model estimated that a tax increase of 25 per cent in the United Kingdom would cost about an extra $4.4 million to administer (see Anderson and Baumberg 2010). This is about 0.17 per cent of the expected revenue increase resulting from a 10 per cent price increase ($2,610 million).

Table 5.2 Summary of costs and benefits of alcohol policy

Costs	Benefits
Implementation costs	Reduced health and welfare costs
$4.4 million	$217 million
Costs to industry	Reduced labour and productivity losses
Not known, but likely to be small	$480 million
Consumer loss not transferred to government in terms of revenue	Reduced non-financial welfare losses
$69 million	$130 million

Source: Anderson and Baumberg (2010).

Note: The original values reported were as follows: cost – €3.7 million, not known, €58 million; benefits – €183 million, €405 million, €110 million in 2009 prices.

The SAPM did not consider transition costs to the alcohol industry, in terms of restructuring staff and capital. However, based on Baumberg (2008), although not exactly known, these are likely to be small, and certainly of an order of magnitude smaller than the estimated benefits of reduced labour and productivity losses. This is an area for further study.

An impact on the loss of some pleasure of drinking alcohol should be included as a potential cost of alcohol policy. The main way that internal benefits of a good are measured economically is through the idea of consumer surplus – how much more people would have been willing to pay for the good than the actual price they paid. The SAP did not estimate losses to consumer surplus. However, the model demonstrated that a 10 per cent price increase would result in an extra spend by consumers of $2,610 million. However, as pointed out in the text, this money, in the presence of a tax increase, and assuming that the tax increases follows through 100 per cent to a price increase, would return to the government as tax revenue, which can be rebated to consumers in a variety of ways. The $2,610 million is thus a transfer rather than a cost. There is though, a loss to consumer surplus, representing the value that consumers place on the foregone consumption that is reduced due to the price increase. Anderson and Baumberg estimated the value of this intangible cost at $69 million. This estimate is based on a view of rational demand for alcohol. But, as has been pointed out, this is not the case, and, in the presence of irrational demand, the loss of the adjusted consumer surplus is more than likely offset by the gain in excise tax revenue; in addition, the tax increase reduces any extra costs of consumption unmatched by consumer surplus benefits.

On the benefit side, there are real tangible benefits due to reduced health and welfare costs ($217 million) and reduced labour and productivity losses ($480 million) estimated from the SAPM. These benefits do not include benefits to people other than the drinker, and may possibly be doubled when doing so.

Finally, there are non-tangible benefits due to the value of reduced health and crime-related quality-adjusted life-years (QALYs) – estimated at $130 million from the SAPM. This estimate would increase if the values of all benefits to people other than the drinker are included.

Putting this altogether, if we just include the tangible costs, at an implementation cost of $4.4 million, a tax increase would bring benefits worth $697 million – a figure that would be even higher if we consider the benefits accruing to people other than the drinker. This favourable balance would need to be adjusted, once accurate estimates of the likely rather small transition costs to the alcohol industry are included. If we consider adding in the non-tangible costs and benefits, the value of benefits ($130 million) outweigh the estimated value of the loss consumer surplus ($69 million).

Impediments to implementation

There appears to be a dissonance between alcohol's health burden on the one hand, and the adequacy of the policy response on the other. If, as mentioned in the introduction, the socially optimum level of alcohol consumption is one where the level of harm is minimized, then the evidence would suggest at a global level that alcohol policy is failing. As mentioned earlier, the relative importance of alcohol as a cause of death and disability increased from eighth place in 1990, to third place in 2010.

There are potentially several reasons for this. They include lack of adequate alcohol policy infrastructures, lack of knowledge of the harms done by alcohol, an overemphasis in public discourse of the presumed benefits of alcohol, and scepticism among the public of the impact of policy measures, in particular, the impact of tax increases (WHO 2009). But, overriding all of these, and probably contributing to them, is too close a relationship between governments and the alcohol industry, and lack of proper regulation of the industry (Anderson 2009a; Gordon and Anderson 2011; Anderson et al. 2013).

Many commentators put great emphasis on corporate social responsibility actions by the alcohol industry to promote joined-up actions with health bodies to reduce the harm done by alcohol. Unfortunately, the incentives are for producers and retailers to be irresponsible rather than responsible. One motivation for social responsibility would be to manage consumer demand. But, this is counterproductive for producers and retailers, since most alcohol is drunk in heavy drinking occasions. For example, in the United Kingdom, 82 per cent of all alcohol is consumed by men who drink >32 g alcohol/day and women >24 g/day, and 55 per cent of all alcohol is consumed by men who drink 64 g alcohol/day and by women who drink more than 48 g/day (Baumberg 2009). This is unfortunate, since such consumption worsens all risks. Another motivation is moral. But here, collective action is either weak (self-regulation does not work) or illegal (the industry itself introducing a minimum price per gram of alcohol), and competition constrains individual action (corporate social responsibility is seen as weakness by competitors).

A third motivation is to avoid legislation, and, here, the evidence shows that the alcohol industry has been effective (Anderson et al. 2013). The alcoholic beverage industry is a pressure group that enters the policy arena to protect its commercial interests (Jernigan 2012). The alcohol industry generally wields a great deal of economic, political and organizational power in the policy arena, globally, but now particularly in emerging economies. The various parts of the industry often form lobbies and coalitions to foster their common interests, and increasingly these interests agree on policy options (Global Actions on Harmful Drinking 2012).

A cornerstone of industry action is to develop, promote and disseminate educational materials and programmes designed to prevent and reduce underage purchase and consumption. However, this is not only inappropriate, but misguided, since systematic reviews have consistently failed to identify educational materials that are capable of reducing underage drinking and alcohol purchases (Anderson 2012b). Another cornerstone of the alcohol industry's strategy is to introduce and frequently revise voluntary marketing codes of practice, including expanding them to include digital media. This action is also misguided, since research on industry self-regulation codes finds that exposure targets and content guidelines of such voluntary codes are systematically violated and the codes are inadequate for protecting vulnerable populations from the negative effects of alcohol marketing (Hastings et al. 2010; Winpenny et al. 2012). The International Centre for Alcohol Policies (ICAP), funded by global alcohol producers, has been involved in the development of national policies for governments in emerging economies. The policies themselves have been found to originate from alcohol producers themselves (Bakke and Endal 2010).

Recommendations

Global alcohol producers have a responsibility for their behaviour all over the world, and should adhere to minimal standards for product design and marketing practices regardless of the country where their products are sold (Anderson et al. 2013). They should stop the development of products that facilitate alcohol intoxication, and withdraw from the market products with demonstrable liability – for example, high alcohol content beers and liquor sachets. The industries themselves cannot legally set a minimum price per gram of alcohol; this is why governments need to act. But they can do similar things, by, for example, reducing bottle and can sizes, and reducing the number of grams of alcohol in a range of popular products – something that some parts of the industry are actually doing, leading to a removal of alcohol from the market (Anderson 2012a). Governments can help set incentives here, also, by, for example, ensuring that taxes are set per gram of alcohol (Doran and Shakeshaft 2008; Anderson et al. 2011a, 2011b).

References

Anderson, P. (2007) *Reducing Drinking and Driving in Europe*. London: Institute of Alcohol Studies.

Anderson, P. (2009a) Global alcohol policy and the alcohol industry, *Current Opinion in Psychiatry*, 22(3): 253–7.

Anderson, P. (2009b) Is it time to ban alcohol advertising?, *Clinical Medicine*, 9(2): 121–4.

Anderson, P. (2012a) Alcohol and the workplace, in P. Anderson, L. Möller and G. Galea (eds) *Alcohol in the European Union: Consumption, Harm and Policy Approaches*. Copenhagen: World Health Organization, pp. 69–82.

Anderson, P. (2012b) Information and education, in P. Anderson, L. Möller and G. Galea (eds) *Alcohol in the European Union: Consumption, Harm and Policy Approaches*. Copenhagen: World Health Organization Regional Office for Europe, pp. 35–9.

Anderson, P. (2012c) The impact of alcohol on health, in P. Anderson, L. Möller and G. Galea (eds) *Alcohol in the European Union: Consumption, Harm and Policy Approaches*. Copenhagen: World Health Organization, pp. 5–9.

Anderson, P. (2014) Alcohol, in W. C. Cockerham, R. Dingwall and S. R. Quah (eds) *The Wiley Blackwell Encyclopedia of Health, Illness, Behavior, and Society*. Chichester: Wiley-Blackwell, pp 55–62.

Anderson, P., Amaral-Sabadini, M. B., Baumberg, B., Jarl, J. and Stuckler, D. (2011a) Communicating alcohol narratives: Creating a healthier relation with alcohol, *Journal of Health Communication*, 16(S2): 27–36.

Anderson, P. and Baumberg, B. (2006) *Alcohol in Europe: A Public Health Perspective.* London: Institute of Alcohol Studies. Available at http://ec.europa.eu/health/ph_ determinants/life_style/alcohol/documents/alcohol_europe.pdf [Accessed 30 June 2009].

Anderson, P. and Baumberg, B. (2010) *Cost Benefit Analyses of Alcohol Policy: A Primer.* Warsaw: Institute of Psychiatry and Neurology.

Anderson, P., Casswell, S., Parry, C. and Rehm, J. (2013) Alcohol, in E. Ollila and S. Pena (eds) *Health in All Policies.* Brussels: European Health Observatory.

Anderson, P., Chisholm, D. and Fuhr, D. C. (2009) Effectiveness and cost-effectiveness of policies and programmes to reduce the harm caused by alcohol, *The Lancet,* 373(9682): 2234–46.

Anderson, P., Harrison, O., Cooper, C. and Jane-Llopis, E. (2011b) Incentives for health, *Journal of Health Communication,* 16(S2): 107–33.

Anderson, P., Möller, L. and Galea, G. (eds) (2012a) *Alcohol in the European Union: Consumption, Harm and Policy Approaches.* Copenhagen: World Health Organization.

Anderson, P., Suhrcke, M. and Brookes, C. (2012b) *An Overview of the Market for Alcoholic Beverages of Potentially Particular Appeal to Minors.* London: Health Action Partnership International.

Babor, T., Caetano, R., Casswell, S. et al. (2010) *Alcohol: No Ordinary Commodity,* 2nd edn. Oxford: Oxford University Press,.

Bakke, O. and Endal, D. (2010) Alcohol policies out of context: Drinks industry supplanting government role in alcohol policies in sub-Saharan Africa, *Addiction,* 105(1): 22–8.

Baumberg, B. (2008) The value of alcohol policies: A review of the likely economic costs and benefits of policies to reduce alcohol-related harm on the global level. Paper prepared for the WHO Department of Mental Health and Substance Abuse.

Baumberg, B. (2009) How will alcohol sales in the UK be affected if drinkers follow government guidelines?, *Alcohol and Alcoholism,* 44(5): 523–8. doi: 10.1093/alcalc/ agp053.

Blomgren, J., Martikainen, P., Mäkelä, P. and Valkonen, T. (2004) The effects of regional characteristics on alcohol-related mortality – a register-based multilevel analysis of 1.1 million men, *Social Science and Medicine,* 58(12): 2523–35.

Bryden, A., Roberts, B., McKee, M. et al. (2012) A systematic review of the influence on alcohol use of community level availability and marketing of alcohol, *Health and Place,* 18(2): 349–57.

Byrnes, J. M., Cobiac, L. J., Doran, C. M., et al. (2010) Cost-effectiveness of volumetric alcohol taxation in Australia, *Medical Journal of Australia,* 192(8): 439–44.

Carrell, S. E., Hoekstra, M. and West, J. E. (2011) Does drinking impair college performance? Evidence from a regression discontinuity approach, *Journal of Public Economics,* 95(1–2): 54–62.

de Bruijn, A. (2012) The impact of alcohol marketing, in P. Anderson, L. Möller and G. Galea (eds) *Alcohol in the European Union: Consumption, Harm and Policy Approaches.* Copenhagen: World Health Organization, pp. 89–95.

Doran, C. M. and Byrnes, J. (2012) The role of health economics in alcohol policy, *Applied Health Economics and Health Policy,* 10(1): 33–5.

Doran, C. M. and Jainullabudeen, T. A. (2010) Economic efficiency of alcohol policy, *Applied Health Economics and Health Policy,* 8(5): 351–4.

Doran, C. M. and Shakeshaft, A. P. (2008) Using taxes to curb drinking in Australia, *The Lancet,* 372(9640): 701–2.

Engels, R. C. M. E., Hermans, R., van Baaren, R. B., Hollenstein, T. and Bot, S. M. (2009) Alcohol portrayal on television affects actual drinking behaviour, *Alcohol and Alcoholism,* 44(3): 244–9.

Gallet, C. A. (2007) The demand for alcohol: A meta-analysis of elasticities, *Australian Journal of Agricultural and Resource Economics*, 51(2): 121–35.

Global Actions on Harmful Drinking (2012) *Reducing harmful use of alcohol: Beer, wine and spirits producers' commitments.* Available at http://www. producerscommitments.org/pdf/Reducing%20Harmful%20Use%20of%20Alcohol.pdf [Accessed October 2014].

Gordon, R. and Anderson, P. (2011) Science and alcohol policy: A case study of the EU Strategy on Alcohol, *Addiction*, 106 Supplement: 55–66.

Hahn, R. A., Kuzara, J. L., Elder, R. et al. (2010) Effectiveness of policies restricting hours of alcohol sales in preventing excessive alcohol consumption and related harms, *American Journal of Preventive Medicine*, 39(6): 590–604.

Hansel, B., Thomas, F., Pannier, B. et al. (2010) Relationship between alcohol intake, health and social status and cardiovascular risk factors in the urban Paris-Ile-De-France Cohort: Is the cardioprotective action of alcohol a myth?, *European Journal of Clinical Nutrition*, 64(6): 561–8. doi:10.1038/ejcn.2010.61.

Hastings, G., Brooks, O., Stead, M., Angus, K., Anker, T. and Farrell, T. (2010) Failure of self regulation of UK alcohol advertising, *British Medical Journal*, 340. doi:10.1136/bmj.b5650.

Herttua, K., Mäkelä, P. and Martikainen, P. (2008) Changes in alcohol-related mortality and its socioeconomic differences after a large reduction in prices: A natural experiment based on register data, *American Journal of Epidemiology*, 168(10): 1110–18.

International Agency for Research on Cancer (IARC) (2010) *Alcohol Consumption and Ethyl Carbamate*. Lyons: IARC.

Jernigan, D. H. (2012) Global alcohol producers, science and policy: The case of the International Center for Alcohol Policy, *American Journal of Public Health*, 102(1): 80–9.

Jones, L., Bellis, M. A., Dedman, D., Sumnall, H. and Tocque, K. (2009) *Alcohol-attributable Fraction for England: Alcohol-attributable Mortality and Hospital Admissions*. Liverpool: Liverpool John Moores University Centre for Public Health and Northwest Public Health Observatory.

Koski, A., Sirén, R., Vuori, E. and Poikolainen, K. (2007) Alcohol tax cuts and increase in alcohol-positive sudden deaths: A time-series intervention analysis, *Addiction*, 102(3): 362–8.

Kypri, K., Jones, C., McElduff, P. et al. (2010) Effects of restricting pub closing times on night-time assaults in an Australian city, *Addiction*, 106(2): 303–10.

Laslett, A.-M., Catalano, P., Chikritzhs, Y. et al. (2010) *The Range and Magnitude of Alcohol's Harm to Others*. Fitzroy, Victoria: AER Centre for Alcohol Policy Research, Turning Point Alcohol and Drug Centre, Eastern Health.

Lim, S. S., Vos, T., Flaxman, A. D. et al. (2012) A comparative risk assessment of burden of disease and injury attributable to 67 risk factors and risk factor clusters in 21 regions, 1990–2010: A systematic analysis for the Global Burden of Disease Study 2010, *The Lancet*, 380(9859): 2224–60.

Ludbrook, A., Petrie, D., McKenzie, L. and Farrar, S. (2012) Tackling alcohol misuse purchasing patterns affected by minimum pricing for alcohol, *Applied Health Economics and Health Policy*, 10(1): 51–63.

Lye, J. and Hirschberg, J. (2010) Alcohol consumption and human capital: A retrospective study of the literature, *Journal of Economic Surveys*, 24(2): 309–38. doi: 10.1111/j.1467-6419.2009.00616.x.

National Health and Medical Research Council (2009) *Australian Guidelines to Reduce Health Risks from Drinking Alcohol*. Canberra: National Health and Medical Research Council.

Nelson, J. P. (2003) Advertising bans, monopoly and alcohol demand: Testing for substitution effects using state panel data, *Review of Industrial Organization*, 22(1): 1–25.

Nelson, J. P. (2010) Alcohol advertising bans, consumption, and control policies in seventeen OECD countries, 1975–2000, *Applied Economics*, 42(7): 803–23.

Norberg, K. E., Bierut, L. J. and Grucza, R. A. (2009) Long-term effects of minimum drinking age laws on past-year alcohol and drug use disorders, *Alcoholism: Clinical and Experimental Research*, 33(12): 2180–90.

Nuffield Council on Bioethics (2007) *Public Health: Ethical Issues*. London: Nuffield Council on Bioethics. Available at http://www.nuffieldbioethics.org [Accessed September 2014].

Österberg, E. (2012a) Availability of alcohol, in P. Anderson, L. Möller and G. Galea (eds) *Alcohol in the European Union: Consumption, Harm and Policy Approaches*. Copenhagen: World Health Organization, pp. 83–8.

Österberg, E. (2012b) Pricing of alcohol, in P. Anderson, L. Möller and G. Galea (eds) *Alcohol in the European Union: Consumption, Harm and Policy Approaches*. Copenhagen: World Health Organization, pp. 96–102.

Purshouse, R. C., Meier, P. S., Brennan, A., Taylor, K. B. and Rafia, R. (2010) Estimated effect of alcohol pricing policies on health and health economic outcomes in England: An epidemiological model, *The Lancet*, 375(9723): 1355–64.

Rabinovich, L., Brutscher, P.-B., Vries, H., Tiessen, J., Clift, J. and Reding, A. (2009) *The Affordability of Alcoholic Beverages in the European Union: Understanding the Link between Alcohol Affordability, Consumption and Harms*. RAND Technical Report. Santa Monica, CA: RAND Corporation.

Rabinovich, L., Hunt, P., Staetsky, L. et al. (2012) *Further Study on the Affordability of Alcoholic Beverages in the EU: A Focus on Excise Duty Pass-through, On- and Off-trade Sales, Price Promotions and Pricing Regulations*. RAND Technical Report. Santa Monica, CA: RAND Corporation.

Rehm, J., Anderson, P., Kanteres, F., Parry, C. D., Samokhvalov, A. V. and Patra, J. (2009a) *Alcohol, Social Development and Infectious Disease*. Toronto, ON: Centre for Addiction and Mental Health.

Rehm, J., Baliunas, D., Borges, G. L. G. et al. (2010) The relation between different dimensions of alcohol consumption and burden of disease: An overview, *Addiction*, 105(5): 817–43.

Rehm, J., Mathers, C., Popova, S., Thavorncharoensap, M., Teerawattananon, Y. and Patra, J. (2009b) Global burden of disease and injury and economic cost attributable to alcohol use and alcohol-use disorders, *The Lancet*, 373(9682): 2223–33.

Rehm, J., Zatonski, W., Taylor, B. and Anderson, P. (2011) Epidemiology and alcohol policy in Europe, *Addiction*, 106 Suppl. 1: 11–19.

Roerecke, M. and Rehm, J. (2010) Irregular heavy drinking occasions and risk of ischemic heart disease: A systematic review and meta-analysis, *American Journal of Epidemiology*, 171(6): 633–44.

Roerecke, M. and Rehm, J. (2012) The cardioprotective association of average alcohol consumption and ischaemic heart disease: A systematic review and meta-analysis, *Addiction*, 107(7): 1246–60.

Rosenquist, J. N., Murabito, J., Fowler, J. H. and Christakis, N. A. (2010) The spread of alcohol consumption behavior in a large social network, *Annals of Internal Medicine*, 152(7): 426–33.

Saffer, H. and Dave, D. (2006) Alcohol advertising and alcohol consumption by adolescents, *Health Economics*, 15(6): 617–37.

Sassi, F (ed.) (2015) Drinking lives away: harmful alcohol use and the economics of public health. Paris: OECD Publishing.

Shield, K. D., Kehoe, T., Gmel, G., Rehm, M. X. and Rehm, J. (2012) Societal burden of alcohol, in P. Anderson, L. Möller and G. Galea (eds) *Alcohol in the European Union: Consumption, Harm and Policy Approaches.* Copenhagen: World Health Organization, pp. 10–28.

Shield, K., Rehm, M., Patra, J., Sornpaisarn, B. and Rehm, J. (2011) Global and country specific adult per capita consumption of alcohol, 2008, *Sucht*, 57(2): 99–117.

Stockwell, T., Auld, C., Zhao, J. and Martin, G. (2012) Does minimum pricing reduce alcohol consumption? The experience of a Canadian province, *Addiction*, 107(5): 912–20. doi: 10.1111/j.1360-0443.2011.03763.x.

Stuckler, D., Basu, S. and McKee, M. (2010) Budget crises, health, and social welfare programmes, *British Medical Journal*, 341: 77–9.

Stuckler, D., Basu, S., Suhrcke, M., Coutts, A. and McKee, M. (2009) The public health effect of economic crises and alternative policy responses in Europe: An empirical analysis, *The Lancet*, 374(9686): 315–23. doi: 10.1016/S0140-6736(09)61124-7.

Vining, A. and Weimer, D. L. (2010) An assessment of important issues concerning the application of benefit-cost analysis to social policy, *Journal of Benefit-Cost Analysis*, 1(1): 1–38. doi: 10.2202/2152-2812.1013.

Weimer, D. L. and Vining, A. R. (2009) *Investing in the Disadvantaged: Assessing the Benefits and Costs of Social Programs.* Washington, DC: Georgetown University Press.

Winpenny, E., Patil, S., Elliott, M. et al. (2012) *Assessment of Young People's Exposure to Alcohol Marketing in Audiovisual and Online Media.* Brussels: European Commission. Available at http://ec.europa.eu/health/alcohol/docs/alcohol_rand_youth_exposure_marketing_en.pdf [Accessed September 2014].

World Economic Forum and World Health Organization (2011) *From Burden to 'Best Buys': Reducing the Economic Impact of NonCommunicable Diseases in Low- and Middle-Income Countries.* Geneva: World Economic Forum and WHO. Available at http://www.who.int/nmh/publications/best_buys_summary.pdf [Accessed September 2014].

World Health Organization (WHO) (2004) *Neuroscience of Psychoactive Substance Use and Dependence.* Geneva: World Health Organization.

World Health Organization (WHO) (2009) *Evidence for the effectiveness and cost-effectiveness of interventions to reduce alcohol-related harm.* Copenhagen: WHO Regional Office for Europe. Available at http://www.euro.who.int/__data/assets/pdf_file/0020/43319/E92823.pdf [Accessed 12 February 2012].

Zatonski, W. (ed.) (2008) *Closing the Health Gap in European Union.* Warsaw: Maria-Sklodowska-Curie Memorial Cancer Center and Institute of Oncology. Available at http://www.hem.home.pl/index.php?idm=87,139&cmd=1 [Accessed 30 June 2009].

Zhao, J., Stockwell, T., Martin, G. et al. (2013) The relationship between minimum alcohol prices, outlet densities and alcohol attributable deaths in British Columbia, 2002 to 2009, *Addiction*, 108(6): 1059–69. doi.10.1111/add.12139.

Promoting physical activity

Michele Cecchini and Fiona Bull

Mortality and the health burden in the European Region

There is clear evidence on the importance of physical activity as a leading factor towards good health (Department of Health 2004; WHO 2004, 2008). Physical inactivity is the fourth leading risk factor for mortality in the European Region (just behind tobacco, high blood pressure and overweight) and the sixth for burden of disease (WHO 2009). Nonetheless, people living in the European Region tend to have low levels of physical activity (Figure 6.1). According to the most recent estimates, more than a third of the population living in the European Region have an insufficient level of physical activity (WHO 2011a). With few exceptions, mainly in Eastern European countries, men tend to be more physically active than women.

Significant differences exist also across different socioeconomic groups, with fairly consistent evidence showing that people with the highest socioeconomic status (with no significant differences between different definitions based on income, occupation, education level or area of residence) are more likely to have higher levels of moderate–vigorous intensity physical activity, compared with lower socioeconomic groups (Dowler 2001; Gidlow et al. 2006). This may, at least to some extent, be explained by the fact that people in low socioeconomic groups may face structural barriers in accessing opportunities, programmes and services that support physical activity. For instance, living in areas where there is less safety (Zubrick et al. 2010), fewer pleasant environments and parks (Crawford et al. 2008; Leslie et al. 2010), or higher cost (Cavill et al. 2006) to access opportunities, may all negatively affect levels of physical activity.

Structural barriers and the broader environment may, again, be a key factor in explaining why city dwellers are significantly more likely not to meet WHO recommended levels of physical activity (Table 1 for full definition) compared to people living in rural areas. This can be shown by looking at the relative index of inequalities in not meeting sufficient levels of physical activity for men and women. In Latvia, for example, men living in cities are 9.3 times more likely

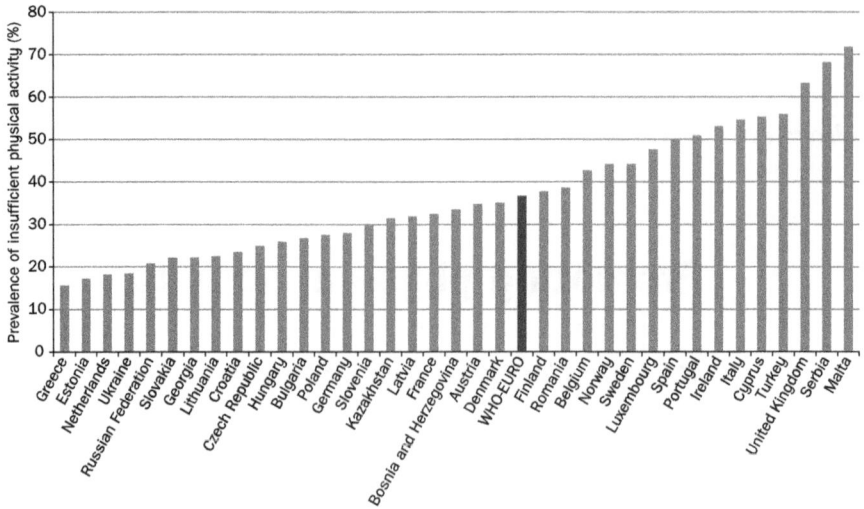

Figure 6.1 Prevalence of people with insufficient levels of physical activity in the European Region, 2008

Source: Authors' analysis on WHO 2011a.

Note: An insufficient level of physical activity is defined as less than 150 minutes per week of moderate-intensity aerobic physical activity, or the equivalent (see Table 6.1 for a full definition).

not to do enough physical activity compared to men living in the countryside. The lowest urban–rural inequalities can be found in Malta and Spain.

At the global level, the presence of physical inactivity is linked to the level of country income (WHO 2011a), with high-income countries having more than double the prevalence of physical inactivity compared to low-income countries (Figure 6.2). Analyses carried out specifically for this chapter, which considered the prevalence of physical inactivity and gross domestic product (GDP) per capita, and adjusted for purchasing power parity, confirmed a similar, but weaker, trend across countries in the European Region. The prevalence of low physical activity increased by 3 per cent for an increase of GDP per capita of 10,000 $PPP, after accounting for sub-region group (i.e. EURO-A, EURO-B, EURO-C) and weighting for countries' population.

Physically fit people have a risk of mortality that is up to 25 per cent lower than the risk of mortality of people with low levels of physical activity (Löllgen et al. 2009). The same analyses show that people with moderate levels of physical activity have a 20 per cent lower risk of all-cause mortality, compared to inactive people. Analysis by sex shows a gender effect, with a stronger reduction of all-cause mortality in women compared to men (Löllgen et al. 2009). Lee and colleagues estimated that complete elimination of physical inactivity would increase life expectancy of the population living in the European Region by about 8 months, ranging from 3–4 months for the Greeks and the Dutch, to up to 18 months for Serbians (Lee et al. 2012). The link between lack of physical activity and a higher risk of developing chronic diseases, such as cardiovascular diseases, Type 2 diabetes, cancer and mental disorders, as

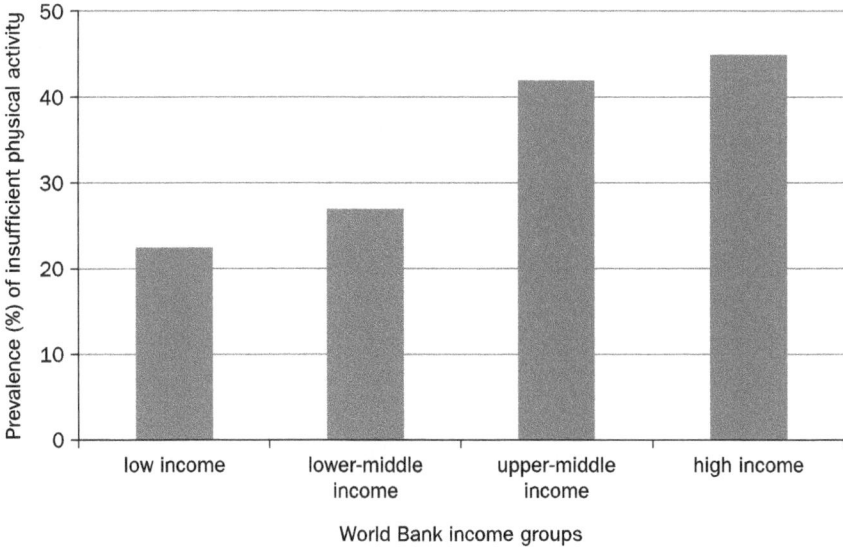

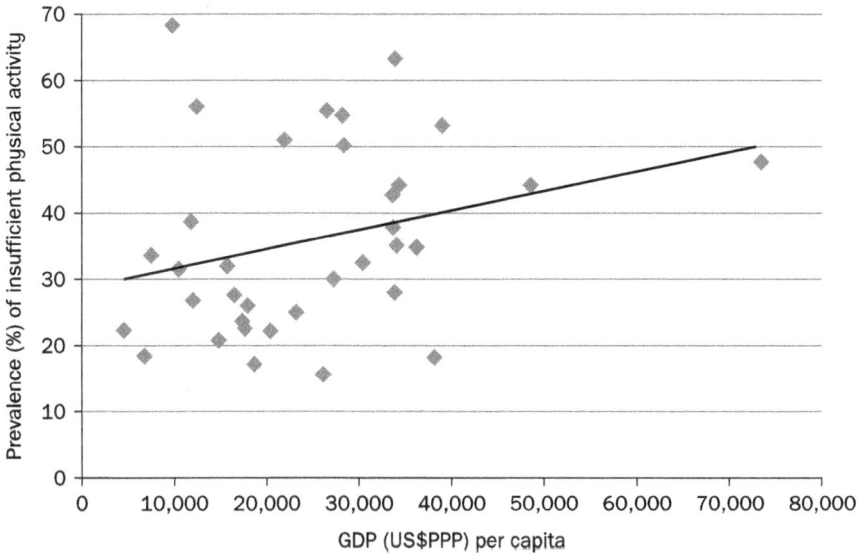

Figure 6.2 Relationship between wealth and level of physical activity, 2008

Physical inactivity levels by World Bank income group

Source: modified from WHO 2011a.

Physical inactivity levels and GDP/capita in the European Region

Source: Authors' analysis.

Note: An insufficient level of physical activity is defined as less than 150 minutes per week of moderate-intensity aerobic physical activity, or the equivalent (see Table 6.1 for a full definition).

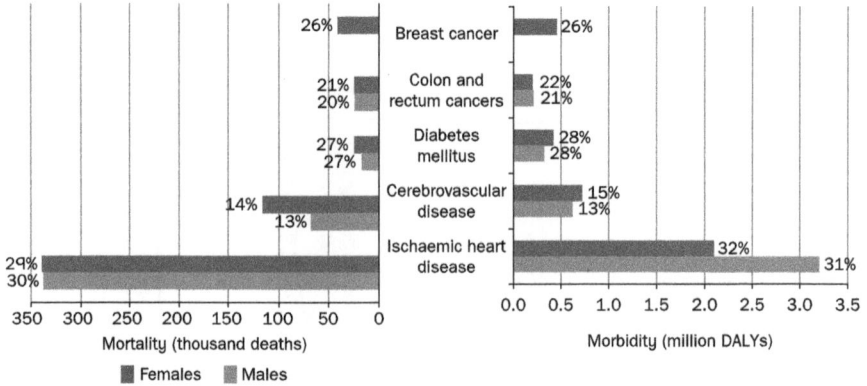

Figure 6.3 Mortality, morbidity and share of the burden of disease attributable to physical inactivity for major noncommunicable diseases in the European Region, 2004

Source: Authors' analysis on WHO 2009.

Note: The percentages represent the contribution of physical inactivity to the total burden for the disease. Insufficient level of physical activity is defined as less than 150 minutes per week of moderate-intensity aerobic physical activity, or the equivalent (see Table 6.1 for a full definition).

well as poor psychological well-being, has been widely documented (Bull et al. 2004). Lack of physical activity is responsible for about 30 per cent of mortality and morbidity due to ischaemic heart diseases, diabetes mellitus and female breast cancer, about one in five cases of colorectal cancer, and 13 per cent to 15 per cent of cerebrovascular disease cases (Figure 6.3). A relationship between sedentary behaviours and increased risk of mental health problems has been documented in children (Biddle and Asare 2011), adults (Teychenne et al. 2010) and older people (Larson et al. 2006). The US Physical Activity Guidelines Advisory Committee (2008) concluded that physical activity has a positive effect on preventing and reducing symptoms of mental disorders such as depression, anxiety, impaired cognitive functioning and dementia.

In children, having a good level of moderate-to-vigorous intensity physical activity is associated with healthy growth and development and a better cardio-metabolic risk profile, which is important for the prevention of the most important noncommunicable diseases (NCDs) (Andersen et al. 2006; Katzmarzyk et al. 2008; Janssen et al. 2010). Evidence also shows a strong dose response, namely that a higher volume of activity provides greater benefits (Anderssen et al. 2007; Ekelund et al. 2007), independently from the time spent doing sedentary activities, such as watching television. Children who spend more time in moderate to vigorous physical activity show significantly lower values of waist circumference, systolic blood pressure, fasting insulin and fasting triglycerides, and higher values of high-density lipoprotein (HDL) cholesterol (Ekelund et al. 2012).

Physical activity directly affects health beyond its impact on weight maintenance and the prevention of obesity. For instance, by lowering blood pressure (Whelton et al. 2002), improving lipid profile (Durstine et al. 2001) and with a positive effect on fibrinolytic activity (Lee and Lip 2003), physical inactivity decreases the risk of ischaemic heart diseases (Sofi et al. 2008) and stroke (Lee et al. 2003; Wendel-Vos et al. 2004). Even small increases in the level of physical activity, particularly in the case of inactive people, may produce sizeable health benefits. In fact, as originally reported in the 1995 US Centres for Disease Control/American College of Sports Medicine guidelines on physical activity (Pate et al. 1995), and reconfirmed (Physical Activity Guidelines Advisory Committee 2008; Warburton et al. 2010), the relationship between levels of physical activity and produced health benefits is not linear but, at the lower level, marginal increases of physical activity produces higher increases of health benefits. For example, Woodcock et al. (2011) calculated that compared with inactive individuals, people engaging in 2.5 hours of moderate physical activity per week had a mortality hazard reduced by 19 per cent; however, almost tripling their own commitment to about 7 hours a week would only produce a further 5 per cent reduction (i.e. to 24 per cent).

Physical activity guidelines and national monitoring systems

One of the barriers to national monitoring of physical activity, and particularly cross country comparisons, has been the use of different instruments to assess behaviour. This problem has been widely recognized (Bauman et al. 2006; Bull and Bauman 2011) and has led to the development of two instruments suitable for national surveillance systems: the international physical activity questionnaire (IPAQ) (Craig et al. 2003) and the global physical activity questionnaire (GPAQ) (Bull et al. 2009). The latter was developed specifically for the WHO STEPS surveillance system, and captures activity across three domains: leisure, work and transport (Armstrong and Bull 2006). Both IPAQ and GPAQ provide countries with information on changing patterns of activity across domains, within countries, and over time. IPAQ has been widely used in the European Region and is the instrument used to provide the currently available regional comparisons (Rütten and Abu-Omar 2004), as well as international studies investigating the determinants of physical activity (Sallis et al. 2009).

Guidelines on physical activity have a long history, with the earliest examples having their origins in the sports science fields and specifically the position statements from the American College of Sports Medicine (ACSM) in the 1970s and 1980s. It was, however, not until the 1990s that many national health departments released statements on physical activity, the most notable being the 1996 guidelines released by the US Surgeon General (US Department of Health and Human Services 1996). This landmark report positioned physical activity as an important risk factor for NCD prevention, shifted the earlier focus of promotion from vigorous-intensity activity to moderate-intensity activity, and specifically paved the way for many countries to focus on promoting '5 × 30' – namely, 30 minutes of moderate physical activity at least 5 days a week. Although this United States report was widely adopted internationally, many European countries have since developed their own national versions to guide the development of their own programmes aimed at increasing physical activity; examples include Denmark, Finland, Norway, Portugal, Slovenia, Switzerland and the United Kingdom. At the European regional level, despite quite a number of policy documents supporting action on physical activity, such as the *Physical Activity and Health in Europe: Evidence for Action* (Cavill et al. 2006), there were no officially endorsed physical activity recommendations for many years. It was only in 2008 that the Sport Unit of the European Union's Directorate for

Education and Culture built on its White Paper on Sport (EU Commission 2007) and developed and issued recommendations and policy-oriented instructions for physical activity promotion to the member states (European Commission 2008).

At the global level, it was only in 2010 that the first official set of global recommendations was launched by the World Health Organization (WHO 2010). These set out specific recommendations on minimal levels of physical activity for the prevention of disease and promotion of well-being. Table 6.1 summarizes the global recommendations for children, adults and older adults on the total amount, frequency, duration, intensity and type of physical activity required to maintain good health.

Table 6.1 WHO recommended levels of physical activity (PA) by age group

	People aged 5–17	*People aged 18–64*	*People aged above 64*
Minimum amount of total PA	60 mins/day of moderate to vigorous intensity PA	150 mins/week of moderate-intensity aerobic PA or 75 mins/week of vigorous-intensity aerobic PA or equivalent combination of moderate- and vigorous-intensity activity	
Amount of aerobic PA	Most of the daily activity should be aerobic	Aerobic activity should be performed in bouts of at least 10 minutes duration	
Other recommendations	Vigorous-intensity activities should be incorporated, including those that strengthen muscle and bone, at least three times per week	Muscle-strengthening activities should be done involving major muscle groups on two or more days a week	
Thresholds for additional benefits	Amounts of PA greater than 60 minutes provide additional health benefits	300 mins/week of moderate-intensity aerobic PA or 150 mins/week of vigorous-intensity aerobic PA or equivalent combination of moderate- and vigorous-intensity activity	
Age group specific recommendations		Older adults, with poor mobility, should perform PA to enhance balance and prevent falls on three or more days per week	
		When older adults cannot do the recommended amounts of PA due to health conditions, they should be as physically active as their abilities and conditions allow	

Source: World Health Organization 2010

Economic impact of physical inactivity

Although there is strong evidence on the positive association between increasing levels of physical activity and a reduction in risk of disease development, there is a paucity of data on the economic impact of inactivity. In recent years, there has been an increase in the reporting of cost-effectiveness of some individual interventions, but to date no comprehensive assessment of the costs of inactivity has been carried out. Indeed, the majority of the available analyses have either been carried out as cost-of-illness studies, which are by nature cross-sectional and assess the cost of physical inactivity in a specific period in time, or have used mathematical models on virtual cohorts. The few notable exceptions, albeit not on countries falling within the European Region, confirm that being physically active can reduce health care costs. For example, results from a prospective cohort study in Japan point out how individuals, free from functional conditions limiting mobility, have 12 per cent lower medical costs if they walk for at least 1 hour per day (Tsuji et al. 2003). While in the United States, Pratt et al. (2000), by employing the Medical Expenditure Panel Survey dataset, found that physically inactive individuals had 24 per cent higher health care costs than active individuals. In Canada, inactive people are 15.4 per cent more likely than active people to use inpatient services; on average, an inactive person spends 38 per cent more days in hospital than an active person. An inactive person also has 5.5 per cent more family physician visits, uses 13 per cent more specialist services, and has 12 per cent more nurse visits than an active individual (Sari 2009).

In developed countries, the impact of physical inactivity on the national health budget has been evaluated to be in the region of 1.5 to 3 per cent (Oldridge 2008). In 2000, physical inactivity in Denmark accounted for $451 million (DKK 3,109 million in 2005 prices) (Juel et al. 2008). This is an underestimation as it does not include outpatient visits and emergency department contacts. This cost roughly corresponds to 2.9 per cent of the total health expenditure of Denmark in the same year. Allender et al. (2007) estimated that direct medical costs due to lack of physical activity would cost $1.92 billion (£1.06 billion in 2002 prices) to the United Kingdom National Health System. This figure would correspond to about 1.2 per cent of the United Kingdom's total public health expenditure in that same year. Other studies from Canada (Katzmarzyk et al. 2000) and the United States (Oldridge 2008) show that 2.5 per cent and 2.5 to 3 per cent respectively, of all direct health care costs, would be attributable to physical inactivity. In Europe, physical inactivity may cost between $193 and $367 (€150 and €300 in 2001 prices) per inhabitant per year (Cavill et al. 2006).

Physical inactivity is also closely linked to household income, the labour market and the wider economy. Evidence from the United States suggests that there is an inverse relationship between healthy behaviours and, specifically, physical activity and the economy. A one percentage point increase in state unemployment is associated with a statistically significant 0.6 percentage point increase in some exercise and a 0.5 point rise in regular physical activity (Ruhm 2000). Inversely, economic expansion is associated with an increase in unhealthy behaviours and producing significant negative impacts on fitness. A 2.5 per cent increase in employment is associated with a decrease in leisure physical activity of 0.5 per cent (Xu and Kaestner 2010). In Denmark, Juel and colleagues (2008) calculated that inactive men would lose three extra days of work compared to the moderately active and the active working population. The same research suggests that a lack of physical activity would also be accountable for about 8 per cent of all social disability pensions, with very small differences between men and women.

Current policies to tackle physical inactivity

There are a number of steps underway to tackle the issues related to the declining levels of physical activity in the European Region. These actions are both at the level of policy and programme delivery (Cavill et al. 2006). A number of European-level actions are in place, aimed at promoting physical activity by educating communities and individuals about the risks associated with physical inactivity, as well as about the health-enhancing benefits of engaging in physical activity.

The European Database on Nutrition, Obesity and Physical Activity (NOPA) compiles information for the WHO European Member States to monitor progress on nutrition, diet, physical activity and obesity (WHO Europe 2011). The country information contains national and subnational surveillance data, policy documents, actions to implement policy, and examples of good practice aimed at improving physical activity. NOPA can be utilized as a reference point to help design and implement successful physical activity promotion policies. Other examples of European initiatives to deal with decreased physical activity rates are the EU Platform for Action on Diet, Physical Activity, and Health and the European Health-Enhancing Physical Activity (HEPA) Network (Martin et al. 2006). Collaborations also exist aimed at monitoring and surveillance, such as the European Physical Activity Surveillance System (EUPASS). In addition, the Lisbon Treaty, enforced in December 2009, tasked the EU with supporting, coordinating and supplementing sport policy actions.

Historically, governments have been more active in trying to influence diet rather than physical activity (Sassi 2010). Most of the countries in the region have reported that they have developed sport policies (e.g. national strategies, action plans) and/or strategies to increase the number of opportunities to increase physical activities (Figure 6.4). However, the least reported interventions areas are: investing in public and private research and use of fiscal tools, such as subsidies for the use of fitness centres, public transportation or cycling. Only France was found to be working on improving standards on service delivery for prevention, diagnosis and treatment of nutrition-related diseases (WHO Europe 2011).

Policy and programmes aimed at increasing physical activity policies are varied and generally aimed at reducing the risk of chronic conditions with a strong focus on counteracting obesity. Interventions can be applied and implemented in various societal settings ranging from that of the environment (e.g. transport, urban planning) education (e.g. schools, children/youth) and sports (e.g. facilities, sports programmes), as well as health (e.g. primary health care). The Bicycle Policy Audit (BYPAD Consortium 2003), TravelSmart (TravelSmart 2002) and the Walk 21 conferences (Walk 21 2012) are three examples of strategies aimed at increasing health and enhancing physical activity by promoting cycling and walking as a means of transport.

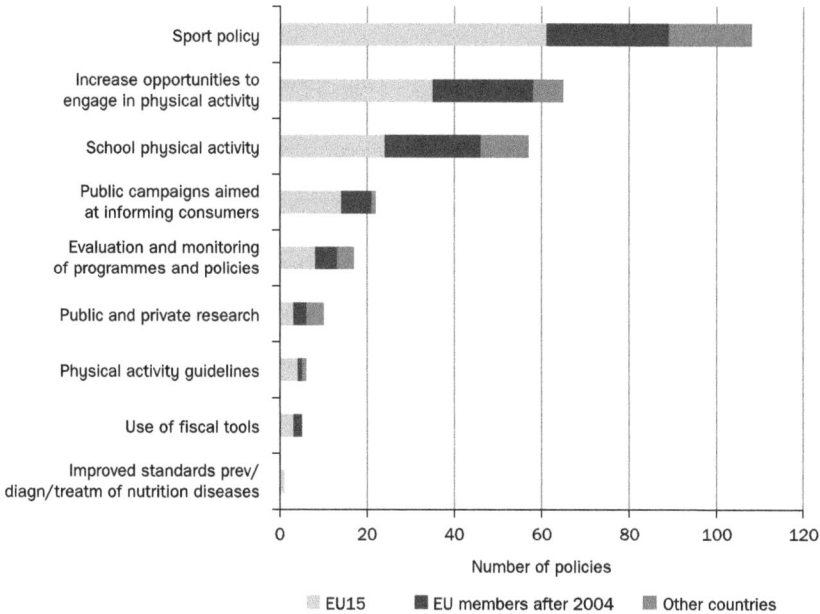

Figure 6.4 Type of policies (and their frequency) currently applied by countries in the European Region

Source: Authors' analysis on the European Database on Nutrition, Obesity and Physical Activity (WHO Europe 2011).

National and regional governments also have a central role, in cooperation with other stakeholders, to create an environment that encourages healthy behaviours by individuals, families and their communities. Stakeholders have started working together to promote local and subnational initiatives to improve rates of physical activity within their communities, as in the Russian Federation and France (see Boxes 6.1 and 6.2). Examples of successful projects include the Finnish national programmes for physical activity promotion (Vuori et al. 2004; Finnish Ministry of Social Affairs and Health 2010).

Box 6.1 Development of physical culture and sports in the Russian Federation 2006–15

In 2006, the Russian Ministry of Sport, Tourism and Youth Policy launched, in collaboration with Federal Agencies for Sport and Education, a ten-year plan to increase the proportion of people doing regular physical activity by 2 per cent each year (Ministry of Sport 2006). This will be achieved by investing $3.3 billion (€2.7 billion in 2006 prices) in infrastructures, advertisements (only at the initial stage) and events. The programme is built to support participation, particularly for low socioeconomic groups and young people. According to the Russian authorities, the programme could generate yearly savings of $407 million (€331 million in 2006 prices) once the impacts on health care expenditure, decreased benefits for temporary disability, and effects on productivity are taken into account.

Box 6.2 Bike sharing in Paris, France

Launched in 2007, the Parisian bike-sharing system (*Vélib*) now includes more than 20,000 bicycles that can be rented in 1,800 stations across Paris and neighbouring municipalities (i.e. one station every 300 metres). The payment system is designed so as to encourage short trips and a quick turnover of bicycles. The use of *Vélib* has increased steadily over time. Before its launch, bikes were used for only 2 per cent of trips in Paris; over four years, shared-bikes have been used for 130 million trips, replacing 8 per cent or 2.2 million of car journeys annually (Gardner 2010). Rabl and de Nazelle (2012) estimated that this programme may have produced benefits of up to $196 million/year (€177 million in 2008 prices).

Effectiveness and cost-effectiveness of interventions: what works and where to invest

In making decisions, policymakers need to know what interventions are effective and which are cost-effective (i.e. the interventions that provide good value for money). Two very important features that should also be taken into account when designing prevention policies are: affordability, and the time frame in which the intervention provides health outcomes. An extremely costly intervention which, for instance, a low- or middle-income country cannot afford, may turn out to be efficient if the high implementation cost is counterbalanced by excellent effectiveness. The time frame also plays an important role. Primary prevention, particularly in the case of physical activity, is often perceived as a long-term investment, while policymakers frequently prefer to invest in policies that produce results in a shorter time frame. Indeed, some interventions, for instance those targeting children, require some time to produce sizeable health effects. Since most of the disease burden produced by physical inactivity is due to NCDs, which start developing in the late thirties, no considerable changes in mortality should be expected before targeted children reach that age. Intermediate effects, such as a decrease in the prevalence of obesity or diabetes, conversely, can be observed in a shorter term. However, there are also interventions that show good effectiveness and cost-effectiveness in the short- to medium-term – for example, those targeting adults, or those focusing on high-risk people (Sassi et al. 2009).

The following section provides an overview of the most common interventions used to tackle physical inactivity: mass media campaigns, school-based interventions, primary care-based interventions, worksite-based interventions, travel and transport-related interventions and community-based interventions. For each of these categories, the most up-to-date evidence on effectiveness, cost-effectiveness and implementation challenges is provided. The final section reports on the costs of some of these interventions across the three European sub-regions and for some countries. Additional quantitative evidence on the effectiveness of interventions can be found in the Appendix to this chapter.

Mass media campaigns

Mass media provides the means for reaching a vast audience in a rapid and direct way. Mass media campaigns are used with the aim of increasing population awareness of the benefits of an active life by providing information, encouraging and 'nudging' (Thaler and Sunstein 2009) towards healthy behaviours. They are not perceived by the population as an invasive approach and may target the whole population or specific groups (e.g. teenagers, sedentary people, etc.). Campaigns may be carried out through single or multiple media such as television, newspapers/magazines, billboards, brochures and may or may not include side-events – for instance, road closures to provide 'pedestrian-only' access at weekends. The length of campaigns varies widely, from a few weeks to continuous promotion. Potential challenges with this approach include the need for careful planning, as well as adequate resources to deliver a sufficient amount of messages for the covered population to make sure that the message is understood and actually induces a change in behaviour. This is particularly important if the focus of the campaign is on individuals with low socioeconomic status, as they would be less able to benefit from health information (Berry et al. 2011). The effectiveness of the intervention can be difficult to monitor, and it is typically conducted using telephone surveys to assess awareness of the campaign and behaviour change. However, study limitations include the wide variation in the measures used to assess awareness, the use of cross-sectional samples, and different time periods of follow-up, with few over durations greater than one year (Leavy et al. 2011).

Nonetheless, various reviews (Kahn et al. 2002; Cavill and Bauman 2004; Leavy et al. 2011) of the potential effects of mass media campaigns consistently conclude that such interventions have a positive, moderate effect on the increase of physical activity in targeted populations. Although there is somewhat limited overall effectiveness on behaviour change, mass media campaigns provide excellent value for money. The OECD calculated that mass media campaigns to increase physical activity are among the best buys to tackle NCDs (WHO 2011a); this is consistent with results from other reviews (Sassi et al. 2009; Lewis et al. 2010), suggesting that mass media campaigns would have a cost-effectiveness ratio below $50,000 per healthy life-year gained and, in a few cases, could even be cost-saving.

School-based interventions

Interventions that use this approach aim at increasing the amount of physical activity in children attending school, mainly by providing additional information on the benefits of increased physical fitness and increased opportunities and time to undertake physical activity. Health education is usually delivered in the classroom setting by providing written material, and often includes a behavioural component (e.g. discussion groups) (Kahn et al. 2002). Additional time for physical activity is achieved by increasing both curricular and extra-curricular activities in this area. For instance, additional classes for physical activity may be included, or a more efficient use of existing classes may be pursued. In some cases, activities outside traditional school time may be encouraged (e.g. sporting events). Growing literature is focused on encouraging walking and cycling to school (Lee et al. 2008; NICE 2008b). Strategies can include: safe routes to school, walking school buses, improvements to the local/school transport environment, community/ parent involvement, walkable school zone maps, school curriculum actions, health education and school travel policies. Cycling interventions do not appear to be as effective as walking interventions in increasing students' physical activity levels. Whenever possible, collaboration with the rest of the family should be obtained as it has been identified as an important driver of success (NICE 2009). Potential challenges of this approach include both legislative and structural barriers. Physical education is compulsory in many countries, but time devoted is generally low and, in some cases, policymakers face increasing pressure to reduce time devoted to it in order to increase time spent on academic subjects. In addition, schools may be old and have inadequate facilities.

A review carried out by Dobbins and colleagues concluded that interventions carried out in school settings produce positive effects on the duration of physical activity and on VO2 max (an indicator for physical fitness), but have no effect on leisure time physical activity (Dobbins et al. 2009). The OECD calculated that school-based interventions exclusively aimed at increasing physical activity have a lower cost-effectiveness ratio compared to other approaches – for instance, mass media campaigns and primary-care interventions (WHO 2011a). Results from other reviews (Sassi et al. 2009; Lewis et al. 2010) suggest that some school-based interventions may be cost-effective (i.e. less than $50,000 per year of life gained in good health), and that efficiency is heavily determined by the design of the intervention. Interventions that combine actions on physical activity and diet seem to be more efficient than interventions focused on single domains.

Primary-care interventions

Primary-care counselling increases awareness of the benefits of being physically active through the provision of information to patients considered at risk of NCDs because of unhealthy behaviours or laboratory test results. Participants tend to be recruited opportunistically during routine visits at the physician's practice, although there are some examples of programmes targeting patients already registered with a chronic disease (Bull and Milton 2010; Boehler et al. 2011). The intervention may be delivered directly by the visiting physician (often through a brief intervention); alternatively, the practitioner may refer the individual to another health specialist (e.g. nurse, exercise specialist, etc.) for sessions that can be held face-to-face or in a group. In some cases, the individual may be provided with a prescription indicating recommended physical exercises, pedometers, written material or vouchers for gyms. The duration of programmes varies between a few minutes (for the brief intervention) to months for the most elaborate approaches. In some cases, general practitioners undergo training before the beginning of the programme. Potential challenges of this approach include the need for careful planning and the high consumption of resources. In addition, as recruitment is usually carried out on an opportunistic basis, reaching a good coverage of the target population may turn out to be difficult.

Interventions carried out in a primary-care setting show a positive and moderate effectiveness on reported levels of physical activity (Williams et al. 2007; Breckon et al. 2008; Fleming and Godwin 2008). In some cases, this is correlated to an improvement of physiological parameters, such as blood pressure or lipid profile. The OECD calculated that, compared to other approaches, primary-care interventions have a good cost-effectiveness ratio (i.e. less than three times GDP/capita per DALY prevented) despite the higher costs of some approaches (WHO 2011c). Other reviews conclude that many interventions falling into this category would present an acceptable, and often good (i.e. less than $50,000 per healthy life-year) cost-effectiveness ratio (Sassi et al. 2009; Lewis et al. 2010; Garrett et al. 2011). However, in an assessment of four interventions, two of which were in primary care (exercise referral and brief interventions), NICE (2006) concluded that only the 'brief intervention' approach should be recommended.

Worksite-based interventions

National and international policy statements have highlighted the significance of workplaces in promoting better health and well-being (Department of Health 2004; Wanless 2004; World Economic Forum 2007), particularly because they offer a setting to reach large population groups and, where needed, to target programmes at specific sub-populations. An early focus of workplace programmes was on promoting aerobic fitness and involved the provision of workplace gyms and employee fitness classes. Initial uptake was almost exclusively in large multinational corporations but, in the last two decades, many medium-sized companies have also adopted programmes. More recently, the focus has shifted away from 'fitness' to lifestyle physical activity, thus decreasing the need of on-site fitness facilities. Typical worksite programmes employ a range of strategies rather than a single action, and they are usually offered to all employees. Examples of approaches include: supporting active travel (i.e. walking and cycling to/from work) through to the provision of adequate facilities (e.g. bike storage, showers); incentives and discounts for fitness clubs; employee walking groups; health education programmes and individual employee health checks and screening programmes (Bull et al. 2008). Compared to other approaches, worksite interventions could offer smaller population coverage. For instance, it was calculated that only 6 per cent of the population in Western Europe (Sassi et al. 2009) and 11 per cent in Russia (Cecchini et al. 2010) would benefit from such interventions. In addition, often the opportunity and availability of programmes to different sections of the workforce can differ and results in different levels of participation.

Early evaluation of workplace programmes from the mid-70s through to the mid-90s concluded that these programmes were not effective (Dishman et al. 1998). More recently, Marshall (2004) also concluded there was 'little evidence to support the long-term effectiveness of workplace physical activity programmes'. However, more recent reviews have reported more consistent positive effects on physical activity behaviour, fitness, anthropometric measures (Proper et al. 2003; Dugdill et al. 2008; Abraham and Graham-Rowe 2009; Conn et al. 2009) and lipids (Conn et al. 2009). On job-related outcomes, such as a reduction of absenteeism and stress, the effect sizes were positive, but not always significant. WHO (2011c) grades worksite interventions as being quite cost-effective (i.e. less than three times GDP/capita per DALY prevented), mainly because of higher implementation costs. Results from analyses carried out for NICE guidelines (NICE 2008c) would suggest a better cost-effectiveness ratio, below a threshold of $50,000 per healthy life-year gained, once other factors (e.g. decreased absenteeism) are taken into consideration (Bending et al. 2008). Findings in this study are broadly in line with the conclusions of a review by Lewis and colleagues (2010).

Travel/transport-related interventions

The promotion of walking and cycling through travel-based interventions has received considerable attention in recent years, with an increasing number of reviews undertaken to assess the evidence of effectiveness (Ogilvie et al. 2007; Pucher et al. 2010; de Nazelle et al. 2011). Ogilvie and colleagues focused on walking interventions, concluding that interventions could increase walking by up to one hour per week. In particular, a workplace intervention, Walk In to Work Out, showed (on a rather small sample) a significant net increase in self-reported walking of 64 mins per week (Mutrie et al. 2002) after a follow-up of six months. TravelSmart™, an 'individualized marketing' approach involving a first phone contact, followed, for interested people, by incentives and support material to switch transport modes, has become very popular and has been tested across Europe and elsewhere (Ogilvie et al. 2007). A review of eleven published studies testing TravelSmart™ concluded that results consistently show a positive increase in walking trips (1 to 21 mins per week) in those joining the programme (Ogilvie et al. 2007).

Other reviews have focussed on interventions aimed at promoting physical activity through interventions that encourage cycling (Yang et al. 2010; Pucher et al. 2010). Interventions vary, and can include health education approaches, but these are often combined with at least some efforts to modify the infrastructure and/or travel conditions. Examples of these include: bike lanes; shared bus/bike lanes; off street paths; Bike Boxes at traffic intersections; and traffic-calming actions. Bike storage/parking and improved end-of-trip facilities (e.g. showers) may also be provided at worksites or at public transport stations to support the integration of cycling with public transport. The evidence of effectiveness of these actions is equivocal. There is, however, good evidence that a comprehensive set of infrastructure can lead to increases in cycling.

For instance, in Delft, the Netherlands, the extension of cycle route networks increased the proportion of bicycle trips by 3 per cent. There are also dis-benefits to walking and cycling, including the increased risk of road-related injuries and increased exposure to poor air quality. The health benefits, risks and costs are therefore complex and have only recently become the focus of investigation (Reynolds et al. 2009; Chillon et al. 2011; de Nazelle et al. 2011).

Evidence on the cost-effectiveness of both walking and cycling and active travel is still developing. An economic assessment (Beale et al. 2007) carried out for the NICE guidelines on creating an environment that supports physical activity (NICE 2008a) suggested that travel/transport-related interventions could be cost-effective and, under a number of assumptions, could fall below a threshold of 50,000 $PPP per healthy life-year gained. Two tools that can assist in the assessment are HEAT Walking and HEAT Cycling. The application of these tools, and further research, is needed to develop the knowledge base in this field (WHO 2011b).

Community-based interventions

Community-based interventions refer to either programmes delivered in the community, and thus available to all, or programmes or actions aimed at the 'whole community' through their reach. This category is diverse and often poorly defined in the literature, and it is therefore often difficult to avoid overlap with evidence reported under other approaches (e.g. mass media, travel programmes). For example, internet-based approaches and telephone-based programmes, as well as walking groups or other activity classes, can all be promoted to and accessed by the whole community.

Pedometer-based programmes have become popular in recent years due to the low cost of the devices and the advantage of an objective measure of activity levels. This approach can be conducted as part of walking group programmes, worksite programmes, or promoted through public awareness campaigns, libraries and other posters. Findings on the effectiveness of pedometers in children and adults by Bravata et al. (2007) and Lubans et al. (2009) indicate that pedometers can be effective, but the evidence is limited to follow-up periods of less than six months. Pedometer interventions were found to be more effective when focused on providing step-based goals (e.g. 10,000 steps per day) rather than time-based goals (e.g. walk for 30 minutes). Moreover, as suggested by many reviews (Ogilvie et al. 2007; Williams et al. 2008), pedometer programmes were more likely to be effective when combined with behaviour change support and goal setting. Pedometers have been modelled to be cost-effective in an Australian context (Vos et al. 2010).

Group-based interventions, such as walking groups, have also been found to be effective by providing an increase of up to 73 minutes per week (Coull et al. 2004). These can use lay leaders and/or education sessions. Reviews by Ogilvie et al. (2007) and Williams et al. (2008) reported studies showing significant benefits, with participants of one study maintaining these effects over ten years. Remote mediated interventions, such as telephone or web-based support and print materials, have also been found to be potentially effective, but there is no clear evidence on whether one method is more effective than another. Williams et al. (2008) concluded that there is modest preliminary evidence that telephone prompts may be helpful in increasing walking behaviour, that the number of contacts may be important (with more contacts being better than less), and that the focus should be on moderate-intensity activity. No comprehensive assessment of the cost-effectiveness of community-based interventions has been carried out (WHO 2011c). A review of the literature (Sassi et al. 2009) concluded that community-based interventions would have a cost-effectiveness ratio that ranges between a few thousand dollars to about $70,000 per DALY/QALY. For children specifically, there is only mixed evidence on the cost-effectiveness of 'walking buses', where groups of children walk to school together along a set route under the supervision of adult 'conductors' (Fordham 2008; Moodie et al. 2009; NICE 2009).

Figure 6.5 reports the cost for some interventions for the three sub-regions of the WHO European Region. Total costs are calculated as the sum of programme costs (i.e. the cost of designing, establishing and maintaining a programme), training costs (i.e. the resources to train the personnel that will deliver the intervention) and patient-level costs (e.g. equipment, incentives, etc.). Details about the employed approach can be found elsewhere (Tan-Torres et al. 2003; Evans et al. 2005; Sassi et al. 2009). Interventions are designed to reflect the descriptions in the previous sections.

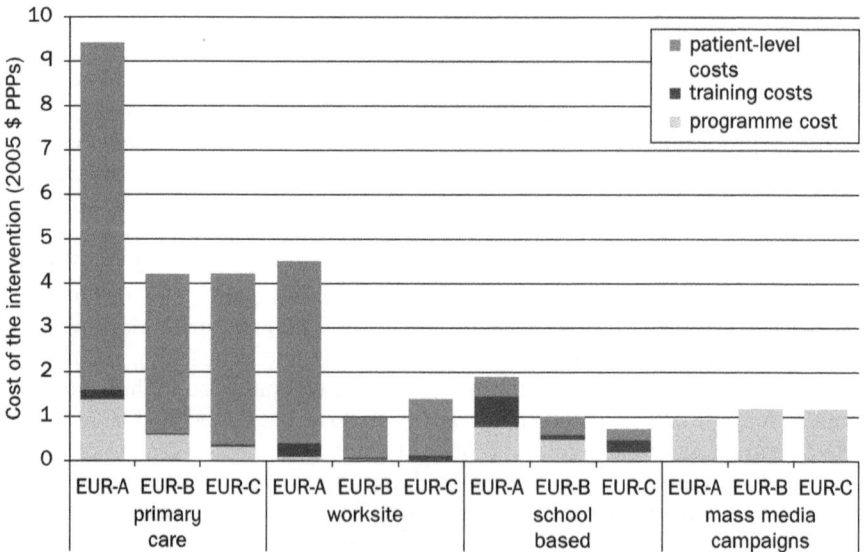

Figure 6.5 Cost of interventions to tackle physical inactivity in the European sub-regions and selected countries (2005 $PPP)

Source: Authors' analysis

Challenges and policy implications

Key challenges

Although the scientific evidence on the importance of physical activity and the burden attributable to inactivity is gaining greater recognition, this is insufficient to guarantee that the problem will be tackled successfully. Better evidence on what interventions work at the population level is needed, as well as more efforts to translate what we already know into policy and action. Both of these tasks require a strong base of support and commitment, but this may be hindered by a number of challenges. Bull and Bauman (2011) identified a set of eight challenges as part of work undertaken in the lead up to the United Nations High Level Meeting on NCD prevention that took place in 2011 (see Box 6.3) (WHO 2012b). Surprisingly, although tobacco and obesity were seen as important risk factors of NCDs, and thus global targets should be set, this was not the case for physical inactivity (NCD Alliance 2012). Greater advocacy and communication of the evidence is required at international and national levels, as well as more targeted efforts to address knowledge gaps that hinder progress.

The most challenging issue is probably that no single institution should be considered fully responsible for increasing physical activity. The review of policies reported in the NOPA database shows how governments tend to

Box 6.3 Causes of insufficient action on physical activity

Physical activity has been defined as the Cinderella of NCD risk factors because of a lack of attention policymakers pay to this issue (Bull and Bauman 2011). They identified eight potential causes of why this has occurred:

1. The strength of the evidence is not known and/or is relatively new and not fully accepted.
2. Lack of consensus-based guidelines on how much activity is needed for disease prevention.
3. Physical activity behaviour is neither understood, nor properly identified, as a discrete risk, because it is a behaviour embedded within everyday life.
4. Physical inactivity cannot be measured reliably to provide valid estimates of risk.
5. Physical inactivity is not recognized as a problem for low- and middle-income countries.
6. Population-wide levels of participation in physical activity cannot be changed.
7. Lack of ownership of the problem and control of the relevant solutions by any single government ministry requires integrated action and partnerships beyond the health sector.
8. Insufficient use of advocacy and communications to make the case strongly and convincingly for physical activity.

assume that physical inactivity is mainly a concern for the ministries of health. On the other hand, it is clear, by looking at the potential policy options that many effective and efficient interventions fall outside the natural scope of the health sector. Physical activity is a clear example of the need for a 'whole-of-government' and, even further, a 'whole-of-society' approach, as no single intervention (and stakeholder) may be sufficiently pervasive in changing behaviours. For instance, interventions aimed at improving transport systems and infrastructure, as well as those aimed at urban design and planning policies, have considerable potential to directly affect physical activity (de Nazelle et al. 2011) while improving the environment and health of the population by other means (e.g. reduction of greenhouse-gas emissions). Thus, a whole of government approach (rather than single allocation to a ministry) with integrated leadership and responsibilities for different strategic actions is the optimal, and far more preferable, way forward to design national actions on physical activity. To date, there is no good example of a sustained cross-government approach underway at a national level within Europe, but, for example, further afield in the State of Western Australia, this approach has been in place for ten years and provides a useful demonstration of what is possible (Physical Activity Taskforce 2011).

The need for an integrated approach becomes an imperative when governments wish to consider strategies aimed at counteracting obesity and thus combining policies on physical activities and diet (which often entails a new, different set of stakeholders). The increasing trends in overweight and obesity will only be reversed when there are sustained and synergistic strategies that address both healthy eating and physical activity with the goals of maintaining a healthy weight (Franz et al. 2007).

Policy implications and conclusions

The health and economic implications of physical inactivity are serious. Insufficient levels of physical activity increase the chances of becoming ill and developing NCDs. This imposes serious costs on health systems, on households and, in general, on the wider economy. John Beard, director of WHO's Department of Ageing and Life Course, has said that prevention may offer the opportunity to 'stretch life in the middle and not just at the end' (WHO 2012a) by keeping people healthy during the central part of their life and allowing them to do the things that they like and that society needs. This chapter reviewed the most common interventions to increase physical activity. It is difficult to change people's attitudes and behaviours; nonetheless, the prevention policies considered generally showed good effectiveness and, in a few cases, even had positive spillover effects in other domains outside the health care sector (e.g. transport policies and climate change). Indeed, tackling physical inactivity can be considered an affordable as well as an efficient approach to increase the health of a population. The currently available evidence shows that, with few exceptions, assessed interventions provide an increased number of life-years in good health for a cost which is comparable to, and in some cases even better than, therapeutic interventions routinely provided by national health systems.

Moving from theory to practice is not easy as there are crucial challenges that have to be overcome. Therefore, prevention and health promotion should be taken seriously. Additional evidence on some interventions, consistent monitoring systems (across countries and over time) and action and cooperation between all the relevant actors (i.e. international organizations, ministries, academia, the private sector and civil society) are all badly needed. Focusing on single interventions, particularly if they are aimed at picking the low-hanging fruit, is not sufficient. Different interventions cover and provide benefits for different groups of people. National policies to tackle physical inactivity should include multiple strategies at once, and all these actions must be coherent, implemented on a sufficiently large scale, and be sustained over time.

References

Abraham, A. and Graham-Rowe, E. (2009) Are worksite interventions effective in increasing physical activity? A systematic review and meta-analysis, *Health Psychology Review*, 3(1): 108–44.

Aittasalo, M., Miilunpalo, S., Kukkonen-Harjula, K. and Pasanen, M. (2006) A randomized intervention of physical activity promotion and patient self-monitoring in primary health care, *Preventive Medicine*, 42(1): 40–6.

Aittasalo, M., Miilunpalo, S. and Suni, J. (2004) The effectiveness of physical activity counseling in a work-site setting: A randomized, controlled trial, *Patient Education and Counseling*, 55(2): 193–202.

Allender, S., Foster, C., Scarborough, P. and Rayner, M. (2007) The burden of physical activity-related ill health in the UK, *Journal of Epidemiology and Community Health*, 61(4): 344–8.

Andersen, L. B., Harro, M., Sardinha, L. B. et al. (2006) Physical activity and clustered cardiovascular risk in children: A cross-sectional study (The European Youth Heart Study), *The Lancet*, 368(9532): 299–304.

Anderssen, S. A., Cooper, A. R., Riddoch, C. et al. (2007) Low cardiorespiratory fitness is a strong predictor for clustering of cardiovascular disease risk factors in children independent of country, age and sex, *European Journal of Cardiovascular Disease Prevention and Rehabilitation*, 14(4): 526–31.

Armstrong, T. and Bull, F. (2006) Development of the World Health Organization Global Physical Activity Questionnaire (GPAQ), *Journal of Public Health*, 14(2): 66–70.

Barilotti, L., Simon, M., Hoecke, H., Schaeffer, M. and Snelling, A. (2002) Motivational impact of pedometers on self-report of physical activity and stage of change, *American Journal of Health Promotion*, 16: 365.

Bauman, A., Phongsavan, P., Schoeppe, S. and Owen, N. (2006) Physical Activity measurement – a primer for health promotion, *Promotion & Education*, 13(2): 92–103.

Beale, S., Bending, M. and Trueman, P. (2007) *An Economic Analysis of Environmental Interventions that Promote Physical Activity*. PDG report. York: York Health Economic Consortium.

Bending, M., Beale, S. and Hutton, J. (2008) *An Economic Analysis of Workplace Interventions that Promote Physical Activity*. PHIAC report. York: York Health Economic Consortium.

Berry, T. R., Spence, J. C., Plotnikoff, R. C. and Bauman, A. (2011) Physical activity information seeking and advertising recall, *Health Communication*, 26(3): 246–54.

Biddle, S. J. and Asare, M. (2011) Physical activity and mental health in children and adolescents: A review of reviews, *British Journal of Sports and Medicine*, 45(11): 886–95.

Boehler, C., Milton, K., Bull, F. C. and Fox-Rushby, J. A. (2011) The cost of changing physical activity behaviour: Evidence from a 'physical activity pathway' in the primary care setting, *BMC Public Health*, 11: 370.

Bonhauser, M., Fernandez, G., Püschel, K. et al. (2005) Improving physical fitness and emotional well-being in adolescents of low socioeconomic status in Chile: Results of a school-based controlled trial, *Health Promotion International*, 20(2): 113–22.

Bravata, D. M., Smith-Spangler, C., Sundaram, V. et al. (2007) Using pedometers to increase physical activity and improve health, *JAMA: The Journal of the American Medical Association*, 298(19): 2296.

Breckon, J. D., Johnston, L. H. and Hutchison, A. (2008) Physical activity counseling content and competency: A systematic review, *Journal of Physical Activity and Health*, 5(3): 398–417.

Brox, J. I. and Fröystein, O. (2005) Health-related quality of life and sickness absence in community nursing home employees: Randomized controlled trial of physical exercise, *Occupational Medicine*, 55(7): 558–63.

Bull, F., Adams, E. and Hooper, P. (2008) *Well@Work: Promoting Active and Healthy Workplaces Final Evaluation Report*. Loughborough: School of Sport and Exercise Sciences, Loughborough University.

Bull, F. C., Armstrong, T. P., Dixon, T., Ham, S., Neiman, A. and Pratt, M. (2004) Physical inactivity, in M. Ezzati, A. D. Lopez, A. Rodgers and C. J. L. Murray, *Comparative Quantification of Health Risks*. Geneva: World Health Organization, pp. 729–881.

Bull, F. C. and Bauman, A. E. (2011) Physical inactivity: The 'Cinderella' risk factor for noncommunicable disease prevention, *Journal of Health Communication*, 16(Suppl. 2): 13–26.

Bull, F. C., Maslin, T. S. and Armstrong, T. (2009) Global physical activity questionnaire (GPAQ): nine country reliability and validity study, *Journal of Physical Activity & Health*, 6(6): 790–804.

Bull, F. C. and Milton, K. (2010) A process evaluation of a 'physical activity pathway' in the primary care setting, *BMC Public Health*, 10: 463.

BYPAD Consortium (2003) BYPAD website: http://www.bypad.org [Accessed September 2014].

Cavill, N. and Bauman, A. (2004) Changing the way people think about health-enhancing physical activity: Do mass media campaigns have a role?, *Journal of Sports Sciences*, 22(8): 771–90.

Cavill, N., Kahlmeier, S. and Racioppi, F. (2006) *Physical Activity and Health in Europe: Evidence for Action*. Copenhagen: WHO Europe.

Cecchini, M., Sassi, F., Lauer, J. A., Lee, Y. Y., Guajardo-Barron, V. and Chisholm, D. (2010) Tackling of unhealthy diets, physical inactivity, and obesity: Health effects and cost-effectiveness, *The Lancet*, 376(9754): 1775–84.

Chillon, P., Evenson, K., Vaughn, A. and Ward, D. (2011) A systematic review of interventions for promoting active transportation to school, *International Journal of Behavioural Nutrition and Physical Activity*, 8: 10.

Coleman, K. J., Tiller, C. L., Sanchez, J. et al. (2005) Prevention of the epidemic increase in child risk of overweight in low-income schools: The El Paso coordinated approach to child health, *Archives of Paediatric and Adolescent Medicine*, 159(3): 217–24.

Conn, V. S., Hafdahl, A. R., Cooper, P. S., Brown, L. M. and Lusk, S. L. (2009) Meta-analysis of workplace physical activity interventions, *American Journal of Preventive Medicine*, 37(4): 330–9.

Coull, A., Taylor, V., Elton, R., Murdoch, P. and Hargreaves, A. (2004) A randomised controlled trial of senior lay health mentoring in older people with ischaemic heart disease: The Braveheart Project, *Age and Ageing*, 33(4): 348–54.

Craig, C., Marshall, A., Sjöström, M. et al. and the IPAQ Consensus Group and IPAQ Reliability and Validity Study Group (2003) International Physical Activity Questionnaire (IPAQ): 12-country reliability and validity, *Medicine and Science in Sports and Exercise*, 35(8): 1381–95.

Crawford, D., Timperio, A., Giles-Corti, B. et al. (2008) Do features of public open spaces vary according to neighbourhood socioeconomic status?, *Health & Place*, 14(4): 889–93.

Da Cunha, C. T. (2002) Impacto de Programa Educativo no Gasto Energético de Escolares nas aulas de Educação Física: Ensaio randomizado controlado São Paulo. Unpublished Masters Thesis, Universidade Federal de São Paulo.

De Cocker, K. A., De Bourdeaudhuij, I. M., Brown, W. J. and Cardon, G. M. (2007) Effects of '10,000 steps Ghent': A whole-community intervention, *American Journal of Preventive Medicine*, 33(6): 455–63.

de Nazelle, A., Nieuwenhuijsen, M. J., Antó, J. M. et al. (2011) Improving health through policies that promote active travel: A review of evidence to support integrated health impact assessment, *Environment International*, 37(4): 766–77.

Department of Health (2004) *A Report of the Chief Medical Officer: At least five a week: Evidence on the Impact of Physical Activity and its Relationship to Health*. London: HM Government.

Dishman, R. K., Oldenburg, B., O'Neal, H. and Shephard, R. J. (1998) Worksite physical activity interventions, *American Journal of Preventive Medicine*, 15(4): 344–61.

Dobbins, M., De Corby, K., Robeson, P., Husson, H. and Tirilis, D. (2009) School-based physical activity programs for promoting physical activity and fitness in children and adolescents aged 6–18. *Cochrane Database Systematic Review*. Jan 21; (1): CD007651.

Dowler, E. (2001) Inequalities in diet and physical activity in Europe, *Public Health Nutrition*, 4(2B): 701–9.

Dugdill, L., Brettle, A., Hulme, C., McCluskey, S. and Long, A. F. (2008) Workplace physical activity interventions: A systematic review, *International Journal of Workplace Health Management*, 1(1): 20–40.

Durstine, J. L., Grandjean, P. W., Davis, P. G., Ferguson, M. A., Alderson, N. L. and DuBose, K. D. (2001) Blood lipid and lipoprotein adaptations to exercise: A quantitative analysis, *Sports Medicine*, 31(15): 1033–62.

Ekelund, U., Anderssen, S. A., Froberg, K. et al. and European Youth Heart Study Group (2007) Independent associations of physical activity and cardiorespiratory fitness with metabolic risk factors in children: The European Youth Heart Study, *Diabetologia*, 50(9): 1832–40.

Ekelund, U., Luan, J., Sherar, L. B., Esliger, D. W., Griew, P. and Cooper, A.; International Children's Accelerometry Database (ICAD) Collaborators (2012) Moderate to vigorous physical activity and sedentary time and cardiometabolic risk factors in children and adolescents, *JAMA*, 307(7): 704–12.

EU Commission (2007) White Paper on a Strategy for Europe on Nutrition, Overweight and Obesity Related Health Issues. Brussels: EU Commission. COM(2007) 279 final. Available at http://ec.europa.eu/health/ph_determinants/life_style/nutrition /documents/nutrition_wp_en.pdf [Accessed September 2014].

European Commission (2008) *EU Physical Activity Guidelines: Recommended Policy Actions in Support of Health-enhancing Physical Activity*. Brussels. European Commission. Available at http://ec.europa.eu/sport/library/policy_documents/eu-physical-activity-guidelines-2008_en.pdf [Accessed 13 October 2014].

Evans, D. B., Edejer, T. T., Adam, T. and Lim, S. S. (2005) Methods to assess the costs and health effects of interventions for improving health in developing countries, *British Medical Journal*, 331(7525): 1137–40.

Finnish Ministry of Social Affairs and Health (2010) *Recommendations for the Promotion of Physical Activity in Finland.* Helsinki: Ministry of Social Affairs and Health.

Fitzgibbon, M. L., Stolley, M. R., Schiffer, L., Sanchez-Johnsen, L. A., Wells, A. M. and Dyer, A. (2005) A combined breast health/weight loss intervention for Black women, *Preventive Medicine*, 40(4): 373–83.

Fleming, P. and Godwin, M. (2008) Lifestyle interventions in primary care: Systematic review of randomized controlled trials, *Canadian Family Physician Medicine*, 54(12): 1706–13.

Fordham, R. (2008) *Promoting Physical Activity for Children: Cost-effectiveness Analysis.* Norwich: University of East Anglia.

Franz, M. J., VanWormer, J. J., Crain, A. L. et al. (2007) Weight-loss outcomes: A systematic review and meta-analysis of weight-loss clinical trials with a minimum 1-year follow-up, *Journal of the American Dietetic Association*, 107(10): 1755–67.

Gardner, G. (2010) Power to the pedals, *World Watch Magazine*, (23)4.

Garrett, S., Elley, C. R., Rose, S. B., O'Dea, D., Lawton, B. A. and Dowell, A. C. (2011) Are physical activity interventions in primary care and the community cost-effective? A systematic review of the evidence, *British Journal of General Practice*, 61(584): e125–33.

Gidlow, C., Johnston, L. H., Crone, D., Ellis, N. and James, D. (2006) A systematic review of the relationship between socioeconomic position and physical activity, *Health Education Journal*, 65(4): 338–67.

Haerens, L., Deforche, B., Maes, L., Cardon, G., Stevens, V. and De Bourdeaudhuij, I. (2006) Evaluation of a 2-year physical activity and healthy eating intervention in middle school children, *Health Education Research*, 21(6): 911–21.

Harrison, R. A., Roberts, C. and Elton, P. J. (2005) Does primary care referral to an exercise programme increase physical activity one year later? A randomized controlled trial, *Journal of Public Health*, 27(1): 25–32.

Heath, E. M. and Coleman, K. J. (2002) Evaluation of the Institutionalization of the Coordinated Approach to Child Health (CATCH) in a US/Mexico Border Community, *Health Education & Behavior*, 29(4): 444–60.

Hemmingsson, E., Udden, J., Neovius, M., Ekelund, U. and Rossner, S. (2009) Increased physical activity in abdominally obese women through support for changed commuting habits: A randomized clinical trial, *International Journal of Obesity*, 33(6): 645–52.

Hendriksen, I., Zuiderveld, B., Kemper, H. and Bezemer, D. (2000) Effect of commuter cycling on physical performance of male and female employees, *Medicine and Science in Sports Exercise*, 32(2): 504–10.

Isaacs, A. J., Critchley, J. A., Tai, S. S. et al. (2007) Exercise Evaluation Randomised Trial (EXERT): A randomised trial comparing GP referral for leisure centre-based exercise, community-based walking and advice only, *Health Technology Assessment*, 11(10): 1–165.

Janssen, I. and LeBlanc, A. G. (2010) Systematic review of the health benefits of physical activity and fitness in school-aged children and youth, *International Journal of Behavioral Nutrition and Physical Activity*, 7: 40.

Juel, K., Sörensen, J. and Brönnum-Hansen, H. (2008) Risk factors and public health in Denmark, *Scandinavian Journal of Public Health*, 36(Suppl. 1): 11–227.

Kahn, E. B., Ramsey, L. T., Brownson, R. C. et al. (2002) The effectiveness of interventions to increase physical activity: A systematic review, *American Journal of Preventive Medicine*, 22(4 Suppl.): 73–107.

Kain, J., Uauy, R., Albala, Vio, F., Cerda, R. and Leyton, B. (2004) School-based obesity prevention in Chilean primary school children: Methodology and evaluation of a controlled study, *International Journal of Obesity and Related Metabolic Disorders*, 28(4): 483–93.

Katzmarzyk, P. T., Baur, L. A., Blair, S. N., Lambert, E. V., Oppert, J.-M. and Riddoch, C. (2008) International conference on physical activity and obesity in children: Summary statement and recommendations, *International Journal of Pediatric Obesity*, 3(1): 3–21.

Katzmarzyk, P. T., Gledhill, N. and Shephard, R. J. (2000) The economic burden of physical inactivity in Canada, *Canadian Medical Association Journal*, 163(11): 1435–40.

Kerse, N., Elley, C. R., Robinson, E. and Arroll, B. (2005) Is physical activity counseling effective for older people? A cluster randomized, controlled trial in primary care, *Journal of the American Geriatrics Society*, 53(11): 1951–6.

Klepp, K. I., Øygard, L., Tell, G. S. and Vellar, O. D. (1994) Twelve year follow-up of a school-based health education programme, *The European Journal of Public Health*, 4(3): 195–200.

Larson, E. B., Wang, L., Bowen, J. D. et al. (2006) Exercise is associated with reduced risk for incident dementia among persons 65 years of age and older, *Annals of Internal Medicine*, 144(2): 73–81.

Leavy, J. E., Bull, F. C., Rosenberg, M. and Bauman, A. (2011) Physical activity mass media campaigns and their evaluation: A systematic review of the literature 2003–2010, *Health Education Research*, 26(6): 1060–85.

Lee, C. D., Folsom, A. R. and Blair, S. N. (2003) Physical activity and stroke risk: A meta-analysis, *Stroke*, 34(10): 2475–81.

Lee, I. M., Shiroma, E. J., Lobelo, F., Puska, P., Blair, S. N., Katzmarzyk, P. T.; Lancet Physical Activity Series Working Group (2012) Effect of physical inactivity on major noncommunicable diseases worldwide: An analysis of burden of disease and life expectancy, *The Lancet*, 380(9838): 219–29.

Lee, K. W. and Lip, G. Y. (2003) Effects of lifestyle on hemostasis, fibrinolysis, and platelet reactivity: A systematic review, *Archives of Internal Medicine*, 163(19): 2368–92.

Lee, M., Orenstein, M. and Richardson, M. (2008) Systematic review of active commuting to school and children's physical activity and weight, *Journal of Physical Activity and Health*, 5(6): 930–49.

Leslie, E., Cerin, E. and Kremer, P. (2010) Perceived neighborhood environment and park use as mediators of the effect of area socioeconomic status on walking behaviors, *Journal of Physical Activity & Health*, 7(6): 802–10.

Lewis, C., Ubido, J., Holford, R. and Scott-Samuel, A. (2010) *Prevention Programmes Cost-Effectiveness Review: Physical activity.* Cost effectiveness review series, number 1. Liverpool: Liverpool Public Health Observatory.

Löllgen, H., Böckenhoff, A. and Knapp, G. (2009). Physical activity and all-cause mortality: An updated meta-analysis with different intensity categories, *International Journal of Sports Medicine*, 30(3): 213–24.

Loughlan, C. and Mutrie, N. (1997) An evaluation of the effectiveness of three interventions in promoting physical activity in a sedentary population, *Health Education Journal*, 56(2): 154–65.

Lubans, D. R., Morgan, P. J. and Tudor-Locke, C. (2009) A systematic review of studies using pedometers to promote physical activity among youth, *Preventive Medicine*, 48(4): 307–15.

Mackett, R.L., Lucus, L., Paskins, J. and Turbin, J. (2005) The therapeutic value of children's everyday travel, *Transportation Research*, part A, 39(2–3): 205–19.

Marshall, A. L. (2004) Challenges and opportunities for promoting physical activity in the workplace, *Journal of Science and Medicine in Sport*, 7(1): 1.

Martin. B. W., Kahlmeier. S., Racioppi, F. et al. (2006) Evidence-based physical activity promotion – HEPA Europe, the European Network for the Promotion of Health-Enhancing Physical Activity, *Journal of Public Health*, 14(2): 53–7.

Matsudo, S. M., Matsudo, V. R., Araujo, T. L. et al. (2003) The Agita São Paulo Program as a model for using physical activity to promote health, *Revista Panamericana de Salud Publica*, 14(4): 265–72.

Matsudo, V., Matsudo, S., Andrade, D. et al. (2002) Promotion of physical activity in a developing country: The Agita Sao Paulo experience, *Public Health Nutrition*, 5(1a): 253–61.

Matsudo, V. K., Matsudo, S. M., Araújo, T. L., Andrade, D. R., Oliveira, L. C. and Hallal, P. C. (2010) Time trends in physical activity in the state of São Paulo, Brazil: 2002–2008, *Medicine & Science in Sports & Exercise*, 42(12): 2231–6.

McKee, R., Mutrie, N., Crawford, F. and Green, B. (2007) Promoting walking to school: Results of a quasi-experimental trial, *Journal of Epidemiology and Community Health*, 61(9): 818–23.

Merom, D., Miller, Y., Lymer, S. and Bauman, A. (2005) Effect of Australia's walk to work day campaign on adults' active commuting and physical activity behavior, *American Journal of Health Promotion*, 19(3): 159–62.

Ministry of Sport, Tourism and Youth Policy. (2006) Programa razvitie fyzicheskoe kultura I sporta v Rossiskoe Federatsie na 2006–2015 [Program of Development of physical culture and sports in the Russian Federation in 2006–2015]. http://www. programs-gov.ru/12_1.php [Accessed 22 February 2012].

Moodie, M., Haby, M., Galvin, L., Swinburn, B. and Carter, R. (2009) Cost–effectiveness of active transport for primary school children – Walking School Bus program, *International Journal of Behavioral Nutrition and Physical Activity*, 6: 63.

Mutrie, N., Carney, C., Blamey, A., Crawford, F., Aitchison, T. and Whitelaw, A. (2002) 'Walk in to Work Out': A randomised controlled trial of a self-help intervention to promote active commuting, *Journal of Epidemiology and Community Health*, 56(6): 407–12.

Napolitano, M., Fotheringham, M., Tate, D. et al. (2003) Evaluation of an internet-based physical activity intervention: A preliminary investigation, *Annals of Behavioral Medicine*, 25(2): 92–9.

National Institute for Health and Clinical Excellence (NICE) (2006) *Four Commonly Used Methods to Increase Physical Activity: Brief Interventions in Primary Care, Exercise Referral Schemes, Pedometers and Community-based Exercise Programmes for Walking and Cycling*. Public Health Intervention Guidance 2. London: NICE.

National Institute for Health and Clinical Excellence (NICE) (2008a) *Promoting and Creating Built or Natural Environments that Encourage and Support Physical Activity*. Public Health Guidance 8. London: NICE.

National Institute for Health and Clinical Excellence (NICE) (2008b) *Promoting PA for Children: Review 5 – Active Transport Interventions*. NICE Public Health Collaborating Centre – PA. (November 2007, revised July 2008)

National Institute for Health and Clinical Excellence (NICE) (2008c) *Workplace Health Promotion: How to Encourage Employees to be Physically Active*. Public Health Guidance 13. London: NICE.

National Institute for Health and Clinical Excellence (NICE) (2009) *Promoting Physical Activity, Active Play and Sport for Pre-school and School-age Children and Young People in Family, Pre-school, School and Community Settings*. Public Health Guidance 17. London: NICE.

NCD Alliance (2012) *Contribution to consultations on proposals for global monitoring framework and targets for NCDs*. Available at http://ncdalliance.org/ [Accessed September 2014].

Nies, M., Chruscial, H. and Hepworth, J. (2003) An intervention to promote walking in sedentary women in the community, *American Journal of Health Behavior*, 27(5): 524–35.

Ogilvie, D., Foster, C. E., Rothnie, H. et al. (2007) Interventions to promote walking: Systematic review, *British Medical Journal*, 334(7605): 1204.

Oja, P., Vuori, I. and Paronen, O. (1998) Daily walking and cycling to work: Their utility as health-enhancing physical activity, *Patient Education and Counseling*, 33(1 Suppl.): S87–S94.

Oldridge, N. B. (2008) Economic burden of physical inactivity: Healthcare costs associated with cardiovascular disease, *European Journal of Cardiovascular Prevention & Rehabilitation*, 15(2): 130–9.

Pate, R. R., Pratt, M., Blair, S. N. et al. (1995) Physical activity and public health: A recommendation from the Centers for Disease Control and Prevention and the American College of Sports Medicine, *Journal of the American Medical Association*, 273(5): 402–7.

Petrella, R. J., Koval, J. J., Cunningham, D. A. and Paterson, D. H. (2003) Can primary care doctors prescribe exercise to improve fitness? The step test exercise prescription (STEP) project, *American Journal of Preventive Medicine*, 24(4): 316–22.

Physical Activity Guidelines Advisory Committee (2008) *Physical Activity Guidelines Advisory Committee Report*. Washington, DC: US Department of Health and Human Services.

Physical Activity Taskforce (2011) *Active Living for All: A Framework for Physical Activity in Western Australia 2012–2016*. Perth: Government of Western Australia.

Pinto, B. M., Goldstein, M. G., Ashba, J., Sciamanna, C. N. and Jette, A. (2005) Randomized controlled trial of physical activity counseling for older primary care patients, *American Journal of Preventive Medicine*, 29(4): 247–55.

Pratt, M., Macera, C. A. and Wang, G. (2000) Higher direct medical costs associated with physical inactivity, *Physician and Sports Medicine*, 28(10): 63–70.

Proper, K. I., Hildebrandt, V. H., Van der Beek, A. J., Twisk, J. W. R. and Van Mechelen, W. (2003) Effect of individual counseling on physical activity fitness and health: A randomized controlled trial in a workplace setting, *American Journal of Preventive Medicine*, 24(3): 218–26.

Pucher, J., Dill, J. and Handy, S. (2010) Infrastructure, programs, and policies to increase bicycling: An international review, *Preventive Medicine*, 50(Suppl. 1): S106–S125.

Rabl, A. and de Nazelle, A. (2012) Benefits of shift from car to active transport, *Transport Policy*, 19(1): 121–31.

Reger-Nash, B., Bauman, A., Booth-Butterfield, S. et al. (2005) Wheeling walks: Evaluation of a media-based community intervention, *Family & Community Health*, 28(1): 64–78.

Reger-Nash, B., Bauman, A., Cooper, L. et al. (2008) WV Walks: Replication with expanded reach, *Journal of Physical Activity & Health*, 5(1): 19–27.

Reis, R. S., Hallal, P. C., Parra, D. C., Ribeiro, I. C., Browson, R. and Ramos, L. (2010) Promoting physical activity through community-wide policies and planning: Findings from Curitiba, Brazil, *Journal of Physical Activity & Health*, 7(Suppl. 2): S137–S45.

Reynolds, C., Harris, M., Teschke, K., Cripton, P. and Winters, M. (2009) The impact of transportation infrastructure on bicycling injuries and crashes: A review of the literature, *Environmental Health: A Global Access Science Source*, 8(1): 47.

Ruhm, C. J. (2000) Are recessions good for your health?, *The Quarterly Journal of Economics*, 115(2): 617–50.

Rütten, A. and Abu-Omar, K. (2004) Prevalence of physical activity in the European Union, *Sozial und Praventivmedizin*, 49(4): 281–9.

Sallis, J. F., Bowles, H. R., Bauman, A. et al. (2009) Neighborhood environments and physical activity among adults in 11 countries, *American Journal of Preventive Medicine*, 36(6): 484–90.

Sari, N. (2009) Physical inactivity and its impact on healthcare utilization, *Health Economics*, 18(8): 885–901.

Sassi, F. (2010) Tackling obesity: The roles of governments and markets, in: F. Sassi, *Obesity and the Economics of Prevention: Fit not Fat*. Paris: OECD Publishing, pp. 147–63.

Sassi, F., Cecchini, M., Lauer, J. and Chisholm, D. (2009) *Improving Lifestyles, Tackling Obesity: The Health and Economic Impact of Prevention Strategies*. OECD Health Working Paper 48. Paris: OECD Publishing.

Schofield, L., Mummery, K. and Schofield, G. (2005) Effects of a controlled pedometer-intervention trial for low-active adolescent girls, *Medicine and Science in Sports and Exercise*, 37(8): 1414–20.

Simoes, E. J., Hallal, P., Pratt, M. et al. (2009) Effects of a community-based, professionally supervised intervention on physical activity levels among residents of Recife, Brazil, *American Journal of Public Health*, 99(1): 68.

Simon, C., Wagner, A., DiVita, C. et al. (2004) Intervention centred on adolescents' physical activity and sedentary behaviour (ICAPS): Concept and 6-month results, *International Journal of Obesity and Related Metabolic Disorders*, 28(Suppl. 3): S96–S103.

Sloman, L., Cavill, N., Cope, A., Muller, L. and Kennedy, A. (2009) *Analysis and Synthesis of Evidence on the Effects of Investment in Six Cycling Demonstration Towns*. London: Department for Transport and Cycling England.

Sofi, F., Capalbo, A., Cesari, F., Abbate, R. and Gensini, G. F. (2008) Physical activity during leisure time and primary prevention of coronary heart disease: An updated meta-analysis of cohort studies, *European Journal of Cardiovascular Prevention and Rehabilitation*, 15(3): 247–57.

Spittaels, H., De Bourdeaudhuij, I. M., Brug, J. and Vandelanotte, C. (2007) Effectiveness of an online computer-tailored physical activity intervention in a real-life setting, *Health Education Research*, 22(3): 385–96.

Tan-Torres, T., Baltussen, T., Adam, T. et al. (2003) *Making Choices in Health: WHO Guide to Cost-effectiveness Analysis*. Geneva: World Health Organization.

Teychenne, M., Ball, K. and Salmon, J. (2010) Sedentary behavior and depression among adults: A review, *International Journal of Behavioural Medicine*, 17(4): 246–54.

Thaler, R. and Sunstein, C. (2009) *Nudge: Improving Decisions about Health, Wealth, and Happiness*. New Haven, CT: Yale University Press.

Transport for London (2004) *Business Case for Cycling in London*. London: Transport for London Street Management.

Transport for London (2005) *Review of Procedures associated with the Development and Delivery of Measures designed to Improve Safety and Convenience for Cyclists*. London: Transport for London.

TravelSmart (2002) TravelSmart Gloucester pilot project. Bristol: Sustrans. Available at http://wdsp.web-labs.co.uk/GetAsset.aspx?id=fAAzADIANwB8AHwARgBhAGwAc wBlAHwAfAA3AHwA0 [Accessed October 2014].

TravelSmart Greater Nottingham (2004) *(Lady Bay and the Meadows): A Report on the Individualised Marketing Project funded through the Department for Transport's Personalised Travel Planning Demonstration Programme*. Bristol: Sustrans.

TravelSmart Sheffield (2004) *(Hillsborough/Middlewood) 2003–04: A report on the Individualised Marketing Project funded through the Department for Transport's Personalised Travel Planning Demonstration Programme*. Bristol: Sustrans.

Troelsen, J. (2005) [Transportation and health: Odense – the national cycling city of Denmark, 1999–2002] [Danish], *Ugeskrift for Laeger*, 167(10): 1164–6.

Troelsen, J., Jensen, S. and Andersen, T. (2004) *Evaluering af Odense – Danmarks nationale cykelby [Evaluation of Odense – Denmark's National Cycle City]* [Danish]. Odense: Odense Kommune.

Tsuji, I., Takahashi, K., Nishino, Y. et al. (2003) Impact of walking upon medical care expenditure in Japan: The Ohsaki Cohort Study, *International Journal of Epidemiology*, 32(5): 809–14.

US Department of Health and Human Services Centres for Disease Control and Prevention (1996) *Physical Activity and Health: A Report of The Surgeon General*. Atlanta, GA: US Department of Health and Human Services Centres for Disease Control and Prevention.

Verstraete, S. J., Cardon, G. M., De Clercq, D. L. and De Bourdeaudhuij, I. M. (2006) Increasing children's physical activity levels during recess periods in elementary schools: The effects of providing game equipment, *The European Journal of Public Health*, 16(4): 415–19.

Vos, T., Carter, R. and Barendregt, J. et al. (2010) *Assessing Cost-effectiveness in Prevention (ACE–prevention)*. Brisbane: University of Queensland.

Vuori, I., Lankenau, B. and Pratt, M. (2004) Physical activity policy and program development: The experience in Finland, *Public Health Reports*, 119(3): 331–45.

Walk 21 (2012) Walk 21 website. Available at http://www.walk21.com [Accessed September 2014].

Wanless, D. (2004) *Securing Good Health for the Whole Population: Final Report*. London: HM Treasury.

Warburton, D. E., Charlesworth, S., Ivey, A., Nettlefold, L. and Bredin, S. S. (2010) A systematic review of the evidence for Canada's Physical Activity Guidelines for Adults, *International Journal of Behavioral Nutritional and Physical Activity*, 7: 39.

Wardman, M., Tight, M. and Page, M. (2007) Factors influencing the propensity to cycle to work, *Transportation Research*, part A, 41(4): 339–50.

Wendel-Vos, G. C., Schuit, A. J., Feskens, E. J. et al. (2004) Physical activity and stroke: A meta-analysis of observational data, *International Journal of Epidemiology*, 33(4): 787–98.

Whelton, S. P., Chin, A., Xin, X. and He, J. (2002) Effect of aerobic exercise on blood pressure: A meta-analysis of randomized, controlled trials, *Annals of Internal Medicine*, 136(7): 493–503.

Williams, D. M., Matthews, C., Rutt, C., Napolitano, M. A. and Marcus, B. H. (2008) Interventions to increase walking behavior, *Medicine and Science in Sports and Exercise*, 40(7 Suppl.): S567.

Williams, N. H., Hendry, M., France, B., Lewis, R. and Wilkinson, C. (2007) Effectiveness of exercise-referral schemes to promote physical activity in adults: Systematic review, *The British Journal of General Practice*, 57(545): 979–86.

Woodcock, J., Franco, O. H., Orsini, N. and Roberts, I. (2011) Non-vigorous physical activity and all-cause mortality: Systematic review and meta-analysis of cohort studies, *International Journal of Epidemiology*, 40(1): 121–38.

World Economic Forum (2007) *Working Towards Wellness: Accelerating the Prevention of Chronic Disease*. A report by Pricewaterhouse Coopers (PwC) and World Economic ForumWorking. Geneva: World Economic Forum. Available at http://www.weforum.org/pdf/Wellness/report.pdf [Accessed September 2014].

World Health Organization (WHO) (2004) *Global Strategy on Diet, Physical Activity and Health*. Geneva: World Health Organization.

World Health Organization (WHO) (2008) *2008–2013 Action Plan for the Global Strategy for the Prevention and Control of Noncommunicable Diseases*. Geneva: World Health Organization.

World Health Organization (WHO) (2009) *Global Health Risks: Mortality and Burden of Disease Attributable to Selected Major Risks*. Geneva: World Health Organization.

World Health Organization (WHO) (2010) *Global Recommendations on Physical Activity for Health*. Geneva: World Health Organization.

World Health Organization (WHO) (2011a) *Global Status Report on Noncommunicable Diseases 2010*. Geneva: World Health Organization.

World Health Organization (WHO) (2011b) *Health Economic Assessment Tools (HEAT) for Walking and Cycling: Economic Assessment of Transport Infrastructure and Policies*. Copenhagen: WHO Regional Office for Europe. Available at http://bit.ly /zJVPYm [Accessed September 2014].

World Health Organization (WHO) (2011c) *Prevention and Control of NCDs: Priorities for Investment*. Geneva: World Health Organization.

World Health Organization (WHO) (2012a) News: The health-care challenges posed by population ageing, *Bulletin of the World Health Organization*, 90(2): 82–3.

World Health Organization (WHO) (2012b) *United Nations High-level Meeting on Noncommunicable Disease Prevention and Control*. Available at http://www.who. int/nmh/events/un_ncd_summit2011/en/ [Accessed September 2014].

World Health Organization (WHO) Europe (2011) *European Database on Nutrition, Obesity and Physical Activity*. Copenhagen: World Health Organization. Available at http://data.euro.who.int/nopa/ [Accessed September 2014].

Xu, X. and Kaestner, R. (2010) The Business Cycle and Health Behaviors. NBER Working Paper No. 15737. Cambridge, MA: NBER.

Yang, L., Sahlqvist, S., McMinn, A., Griffin, S. J. and Ogilvie, D. (2010) Interventions to promote cycling: Systematic review, *British Medical Journal*, 341(7778): 870.

Zubrick, S., Wood, L., Villanueva, K., Wood, G., Giles-Corti, B. and Christian, H. (2010) *Nothing but Fear Itself: Parental Fear as a Determinant Impacting on Child Physical Activity and Independent Mobility*. Melbourne, Victoria: Victorian Health Promotion Foundation.

Appendix: # Chapter 6

Effectiveness of interventions for physical activity

Note: versus (vs), minutes (mins), socioeconomic status (SES), odds ratio (OR), confidence interval (CI), physical activity (PA), moderate-to-vigorous physical activity (MVPA), moderate-level physical activity (MPA), Intervention (I), Control (C)

Table A.1 Mass media campaigns

	Author	Country	Key change result
1	Matsudo et al. 2003 and 2010	Brazil	Pre-2002–post-2008 (6 years) % defined as '<150 mins/week' – 43.7%–15.7% (p<0.001) 1. Showed greater effect for women vs men in improvements to moderate intensity PA (no data provided), and 2. among lower SES for walking. Specific data provided are: % 'zero walking' – SES A+B (wealthy) 26.9% dropped to 17.0% Versus SES D+E (poorest) 26.2% to 9.2% [Linear test for trend over time significant]
2	Reger-Nash et al. 2005	United States	Pre-Apr. 2001–post-Mar. 2002 (= 12 months) • % of population who were 'sedentary non-walkers' after 12 months dropped – 32%–18% • Probability that least active group will increase daily walking after 12 months – OR 1.72 (CI: 1.01–2.95) • Probability that least active group will achieve 'sufficient active walking' after 12 months OR 1.94 (CI: 1.06–3.55)
3	Reger-Nash et al. 2008	United States	Pre-Mar. 2005–post-Apr. 2005 (= 8 weeks intervention) Two outcomes: • % 'non active walker' (defined as 0–29 mins/day)* – 27.1%–15.3% [a change of 12.2%] • Adults 'insufficiently active' (defined as <30 mins/5 days a week) in intervention community were 82% more likely to become 'active walkers' compared with insufficiently active in comparison community (OR 1.82 (1.05-3.17) * this means a 'walker' does at least ≥30 mins/day

4	Merom et al. 2005	Australia	Pre-Sept. 15 2003–post-Oct. 3 2003 (= 3 weeks)

4 Merom et al. 2005 — Australia — Pre-Sept. 15 2003–post-Oct. 3 2003 (= 3 weeks)
- % inactive (amongst employed) dropped 15.3%–11.3% (p<0.05) vs % unemployed 16.2%–16.9%
- % 'sufficient' (among employed) increased 52.0% to 57% (non–significant increase)

(Other results on travel to work modal shift in table)

5 De Cocker et al. 2007 — Belgium — Pre-2005–post–2006 (= 12 months)
- Meet 10,000 steps/day (deemed equivalent to 150 mins = recommended level)
- % of adults reaching 10,000 steps/day target increased – 42%–50% (p<0.001)

Table A.2 School-based interventions

	Author	Country	Key change result
1	Haerens et al. 2006	Belgium	Number of mins of school-based activity: Boys only – significant increase of 6.9 mins
2	Klepp et al. 1994	Norway	% meeting 'PA $\geq$ 2x week' Net increase of 9% physically more active in intervention group
3	Simon et al. 2004	France	% engaged in 'leisure supervized PA' Girls: net increase by 22% Boys: net increase by 13%
4	Verstraete et al. 2006	Belgium	% time in morning recess spent in MVPA Difference between I vs C % change is 9.3% % time in morning recess spent in MVPA In girls, only difference between I vs C % change is 22.4%
5	Bonhauser et al. 2005	Chile	VO2 change Difference between I vs C in VO2 % change = 6.7%
6	Coleman et al. 2005	Texas/United States and New Mexico	% 'passing' fitnessgram 1 mile run Boys only – difference in % change between I vs C = 16% Girls only – difference in % change between I vs C = 3%
7	Da Cunha 2002	Brazil	% walk to school Result has to be estimated (conservatively) from Figure 1 in paper – 6% net increase
8	Heath and Coleman 2002	Texas/United States and Eastern New Mexico	% time spent in MVPA in PE class net change for I vs C = 20.1% % time spent in VPA in PE class net change for I vs C = 4.5%
9	Kain et al. 2004	Chile	% change in level achieved on aerobic capacity test Boys only – net change I vs C = 35% Girls only – net change I vs C = 37.2%

Table A.3 Primary-care interventions

	Author	Country	Key change result
1	Harrison et al. 2005	United Kingdom	At 6 months, net increase of 9%
2	Isaacs et al. 2007	United Kingdom	Leisure centre group 36.2% increase in those achieving >150 mins/week of MPA
			Walking group 6.5% increase in those achieving >150 mins/week of MPA
			In walking group, 84% increase in MVPA
			In walking group, 28% in total mins of activity
3	Petrella et al. 2003	United Kingdom	VO2 net change after 12 months = 11% ml/kg/min (p <0.001)
4	Aittasalo et al. 2006	Finland	Net increase in PA sessions per week of 20.81%
5	Proper et al. 2003	The Netherlands	Net change in aerobic fitness is 3.48%
6	Fitzgibbon et al. 2005	USA	Net increase of PA sessions in cohort 2 is 472.3% per week
7	Pinto et al. 2005	USA	Net increase in moderate PA mins/week
			From baseline to 3 months = 123.12%
			From baseline to 6 months = 119.76%
8	Kerse et al. 2005	New Zealand	Leisure moderate-vigorous hours/week
			From baseline to 12 months 55.3%

Table A.4 Worksite interventions

	Author	Country	Key change result
1	Aittasalo et al. 2004	Finland	Change in amount of leisure time PA
			Difference between intervention group 1 and control d = 0.1534
			Difference between intervention group 2 and control d = 0.0660
2	Brox and Fröystein 2005	Norway	Change in performance on the UKK walking test
			Difference between intervention group and control d = 0.3141
3	Hendriksen et al. 2000	The Netherlands	Change in maximal physical performance level
			Difference between intervention group and control in females d = 0.2727
			Difference between intervention group and control in males d = 0.5030

(*Continued overleaf*)

Table A.4 Worksite interventions (*continued*)

	Author	Country	Key change result
4	Loughlan and Mutrie 1997	Scotland, United Kingdom	Change in self-reported PA using an amended version of the seven-day recall of leisure time PA questionnaire
			Difference between intervention group one and control d = 0.7753
			Difference between intervention group two and control d = 0.8687
5	Mutrie et al. 2002	Scotland, United Kingdom	Change in self-reports of cycling and walking to and from work from a seven-day recall questionnaire
			Difference between intervention group and control d = 0.5232
6	Oja et al. 1998	Finland	Change in the VO2 max
			Difference between the intervention group compared to control d = 0.0948
7	Proper et al. 2003	The Netherlands	Change in sub-maximal heart rate (PA fitness measure)
			Difference between the intervention group compared to control d = 0.3642
8	Spittaels et al. 2007	Belgium	Change in self-reported PA
			Difference between intervention group one and control d = 0.0533
			Difference between intervention group two and control d = 0.1289

Table A.5 Active travel interventions

	Author	Country	Key change result
1	Mutrie et al. 2002	Scotland, United Kingdom	'Walk in to Work Out'
			Increase of 64 mins/week (P<0.05)
2	TravelSmart Gloucester 2002; TravelSmart Greater Nottingham 2004; TravelSmart Sheffield 2004	England, United Kingdom	Travel Smart UK
			Gloucester: Reported net effect: +25 trips/year, +7 mins/week
			Nottingham: Reported net effect: +2 mins/day (in one area), +3 mins/day (in another), +18 mins/week
			Sheffield: Reported net effect: +2 mins/day (SSNR), +14 mins/week
3	Hemmingsson et al. 2009	Sweden	Prevalence of cycling >2 km/day at follow-up: 38.7% vs 8.9% (OR 7.8, 95% CI 4.0 to 15.0; P<0.001)
			Prevalence of cycling >4 km/day at follow-up: 24.8% vs 4.6% (P<0.001)

4	Sloman et al. 2009	England, United Kingdom	Prevalence of cycling ≥30 mins once a month or more: Intervention group +2.78% compared to control (+1.89% if adjusted to most similar control area)
			Prevalence of cycling ≥30 mins 12 times a month or more: Intervention group +0.97% compared to control (+1.65% if adjusted to most similar control area)
5	Troelsen et al. 2004 and Troelsen 2005	Denmark	Proportion of all trips made by cycle (percentage point change): Intervention group +3.4% compared to control
			Cycling trip frequency per person: Intervention group +0.06/day compared to control
			Distance cycled per person: Intervention group +0.1 km/day compared to control
6	Transport for London 2004 and 2005	United Kingdom	Cycle tracks
			An evaluation of a two-way cycletrack in London showed a decrease in the rate of cycling crashes (Transport for London, 2005) and a 58% increase in the number of cyclists on the roadway in 3.5 years (Transport for London, 2004).
7	Wardman et al. 2007	United Kingdom	End-of-trip facilities impacting cycling to work
			Compared to base bicycle mode share of 5.8% for work trips, outdoor parking would raise share to 6.3%, indoor secure parking to 6.6%, and indoor parking plus showers to 7.1%
8	McKee et al. 2007	Scotland, United Kingdom	Increase of 389% of children's 'days walked to school' in intervention group, compared to 17% increase in control group
9	Mackett et al. 2005	United Kingdom	About 63% of children using walking buses had previously travelled to school by car. On average, each child who switched mode of transport walked for 22 mins each trip. This is nearly 2 hours of extra PA a week.

Table A.6 Whole-of-community interventions

	Author	Country	Key change result
1	Schofield et al. 2005	Australia	Pedometer The intervention group compared to the control reported an increase of 2,591 steps a day OR 181 mins/week of PA
2	Barilotti et al. 2002	USA	Pedometer with 10,000 step goal The intervention group compared to the control reported an increase of 57.5 mins/week of PA
3	Coull et al. 2004	Scotland, United Kingdom	Community walking group Increase of 73 mins/week of PA in participants who joined a walking group
4	Nies et al. 2003	USA	Remote telephone intervention support Increase of 4.6 mins/day or 32 mins/week of PA
5	Napolitano et al. 2003	USA	Remote internet intervention support Increase of 62 mins/week of PA
6	Simoes et al. 2009	Recife, Brazil	Whole of community Prevalence OR for moderate to high levels of leisure time PA were higher among former (OR = 2.0), current (OR = 11.3) intervention participants and those who had heard about or seen the intervention activity (OR = 1.8)
7	Reis et al. 2010	Curitiba, Brazil	Whole of community Exposure to community programs was associated with leisure-time PA (Prevalence OR = 2.9) and walking for leisure (Prevalence OR = 2.4)
8	Matsudo et al. 2002	Sao Paulo, Brazil	Whole of community Risk of being inactive was greater for those who had not heard of the intervention *Agita* (13.1%) compared with those that had known the programme's objectives (7.1%)

chapter seven

Improving the quality
of nutrition

Corinna Hawkes and
Franco Sassi

The burden of diet-related disease

It is well-established that a 'healthy diet' is required to maintain and improve
human health. In general terms, a 'healthy' diet can be defined as one that
includes the right balance between the necessary dietary constituents
(Table 7.1). Governments and scientific bodies have developed both food-
based and nutrient-based dietary guidelines to help guide intake by populations
and individuals. While not without controversy, nutrient-based guidelines
generally suggest that diets high in fats – particularly saturated and trans-fats
relative to polyunsaturated fats, free (added) sugars, sodium (salt), and low
in dietary fibre – do not promote good health (Table 7.1). Diets in which
energy (caloric) intake exceeds energy use, leading to weight gain, are also
not considered health promoting. In terms of foods, diets high in energy-dense
and nutrient-poor foods, red meat, processed meats, and low in fruit and
vegetables, legumes and wholegrain cereals, are not considered beneficial for
health.

Despite existing scientific knowledge about healthy eating, there is clear
evidence that the leading energy sources in the human diet have shifted away
from wholegrain cereals and complex carbohydrates towards fats, sweeteners,
refined carbohydrates and salt, with greater intake of meat and high-calorie
and/or nutrient-poor processed foods (Popkin 2006). This shift has been taking
place in Western Europe since the nineteenth century, and at a faster pace over
past decades in developing nations (Grigg 1995; Popkin 2002).

Although there are important dietary differences between European countries,
there have also been some common trends over past decades. The availability
of energy has increased (albeit not everywhere) and the proportion of calories
obtained from fats, especially vegetable fats, has increased significantly
(Branca et al. 2007). Excessive consumption of saturated fats, cholesterol and
sugars has increased over time in almost all countries (Schmidhuber and Traill
2006). The proportion of energy intake from fat is now typically around 30–40

Table 7.1 Nutrient and food-based dietary guidelines

a) Population-level nutrient-based guidelines (adults)

Nutrient	Recommendation
Protein	10–15% of caloric intake
Carbohydrates	55–75% of caloric intake
Free (added) sugars	<10% of caloric intake
Fats	
Total	15–30% of caloric intake
Saturated fats	<10% of caloric intake
Polyunsaturated fats (PUFA)	6–10% of caloric intake
Trans-fats	<1% of caloric intake
Cholesterol	<300 mg per day
Sodium chloride (salt)	<5 g per day
Dietary fibre	25 g/25–3 g per day

Source: WHO/FAO 2003; WCRF/AICR 2007 and USDA 2010 for dietary fibre.

b) Food-based dietary guidelines (adults)

Food	Recommendation
Meat	
Red meat	Less than 500 g cooked weight (about 700–750 g raw weight) per week[a].
Processed meats	Avoid processed meats such as bacon, ham, salami, corned beef and some sausages[a].
Fish	Increase the amount and variety of seafood consumed by choosing seafood in place of some meat and poultry.
Fruits and vegetables	=/> 400 g per day. The most appropriate source of dietary carbohydrate along with legumes and wholegrain cereals. Eat a variety of vegetables, especially dark-green and red and orange vegetables and beans and peas.
Legumes	The most appropriate source of dietary carbohydrate along with fruits and vegetables and wholegrain cereals.
Whole-grain cereals	The most appropriate source of dietary carbohydrate along with legumes and fruits and vegetables; at least half of all grains consumed should be wholegrains.
Refined grains	Limit the consumption of foods that contain refined grains ('refined starchy foods'), especially refined grain foods that contain solid fats, added sugars, and sodium.
High calorie/energy-dense foods with added sugar	Avoid/drink fewer sugar-sweetened drinks; reduce portion size of high calorie foods with added sugars.

Sources: WHO/FAO 2003; WCRF/AICR 2007; USDA 2010.

[a] WCRF/AICR 2007 for cancer prevention.

per cent, compared to the recommended intake of 15–30 per cent (Branca et al. 2007; Table 7.1). Both national and household data show that sugar use in the home has declined, but foods containing added sugars have increased, with the notable example of soft drinks (Naska et al. 2010). Intake of fruits and vegetables remains below recommended levels in most countries; fibre intake is also below recommended levels (Branca et al. 2007). The picture is somewhat different in Eastern Europe, and the newly independent states (NIS), where energy levels fell rapidly during the transition period.

These dietary patterns developed alongside an increasing burden of diet-related chronic noncommunicable diseases (DRNCDs) in Europe. Cardiovascular disease is the leading cause of death in Europe, causing more than half of all deaths across the Region, with heart disease or stroke being the leading cause of death in all Member States (WHO EURO 2006). Noncommunicable diseases (NCDs) as a group are the leading cause of death, disease and disability in the WHO European Region, accounting for nearly 86 per cent of deaths and 77 per cent of the disease burden (WHO EURO 2011). This burden, which has also existed for a long time in North America, has now spread to other world regions. In 2008, over 80 per cent of cardiovascular and diabetes deaths actually occurred in low- and middle-income countries. Globally, deaths from NCDs are predicted to increase by 15 per cent between 2010 and 2020 (WHO 2010).

Associated with these patterns of disease are changes in diet-related metabolic risk factors. Particularly notable is the over-three-fold rise in overweight/obesity prevalence since the 1980s in the WHO European Region, even in countries with traditionally low rates (Branca et al. 2007). The steepest rises appear to have occurred since the early 1980s. Other key metabolic risk factors are high blood pressure, which is present among over 40 per cent of adults in the European Region, and elevated levels of cholesterol, which affects over 50 per cent of adults (WHO 2010).

When combined, the leading behavioural and metabolic risk factors (high blood pressure, high blood glucose, overweight and obesity, high cholesterol, low fruit and vegetable intake) plus physical inactivity, are estimated to be responsible for almost 80 DALYs per 1,000 population over age 30 in the European Region, which is more than any other world region (WHO 2009).

Objectives and scope of the chapter

The aim of this chapter is to present the economic case for population-based policies to change food environments as a means of preventing and controlling DRNCDs. The chapter briefly reviews the current problem of diet-related disease and explains why dietary patterns are an economic issue. Based on an economic framework, the chapter presents a taxonomy of policy options to address poor diet and reviews the evidence of the effectiveness and cost-effectiveness of these policies. It ends by discussing the issues and challenges of the available evidence and making recommendations. The main geographical focus of the chapter is the broader European Region – the 53 Member States of the WHO European Region ('Europe') – but many of the findings are relevant to the rest of the world.

Unhealthy diets as an economic issue

Health care and productivity costs

The management of diet-related ill health within European health care systems is increasingly expensive. The labour market and productivity impacts of ill health contribute further to the economic burden of DRNCDs. Obesity alone is estimated to account for approximately 1 per cent to 3 per cent of total health expenditure in most countries (and more in the United States) (Tsai et al. 2010). At the individual level, an obese person incurs health care expenditures at least 25 per cent higher than those of a normal weight person, according to a range of studies from a variety of countries (Withrow and Alter 2010). When production losses are added to health care costs, obesity accounts for a fraction of a percentage point of GDP in most countries, and over 1 per cent in the United States (WHO 2007).

Economic determinants of unhealthy diets

The economic relevance of unhealthy diets extends beyond their economic burden. Dietary patterns also have economic determinants, both on the demand side – changes in the economic status of populations, communities and households – and on the supply side – the economic organization of the food supply chain.

On the demand side, real consumer income is one of the main determinants of food consumption: as income increases, so does consumption, with faster increases at lower levels of income. For example, lower-income countries in Europe experienced a faster growth in fat intake between 1961–63 and 2001–3 relative to countries with higher levels of income (Schmidhuber and Shetty 2010). In addition, as incomes rise, the share of income spent on non-cereals/starchy foods rises (Bennett's Law). This is exemplified on a global scale by the relationship between national income and meat and dairy intake (Regmi et al. 2001), sweeteners use (Popkin and Nielsen 2003), and the size of the packaged food market (Goldman Sachs Group Inc. 2007).

On the supply side, food systems have undergone tremendous changes over past decades, with radical shifts in the way supply chains are organized (Vorley 2003). Core changes include a convergence in the actors supplying food (Regmi 2008); more open sourcing of food (Hawkes et al. 2010); a larger gap between producer and retail prices (Vorley 2003); and more intensive food advertising and promotion (Kelly et al. 2010) (Table 7.2). These changes in the food supply chain have been facilitated by a major paradigm shift in economic policy: the shift from the notion that there should be intervention in agri-food markets, to the preference for removing state intervention in order to allow private, open and competitive markets to flourish (consistent with trends towards a globalized economy). In Europe, for example, reforms to the

Table 7.2 Examples of key changes in the economic organization of the food supply chain and implications for the consumer food environment

Change in the food supply chain	Implication for the consumer food environment
Convergence in supply chain towards more transnational companies and supermarkets	Increased availability of processed foods (fast foods, snacks, soft drinks) through growth of fast food outlets, supermarkets and food advertising/ promotion; growth of transnational supermarkets changes food availability, affordability, and way food is promoted (acceptability).
More open sourcing of food	Increased ability to import and export changes availability of foods, their nutritional quality and/or their affordability.
Greater value accrued in the supply chain by processors manufacturers and retailers	Increased incentive to make 'high-value' foods available to consumers and affects affordability.
More food advertising and promotion	Shapes food choices by affecting acceptability of different foods.

Source: Adapted from Hawkes et al. 2009

Common Agricultural Policy (CAP) have resulted in substantial declines of income support to farmers since the 1980s (OECD 2011).

Further up the food supply chain, marketing channels have transformed, with shifting of power to food processors, manufacturers, caterers and (particularly) retailers which move farm products through the market. Supply chains have become more tightly coordinated, increasing the ability of these industries to cut purchasing costs from the agricultural sector, and then transform farm products into highly-differentiated, processed products. With consumers being willing to pay more for these 'value-added' products relative to primary foods, companies now have a greater incentive not just to meet demand, but to mobilize and create it through product innovation and marketing.

Economic rationale for intervention

Economics also has a role to play in diet by guiding policy interventions. From an economic standpoint, government intervention in the food sector, as in any other sector of the economy, may be justified when free markets fail to operate efficiently (termed 'market failure'). In the case of food markets, it is difficult to explain consumer eating behaviours as the result of rational action within an efficient market environment. Insights from psychology and sociology, as well as from developments in behavioural economics, have shown that many consumers' food choices are driven by forces unlikely to lead to optimal nutrition and health outcomes (Sassi and Hurst 2008; Grunert et al. 2012). For instance, there is evidence that unhealthy dietary habits are partly linked to inconsistencies in time preferences, leading to poor self-control in health-related consumption, and a biased perception of risk (e.g. Brunello et al. 2008).

Markets may also fail when consumers do not bear the full cost of their consumption choices and generate 'externalities'. The argument that unhealthy diets produce societal costs because of higher health care expenditures for treating disease consequences, collectively funded through insurance or tax-funded systems, has been somewhat controversial (e.g. Philipson and Posner 2008). Some existing empirical evidence suggests these external costs are unlikely to be large enough to require specific government intervention (e.g. Bhattacharya and Sood 2005). A different source of externalities, less commonly identified as such, is associated with the spread of unhealthy dietary habits, and even conditions such as obesity, within families and social networks, as a contagion effect acting as a social multiplier of the negative effects of unhealthy diets and obesity (e.g. Christakis and Fowler 2007; Sassi et al. 2009b).

In addition, there is evidence that many consumers are not fully informed about the potential health consequences of their food choices, partly because the science is not so strong in many areas and consumers are exposed to often conflicting messages from different sources. Whether existing information failures are sufficiently important to justify government intervention is a matter of debate, with some arguing that the main problem is people's ability to process the relevant information, rather than the availability of information itself (e.g. Cawley 2004). The targeting of specific market failures in the design of prevention policies may be justified when these failures have a sufficiently large impact to warrant government intervention and when failures are amenable to correction through appropriate policies (Sassi 2010).

Policy options

An economic rationale for government intervention emerges from the above analysis. First, interventions on the *information environment*, aimed at ensuring more, and more balanced, information to enable consumers to make efficient choices in the food marketplace (Sassi 2010). Second, interventions on the *market environment* (i.e. the foods sold in the marketplace, the product composition of those foods, and the prices of those foods). Taking action in this market environment also serves to reinforce messages provided through information, or prevent messages that undermine that information, thus increasing the efficiency of information provision.

Together, the 'information environment' and 'market environment' form what can be termed the 'consumer food environment' (see also taxonomy in Capacci et al. 2012). Policies that have the potential to improve the consumer food environment are listed in Table 7.3, and fall into seven policy domains: public awareness campaigns; labelling; food marketing; food availability in specific settings; pricing instruments; retail environment; and food composition across food supply. Within each domain there are a range of policy actions that can be taken. Policies can target different foods or nutrients, with different policy actions being potentially more effective for different foods and nutrients

Table 7.3 Taxonomy of policies to target the consumer food environment

Domain of policy action	Examples of policy actions
Public awareness campaigns	Food-based dietary guidelines; mass media; social marketing; community campaigns.
Labelling	Nutrient lists on food packages; 'interpretative' and calorie labels; menu, shelf labels; rules on nutrient and health claims.
Food marketing	Restrict advertising to children in all forms of media; sales promotions; packaging; sponsorship.
Food availability in specific settings	Fruit and vegetable programmes; standards in education, work, health facilities; award schemes; choice architecture.
Food prices	Targeted subsidies; price promotions at point of sale; unit pricing; food taxes.
Retail environment	Incentives for shops to locate in underserved areas; planning restrictions on food outlets; in-store promotions.
Food composition across food supply	Reformulation; elimination of transfats; calorie reduction; portion size limits; agricultural and food chain incentives.

(e.g. altering product composition of foods may be more effective as a means of reducing excessive dietary intake of salt, relative to sugar). Some policies may be best targeted at whole food groups, with others taking a nutrient-based approach. The effectiveness of policies may also vary with population groups. For example, subsidies affecting food prices may be best targeted at certain groups, as may promotional campaigns for under-consumed foods. Different policy actions can also be combined – such as mass media campaigns combined with product composition restrictions, or public information campaigns in specific settings combined with non-environmental, more personal-oriented policies, such as nutrition education or dietary advice ('multi-component' actions).

The effectiveness and cost-effectiveness of policies targeting the consumer food environment

The remainder of this chapter contains a review of what is known about the effectiveness and cost-effectiveness of policies that aim to change the consumer food environment (listed in Table 7.3), potentially underpinning the rationale for action. Only policy options with available evidence on cost-effectiveness are included.

An initial consideration when examining the effectiveness of policies is the outcome with respect to which effectiveness is measured. Ultimately, the goal is to reduce disease burden, but there is a hierarchy of potential outcomes. For example, some research may measure the impact of the policy on some aspect of the food environment, while other studies examine the impact on dietary intake. Clear associations between policy actions that aim to change the food environment and health outcomes, or even dietary intake, can be methodologically difficult to establish, so effectiveness can also be measured using dietary precursors, such as consumer attitudes, or changes in the food environment itself. Cost-effectiveness studies often use model-based techniques to establish a link between action, diet, and health outcome, when direct evidence is not available, by combining existing evidence on each step of the process that leads to health outcomes (e.g. combining evidence of dietary changes following an intervention, with separate evidence of health improvements following a similar dietary change).

The information for effectiveness was obtained from three sources: (1) a systematic 'review of reviews' of the evidence on effectiveness, which included strict inclusion and exclusion criteria and quality assessment, completed in September 2011; (2) a more recent systematic review by Mozaffarian et al. (2012); (3) where there was no systematic review, or where studies had been published since the most recent systematic review, non-systematic summaries of the evidence, notably by Capacci et al. (2012), and original studies. The evidence on cost-effectiveness was based on a comprehensive review of the literature. While the search and reporting of evidence is from all countries, particular emphasis is placed on reporting the results from the broader European Region.

Public awareness campaigns

Effectiveness

Public awareness campaigns aim to change the consumption of specific foods or nutrients, or to encourage healthy eating more generally. They can be conducted at the national or community level through the mass media, or in specific settings, such as schools, worksites, supermarkets, etc. In Europe, there have been a number of campaigns targeted at specific nutrients, notably salt and fruit and vegetables (Capacci et al. 2012). Most countries have some form of public awareness campaign for fruits and vegetables, typically based on the 'five portions a day' message (Fulponi 2009; Capacci et al. 2012).

According to Mozaffarian et al. (2012), the weight of evidence suggests that sustained and focused media and educational campaigns, using multiple channels to increase consumption of specific healthy foods (e.g. fruit and vegetables, as well as other 'eat more of' foods, as reviewed below) are likely to be effective at changing knowledge. A systematic review published by the WHO concluded that intensive mass media campaigns using one simple message, and long-tem intensive campaigns promoting healthy diets, are moderately effective interventions (Anderson et al. 2009). According to a review of studies based in Europe, most public campaigns were evaluated on the basis of their effects on dietary precursors (knowledge and awareness), rather than on dietary intake, therefore they are not conclusive about the effects of campaigns on behaviour and dietary patterns (Capacci et al. 2012).

Cost-effectiveness

Several economic analyses of public awareness campaigns are available, some of which assessed campaigns combined with other policy actions, e.g. with interpretive labelling schemes (Sacks et al. 2011), or product reformulation (Eatwell 2011). Five studies estimated the cost-effectiveness of information campaigns alone, two of these using data from intervention studies (Wootan et al. 2005; Cobiac et al. 2010b), the rest using models to combine evidence from multiple studies (Willet et al. 2006; Sassi et al. 2009a; Ha and Chisholm 2011). One examined fruits and vegetables in workplace settings (Cobiac et al. 2010b), and one at a population-level (Sassi et al. 2009a); one focused on milk in a community setting (Wootan et al. 2005); the remainder examined fats and salt at a population-level in developing countries (Willett et al. 2006; Ha and Chisholm 2011).

The effects of a mass media campaign aimed at increasing fruit and vegetable intake, as well as physical activity, were assessed in a multi-country study based on a microsimulation approach (Sassi et al. 2009a; Sassi 2010). The study concluded that the implementation costs of the campaign would be modest, compared to those of alternative strategies to improve diet or increase physical activity, but would nevertheless be greater than any reductions in health care expenditure that may result from reduced morbidity. The campaign would have a favourable cost-effectiveness ratio starting from about ten years from its initial implementation, but its health effects would be smaller than those of any of the other strategies examined.

The cost-effectiveness of worksite information campaigns, generally coupled with interventions like changes in catering arrangements, were also assessed in the above studies (targeting fat, as well as fruit and vegetable, consumption), and in the Australian ACE Prevention programme, for fruit and vegetables only (Cobiac et al. 2010b). OECD studies concluded that the cost-effectiveness of such programmes would only drop to commonly acceptable levels after over 30 years from the initial implementation. The ACE Prevention study, which assessed interventions at their steady state, sourced data on programme effectiveness from seven worksite interventions in the United States and United Kingdom, and concluded that only one in seven estimates (based on Engbers et al. 2006) was within acceptable limits.

A study of the cost-effectiveness of different media strategies to promote low-fat milk consumption in the United States assessed their impact (based on local experiments) on the cost per person switching from high- to low-fat milk (Wootan et al. 2005). The study concluded that a combination of paid advertising and media relations provided the best value for money, although a comprehensive assessment of how unobserved local factors may have affected the costs and outcomes of the campaigns was not reported. The study did not include impacts on health and health care expenditures.

In developing country settings, model-based studies found that mass media campaigns for salt, saturated fat, and cholesterol reduction had a more favourable cost-effectives profile (Willet et al. 2006; Ha and Chisholm 2011), although an OECD study of a campaign to promote fruit and vegetable intake and physical activity provided a mixed picture of the potential cost-effectiveness of this strategy in different countries (Cecchini et al. 2010).

Labelling

Effectiveness

Lists of nutrients can be provided on foods, menus, retail shelves, etc. In Europe, the regulations on nutrient labelling changed in 2011. Previously, the provision of a nutrient list was required only when a nutrient claim was made, but nutrient labelling will become mandatory in December 2016 (EC 2011). Other countries, notably the United States, have required mandatory labelling for a much longer time period (Hawkes 2010). Even though labelling is not yet mandatory in Europe, food companies already apply nutrition lists on the vast majority of their products (Bonsmann et al. 2010).

There is a significant body of literature on the effects of application of nutrient lists, which includes five systematic reviews and around 300 papers (Cowburn and Stockley 2005; Grunert and Wills 2007; Ni Mhurchu and Gorton 2007; Campos et al. 2011; Mozaffarian et al. 2012). The largest proportion of evidence comes from the United States, but a considerable amount is from Western Europe (Grunert and Wills 2007). Impact on label use and understanding (dietary precursors) are typically measured, rather than dietary intake, with the exception of some more recent studies from the United States.

Existing studies show there is convincing evidence that consumers use nutrient lists. Consumers look more closely at nutrients they wish to avoid, notably fat and energy, but also different types of fat, cholesterol, and sodium (salt) (Campos et al. 2011). But there is also strong evidence that label use is considerably lower along lower socioeconomic status (SES) groups and people with little nutritional knowledge, especially consumers of low SES – suggesting that the application of nutrient lists absent of other measures may have negative implications for dietary inequalities (see Chapter 12).

Evidence on how well nutrient lists are understood is not uniform, although it is clear that consumers can find nutrient lists confusing and hard to understand (Cowburn and Stockley 2005). With regard to dietary intake, a small number of studies from the United States find positive associations between label use and intake of dietary fibre, and inconsistent results for saturated fat and cholesterol (Capacci et al. 2012).

In large part arising from concerns about lack of consumer understanding of nutrient lists, a range of different mechanisms have emerged for presenting nutrition information in ways that are more likely to be understood by the consumer, and/or directly influence their food choices. These 'interpretative labels' (sometimes referred to as 'front-of-pack' labels) either make nutrient information more prominent on the front of food packages or menus – e.g. calorie labelling, guideline daily amount (GDA) labelling – indicate that levels of nutrients are high, medium or low (e.g. 'traffic light' labelling), and/or display symbols that integrate the presence/absence of selected nutrients into one symbol or score (e.g. the Choices symbol, the Keyhole). These mechanisms are now used on a voluntary basis throughout Europe by food companies, notably GDA labelling (CIAA, cited in Hawkes 2010). Labelling schemes have also been developed by governments, such as guidance on 'traffic light' labelling in the United Kingdom, or via government-industry collaboration, such as the 'Keyhole' scheme in Sweden, Norway, and Denmark.[1]

Less evidence is available on the effects of interpretative labels relative to nutrient lists, and what there is varies according to whether it measures dietary precursors (e.g. 'liking' and understanding), or actual effects on sales or dietary intake. Systematic reviews of the evidence to date suggest that consumers have a greater liking and understanding of simplified front-of-pack information (Borgmeier and Westenhoefer 2009; Campos et al. 2011; Hawley et al. 2013). The first systematic review that considered label formats found that liking varied between label formats (Grunert and Wills 2007), but a later systematic review published in 2013 concluded that out of all the labels studied, 'traffic light' labels, including those with additional features, were the most liked and readily understood by consumers (Roberto et al. 2012; Hawley et al. 2013).

Mozaffarian et al. (2012) and Hawley et al. (2013) also reviewed studies on the effects of front-of-package labels on sales and consumption, finding that results varied with study design, type of label, and context. For example, results from two studies of the effects of traffic light labelling on sales have conflicting results, but the study designs were very different (Sacks et al. 2009; Thorndike et al. 2012). One study of 'shelf-labelling' showed no effect on sales, but another – a very different front-of-package icon system in a United States supermarket – showed positive effects (Sutherland et al. 2010; Steenhuis, cited in Capacci et al. 2012). On menu labelling, individual studies have identified some limited positive effects (Dumanovsky et al. 2011; Bruemmer et al. 2012), but a systematic review of the evidence concluded that, to date, calorie labelling does not have the intended effect of decreasing calorie purchasing or consumption (Swartz et al. 2011). Although finding the evidence inconclusive overall, Hawley et al. (2013) reported that labels on supermarket shelves appeared to hold promise, while Mozaffarian et al. (2012) concluded that the most promising evidence to date was on the impact of labelling on industry behaviour and product formulation. Of note, a review by Vyth et al. (2012) concluded that the methodological quality of published front-of-pack labelling research is generally low to mediocre.

Cost-effectiveness

Despite the widespread application of nutrient lists, very limited evidence of cost-effectiveness is currently available, with just one multi-country modelling study identified (Sassi et al. 2009a). This study was based on the assumption that implementation would be mandatory (as will be the case in the EU as of 2016), and only 65 per cent of the population would use labels, in line with established evidence. Costs were assumed to be $3.18 per target individual, and effects were assumed to influence fruit and vegetable and fat intake, and consequently body mass index (BMI). The study found that mandatory labelling would have a favourable cost-effectiveness ratio in the EUR-A WHO Region, as well as in a number of non-European countries at different levels of income. In major emerging economies, labelling was shown to be potentially cost-effective in the 20 years after implementation, and to become cost saving in 4 out of 6 countries within 50 years from the initial implementation. Although cost-effective, nutrient lists were estimated to have smaller health effects than fiscal measures (see the section 'Pricing mechanisms').

The evidence on cost-effectiveness is also relatively limited for interpretative labels. But it is consistent: both identified studies found interpretive labelling to be cost-effective. Sacks et al. (2011) examined the cost-effectiveness of 'traffic light' labels in Australia. The study assumed that implementation was mandatory on several categories of high-fat foods, and would be accompanied by a campaign to inform consumers how to use the labels. Owing to the conflicting evidence on the effects of interpretive labels, as reviewed here, the study assumed an effect somewhere between 'no effect' and 'significant effect'. It was also assumed the effect would only be experienced by 10 per cent of the population. Costs included those incurred by government and industry. Data on government costs were taken from other legislative actions (alcohol), and included costs of implementing, administering and enforcing, plus the information campaign. Data on industry costs were taken from the cost of application of country-of-origin labelling. The study found that the 'traffic light' labelling was cost-effective and, on the basis of net costs, dominant (interventions improve health and save money).

A second study, also from Australia, examined the cost-effectiveness of using a 'tick' symbol to indicate products low in salt (Cobiac et al. 2010a). The study compared the cost-effectiveness of the use of the tick between voluntary and mandatory policy regimes. The effects were measured by estimating by how much the use of the tick led food companies to reduce the salt content of their foods, with the assumption that mandatory application would result in a much more significant decline. Data on the costs of the voluntary measures included programme costs borne by industry, but not the costs of adding less salt; the cost of legislation was taken from WHO estimates of the number of resources used in making and enforcing legislative changes, coupled with the unit costs of the resources. The study found the programme to be effective and cost saving, especially when implemented on a mandatory basis (figures not provided).

Food marketing

Effectiveness

There has been considerable interest in Europe on restricting the commercial promotion of high fat, high sugar, or high salt foods to children. More countries are developing policies on food marketing to children, although these mainly involve the encouragement of industry self-regulation. At least 22 countries around the world have developed explicit policies on marketing to children, over half of which are in Europe (Hawkes and Lobstein 2011). Although none are comprehensive, they include specific restrictions and/or require messaging on advertising. The most restrictive approach is found in the United Kingdom, where broadcast advertising of high fat, sugar or salt foods is prohibited to children aged under 16. The food industry has also been active in this area – there are at least 20 pledges by food companies to restrict advertising to children under the age of 12, including the 'EU Pledge', which covers the whole EU region (Rudd Center 2013).

The development of policies restricting food marketing to children has been based in part on the moderate–strong evidence that food television advertising influences food and beverage preferences, purchase requests, beliefs and dietary intake risk (McGinnis et al. 2006; Cairns et al. 2009). Yet evidence on the actual effectiveness of these policies is still emerging, with no systematic reviews having been conducted on the topic. Nevertheless, there are a range of studies which have monitored and/or evaluated government- and industry-led policies on food marketing to children in a number of countries (PAHO 2012). These include monitoring reports written or commissioned by the secretariats of voluntary industry pledges and self-regulatory organizations, academic studies by independent researchers, and reports by non-governmental organizations (NGOs). The studies use a range of different methodologies (e.g. some apply to all advertising, others to advertising by select companies; evaluations use different methods to define 'unhealthy foods'), and outcome indicators (e.g. compliance, expenditure, exposure). Put together, it can be concluded from these studies that:

- Compliance with existing regulations, self-regulations, and pledges is generally high (e.g. IFBA 2009; Landmark Europe 2010; Accenture 2012; Tymms 2012). Where low compliance was found, this is the result of either a small number of repeated non-compliant advertisements, or failure to adhere to a very specific provision (e.g. Romero-Fernández et al. 2010; Roberts et al. 2012).
- Restrictions on specific communications channels and marketing techniques have led to declines in the amount of advertising according to the criteria adopted in the policy or pledge. This is the case for both statutory and self-regulatory approaches (e.g. Ofcom 2010; EU Pledge 2012; Kim et al. 2013). Importantly, however, these declines are measured according to the criteria of the policy, rather than declines of total exposure across the marketing mix. Thus, restrictions may reduce: some high-calorie foods from being advertised but not all (e.g Harris et al. 2010; Effertz and Wilcke 2011; Hebden et al. 2011; Powell et al. 2011); or prevent some companies from advertising but not all (e.g. King et al. 2011); advertising on TV directly targeted at children but lead to increases during family-oriented TV to which they are exposed (e.g. Potvin Kent et al. 2011; Adams et al. 2012); and/or marketing through some communications channels, but lead to increases elsewhere (e.g. UK Department of Health 2008; FTC 2012).
- Evidence is available from models of the effects of restrictions on dietary precursors or intake. All available studies suggest that restrictions have positive outcomes for dietary intake (e.g. Dhar and Baylis 2011 for fast food) or obesity (Chou et al. 2008; Magnus et al. 2009; Veerman et al. 2009).

Cost-effectiveness

Although there is no high-quality effectiveness evidence on dietary intake or obesity, there are two cost-effectiveness studies on restricting food marketing to children. One of these compared the cost-effectiveness of restricting commercial promotion through mandatory and self-regulatory approaches (Sassi et al. 2009a; Cecchini et al. 2010; Sassi 2010). The study assumed that the restrictions would affect children up to age 18 years – i.e. 20–35 per cent of the population – and covered five countries. Evidence of effectiveness was derived from evaluations of the effects of the United Kingdom ban implemented by the regulator OFCOM, and from a United States-based study (Chou et al. 2008), adapted to account for the influence of non-TV advertising. Effects were assumed to continue in a reduced form into adulthood. The effects of self-regulation were assumed to be half on the assumption that restrictions would be weaker and compliance would be lower. Costs to government included basic administration and planning costs at the national and local levels, as well as monitoring and enforcement costs. Costs of self-regulation were reduced significantly to allow for lower enforcement costs, but did not include costs to industry (from $7.51 to $0.51 per individual). The study found that restrictions were highly cost-effective in the 20 years after implementation, especially in low- and middle-income countries, where they may even be cost saving in some instances. The measure was more cost-effective after 50 years. Even though statutory regulations were assumed to have a greater health impact, self-regulation was found to be significantly more cost-effective as a result of its significantly lower costs.

Another model-based study examined the cost-effectiveness of the extension of existing regulations in Australia to include food advertising during specified children's TV viewing hours (Magnus et al. 2009). Effectiveness data was interpreted from modelling evidence combined with evidence of the effects of advertising on food preferences. Costs were estimated to be minimal, as compliance costs in Australia rest with industry, and these costs were not included. The study estimated that restricting commercial food promotion was highly cost-effective and dominant for net costs.

Fruit and vegetable initiatives in schools

Effectiveness

Promoting the availability of fruits and vegetables in schools has been a particularly significant policy action in Europe. The EU School Fruit Scheme, established in 2009, co-finances distribution of free fruit and vegetables to schools and participation is voluntary. In 2010/11, it had been taken up by 24 of the 27 EU Member States (European Commission 2012a).

There is convincing evidence that fruit and vegetable initiatives in schools have a positive, albeit modest, effect on dietary intake. The development of the EU School Fruit Scheme was based on a systematic review of the effects of fruit and vegetable programmes in schools (de Sa and Lock 2008), which concluded that school fruit and vegetable programmes are effective in increasing dietary knowledge and intake. Initial results from the scheme suggest it has led to an increase in the amount of fruits and vegetables consumed by children (European Commission 2012b). Evaluations at the national level suggest that the consumption effect varies between different groups of children – e.g., girls consume more than boys.

A more recent systematic review of 42 school-based interventions in Europe concluded that there is strong evidence of effect for 'multicomponent interventions' (i.e., those that combine changes to the food environment with education interventions) on fruit and vegetable intake, with more limited evidence of the effect of interventions that changed provision or provided education alone (Van Cauwenberghe et al. 2010). Other systematic reviews concluded that interventions designed to increase fruit and vegetable intake have a modest, but positive, effect (Howerton et al. 2007; Evans et al. 2012; Mozaffarian et al. 2012). Another systematic review focused on whether school-based interventions had the effect of widening or narrowing inequalities, with no conclusive evidence of effects (Oldroyd et al. 2008).

Cost-effectiveness

Despite the widespread use of measures to promote the availability of fruit and vegetables, and the reasonably large number of evaluations of the effects of these actions, very limited evidence of cost-effectiveness is currently available. In particular, one study assessed two programmes, each covering over 700 school children in the Netherlands, using a model to extrapolate the effects on consumption observed in the context of randomized controlled trials (RCTs) over the lifetime of the children exposed to the programmes (te Velde et al. 2011). The study assumed that 30 per cent of the effect on fruit and vegetable consumption would be permanent. One intervention (Pro Children) turned out to be dominant (lower cost and higher effectiveness) over the other. This intervention entailed multiple components, including provision of free fruit and vegetables twice weekly, delivery of health education as part of the school curriculum, with feedback and parental involvement. In the less effective intervention, the latter components were absent and schools were encouraged, but not mandated, to provide health education. Children were targeted at age 10 to 12. Both interventions were cost-effective in comparison with doing nothing, with Pro Children showing an incremental cost-effectiveness ratio of $6,629 (€5,728 in 2008 prices) per DALY saved, including future reductions in health care expenditures discounted at 3 per cent (same as health outcomes). The ratio would increase to $31,142 (€26,908 in 2008 prices) if only 10 per cent of the effect of consumption were to become permanent.

Pricing mechanisms

Effectiveness

Studies have assessed the impact of food taxes, subsidies and financial incentives. Food taxes have been discussed as a potential mechanism for encouraging healthier eating habits for over a decade (Jacobsen and Brownell

2000; Marshall 2000), and many jurisdictions have some form of taxes on all foods, or specific foods. But it is only very recently that they have been applied in Europe in the context of healthier eating, and even in these circumstances fiscal reasons appear to be the more important motivation.

Denmark introduced a tax on foods containing more than 2.3 per cent saturated fats (meat, cheese, butter, edible oils, margarine, spreads, snacks, etc.) in 2011, although it repealed the tax one year later. Hungary has introduced a tax on selected manufactured foods with high sugar, salt or caffeine content, including carbonated sugary drinks, Finland a tax on confectionery products, combined with a raised excise tax on soft drinks, and France a tax on soft drinks, affecting both drinks with added sugars and drinks with artificial sweeteners. Other countries are currently considering similar measures.

The evidence-base on the potential effects of taxes on nutrition and health has grown considerably in the past few years. A recent review concluded that taxes have the potential to shift consumer behaviour towards healthier dietary patterns, but the effects of taxes depend largely on 'the details of the policy design' (Thow 2012). A review of simulation models concluded that taxes on carbonated drinks and saturated fat and subsidies on fruit and vegetables would be associated with beneficial dietary change (Eyles et al. 2012). A systematic review of earlier, mainly lower quality, studies on taxes/subsidies concluded that taxes influence consumption in the intended direction, but found a wide range of predicted effects (Thow et al. 2010).

Empirical estimates of the responsiveness of consumers to price changes (price elasticity) in the long term suggest that taxes would influence food purchases, but to differing degrees depending on the study and nutrient/food in question, ranging from 'negligible' for a fat tax in the United Kingdom (Tiffin and Arnoult 2011), 'small and ambiguous' for a fat tax in France (Allais et al. 2010), to relatively significant effects for a beverage tax in the United Kingdom (Ng et al. 2011). Studies of beverage price elasticities in the United States, Brazil and Mexico likewise suggest that a beverage tax would be effective in reducing consumption of sugar sweetened beverages, with a larger tax having a larger effect (Barquera et al. 2008; Duffey et al. 2010; Dharmasena and Capps 2011; Claro et al. 2012; Finkelstein et al. 2013; Zhen et al. 2013), but with some authors concluding that the effect depends on the nature of the substitutions for different drinks (Hawkes 2012). A recent systematic review of price elasticities in the United States suggests that the demand for sugar-sweetened beverages is elastic, unlike the demand for fast food, fruit and vegetables, making substitutions more likely (Powell et al. 2013).

However, the demand for most foods has a low price elasticity, which means that people will cut their consumption of the taxed foods somewhat but spend a larger share of their income on these, with a lesser likelihood of substitutions. Model-based studies show, among other things, the extent of the potential knock-on effects of taxes on nutrients other than those targeted. For example, taxing fats was shown to have a potential for increasing sugar intake (Jensen and Smed 2007) or salt intake (Mytton et al. 2007). Taxing foods according to their nutrient profile may make undesirable substitutions less likely (Mytton et al. 2007), although Nnoaham et al. (2009) found that the latter approach would only have positive impacts on consumption if it was accompanied by a subsidy for fruit and vegetables.

Recent laboratory choice studies in the Netherlands and the United States found that consumers respond to taxes by reducing purchases (e.g. Epstein et al. 2010; Giesen et al. 2011, 2012; Nederkoorn et al. 2011; Temple et al. 2011). A recent review of experimental studies concluded that 'research on the overall nutritional quality of purchases is mixed because of substitution effects' (Epstein et al. 2012). Food substitutions are difficult to investigate and predict, and they may hinder the effectiveness of taxes when the latter are not carefully designed.

From an equity perspective, most existing studies find that taxes are regressive, although disadvantaged socioeconomic groups will also benefit disproportionately in terms of health outcomes (Sassi 2010).

Food subsidies can either be targeted at specific food commodities, or at consumers (all or selected groups). In the former case, the challenge is to ensure that subsidies effectively translate into reduced market prices; in the latter, that consumers spend the extra money to purchase healthy foods. Population-wide subsidies have not been implemented with the aim of promoting healthier eating thus far, but there are examples of subsidies targeting specific groups of consumers. The Healthy Start programme in the United Kingdom provides vouchers for fruit, vegetables and milk to certain groups of pregnant women and families with young children. In the United States, the Women, Infants, and Children program provides supplemental foods designed to meet the special nutritional needs of low-income pregnant women, postpartum women, infants, and children up to five years of age who are at nutritional risk.

The effects of the Women, Infants and Children (WIC) Fruit and Vegetable Voucher Campaign (farmers' market or supermarket food vouchers) in the United States have been tested in a controlled trial. Total consumption of fruit and vegetables increased in all groups over the course of the study and six months after the intervention (Herman et al. 2008). Studies of the effects of population-level food subsidies, reviewed in Thow et al. (2010), suggest that subsidies influence consumption in the intended direction, and that taxes are more effective when combined with subsidies. For example, a United Kingdom study predicted relatively small effects of taxes on saturated fat, and larger effects of subsidies on fruit and vegetable intake (Tiffin and Arnoult 2011). OECD analyses on multiple countries also showed that coupling taxes on foods high in fat with subsidies on fruit and vegetables would lead to larger health and economic benefits (Cecchini et al. 2010; Sassi 2010). However, a Swedish study found that subsidizing wholewheat bread and cereal products in Sweden led to greater intake, but mostly among those who already consumed these products. It also led to greater intake of less healthy nutrients, such as salt and fat (Nordström and Thunström 2009, 2011). A small experimental study carried out in France suggests that subsidies for healthy foods are likely to be regressive, especially when combined with food taxes (Lacroix et al. 2010).

A recent systematic review of 'prices, demand and body weight outcomes' of a range of fiscal policies found that lower prices of fruit and vegetables were generally associated with lower weight outcomes, especially for children in low-income groups and for those with the highest levels of BMI (Powell et al. 2013).

Another action through which healthy foods could be made more affordable is to introduce financial incentives at the point of sale, such as price discounts and other promotions. European retailers have included this approach in their 'health and wellness' activities, but government policymakers have not given it major consideration.

A systematic review, which included only RCTs, found that incentives at point-of-sale have a positive effect on food purchasing patterns, though the evidence in support of sustained effects is more tenuous. It concluded that 'the small number of relevant studies precludes conclusions regarding the optimal characteristics, level or form of an incentive to achieve effect, particularly in diverse populations' (Wall et al. 2006). More experimental studies in the United States on price discounts in vending machines and other discrete settings confirm previous findings (French et al. 2010).

More recent studies on discounting in supermarkets and web-based simulated supermarkets indicate complex dynamics on impacts beyond the targeted food or nutrient. An RCT from New Zealand found that that subjects randomly assigned to receive price discounts in supermarkets bought significantly more predefined healthier foods at 6 months (11 per cent more) and 12 months (5 per cent more), whereas education had no effect on food purchases. Still, neither intervention had an effect on the amount of purchased saturated fat (Ni Mhurchu et al. 2010). In the Netherlands, an RCT in a web-based supermarket found that a 25 per cent price discount increased the purchased amount of fruit and vegetables, but did not change the purchasing of unhealthier food categories (Waterlander et al. 2012a). Another RCT in the same web-based supermarket, which included a combination of price discounts and price increases, found that discounts had the effect of increasing purchases of vegetables, but was associated with purchasing more calories overall, and there was no effect of increases in the prices of unhealthier foods (Waterlander et al. 2012b).

There is thus a moderate amount of evidence that financial incentives and disincentives at point of sale can influence purchasing patterns, but the full range of impacts on consumers is yet to be fully understood and appears to vary with intervention type.

Cost-effectiveness

The cost-effectiveness of food taxes has been assessed in a small number of modelling studies, all of which find taxes to have favourable cost-effectiveness ratios. A United States study comparing a sodium tax (assumed to produce a 6 per cent reduction in intake) with those of a voluntary sodium reduction programme by food manufacturers (assumed to produce a 9.5 per cent reduction) reached the conclusion that both strategies were cost-saving, with reduced medical expenditures of $22.4 billion ($22 billion in 2008 prices) and $32.6 billion ($32 billion in 2008 prices), respectively, and QALY gains of 1.3 and 2 million, over the lifetime of a cohort of individuals aged 40 to 85 (Smith-Spangler et al. 2010). An Australian study – part of the ACE Prevention programme – compared the effects of a tax on seven 'junk food' categories, leading to a 10 per cent price increase for all targeted products with those of a mandatory 'traffic-light' labelling scheme. Simulated steady-state policy scenarios were compared with current practice and were found to be cost-saving, with predicted reductions in health expenditures of $4,750 million ($A5,550 in 2003 prices) and $390 ($A455 million in 2003 prices), respectively for taxes and labelling, and DALY gains of 559,000 and 45,100 (Sacks et al. 2011).

Two of the cost-effectiveness studies examined the effects of taxes combined with subsidies. A series of multi-country studies of a tax on foods with high fat content leading to a 10 per cent price increase, combined with a subsidy on fruit and vegetables leading to a 10 per cent price reduction, found the strategy to be potentially cost-saving in all of the countries examined (Sassi et al. 2009a; Cecchini et al. 2010; Sassi 2010). The latter studies also showed that fiscal measures generate health gains more quickly than other policies aimed at improving nutrition, and have the potential for improving the health of people in disadvantaged socioeconomic conditions more than that of their better-off counterparts.

Cost-effectiveness analyses typically neglect broader welfare effects, which may be important in the case of taxation. A study that examined taxes on fats and sugar, tax reductions on fruit and vegetables, and subsidies on fibres, as well as revenue-neutral combinations of taxes and subsidies in Denmark (Jensen and Smed 2007), provided an assessment of net welfare costs, defined as the algebraic sum of variations in consumer surplus and fiscal revenues. For the same net welfare cost, a strategy involving a subsidy on fibres and a tax on saturated fat and sugar was predicted to yield the most desirable changes in nutrient consumption. A recent study of taxes on sugar-sweetened beverages in the United States estimated the welfare losses associated with a half-cent tax per ounce to amount to an average of $23.70 per household (Zhen et al. 2013), while a study assessing a range of possible food taxes in the United States concluded that the value of welfare losses would amount to up to half of the savings in health care expenditure generated by the tax (Okrent and Alston 2012).

Two cost-effectiveness studies were identified which examined subsidies alone, both for fruit and vegetables. An ACE Prevention study assessed the potential impact in Australia of a programme modelled on the above WIC scheme, assuming an equivalent effectiveness in changing consumer behaviour (although the evidence of such effectiveness provided by Herman et al. 2008, was found to be of limited strength). The study reached the conclusion that the programme would have an unfavourable cost-effectiveness ratio of $231,101 and $564,914 ($A270,000 and $A660,000 in 2003 prices) per DALY saved, respectively, for farmers' market and supermarket vouchers, but counting the subsidies delivered as costs (Cobiac et al. 2010b). Had subsidies been (more correctly) classified as transfers, the programme would have been shown to be cost saving.

A second study compared the effects on fruit and vegetable consumption and health of a €100/year stamp subsidy policy for low-income earners, a 3.4 per cent targeted VAT reduction, and a €10 million information campaign in France (Dallongeville et al. 2011). The study was based on an economic model accounting also for the effects of providing subsidies on market prices, which affect all consumers, but without accounting for impacts on health care expenditure and still counting subsidies and tax revenue reductions as costs (as in Cobiac et al. 2010b). The results of this study are broadly similar to those obtained in the Australian analysis, with an estimated cost-effectiveness ratio of $553,513 (€474,000 in 2006 prices) per life-year gained, substantially higher than those of reducing VAT of $116,774 (€100,000 in 2006 prices) and delivering an information campaign of $3,503–$31,529 (€3,000–€27,000 in 2006 prices). However, subsidies were shown to have the potential for reducing health disparities to some degree, while other strategies provided greater benefits to the better off.

Finally, in a study conducted in a United States supermarket, price discounts on fruit and vegetables, combined with promotional activities, were found to have a cost-effectiveness ratio of $2.14 million ($A2.5 million in 2003 prices) per DALY saved (Cobiac et al. 2010b).

Food product reformulation

Effectiveness

Potentially, food product reformulation could include any nutrient (or calories), but in practice, action in this area has concentrated on reduction in the level of salt and trans-fats in processed foods, with some attention being paid to portion size. At least 19 European countries have implemented salt reduction strategies (as well as over 10 other countries), all of which include targets for reformulation, usually by voluntary means (Webster et al. 2011). There has been far less action in Europe on trans-fats (Mendis et al. 2011), with the notable exception of Denmark, where the government imposed a maximum level of 2 g/100 g fat on industrially produced trans-fats in 2003. In the Netherlands there is also a Task Force for the Improvement of the Fatty Acid Composition, which encourages product reformulation on a voluntary basis. Outside of Europe there has been action in trans-fats in Latin America (Monge-Rojas et al. 2011) and North America. In Canada, there are voluntary targets for reduction, and in the United States there are some local bans on trans-fats. Mandatory labelling of trans-fats has also been reported to have stimulated voluntary reformulation by the food industry (Unnevehr and Jagmanaite 2008).

There are no systematic reviews of the effects of actions to reduce salt intake on dietary outcomes, but there are three reviews with examples of national actions taken to reduce salt, with information on the effects (He and MacGregor 2009; Mohan et al. 2009; Webster et al. 2011). Webster et al. (2011) reported that five countries, Finland, France, Ireland, Japan and the United Kingdom have demonstrated some impact of their salt reduction initiatives. In four cases, this includes evidence of changes in population salt consumption; in another four, changes in the salt levels in foods; and in two, changes in consumer awareness. Further analysis of the United Kingdom data conclude that the salt reduction initiative can be associated with reduced salt intakes, by approximately 10 per cent, with stronger impacts among women than among men (Shankar et al. 2012) and 'modest reductions in salt intake, although it is not clear precisely which aspects of the strategy contributed to this' (Millett et al. 2012).

There is no systematic review of the effectiveness of reformulation to reduce trans-fats, although there are general overviews (Unnevehr and Jagmanaite 2008; Mozaffarian et al. 2010; Remig et al. 2010; Tan 2011) and several evaluations of policy actions which indicate effects. An assessment of Denmark's trans-fat ban found that it virtually eliminated artificial trans-fat in the food supply by 2005, and lowered the average population intake of trans-fat to 0 g per day, with no disparity in the policy benefits across subgroups (Leth et al. 2006). There has also been a significant decline in trans-fat intake in the Netherlands, Canada, and the United States (Ratnayake et al. 2009; van Rossum et al. 2011; Vesper et al. 2012).

Cost-effectiveness

There are more studies on the cost-effectiveness of reformulation for salt than any other policy action, with all studies finding it to be cost-effective. One uses the WHO-CHOICE modelling methodology to make estimates for different world regions, including Europe, for both voluntary and legislative reduction of salt in processed foods (Murray et al. 2003).[2] The study assumed that the whole population (95 per cent) would be affected and would result in a 15 per cent reduction in salt intake for voluntary reduction, and 30 per cent for legislation. Costs included central administration and planning costs for voluntary reduction, and central administration, planning and enforcement costs for legislation – but in practice, the actual costs are assumed to be the same for both legislation and voluntary reduction. The study found that both voluntary and legislative reductions would be cost-effective, but legislation would be more cost-effective. The finding reflects the assumptions that the costs would be the same between voluntary reduction and legislation, but that the effects of legislation would be stronger.

Two studies were identified for specific European countries. One was a model-based study of a multi-component intervention in Norway. Selmer et al. (2000) modelled the effect of industry reformulation combined with an information campaign. The assumptions behind the effectiveness parameter were not explained. Costs were assumed to be $2.9 million per year on the basis of expert opinion. The actions were estimated to be cost saving.

The second study from a specific European country was based on actual data of costs and effects of the salt reduction initiative in the United Kingdom (Eatwell 2011). The estimate was made for both voluntary salt reduction by industry and an information campaign. The effects were based on actual measured declines of sodium intake (by around 10 per cent), and the costs used were those actually incurred by the relevant government agency, the Food Standards Agency. They included: costs incurred by research and development, production, media, marketing and PR and grants/partner funding. These costs were actually for the information campaign (industry costs were not included), and amounted to £20 million. On the basis that the salt reduction initiative saved 44,000 QALYs, it was found to be cost-effective. If savings to the National Health Service are included (£116 million), it was found to be 'dominant'.

Another study estimated the cost-effectiveness of a government industry initiative to reduce salt content in bread in Argentina (Rubinstein et al. 2010). The intervention was assessed alongside other interventions to reduce the burden of cardiovascular disease. It is not clear what the effectiveness parameter was; costs were reported to include programme-level expenses associated with management of the interventions and patient-level costs, although the source was not provided. Reducing salt in bread was found to be cost saving, and more cost-effective than any of the other interventions analysed.

Another study focused on developing countries only. It was a modelling study, but the assumptions and methods could not be identified. It found that a legislated reduction in salt content of manufactured foods and an accompanying public education campaign would be cost-effective (Willett et al. 2006).

There are also two studies for the United States – both modelling studies – though one was based on United Kingdom data. Smith-Spangler et al. (2010) assumed that the effects of voluntarily working with the food industry would be the same as in the United Kingdom (a reduction in intake of 9.5 per cent), and estimated costs by taking 15 per cent of the annual budget of the UK Food Standards Agency and converting it for the United States population. The intervention was assumed to affect the whole population aged between 40 and 85. Costs to food manufacturers were not included. The study found that voluntary reductions were cost-effective, and more cost-effective than a sodium tax. Bibbins-Domingo et al. (2010) also conducted a cost-effectiveness analysis of salt reduction in the United States, but for a 'population-wide regulatory approach to salt reduction' without any reference to any particular policy actions. It assumed that a national effort to reduce salt would lead to either a 1 g or 3 g decline in intake and that the cost would be \$1 per person per year (which does not include costs to industry). It found that salt reduction would be cost saving.

Most of these studies were included in a recent systematic review by Wang and Labarthe (2011), which concluded that 'literature provided economic evidence that was in favour of population-wide interventions designed to reduce sodium intake. Reducing the intake of sodium through such initiatives might be one of the best buys in public health. However, the small body of literature and hypothetical scenarios in most studies might limit policy implications of the findings.' (p.1693).

Just one study was identified that assessed the cost-effectiveness of the replacement of 2 per cent of dietary trans-fat from partial hydrogenation with polyunsaturated fat in manufactured foods. The methods were not described. The study found the measure to be cost-effective (Willett et al. 2006).

Conclusions

A considerable amount of evidence on the effectiveness and cost-effectiveness of policy actions to address unhealthy diets has become available since the mid-2000s. This chapter presents a review and assessment of that evidence. It finds a heterogeneous set of studies covering some, but not all, of the potential policy options.

The economic evidence available on policies aimed at affecting the market environment of food choices reveals generally positive results. Policies aimed at making fruit and vegetables more available in schools were found to have positive, albeit modest, effects on dietary intake. An evaluation in the Netherlands found these initiatives to be cost-effective, although the finding was sensitive to assumptions regarding the sustainability of dietary changes in the long term. Policies aimed at altering the prices of less healthy foods through the use of taxes were more thoroughly investigated by means of economic models. Existing studies show that taxes on foods high in salt, sugar and fat, and more broadly on 'junk food', are consistently cost saving – i.e. they cost less to implement than they save in terms of reduced health care expenditures, and they have a favourable health impact at the population level. Food taxes are likely to be regressive, although the less well-off also benefit disproportionately from their effects. The evidence shows they need to be designed carefully in order to avoid undesirable substitution effects in food consumption. Both the effectiveness and the distributional impact of taxes appear to be enhanced by coupling them with subsidies targeting healthy foods or disadvantaged consumers. Finally, product reformulation policies aimed at reducing the salt content of processed foods were found to be cost saving or to have a favourable cost-effectiveness ratio in several economic evaluations, although the economic evidence on other instances of reformulation (e.g. to reduce trans-fat content) is very limited.

The evidence from economic studies of information campaigns is more mixed. Some studies conclude that information campaigns can be cost-effective, but this is based on the low cost of these actions, with actual effectiveness being limited largely to impacts on knowledge and specific populations. Food labelling schemes were found to perform better in terms of cost-effectiveness, especially when implemented on a mandatory basis, but the studies available to support this claim are few and vary in the types of schemes assessed and methods applied. Restrictions in the commercial promotion of food, shown to be cost-effective in a small number of model-based economic studies focusing on food advertising to children, also appear to work better and are more efficient when implemented on a mandatory basis than through industry self-regulation.

The cost-effectiveness of some of the potential policy options has not been studied at all. Examples include interventions to change the 'architecture' of food choices, and which impose restrictions on the availability of snacks and drinks in schools (e.g. Jaime and Lock 2009; Chriqui 2012; Gittelsohn et al. 2012). Many also lack substantial effectiveness evidence. Particularly, critical gaps in the effectiveness evidence are those regarding agricultural and food-chain incentives, and more generally the effects of supply-side changes triggered by government policies, including, for instance, regulation of labelling and health claims. A further important gap is the broader effects of interventions on people's overall preferences and dietary habits, rather than specific foods or nutrients. This is especially challenging, because individuals make substitutions across different types of foods, which may cause interventions to have unintended consequences. In addition, heterogeneous intervention effects across individuals may produce undesirable distributional impacts. Finally, even where evidence is available it can suffer from a lack of generalizability and reliance on relatively weak investigation approaches.

The availability of evidence of effectiveness is a pre-requisite for sound economic evaluations. Where the former is weak, the latter will fail to provide the evidence required for action, and the review reported in this chapter shows that several of the existing economic evaluations had to make up for gaps in the effectiveness evidence by making extrapolations and assumptions.

The evidence reviewed in this chapter provides initial support for a limited set of policy actions aimed at improving the quality of people's diets. It is a useful starting point for setting a detailed research agenda, which will enable policymakers to consider a broader range of actions in the future, with a better knowledge base than we have at present of the full range of consequences those actions may produce.

Notes

1 National governments in the EU are not permitted to mandate such schemes, since nutrition labelling is regulated at the European level; European ministers voted to reject the requirement of front-of-pack labelling in the new regulations of 2011.
2 Ortegón et al. (2012) also generates estimates for voluntary and legislative reductions, but the results are not reported.

References

Accenture (2012) *2012 Compliance Monitoring Report For the International Food & Beverage Alliance On Global Advertising on Television*. Available at https://www.ifballiance.org/sites/default/files/AccentureMonitoringReport2012FINALDecember 2012.pdf [Accessed 13 October 2014].
Adams, J., Tyrrell, R., Adamson, A. J. and White, M. (2012) Effect of restrictions on television food advertising to children on exposure to advertisements for 'less healthy' foods: Repeat cross-sectional study, *PLoS ONE*, 7(2): e31578. doi:10.1371/journal.pone.0031578.
Allais, O., Bertail, P. and Nichele, V. (2010) The effects of a fat tax on French households' purchases: A nutritional approach, *American Journal of Agricultural Economics*, 92(1): 228–45.
Anderson, J., Parker, W., Steyn, N. P. et al. (2009) *Interventions on Diet and Physical Activity: What Works*. Geneva: World Health Organization.
Barquera, S., Hernandez-Barrera, L., Tolentino, M. L. et al. (2008) Energy intake from beverages is increasing among Mexican adolescents and adults, *Journal of Nutrition*, 138(12): 2454–61.
Barton, P., Andronis, L., Briggs, A., McPherson, K. and Capewell, S. (2011) Effectiveness and cost-effectiveness of cardiovascular disease prevention in whole populations: Modelling study, *British Medical Journal*, 343: d4044.
Bhattacharya, J. and Sood, N. (2005) *Health Insurance and the Obesity Externality*. NBER Working Paper No. 11529. Cambridge, MA: National Bureau of Economic Research.
Bibbins-Domingo, K., Chertow, G. M., Coxson, P. G. et al. (2010) Projected effect of dietary salt reductions on future cardiovascular disease, *New England Journal of Medicine*, 362(7): 590–9.
Bonsmann, S. S. G., Celemín, L. F., Larrañaga, A. et al. (2010) Penetration of nutrition information on food labels across the EU–27 plus Turkey, *European Journal of Clinical Nutrition*, 64(12): 1379–85.
Borgmeier, I. and Westenhoefer, J. (2009) Impact of different food label formats on healthiness evaluation and food choice of consumers: A randomized-controlled study, *BMC Public Health*, 9: 184.

Branca, F., Nikogosian, H. and Lobstein, T. (2007) *The Challenge of Obesity in the WHO European Region and the Strategies for Response.* Copenhagen: World Health Organization Regional Office for Europe.

Brownell, K. D., Farley, T., Willett, W. C. et al. (2009) The public health and economic benefits of taxing sugar-sweetened beverages, *The New England Journal of Medicine* Health Policy Report, 1–7.

Bruemmer, B., Krieger, J., Saelens, B. E. and Chan, N. (2012) Energy, saturated fat, and sodium were lower in entrées at chain restaurants at 18 months compared with 6 months following the implementation of mandatory menu labeling regulation in King County, Washington, *Journal of the Academy of Nutrition and Dietetics,* 112(8): 1169–76.

Brunello, G., Michaud, P. C. and Sanz-de-Galdeano, A. (2008) *The Rise in Obesity Across the Atlantic: An Economic Perspective.* IZA Discussion Paper No. 3529. Bonn: IZA.

Cairns, G., Angus, K. and Hastings, G. (2009) *The Extent, Nature and Effects of Food Promotion to Children: A Review of the Evidence to December 2008.* Geneva: World Health Organization.

Campos, S., Doxey, J. and Hammond, D. (2011) Nutrition labels on pre-packaged foods: A systematic review, *Public Health Nutrition,* 14(8): 1496–506.

Capacci, S., Mazzocchi, M., Shankar, B. et al. (2012) Policies to promote healthy eating in Europe: A structured review of policies and their effectiveness, *Nutrition Reviews,* 70(3): 188–200.

Cawley, J. (2004) An economic framework for understanding physical activity and eating behaviors, *American Journal of Preventive Medicine,* 27(3S): 117–25.

Cecchini, M., Sassi, F., Lauer, J. A., Lee, Y. Y., Guajardo-Barron, V. and Chisholm, D. (2010) Tackling of unhealthy diets, physical inactivity, and obesity: Health effects and cost-effectiveness, *The Lancet,* 376: 1775–84.

Chou, S.-Y., Rashad, I. and Grossman, M. (2008) Fast-food restaurant advertising on television and its influence on childhood obesity, *Journal of Law & Economics,* 51(4): 599–618.

Chriqui, J. (2012) *Influence of Competitive Food and Beverage Policies on Children's Diets and Childhood Obesity.* Healthy Eating Research Issue Brief No. 12. Minnesota: Healthy Eating Research. Available at http://healthyeatingresearch.org/wp-content/uploads/2013/12/Competitive_Foods_Issue_Brief_HER_BTG_7-2012-WEB.pdf [Accessed September 2014].

Christakis, N. A. and Fowler, J. H. (2007) The spread of obesity in a large social network over 32 years, *New England Journal of Medicine,* 357(4): 370–9.

Claro, R. M., Levy, R. B., Popkin, B. M. and Monteiro, C. A. (2012) Sugar-sweetened beverage taxes in Brazil, *American Journal of Public Health,* 102(1): 178–83.

Cobiac, L. J., Vos, T. and Veerman, J. L. (2010a) Cost-effectiveness of interventions to reduce dietary salt intake, *Heart,* 96(23): 1920–5.

Cobiac, L. J., Vos, T. and Veerman, J. L. (2010b) Cost-effectiveness of interventions to promote fruit and vegetable consumption, *PLoS One,* 5(11): e14148.

Cowburn, G. and Stockley, L. (2005) Consumer understanding and use of nutrition labelling: A systematic review, *Public Health Nutrition,* 8(1): 21–8.

Dallongeville, J., Dauchet, L., de Mouzon, O., Réquillart, V. and Soler, L. G. (2011) Increasing fruit and vegetable consumption: A cost-effectiveness analysis of public policies, *European Journal of Public Health,* 21(1): 69–73.

de Sa, J. and Lock, K. (2008) Will European agricultural policy for school fruit and vegetables improve public health? A review of school fruit and vegetable programmes, *European Journal of Public Health,* 18(6): 558–68.

Dhar, T. and Baylis, K. (2011) Fast-food consumption and the ban on advertising targeting children: The Quebec experience, *Journal of Marketing Research,* 48(5): 799–813.

Dharmasena, S. and Capps, O. Jr. (2011) Intended and unintended consequences of a proposed national tax on sugar-sweetened beverages to combat the US obesity problem, *Health Economics*, 21(6): 669–94.

Duffey, K. J., Gordon-Larsen, P., Shikany, J. M. et al. (2010) Food price and diet and health outcomes: 20 years of the CARDIA Study, *Archives of Internal Medicine*, 170(5): 420–6.

Dumanovsky, T., Huang, C. Y., Nonas, C. A., Matte, T. D., Bassett, M. T. and Silver, L. D. (2011) Changes in energy content of lunchtime purchases from fast food restaurants after introduction of calorie labelling: Cross sectional customer surveys, *British Medical Journal*, 343: d4464.

Eatwell (2011) *D2.3: Evaluation of Cost Utility of Policy Interventions*. Eatwell Project Report. Reading: Eatwell Project. Available at http://eatwellproject.eu/en/upload/Reports/D2.3_Evaluation_of_cost_utility_of_policy_interventions0%201.pdf [Accessed September 2014].

Effertz, T. and Wilcke, A.-C. (2011) Do television food commercials target children in Germany?, *Public Health Nutrition*, 15(8): 1466–73.

Engbers, L., van Poppel, M., Paw, M. and van Mechelen, W. (2006) The effects of a controlled worksite environmental intervention on determinants of dietary behavior and self-reported fruit, vegetable and fat intake, *BMC Public Health*, 6: 253.

Epstein, L. H., Dearing, K. K., Roba, L. G. and Finkelstein, E. (2010) The influence of taxes and subsidies on energy purchased in an experimental purchasing study, *Psychological Science*, 21(3): 406–14.

Epstein, L. H., Jankowiak, N., Nederkoorn, C., Raynor, H. A., French, S. A. and Finkelstein, E. (2012) Experimental research on the relation between food price changes and food-purchasing patterns: A targeted review, *American Journal of Clinical Nutrition*, [epub ahead of print].

EU Pledge (2012) *2012 Monitoring Report*. EU Pledge.

European Commission (EC) (2006) *Regulation (EC) No. 1924/2006 of the European Parliament and of the Council of 20 December 2006 on nutrition and health claims made on foods*. Available at http://eur-lex.europa.eu/LexUriServ/LexUriServ.do?uri=CONSLEG:2006R1924:20080304:EN:PDF [Accessed September 2014].

European Commission (EC) (2011) *Regulation (EU) No 1169/2011 of the European Parliament and of the Council of 25 October 2011 on the provision of food information to consumers*. Available at http://eur-lex.europa.eu/LexUriServ/LexUriServ.do?uri=CELEX:32011R1169:EN:NOT [Accessed September 2014].

European Commission (EC) (2012a) *European School Fruit Scheme: A Success Story for Children*. Brussels: European Union. Available at http://ec.europa.eu/agriculture/sfs/documents/leaflet_en.pdf [Accessed September 2014].

European Commission (EC) (2012b) *Report from the Commission to the European Parliament and the Council in Accordance with Article 184(5) of Council Regulation (EC) No. 1234/2007 on the Implementation of the European School Fruit Scheme*. Brussels: European Commission. Available at http://ec.europa.eu/agriculture/sfs/documents/documents/com2012–768_en.pdf [Accessed September 2014].

Evans, C. E., Christian, M. S., Cleghorn, C. L., Greenwood, D. C. and Cade, J. E. (2012) Systematic review and meta-analysis of school-based interventions to improve daily fruit and vegetable intake in children aged 5 to 12 y, *American Journal of Clinical Nutrition*, 96(4): 889–901.

Eyles, H., Ni Mhurchu, C., Nghiem, N. and Blakely, T. (2012) Food pricing strategies, population diets, and noncommunicable disease: A systematic review of simulation studies, *PLoS Medicine*, 9(12): e1001353. doi: 10.1371/journal.pmed.1001353.

Ezzati, M., Vander Hoorn, S., Lawes, C. M. M. et al. (2005) Rethinking the 'diseases of affluence' paradigm: Global patterns of nutritional risks in relation to economic development, *PLoS Medicine*, 2(5): 404–12.

FAO (2010) *Fats and Fatty Acids in Human Nutrition*. Food and Nutrition Paper 91. Rome: FAO.

Federal Trade Commission (FTC) (2012) *A Review of Food Marketing to Children and Adolescents: Follow-Up Report*. Washington, DC: Federal Trade Commission.

Finkelstein, E. A., Zhen, C., Bilger, M. et al. (2013) Implications of a sugar-sweetened beverage (SSB) tax when substitutions to non-beverage items are considered, *Journal of Health Economics*, 32(1): 219–39.

French, S. A., Hannan, P. J., Harnack, L. J., Mitchell, N. R., Toomey, T. L. and Gerlach, A. (2010) Pricing and availability intervention in vending machines at four bus garages, *Journal of Occupational and Environmental Medicine*, 52(Suppl. 1): S29–S33.

Fulponi, L. (2009) *Policy Initiatives Concerning Diet, Health and Nutrition*. OECD Food, Agriculture and Fisheries Working Papers, No. 14. Paris: OECD Publishing.

Giesen, J. C., Havermans, R. C., Nederkoorn, C. and Jansen, A. (2012) Impulsivity in the supermarket: Responses to calorie taxes and subsidies in healthy weight undergraduates, *Appetite*, 58(1): 6–10.

Giesen, J. C., Payne, C. R., Havermans, R. C. and Jansen, A. (2011) Exploring how calorie information and taxes on high-calorie foods influence lunch decisions, *American Journal of Clinical Nutrition*, 93(4): 689–94.

Gittelsohn, J., Rowan, M. and Gadhoke, P. (2012) Interventions in small food stores to change the food environment, improve diet, and reduce risk of chronic disease, *Preventing Chronic Disease*, 9:110015. doi: http://dx.doi.org/10.5888/pcd9.110015.

Goldman Sachs Group Inc. (2007) *Global: Food and Beverages*. London: Global Investment Research.

Grigg, D. (1995) The nutritional transition in Western Europe, *Journal of Historical Geography*, 21(3): 247–61.

Grunert, K. (2007) A review of European research on consumer response to nutrition information on food labels, *Journal of Public Health*, 15(5): 385–9.

Grunert, K. G., Sheperd, R., Traill, W. B. and Wold, B. (2012) Food choice, energy balance and its determinants: Views of human behaviour in economics and psychology, *Trends in Food Science and Technology*, 28(2): 132–42.

Grunert, K. G. and Wills, J. M. (2007) A review of European research on consumer response to nutrition information on food labels, *Journal of Public Health*, 15(5): 385–99.

Ha, D. A. and Chisholm, D. (2011) Cost-effectiveness analysis of interventions to prevent cardiovascular disease in Vietnam, *Health Policy Plan*, 26(3): 210–22

Harris, J. L., Schwartz, M. B., Brownell, K. D. et al. (2010) *Fast Food FACTS: Evaluating Fast Food Nutrition and Marketing to Youth*. New Haven, CT. Rudd Center for Food Policy and Obesity, Yale University.

Hawkes, C. (2010) Government and voluntary policies on nutrition labelling: A global overview, in J. Albert (ed.) *Innovations in Food Labelling*. Woodhead Food Series No. 184. Cambridge: Woodhead Publishing Limited.

Hawkes, C. (2012) Food taxes: What type of evidence is available to inform policy development?, *Nutrition Bulletin*, 37(1): 51–6.

Hawkes, C., Blouin, C., Henson, S., Drager, N. and Dubé, L. (eds) (2010) *Trade, Food, Diet and Health: Perspectives and Policy Options*. Oxford: Wiley Blackwell.

Hawkes, C., Chopra, M. and Friel, S. (2009) Globalization, trade and the nutrition transition, in R. Labonté, T. Schrecker, V. Runnels and C. Packer (eds) *Globalization and Health: Pathways, Evidence and Policy*. New York: Routledge, pp. 235–62.

Hawkes, C. and Lobstein, T. (2011) Regulating the commercial promotion of food to children: A survey of actions worldwide, *International Journal of Pediatric Obesity*, 6(2): 83–94.

Hawley, K. L., Roberto, C. A., Bragg, M. A., Liu, P. J., Schwartz, M. B. and Brownell, K. D. (2013) The science on front-of-package food labels, *Public Health Nutrition*, 16(3): 430–9.

He, F. J. and MacGregor, G. A. (2009) A comprehensive review on salt and health and current experience of worldwide salt reduction programmes, *Journal of Human Hypertension*, 23(6): 363–84.

Hebden, L., King, L., Grunseit, A., Kelly, B. and Chapman, K. A. (2011) Advertising of fast food to children on Australian television: The impact of industry self-regulation, *Medical Journal of Australia*, 195(1): 20–4.

Herman, D. R., Harrison, G. G., Afifi, A. A. and Jenks, E. (2008) Effect of a targeted subsidy on intake of fruits and vegetables among low-income women in the special supplemental nutrition program for women, infants, and children, *American Journal of Public Health*, 98(1): 98–105.

Howerton, M. W., Bell, B. S., Dodd, K. W., Berrigan, D., Stolzenberg-Solomon, R. and Nebeling, L. (2007) School-based nutrition programs produced a moderate increase in fruit and vegetable consumption: Meta and pooling analyses from 7 studies, *Journal of Nutrition Education and Behavior*, 39(4):186–96.

IFBA (2009) Compliance Monitoring of Global Advertising for Television, Print, and Internet for the International Food & Beverage Alliance. Brussels: IBFA. Available at https://www.ifballiance.org/sites/default/files/IFBA%20Compliance%20 Monitoring%20Report%2010%20Nov09.pdf [Accessed September 2014].

Jacobson, M. F. and Brownell, K. D. (2000) Small taxes on soft drinks and snack foods to promote health, *American Journal of Public Health*, 90(6): 854–7.

Jaime, P. C. and Lock, K. (2009) Do school based food and nutrition policies improve diet and reduce obesity?, *Preventive Medicine*, 48(1): 45–53.

Jensen, J. D. and Smed, S. (2007) Cost-effective design of economic instruments in nutrition policy, *International Journal of Behavioral Nutrition and Physical Activity*, 4(10). Available at http://www.ijbnpa.org/content/pdf/1479-5868-4-10.pdf [Accessed September 2014].

Kelly, B., Halford, J. C., Boyland, E. J. et al. (2010) Television food advertising to children: A global perspective, *American Journal of Public Health*, 100(9): 1730–6.

Kim, S., Lee, Y., Yoon, J., Chung, S. J., Lee, S. K. and Kim, H. (2013) Restriction of television food advertising in South Korea: Impact on advertising of food companies, *Health Promotion International*, 28(1): 17–25.

King, L., Hebden, L., Grunseit, A., Kelly, B., Chapman, K. and Venugopal, K. (2011) Industry self regulation of television food advertising: Responsible or responsive?, *International Journal of Pediatric Obesity*, 6(2): 390–8.

Lacroix, A., Muller, L. and Ruffieux, B. (2010) *To What Extent would the Poorest Consumers Nutritionally and Socially Benefit from Global Food Tax and Subsidy Reform? A Framed Field Experiment based on Daily Food Intake*. Grenoble: INRA-GAEL.

Landmark Europe (2010) *EU Pledge Monitoring Report 2010*. Brussels: Landmark Europe. Available at http://www.eu-pledge.eu/ [Accessed September 2014].

Leth, T., Jensen, H. G., Mikkelsen, A. A. and Bysted, A. (2006) The effect of the regulation on trans fatty acid content in Danish food, *Atherosclerosis Supplements*, 7: 53–6.

Magnus, A., Haby, M. M., Carter, R. and Swinburn, B. (2009) The cost-effectiveness of removing television advertising of high-fat and/or high-sugar food and beverages to Australian children, *International Journal of Obesity (Lond)*, 33(10): 1094–102.

Mann, J., Cummings, J. H., Englyst, H. N. et al. (2007) FAO/WHO scientific update on carbohydrates in human nutrition: conclusions, *European Journal of Clinical Nutrition*, 61(Suppl. 1): S132–S137.

Marshall, T. (2000) Exploring a fiscal food policy: The case of diet and ischaemic heart disease, *British Medical Journal*, 320(7230): 301–5.

McGinnis, J. M., Gootman, J. A. and Kraak, V. I. (2006) *Food Marketing to Children and Youth: Threat or Opportunity?* Washington, DC: National Academies Press.

Mendis, S., Puska, P. and Norrving, B. (eds) (2011) *Global Atlas on Cardiovascular Disease Prevention and Control.* Geneva: World Health Organization in collaboration with the World Heart Federation and the World Stroke Organization. Available at http://www.world-heart-federation.org/fileadmin/user_upload/documents/Publications/Global_CVD_Atlas.pdf [Accessed September 2014].

Millett, C., Laverty, A. A., Stylianou, N., Bibbins-Domingo, K. and Pape, U. J. (2012) Impacts of a national strategy to reduce population salt intake in England: Serial cross sectional study, *PLoS One*, 7(1): e29836. Epub 2012 Jan 4.

Mohan, S., Campbell, N. R. and Willis, K. (2009) Effective population-wide public health interventions to promote sodium reduction, *Canadian Medical Association Journal*, 181(9): 605–9.

Monge-Rojas, R., Colón-Ramos, U., Jacoby, E. and Mozaffarian, D. (2011) Voluntary reduction of trans-fatty acids in Latin America and the Caribbean: Current situation, *Revista Panamericana de Salud Publica*, 29(2): 126–9.

Mozaffarian, D., Afshin, A., Benowitz, N. L. et al. (2012) Population approaches to improve diet, physical activity, and smoking habits: A scientific statement from the American Heart Association, *Circulation*, 126(12): 1514–63.

Mozaffarian, D., Jacobson, M. F. and Greenstein, J. S. (2010) Food reformulations to reduce trans fatty acids, *New England Journal of Medicine*, 362(21): 2037–9.

Murray, C. J., Lauer, J. A., Hutubessy, R. C. et al. (2003) Effectiveness and costs of interventions to lower systolic blood pressure and cholesterol: A global and regional analysis on reduction of cardiovascular-disease risk, *The Lancet*, 361(9359): 717–25.

Mytton, O., Gray, A., Rayner, M. and Rutter, H. (2007) Could targeted food taxes improve health?, *Journal of Epidemiology and Community Health*, 61(8): 689–94.

Naska, A., Bountziouka, V. and Trichopoulou, A.; DAFNE Participants (2010) Soft drinks: Time trends and correlates in twenty-four European countries: A cross-national study using the DAFNE (Data Food Networking) databank, *Public Health Nutrition*, 13(9): 1346–55.

Nederkoorn, C., Havermans, R. C., Giesen, J. C. and Jansen, A. (2011) High tax on high energy dense foods and its effects on the purchase of calories in a supermarket: An experiment, *Appetite*, 56(3): 760–5.

Nethe, A., Dorgelo, A., Kugelberg, S. et al. (2012) Existing policies, regulation, legislation and ongoing health promotion activities related to physical activity and nutrition in pre-primary education settings: An overview, *Obesity Reviews*, 13(Suppl. 1): 118–28.

Ng, S. W., Ni Mhurchu, C., Jebb, S. A. and Popkin, B. M. (2011) Patterns and trends of beverage consumption among children and adults in Great Britain, 1986–2009, *British Journal of Nutrition*, 1–16. (Epub ahead of eprint)

Ni Mhurchu, C., Blakely, T., Jiang, Y., Eyles, H. C. and Rodgers, A. (2010) Effects of price discounts and tailored nutrition education on supermarket purchases: A randomized controlled trial, *American Journal of Clinical Nutrition*, 91(3): 736–47.

Ni Mhurchu, C. and Gorton, D. (2007) Nutrition labels and claims in New Zealand and Australia: A review of use and understanding, *Australian and New Zealand Journal of Public Health*, 31(2): 105–12.

Nnoaham, K. E., Sacks, G., Rayner, M., Mytton, O. and Gray, A. (2009) Modelling income group differences in the health and economic impacts of targeted food taxes and subsidies, *International Journal of Epidemiology*, 38(5): 1324–33.

Nordström, J. and Thunström, L. (2009) The impact of tax reforms designed to encourage healthier grain consumption, *Journal of Health Economics*, 28(3): 622–34.

Nordström, J. and Thunström, L. (2011) Economic policies for healthier food intake: The impact on different household categories, *European Journal of Health Economics*, 12(2): 127–40.

OECD (2011) *Evaluation of Agricultural Policy Reforms in the European Union*. Paris: OECD.

Ofcom (2010) *HFSS Advertising Restrictions: Final Review*. London: Ofcom.

Okrent, A. M. and Alston, J. M. (2012) The effects of farm commodity and retail food policies on obesity and economic welfare in the United States, *American Journal of Agricultural Economics*, 94(3): 611–46.

Oldroyd, J., Burns, C., Lucas, P., Haikerwal, A. and Waters, E. (2008) The effectiveness of nutrition interventions on dietary outcomes by relative social disadvantage: A systematic review, *Journal of Epidemiology & Community Health*, 62(7): 573–9.

Ortegón, M., Lim, S., Chisholm, D. and Mendis, S. (2012) Cost effectiveness of strategies to combat cardiovascular disease, diabetes, and tobacco use in sub-Saharan Africa and South East Asia: Mathematical modelling study, *British Medical Journal*, 344: e607. doi: 10.1136/bmj.e607.

PAHO (2012) *Recommendations from a Pan American Health Organization Expert Consultation on the Marketing of Food and Non-Alcoholic Beverages to Children in the Americas*. Washington, DC: PAHO.

Philipson, T. J. and Posner, R.A. (2008) Is the obesity epidemic a public health problem? A review of Zoltan J. Acs and Alan Lyles's *Obesity, Business and PublicPolicy*, *Journal of Economic Literature*, 46(4): 974–82.

Popkin, B. M. (2002) The shift in stages of the nutrition transition in the developing world differs from past experiences!, *Public Health Nutrition*, 5: 205–14.

Popkin, B. M. (2006) Global nutrition dynamics: The world is shifting rapidly toward a diet linked with noncommunicable diseases, *American Journal of Clinical Nutrition*, 84: 289–98.

Popkin, B. M. and Nielsen, S. J. (2003) The sweetening of the world's diet, *Obesity Research*, 11(11): 1325–32.

Pothoulaki, M.and Chryssochoidis, G. (2009) Health claims: Consumers' matters, *Journal of Functional Foods*, 1(2): 222–8.

Potvin Kent, M., Dubois, L. and Wanless, A. (2011) Food marketing on children's television in two different policy environments, *International Journal of Pediatric Obesity*, 6(2–2): e433–41.

Powell, L. M., Chriqui, J. F., Khan, T., Wada, R. and Chaloupka, F. J. (2013) Assessing the potential effectiveness of food and beverage taxes and subsidies for improving public health: A systematic review of prices, demand and body weight outcomes, *Obesity Reviews*, 14: 110–28.

Powell, L. M., Schermbeck, R. M., Szczypka, G., Chaloupka, F. J. and Braunschweig, C. L. (2011) Trends in the nutritional content of television food advertisements seen by children in the United States: Analyses by age, food categories, and companies, *Archives of Pediatrics and Adolescent Medicine*, 165(12): 1078–86.

Ratnayake, W. M., L'Abbe, M. R., Farnworth, S. et al. (2009) Trans fatty acids: Current contents in Canadian foods and estimated intake levels for the Canadian population, *Journal of AOAC International*, 92(5): 1258–76.

Regmi, A. (2008) *Convergence in Global Food Demand and Delivery*. Economic Research Report Number 56. Washington, DC: United States Department of Agriculture.

Regmi, A., Deepak, M. S., Seale, J. L. Jr. and Bernstein, J. (2001) Cross-country analysis of food consumption patterns, in A. Regmi (ed.) *Changing Structure of Global Food Consumption and Trade*. Washington DC: USDA, pp.14–22.

Remig, V., Franklin, B., Margolis, S., Kostas, G., Nece, T. and Street, J. C. (2010) Trans fats in America: A review of their use, consumption, health implications, and regulation, *Journal of the American Dietetic Association*, 110(4): 585–92.

Roberto, C. A., Bragg, M. A., Seamans, M. J., Mechulan, R. L., Novak, N. and Brownell, K. D. (2012) Evaluation of consumer understanding of different front-of-package nutrition labels, 2010–2011, *Preventing Chronic Disease*, 9: E149. doi: 10.5888/pcd9.120015.

Roberts, M., Pettigrew, S., Chapman, K., Miller, C. and Quester, P. (2012) Compliance with children's television food advertising regulations in Australia, *BMC Public Health*, 12: 846.

Romero-Fernández, M. M., Royo-Bordonada, M. A. and Rodríguez-Artalejo, F. (2010) Compliance with self-regulation of television food and beverage advertising aimed at children in Spain, *Public Health Nutrition*, 13(7): 1013–21.

Rubinstein, A., Colantonio, L., Bardach, A. et al. (2010) Estimation of the burden of cardiovascular disease attributable to modifiable risk factors and cost-effectiveness analysis of preventative interventions to reduce this burden in Argentina, *BMC Public Health*, 10: 627.

Rudd Center for Food Policy and Obesity (2013) *Pledges on food marketing to children worldwide*. Online resource available at http://www.yaleruddcenter.org/marketingpledges/ [Accessed September 2014].

Sacks, G., Rayner, M. and Swinburn, B. (2009) Impact of front-of-pack 'traffic-light' nutrition labelling on consumer food purchases in the UK, *Health Promotion International*, 24(4): 344–52.

Sacks, G., Veerman, J. L., Moodie, M. and Swinburn, B. (2011) 'Traffic-light' nutrition labelling and 'junk-food' tax: A modelled comparison of cost-effectiveness for obesity prevention, *International Journal of Obesity (Lond)*, 35(7).

Sassi, F. (2010) *Obesity and the Economics of Prevention: Fit not Fat*. Paris: OECD.

Sassi, F., Cecchini, M., Lauer, J. and Chisholm, D. (2009a) *Improving Lifestyles, Tackling Obesity: The Health and Economic Impact of Prevention Strategies*. OECD Health Working Papers, No. 48. Paris: OECD Publishing. Available at http://dx.doi.org/10.1787/220087432153 [Accessed September 2014].

Sassi, F., Devaux, M., Cecchini, M. and Rusticelli, E. (2009b) *The Obesity Epidemic: Analysis of Past and Projected Future Trends in Selected OECD Countries*. OECD Health Working Papers, No. 45. Paris: OECD Publishing. Available at http://dx.doi.org/10.1787/225215402672 [Accessed September 2014].

Sassi, F. and Hurst, J. (2008) *The Prevention of Lifestyle-Related Chronic Diseases: An Economic Framework*. OECD Health Working Papers, No. 32. Paris: OECD Publishing. Available at http://dx.doi.org/10.1787/243180781313 [Accessed September 2014].

Schmidhuber, J. and Shetty, P. (2010) The European Union's Common Agricultural Policy and the European diet: Is there a link?, in C. Hawkes, C. Blouin, S. Henson, N. Drager and L. Dubé (eds) *Trade, Food, Diet and Health: Perspectives and Policy Options*. Oxford: Wiley Blackwell, pp. 131–46.

Schmidhuber, J. and Traill, W. B. (2006) The changing structure of diets in the European Union in relation to healthy eating guidelines, *Public Health Nutrition*, 9(5): 58–9.

Selmer, R. M., Kristiansen, I. S., Haglerod, A. et al. (2000) Cost and health consequences of reducing the population intake of salt, *Journal of Epidemiology and Community Health*, 54(9): 697–702.

Shankar, B., Brambila-Macias, J., Traill, W. B., Mazzocchi, M. and Capacci, S. (2012) An evaluation of the UK Food Standards Agency's salt campaign, *Health Economics*, 22(2): 243–50.

Shepherd, J., Harden, A., Rees, R. et al. (2001) *Young People and Healthy Eating: A Systematic Review of Research on Barriers and Facilitators.* London: EPPI-Centre, Institute of Education, University of London.

Smith-Spangler, C. M., Juusola, J. L., Enns, E. A., Owens, D. K. and Garber, A. M. (2010) Population strategies to decrease sodium intake and the burden of cardiovascular disease: A cost-effectiveness analysis, *Annals of Internal Medicine*, 152(8): 481–7, W170–3.

Snelling, A. M. and Yezek, J. (2012) The effect of nutrient-based standards on competitive foods in 3 schools: Potential savings in kilocalories and grams of fat, *Journal of School Health*, 82(2): 91–6. doi: 10.1111/j.1746–1561.2011.00671.x.

Sutherland, L. A., Kaley, L. A. and Fischer, L. (2010) Guiding stars: The effect of a nutrition navigation program on consumer purchases at the supermarket, *American Journal of Clinical Nutrition*, 91(4): 1090S–1094S.

Swartz, J. J., Braxton, D. and Viera, A. J. (2011) Calorie menu labeling on quick-service restaurant menus: An updated systematic review of the literature, *International Journal of Behavioral Nutrition and Physical Activity*, 8: 135.

Tan, A. S. L. (2011) An approach to building the case for nutrition policies to limit trans-fat intake – A Singapore case study, *Health Policy*, 100(2–3): 264–72.

Temple, J. L., Johnson, K. M., Archer, K., Lacarte. A., Yi, C. and Epstein, LH. (2011) Influence of simplified nutrition labeling and taxation on laboratory energy intake in adults, *Appetite*, 57(1): 184–92.

te Velde, S. J., Lennert Veerman, J., Tak, N. I., Bosmans, J. E., Klepp, K. I. and Brug, J. (2011) Modeling the long term health outcomes and cost-effectiveness of two interventions promoting fruit and vegetable intake among schoolchildren, *Economics and Human Biology*, 9(1): 14–22.

Thorndike, A. N., Sonnenberg, L., Riis, J., Barraclough, S. and Levy, D. E. (2012) A 2-phase labeling and choice architecture intervention to improve healthy food and beverage choices, *American Journal of Public Health*, 102(3): 527–33.

Thow, A. M. (2012) *Fiscal Policy Levers to Improve Diets and Prevent Obesity.* AHHA Health Policy Research Institute, Evidence Brief no. 2. Available at http://ahha.asn. au/system/files/docs/publications/20120321_deeble_institute_evidence_brief_fiscal_ policy_measures_for_obesity.pdf [Accessed September 2014].

Thow, A. M., Jan, S., Leeder, S. and Swinburn, B. (2010) The effect of fiscal policy on diet, obesity and chronic disease: A systematic review, *Bulletin of the World Health Organization*, 88(8): 609–14.

Tiffin, R. and Arnoult, M. (2011) The public health impacts of a fat tax, *European Journal of Clinical Nutrition*, 65: 427–33.

Tsai, A. G., Williamson, D. F. and Glick, H. A. (2011) Direct medical cost of overweight and obesity in the USA: A quantitative systematic review, *Obesity Reviews*, 12(1): 50–61.

Tymms, S. (2012) *Responsible advertising to children: An independent review of the Australian food and beverage industry self-regulatory codes.* Available at http:// www.afgc.org.au/media-releases/1306-industry-surpassing-advertising-to-children-self-regulatory-initiatives.html [Accessed September 2014].

UK Department of Health (2008) *Changes in Food and Drink Advertising and Promotion to Children: A Report Outlining the Changes in the Nature and Balance of Food and Drink Advertising and Promotion to Children, from January 2003 to December 2007.* London: Department of Health.

Unnevehr, L. J. and Jagmanaite, E. (2008) Getting rid of trans fats in the US diet: Policies, incentives and progress, *Food Policy*, 33(6): 497–503.

US Department of Agriculture (USDA) and US Department of Health and Human Services (2010) *Dietary Guidelines for Americans, 2010*, 7th edn. Washington, DC: US Government Printing Office.

Van Cauwenberghe, E., Maes, L., Spittaels, H. et al. (2010) Effectiveness of school-based interventions in Europe to promote healthy nutrition in children and adolescents: Systematic review of published and 'grey' literature, *British Journal of Nutrition*, 103(6): 781–97.

van Rossum, C., Fransen, H. P., Verkaik-Kloosterman, J., Buurma-Rethans, E. J. M. and Ocké, M. (2011) *Dutch National Food Consumption Survey 2007–2010: Diet of Children and Adults aged 7 to 69 Years*. Bilthoven: National Institute for Public Health and the Environment. Available at http://www.rivm.nl/bibliotheek/rapporten/350050006.pdf [Accessed September 2014].

Veerman, J. L., Van Beeck, E. F., Barendregt, J. J. and Mackenbach, J. P. (2009) By how much would limiting TV food advertising reduce childhood obesity?, *European Journal of Public Health*, 19(4): 365–9.

Vesper, H. W., Kuiper, H. C., Mirel, L. B., Johnson, C. L. and Pirkle, J. L. (2012) Levels of plasma trans-fatty acids in non-Hispanic white adults in the United States in 2000 and 2009, *JAMA*, 307(6): 562–3.

Vorley, B. (2003) *Food, Inc.: Corporate Concentration from Farm to Consumer*. London: IIED.

Vyth, E. L., Steenhuis, I. H., Brandt, H. E., Roodenburg, A. J., Brug, J. and Seidell, J. C. (2012) Methodological quality of front-of-pack labeling studies: A review plus identification of research challenges, *Nutrition Reviews*, 70(12): 709–20.

Wall, J., Mhurchu, C. N., Blakely, T., Rodgers, A. and Wilton, J. (2006) Effectiveness of monetary incentives in modifying dietary behavior: A review of randomized, controlled trials, *Nutrition Reviews*, 64(12): 518–31.

Wang, G. and Labarthe, D. (2011) The cost-effectiveness of interventions designed to reduce sodium intake, *Journal of Hypertension*, 29(9): 1693–9.

Waterlander, W. E., Steenhuis, I. H., de Boer, M. R., Schuit, A. J. and Seidell, J. C. (2012a) The effects of a 25% discount on fruits and vegetables: Results of a randomized trial in a three-dimensional web-based supermarket, *International Journal of Behavioral Nutrition and Physical Activity*, 9(1): 11.

Waterlander, W. E., Steenhuis, I. H., de Boer, M. R., Schuit, A. J. and Seidell, J. C. (2012b) Introducing taxes, subsidies or both: The effects of various food pricing strategies in a web-based supermarket randomized trial, *Preventive Medicine*, 54(5): 323–30.

Webster, J. L., Dunford, E. K., Hawkes, C. and Neal, B. C. (2011) Salt reduction initiatives around the world, *Journal of Hypertension*, 29(6): 1043–50.

Willett, W. C., Koplan, J. P., Nugent, R., Dusenbury, C., Puska, P. and Gaziano, T. A. (2006) Prevention of chronic disease by means of diet and lifestyle changes, in D. T. Jamison, J. G. Breman, A. R. Measham et al. (eds) *Disease Control Priorities in Developing Countries*. Washington, DC: World Bank, pp. 833–50.

Williams, P. (2005) Consumer understanding and use of health claims for foods, *Nutrition Reviews*, 63(7): 256–64.

Wills, J. M., Storcksdieck Genannt Bonsmann, S., Kolka, M. and Grunert, K. G. (2012) European consumers and health claims: Attitudes, understanding and purchasing behaviour, *Proceedings of the Nutrition Society*, 5: 1–8. [Epub ahead of print]

Withrow, D. and Alter, D. (2010) The economic burden of obesity worldwide: A systematic review of the direct costs of obesity, *Obesity Reviews* (epub ahead of print).

Wootan, M. G., Reger-Nash, B., Booth-Butterfield, S. and Cooper, L. (2005) The cost-effectiveness of 1% or less media campaigns promoting low-fat milk consumption, *Preventing Chronic Disease*, 2(4): A05.

World Cancer Research Fund (WCRF) and American Institute for Cancer Research (AICR) (2007) *Food, Nutrition, Physical Activity and the Prevention of Cancer: A Global Perspective: Second Expert Report*. Washington, DC: AICR.

World Health Organization (WHO) (2007) Economic consequences of obesity, in F. Branca, H. Nikogosian and T. Lobstein (eds) *The Challenge of Obesity in the European Region and the Strategies for Response.* Copenhagen: World Health Organization Regional Office for Europe, pp. 28–34.

World Health Organization (WHO) (2009) *Global Health Risks: Mortality and Burden of Disease Attributable to Selected Major Risks.* Geneva: WHO. Available at http://www.who.int/healthinfo/global_burden_disease/GlobalHealthRisks_report_full.pdf [Accessed September 2014].

World Health Organization (WHO) (2010) *Global Status Report on Noncommunicable Diseases 2010.* Geneva: World Health Organization.

World Health Organization (WHO)/FAO (2003) *Diet, Nutrition and the Prevention of Chronic Diseases: Report of a Joint WHO/FAO Expert Consultation.* WHO Technical Report Series, 916. Geneva: World Health Organization.

World Health Organization Regional Office for Europe (WHO EURO) (2006) *Gaining Health: The European Strategy for the Prevention and Control of Noncommunicable Diseases.* Copenhagen: World Health Organization Regional Office for Europe.

World Health Organization Regional Office for Europe (WHO EURO) (2011) Action plan for implementation of the European Strategy for the Prevention and Control of Noncommunicable Diseases 2012–2016. Regional Committee for Europe EUR/RC61/12, Sixty-first session, Baku, Azerbaijan, 12–15 September.

Zhen, C., Finkelstein, E. A., Nonnemaker, J. M. et al. (2013) Predicting the effects of sugar-sweetened beverage taxes on food and beverage demand in a large demand system, *American Journal of Agricultural Economics*, advanced access.

chapter eight

Addressing environmental risks for child health

Leonardo Trasande and
Zachary Brown

Introduction

The unique vulnerability of children to environmental hazards has been documented in many scientific studies and government reports, including a landmark 1993 US National Academy of Sciences report on pesticide exposures (National Research Council 1993). Children drink more water, breathe more air and eat more food per unit of body weight, exposing their organ systems to a range of environmental hazards – from unsafe drinking water to air pollution – at relatively high rates compared to adults (Thurlbeck 1982; Trasande and Thurston 2005). Furthermore, behaviours specific to young children, such as crawling on the ground and frequent hand-to-mouth activity, expose them to some toxins, such as lead paint in homes, at rates which are high by any measure (Grandjean and Landrigan 2007). Their developing organs and immune systems are also more susceptible to the hazardous effects of these exposures (Goldman et al. 2004). Children also have greater years of life in which chronic conditions can occur as a result of early life exposures to environmental hazards (Bearer 1995). Both higher exposure to these hazards and their more far-reaching impacts for children increase the likelihood of lifelong impairment of respiratory, neurologic, immune, and other organ systems (Martinez 2009).

This chapter presents scientific and economic evidence on the impacts of environmental hazards to child health, and interventions for their prevention. While environmental hazards can be broadly defined, this chapter concentrates on environmental chemical contaminants which are intentionally or unintentionally produced by human activities.[1] Quantitative estimates of disease burden and intervention effectiveness associated with four specific risks are summarized:

- Impacts on children due to mercury emitted from anthropogenic sources.
- Children's exposure to lead.
- Respiratory health consequences of air pollution exposure in early life.
- Children's exposure to commercial chemicals in the environment.

These risks were selected based on evidence of their substantial (if sometimes poorly understood) health impacts, the availability of effective interventions to control them, and their relevance in current global policy discourses. In addition, these hazards illustrate unique aspects of environmental hazards for child health, since the dominant interventions consist of policies to regulate and incentivize pollution abatement.

Evidence is first presented on how mercury pollution, lead exposure, outdoor air pollutants and uncontrolled diffusion of commercial chemicals into the environment, affect children's health and their future well-being. In contrast to much of the other evidence in this book, with the exception of the chapter on road-related injuries, the research summarized here often evaluates the health impacts of these exposures in monetary terms (e.g., reduction in wages due to intelligence quotient (IQ) loss associated with early life exposure) rather than disability-adjusted life-years (DALYs) or quality-adjusted life-years (QALYs), the morbidity measures used in the majority of this book.[2] The chapter then presents available policy interventions for abating mercury, lead and outdoor air pollution, as well as for improving the control of hazards from commercial chemicals. For each intervention described, the estimated effectiveness and economic cost is presented. Throughout the chapter, important limitations are highlighted concerning the scientific evidence on environmental hazards to children, as well as historical and political factors that have led to evidence being translated to action.

Impacts on children of selected environmental contaminants

Mercury emissions from anthropogenic sources

Mercury (Hg) is a ubiquitous environmental toxicant (Goldman and Shannon 2001) which exists in three general forms with different bioavailability and toxicity profiles: the metallic element, inorganic Hg and organic Hg. Coal-fired power and chloralkali plants are major point sources of elemental and inorganic Hg release to the environment (EPA 1997, 2003). Other sources include: artisanal mining, which is usually small-scale independent mining relying on the use of hand-held tools (Roulet et al. 1999, 2000), volcanic emissions (Nriagu and Pacyna 1988; Nriagu 1989), and forest fires (Fostier et al. 2000; Roulet et al. 2000). In the atmosphere, elemental Hg is converted to inorganic ('reactive') forms that eventually deposit into soil/water through rain, snow or terrestrial run-off. A portion of the Hg is then microbially transformed to an organic form, methylmercury (MeHg) (Guimaraes et al. 2000). MeHg biomagnifies in the marine food chain, and the highest concentrations are generally found in predatory fish such as swordfish, carp, king mackerel and shark (Mason et al. 1995; Neumann and Ward 1999; Dietz et al. 2000; Gilmour and Riedel 2000). Consumption of contaminated fish is the most important route of human exposure to MeHg (Trasande et al. 2005).

The health burden of mercury emissions from coal burning has been estimated to be substantial. In the USA, Trasande et al. (2005) used an environmentally attributable fraction model to quantify the impact of methylmercury toxicity to the cohort of children born in 2000. Using a cost-of-illness approach, they then quantified lost economic productivity produced as a result of methylmercury-associated cognitive impairment, and identified the fractions of the lost economic productivity that could be attributed to all anthropogenic sources, including American anthropogenic sources and, in particular, American coal-fired power plants. They found that over 600,000 children suffered decrements in IQ ranging from 0.2 to 5.1 points, with a resultant $10.75 billion ($8.7 billion in 2000 prices) loss in economic productivity. Of this total, 15 per cent ($2.1 to $1.3 billion in 2000 prices) could be attributed to American coal-fired power plant emissions. Subsequent analyses quantified additional costs attributable to increases in the number of children with subnormal IQs (and who receive additional health, education and other services due to intellectual disability) as well as estimates of economic benefits that would be produced by proposed regulations on mercury emissions (Landrigan et al. 2006; Trasande et al. 2006).

In Europe, as in the United States, coal burning remains a dominant source of electricity, with similar implications for childhood exposure to mercury. Ronchetti et al. (2006) report that in five European countries – Belgium, Germany, Italy, Norway and Portugal – average daily intake of methylmercury among adults is in excess of the threshold of 0.1 µg/kg of body mass set by the US Environmental Protection Agency (EPA). The EPA threshold is set based on studies analyzing, among other things, the effect of maternal mercury exposure on childhood development (EPA 2010).

In other parts of the world, mercury emissions are an increasing concern with the need to produce a larger amount of electricity in the rapidly industrializing countries. The global costs from loss of productivity due to mercury pollution have been documented to amount to as much as $32.4 billion ($29.4 billion in 2005 prices) by 2020 (Pacyna et al. 2008), while reductions in emissions could contribute $2.0 to 2.4 billion ($1.8 to $2.2 billion in 2005 prices) annually in global economic benefits in 2020, with similar benefits for subsequent cohorts of children born with lower levels of exposure from their mothers who ingest less contaminated fish (Sundseth et al. 2010).

Lead in petrol and paint

Lead is similar to methylmercury in that it is a toxic element which can impair neurological and cognitive function when absorbed by the human body. The dominant exposure pathways for lead, however, differ from those associated with mercury. Modern-day exposure pathways in children have been mostly through leaded petrol (gasoline) and lead-based paint in older homes.

Estimates from various sources compiled in Table 8.1 show that 17 per cent of children under 15 years of age in low- and middle-income countries in the European region had blood lead levels (BLLs) above 5 µg/dL, while 2 per cent had levels above 10 µg/dL. The BLL is a measure of how much lead is circulating in a person's bloodstream, which provides an indicator of exposure. Although BLLs above 10 µg/dL are generally viewed as causing serious impairment, government studies have found no level of lead exposure which is 'safe', and cognitive impairment has been documented at levels between 2 and 10 µg/dL

(Lanphear et al. 2005; Binns et al. 2007; Bellinger 2008). In terms of mortality and morbidity effects, 34,000 DALYs were lost in 2004 among low- and middle-income countries of the European region due to lead exposure among children less than five years of age (WHO 2012).

In previous decades, the primary source of lead exposure in high-income countries was from petrol, but at the time of writing only seven countries worldwide do not require the de-leading of petrol (UNEP 2013a). Indeed, this signifies one of the landmark successes in children's environmental health. A short history and economic evaluation of de-leading gasoline is taken up in a subsequent section of this chapter.

Today, lead paint in homes is the major source of childhood lead exposure globally, including in high-income countries. In the United States, it has been estimated that $12 to $57 billion ($11 to $53 billion in 2006 prices) in annual health care costs can be attributed to lead poisoning in children under 6 years of age, primarily via paint in homes (Gould 2009). Additionally, Gould calculated the present value of lost lifetime earnings to exceed $176 billion ($165 billion in 2006 prices) among the 24.7 per cent of United States children estimated to have BLLs between 2 and 10 µg/d L at the time of the study. For this calculation, the author used a relationship between childhood BLLs and future IQ that had previously been estimated based on pooled international data (Lanphear et al. 2005). This empirical relationship is useful to note when considering extrapolation of lead poisoning burden estimates to other countries.

For other countries, few reports are available concerning the health burden attributable to childhood exposure to lead-based paint. For France, Pichery et al. (2011) conducted an exercise, similar to Gould's, and estimated the total monetized benefits in 2008 of lead abatement in homes to be in excess of $25.2 billion (€22.72 billion in 2008 prices), using a threshold BLL value of 15 µg/dL (well above that at which cognitive impairment is known to occur). If United States-based estimates provide any guide for European exposure sources, then the majority of lead exposure in children in Europe can be attributed to lead in the home. It is therefore reasonable to infer that contaminated homes are the likely cause of the BLLs observed for some European countries, and displayed in Table 8.1.

Early life exposure to outdoor air pollution

The biological basis of children's unique vulnerability to outdoor air pollution (e.g. ozone and fine particulate matter) is well documented (National Research Council 1993). Higher minute ventilation and food/water ingestion per unit of body weight, the vulnerability of developing organ systems (Thurlbeck 1982), and the greater number of years of life in which children can manifest consequences are among the biological bases for this vulnerability. Birth to the age of two to three years is the period of greatest alveolar multiplication (Thurlbeck 1982). Injury to alveoli (the gas-exchange structure of the lungs) during this period can produce an acquired deficit in lung growth, accelerated decline in lung function (Gauderman et al. 2004) and predispose a child to the development of chronic obstructive pulmonary disease in adulthood (Martinez 2009). The evidence is greatest for exacerbation of asthma in already affected children, though at

Table 8.1 Data available on blood lead levels in children/adults in European population surveys; NR = not recorded; P95 = 95th percentile

Country	Mean/median blood Pb (micrograms/dL)	95% CI for mean (or 95th percentile)	Age group	Gender	Year	Source
Belgium	1.82	P95 = 4.79	14–15 years	female	2002–2006	(Smolders et al. 2010)
Cyprus	1.7	NR	2–6 years	non-specified	2001	(Demoliou and Charalambous 2004)
Cyprus	2.2	NR	2–6 years	non-specified	2010	(Demoliou and Charalambous 2004)
Czech Republic	2.48	NR	adults	female	2007	(Bierkens et al. 2011)
Denmark	26.39		adults	female	1994	(Smolders et al. 2010)
Finland	2.23	NR	pre-school children	non-specified	1999	(Bierkens et al. 2011)
France	1.51	NR	children	non-specified	2008–9	(Pichery et al. 2011)
Germany	3.1	P95 = 5.7	6-year-old children	non-specified	2000	(Schulz et al. 2009)
Italy	2.35	P95 = 5.2	adults	female	2004	(Smolders et al. 2010)
Netherlands	2.4	P95 = 45	pre-school children	non-specified	2001	(Smolders et al. 2010)
Poland	3.48	NR	pre-school children	non-specified	2002 and 2004	(Bierkens et al. 2011)
Portugal	2.4 (median)	P95 = 5.0	1–2 years	non-specified	2006–7	(Smolders et al. 2010)
Slovakia	2.79 (median)	P95 = 6.2	adults	female	2001–5	(Smolders et al. 2010)
Sweden	1.53 (median)	P95 = 5.3	adults	female	2004	(Smolders et al. 2010)
United Kingdom	1.7	0.6–2.4	2 years old	non-specified	1991	(Bost et al. 1999)

European countries with air pollution attributable consequences

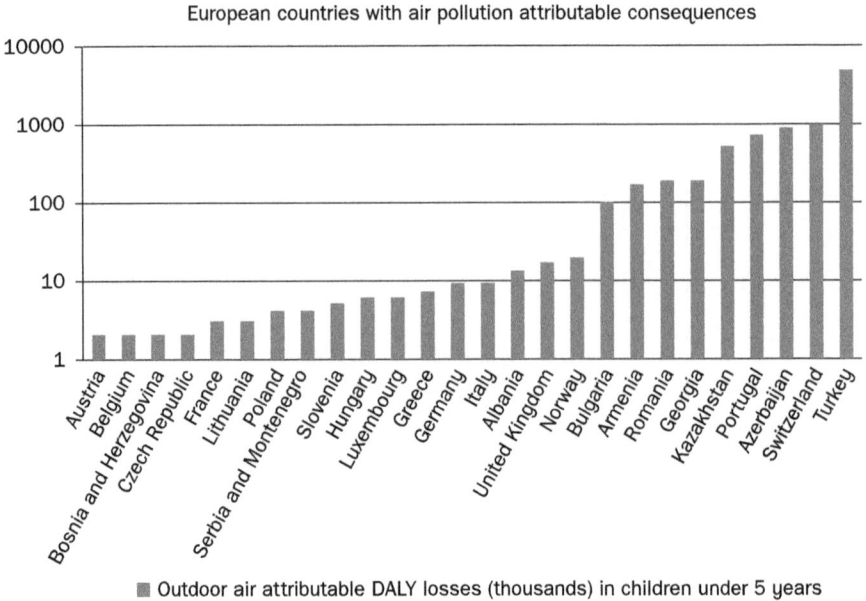

■ Outdoor air attributable DALY losses (thousands) in children under 5 years

Figure 8.1 Disability life-year losses in children <5 years of age, by country within the European Region

least one study has suggested a possible role for ozone in the development of childhood asthma (Thurston et al. 1997; Trasande and Thurston 2005).

Figure 8.1 presents data on outdoor air pollution associated losses in DALYs as has been quantified across the European region by the World Health Organization. Across the European Region, 8.7 million DALYs were lost in children under five years of age due to outdoor air pollution. These losses are concentrated in low- and middle-income countries in the region. Furthermore, despite progressively stricter vehicle emissions standards and higher motor fuel taxes in the last several decades, ground-level ozone – a major air pollutant associated with motor vehicle emissions – is expected to increase by 35 per cent in large cities throughout OECD countries between 2010 and 2050, assuming no new policies are introduced to control this pollution (OECD 2012b).

Early life exposure to commercial chemicals

Many commercial chemical ingredients in pesticides, flame retardants, and plastics are known to cause chronic and acute diseases in children (and adults) under certain exposure scenarios. Prüss-Ustun and colleagues estimate that the global burden of disease attributable to unintentional acute chemical poisoning and preventable through improved safety standards in 2004 was 5.2 million DALYs, with 19 per cent of this total being concentrated in children (Prüss-Ustun et al. 2011). They also conclude that over three-quarters of this burden could have been avoided through improved chemicals safety standards.

In addition to their acute impacts, commercial chemicals are likely to have a range of negative chronic impacts, though measuring them is more difficult than for acute effects. In the absence of a regulatory structure that assesses toxicity prior to approval of any chemicals for their widespread use (EPA 2012c), decades of epidemiologic data typically are required before acknowledgement of possible causation is typically made (Trasande 2011; Trasande and Liu 2011). Outcomes of concern routinely have multiple potential confounders, and satisfying criteria of reproducibility and consistency (Hill 1965) before proactive policy prevention further widens the time lag between harmful exposures and confirmation of health impacts.

Nevertheless, a growing body of peer-reviewed research is identifying negative health outcomes from exposure to a range of useful chemicals. In industrialized countries, the prevalence and incidence of chronic health conditions have increased with temporal consistency to suggest potential causation by chemical exposure. Asthma prevalence has tripled (Akinbami et al. 2009), increases in certain birth defects have been detected (Paulozzi et al. 1997; Williams et al. 2005), and increases in leukemias (Matasar et al. 2006), as well as brain (Schechter 1999) and testicular cancer have been observed (Devesa et al. 2003). Obesity has tripled in prevalence among US children (Hedley et al. 2004; Ogden et al. 2010), with emerging laboratory and modest epidemiologic evidence raising cause for concern about the role of endocrine disrupting chemicals (Trasande et al. 2009). The US National Academy of Sciences has estimated that 28 per cent of developmental disabilities are due, at least in part, to environmental factors (National Academy of Sciences 2000). Epidemiologic studies have associated exposure to benzene (Savitz and Feingold 1989; Knox 2005), certain pesticides (Lee et al. 2004; Rudant et al. 2007), polychlorinated biphenyls (Ward et al. 2009), and 1,3-butadiene (Robison et al. 1995) with increases in childhood malignancies.

Effective interventions to limit environmental hazards to children's health

Reducing childhood exposure to mercury

Because most childhood mercury exposure in high- and middle-income countries is due indirectly to the burning of coal (as summarized above), the logical approach to dealing with mercury hazards is to abate emissions at coal-fuelled power plants. This can be done by burning less or cleaner coal, or by capturing mercury during combustion. Table 8.3 presents the economic burden of mercury pollution prevention alongside potential intervention costs and benefits.

Currently, the most effective technology for removal during combustion is via the use of activated carbon injection (ACI) filters, which remove over 80 per cent of mercury from emissions (EPA 2007). The long-run cost of mercury removal via ACI is difficult to estimate, because it has been introduced relatively recently and because little legislation has been enacted to incentivize cost-saving research and development: one study, funded by the US Department of

Table 8.2 Summary of impacts of selected environmental risks to children's health

Risk factor	Estimated impacts and costs of risk factor in Europe	Source
Exposure to lead (e.g. through air pollution and lead-based paint and plumbing in homes)	37,189,000 DALYs lost globally in 2004 due to cognitive impairment from childhood exposure.	(Prüss-Ustun et al. 2011)
Methylmercury exposure from coal-fired power plants	Global loss of productivity due to cognitive impairment from childhood exposure could amount to as much as $32.7 billion by 2020.	(Pacyna et al. 2008)
Exposure to air pollution from vehicle emissions	In 2004, 8.7 million DALYs were lost in European children under five years of age due to outdoor air pollution.	(WHO 2012)
Childhood exposure to commercial chemicals	1.4 million DALYs lost in 2004 worldwide due to acute chemical poisonings in children.	(Prüss-Ustun et al. 2011)

Energy, estimated that the cost of using ACI in United States coal-fired power plants was between $8,735 and $381,000 ($8,400 and $366,000 in 2007 prices) per kg of mercury removed (Jones et al. 2007).

Mercury removal is also a 'co-benefit' of other emissions abatement technologies for coal burning, such as the use of SO_2 and NO_x scrubbers. It has been alleged, for example, that European mercury emissions declined by as much as 70 per cent since the 1970s as the result of particulate matter controls (Sloss 2003). Experts generally agree these co-benefit approaches currently provide the cheapest means of mercury abatement in emissions, but are unlikely to achieve the levels of effectiveness possible with a dedicated mercury-removal technology (Pacyna et al. 2010). The EPA maintains cost and mercury removal information on ACI as well as on other technologies in its freely distributed software program CUECost (Yelverton 2009).

The large uncertainty in the economic costs of mercury abatement reflects a short history and lack of experience with direct regulation of mercury emissions. In general, establishing a tax or a tradable permit system for mercury emissions from power plants would provide an economic mechanism by which to drive down the costs of abatement, as has been shown with SO_2 and NO_x control in the USA and Europe. A review by Burtraw and Szambelan (2009) of the effectiveness of the US SO_2 tradable permit system concludes that the program decreased costs by 43–55 per cent relative to a counterfactual policy of capping SO_2 emissions at each power plant. Rezek and Campbell (2007) caution, however, that homogeneity of mercury abatement costs across power plants in the USA may limit similar cost savings from a tradable permit system for mercury, relative to a simple 'command-and-control' regulation (i.e., a plant-level cap). Economic models have been formulated to forecast the permit price for emitting 1 kg of mercury (since the permit price should reflect the opportunity cost of mercury emissions), but these forecasts exhibit levels of uncertainty even larger than those associated with ACI costs, e.g. $3,773 to $327,600 ($2,943 to $255,526 in 1998 prices) per kg of mercury emitted (Rezek and Campbell 2007). Furthermore, research in the EU has suggested that *ex ante* forecasts like these often overestimate the *ex post* compliance costs for proposed environmental policies (OECD 2006).

Only a few published estimates are available of either the cost-effectiveness (CE) or return on investment (ROI) from mercury abatement, both of which require an impact assessment of proposed or existing interventions. Part of the reason for this gap in the literature is because the impact on human health from mercury emitted through coal combustion is mediated by complex ecological factors, since most exposure occurs through fish consumption. The only impact assessment and subsequent ROI analysis which the authors are aware of was published in 2011 by the US Environmental Protection Agency as part of its Mercury and Air Toxics Standards (MATS), which enter into force in 2016. These standards set the first-ever limits on mercury emissions from electricity generation in the United States. In this document, the EPA estimates initial annualized compliance costs associated with these standards are $10 billion ($9.6 billion in 2007 prices) in 2015, whereas the predicted health benefits of MATS – which account for avoided IQ loss only among children exposed to recreationally caught freshwater fish – are forecast to exceed $38 billion ($37 billion in 2007 prices) per year. However, it is important to note that the majority of predicted health impacts of MATS derive from co-benefits associated with a reduction in very fine particulate matter pollution, not from the abatement of mercury itself (EPA 2011).

Internationally, the United Nations Environment Programme (UNEP) coordinated negotiations towards a legally binding global mercury treaty, including standards for mercury abatement from coal combustion (UNEP 2011). This resulted in the Minimata Convention on Mercury being formally adopted in international law in October 2013 (UNEP 2013b). The treaty is named after the Japanese city of Minimata, which experienced one of the world's worst cases of mercury poisoning in the 1950s. However, the authors of this chapter are not aware of any impact analyses of the policies contained in this treaty.

Aside from abatement of emissions from coal burning, there is also a role for alternative approaches to reducing mercury contamination in certain contexts – for example, adopting mercury-free gold-mining technologies (Rickford 2006) and reducing mercury emissions from incineration. Insofar as the costs of implementation are modest and the technology is easily transferred to the developing world context, the benefits of such an intervention, even at slightly higher cost, could produce long-term cognitive and economic productivity benefits that outweigh these costs. Again, formal *ex post* impact analyses on these technologies remain lacking.

Reducing childhood exposure to lead

As discussed above, childhood exposure to lead from petrol combustion has been drastically reduced, while lead-based paint and plumbing in homes continues to impose a significant health burden. We first review *ex post* analyses of policies eliminating lead from petrol, before turning to *ex ante* analyses of proposed policies for eliminating lead contamination in homes.

The phase-out of lead in petrol remains to this day one of the major watershed moments in childhood disease prevention in the twenty-first century. The story behind this landmark policy intervention, however, is more parochial than it appears today. A major driver for the initial phase-out in the United States during the 1970s was that lead impeded the function of catalytic converters, which were being introduced into cars at the time. Approximately five years later, a technological work-around was identified, permitting the reincorporation of lead into petrol. Policy debate about the reintroduction of lead into petrol only ceased when data from serial surveys of the US National Health and Nutrition Examination Survey documented a lock-step decrease of BLLs with the average concentration of lead in petrol.

Retrospectively, this decision proved tremendously smart from an economic perspective. Scott Grosse and colleagues at the Centers for Disease Control and Prevention compared BLLs of children born in the 1970s with children born in the 2000s, and identified approximately a 12–15 µg/dL difference in the average blood lead between these two cohorts of children. Utilizing available literature on decrements of IQ per increment in blood lead, estimates of increased percent lifetime earnings per IQ point, and lifetime earnings estimates, he estimated that the cohort of children born in 2000 would be $263 billion ($213 billion in 2000 prices) more economically productive than the cohort of children born 30 years earlier. Accounting for uncertainty in lead-IQ and IQ-earnings associations, they estimated a possible range of economic benefits between $136 to $393 billion ($110 to $318 billion in 2000 prices) (Grosse et al. 2002). These benefits compare to an *ex ante* $6.25 billion ($6 billion in 2007 prices) cost estimate of the regulations, published by the US Department of Energy (Nichols 1997).[3]

Only six countries have currently failed to eliminate lead from gasoline. Tsai and Hatfield (2011) have quantified the economic benefit of removing lead from gasoline globally, extending the findings of Grosse et al. and accounting for other benefits such as reduced health care costs and criminality. They estimate that the benefits of removing lead in gasoline are $2.86 trillion/year ($2.45 trillion in 2003 prices), or 4 per cent of global gross domestic product. Using the most conservative inputs to their estimates, they suggest that the economic benefits can be no lower than $1.17 trillion/year ($1 trillion in 2003 prices), and might be as much as sixfold higher. Even if the costs of these regulations are only orders of magnitude within the estimated United States phase out costs (adjusting of course for demographic, economic, and geographic differences), then these phase outs have enjoyed unambiguously favourable ROIs.

The dominant intervention for reducing lead exposure in the home is the removal of lead paint and plumbing. Other possible measures include the control of dust and educational interventions with households, but none of these have been shown to be effective (Yeoh et al. 2012). Table 8.3 presents the burden of disease for childhood lead poisoning alongside the costs and benefits of lead abatement in homes. This can be a tricky and costly operation, and it is important that safe work practices are used during the removal process (Jacobs et al. 2003). Assuming safe practices are followed, the average cost of lead removal in the United States is between $1,281 and $11,528 ($1,200 and $10,800 in 2006 prices) per housing unit (President's Task Force on Environmental Health Risks and Safety Risks to Children 2000). In France, Pichery et al. (2011) calculate the average costs of lead decontamination to be $3,952 to $10,171 (€3,560 to €9,162 in 2008 prices) per home. On a per home basis, the estimated present-value benefits of lead abatement in United States homes is $201,324–$283,024 ($188,608–$265,147 in 2006 prices) (Gould 2009), and Pichery et al. (2011) report benefits of approximately $9,800–$57,000 (€8,828 to €51,361 in 2008 prices) per decontaminated home. For both studies, these benefits are calculated as avoided cost of illness (COI) owing to lead exposure in children under the age of six. In contrast to the estimated benefits of the EPA's newly published mercury standards for the USA, the benefits from lead decontamination are calculated to accrue entirely to young children (including increases in their future incomes as a result of higher cognitive ability).

Reducing outdoor air pollution from traffic congestion

The 1990 US Clean Air Act Amendments (CAAA) permitted the EPA to reduce vehicle emissions, a major source of outdoor air pollution (EPA 2012a, 2012b), producing large economic benefits annually in reduced morbidity and expenditures for childhood asthma treatment. Compared with 1997 asthma costs that could be attributed to air pollution and other environmental factors, annual costs in 2008 were reduced by over 30 per cent, from $3.1 billion to $2.2 billion ($3.0 to $2.2 billion in 2008 prices). While it is important to recognize that, at the same time, asthma management shifted to emphasize less costly outpatient management of the condition (National Heart Lung and Blood Institute 2007), childhood asthma care costs may have fallen, in part, as a result of nationwide reductions in outdoor air pollution observed between 1990 and 2005 and attributed to the CAAA. The compliance costs of the CAAA, in turn, were estimated to be $29 billon in 2000 ($19 billion in 1990 prices), and projected to rise to $41.5 billion per year ($27 billion in 1990 prices) by 2010. The United States Government benefit-cost analysis of CAAA reported that the central estimate of CAAA yearly benefits (accounting for health impacts across all ages) exceeded yearly costs by a factor of four (EPA 1999).

Potential cost savings also exist for other respiratory diseases which are typically considered to be infectious in origin. While bronchiolitis is typically considered an infectious disease, multiple studies have suggested particulate matter and nitrous dioxide as potential risk factors for bronchiolitis hospitalization (Pino et al. 2004; Karr et al. 2007, 2009a, 2009b), supplementing laboratory studies that document increased inflammation produced by air pollutants, especially with coexistent viral infection (Castranova et al. 2001). In a cross-sectional, multi-year study of United States paediatric hospitalizations, Sheffield et al. estimate that if the United States were to reduce levels of fine particulate matter (<2.5 µm in diameter) to 7 per cent below the current annual standard, the nation could save $16.4 million ($15 million in 2005 prices) annually in reduced health care costs from hospitalizations of children with bronchiolitis living in urban areas (Sheffield et al. 2011).

Taxes on vehicles to reduce economic externalities associated with traffic congestion have also been shown to have positive health impacts (in addition to other benefits such as greenhouse gas reductions, improved economic productivity, etc.). Two well-known examples of these so-called congestion-charging schemes have been implemented in London and Stockholm. In the United Kingdom, data on the implementation of the congestion charge in London suggest large economic rewards from avoided health impacts associated with reducing traffic emissions. Compared with the two-year period preceding the scheme, bronchiolitis hospitalizations decreased by 9 per cent, controlling for multiple potential coincident phenomena over the natural experiment study period. No other hospitalization type studied had any significant change over the same timespan (Tonne et al. 2010). Meanwhile, the collection costs for the London scheme were estimated to be $223 million per year (€175.7 in 2003 prices) (Prud'homme and Bocarejo 2005). Ongoing study of the low-emission zone requirements implemented over a broader geographic region may identify similar economic rewards (Woodcock et al. 2009). In Stockholm, the congestion charge had a noticeable effect on air pollution, reducing emissions of major pollutants by over 10 per cent (slightly less for NO_x). This reduction in pollution was estimated to translate into 27 avoided deaths per year (Johansson et al. 2009). Estimated health gains specifically for children from the charge are not available. The costs of Stockholm's programme were estimated at $39.7 million (SEK 340 million in 2006 prices) per year (Eliasson 2009).

The potential benefits of improved chemical safety regulations

Until very recently, United States regulatory policies and procedures for chemical regulation – embodied, most notably, by the Toxic Substances Control Act (TSCA) of 1976 – has provided the basis for global policy in this area (EPA 2012c). When the TSCA was enacted, tens of thousands of chemicals in commerce were largely exempted from any retrospective review of potential hazards. Furthermore, United States law does not require systematic premarket testing of chemicals and, as a result, most recently available data suggest that the majority of high production volume (HPV) chemicals have no toxicity testing data whatsoever. Indeed, data on developmental impacts are available in the United States for less than 20 per cent of such chemicals (EPA 1998). As of 2009, only around a quarter of the 4,637 chemicals that OECD has designated as HPV are known to have hazard screening data (OECD 2009).

More recently, the European Union has become best positioned to obtain childhood health benefits from improved regulation of chemicals, through its implementation of the Regulation on Registration, Evaluation, Authorisation and Restriction of Chemicals (REACH), beginning in 2007. REACH supersedes TSCA in that it requires premarket testing of chemicals and substitution with safer alternatives when less toxic alternatives exist. A European Commission Extended Impact Assessment estimated the costs of implementing REACH to be between $3.6 and $6.7 billion (€2.8 to €5.2 billion in 2003 prices) (European Commission 2003), with economic benefits of $34 to $68 billion (€27 to €54 billion in 2003 prices) over the next 30 years (Risk and Policy Analysts Ltd

Table 8.3 Economic burden of children's exposure to hazardous chemicals alongside intervention costs, effectiveness and potential benefits. US $ 2010 prices. Sources in parentheses where appropriate. Note that different studies often used different discount rates so that dollar values are not directly comparable between studies.

Risk factor	Current and proposed policies and interventions	Economic costs of intervention	Effectiveness or economic benefit of intervention
Methylmercury exposure from coal-fired power plants	• US Air Act (1970 USA, co-benefit). • Mercury and Air Toxics Standards (2011 USA). • European Emissions Trading Scheme (2005 EU, co-benefit).	• $3,773 to $327,600 per kg Hg emitted (Rezek and Campbell 2007, projected permit price). • $186,510 in 2010, $37,674 in 2015, per kg Hg emitted (Palmer et al. 2007, projected permit price). • $9,391 to $130,405 per kg Hg removed (Sloss 2008, engineering cost using ACI).	• Research generally lacking on how mercury emissions reductions translate into reduced childhood exposure. • USA 2011 Mercury and Air Toxics Standards estimated to yield benefits in excess of $38.5 billion per year across USA.
Exposure to lead-based paint and plumbing in homes	• De-leading homes in at-risk neighbourhoods.	• In France $3,952 to $10,171 per de-leaded home (Pichery et al. 2011). • In the US, $1,281 and $11,528 per de-leaded home (President's Task Force on Environmental Health Risks and Safety Risks to Children 2000). • $3,291 per de-leaded home (Taha et al. 1999).	• In France, $9,800 to $57,000 reduction in COI per de-leaded home (Pichery et al. 2011). • In the US, $201,324 to $283,024 reduction in COI per de-leaded home (Gould 2009).
Exposure to air pollution from vehicle emissions	• Designate congestion charging schemes and low-emission zones in metro areas (London and Stockholm). • Air quality standards (US Clean Air Act 1970).	• *London congestion charge:* $223 million per year (Prud'homme and Bocarejo 2005). • *Stockholm congestion charge:* $9.7 million per year (Eliasson 2009).	• *London traffic congestion charge:* 9 per cent reduction in bronchiolitis hospitalizations. • *Stockholm congestion charge:* reducing emissions of major pollutants by over 10 per cent; 27 fewer deaths per year (Eliasson 2009). *(Continued overleaf)*

Table 8.3 Economic burden of children's exposure to hazardous chemicals alongside intervention costs, effectiveness and potential benefits. US $ 2010 prices. Sources in parentheses where appropriate. Note that different studies often used different discount rates so that dollar values are not directly comparable between studies. *(continued)*

Risk factor	Current and proposed policies and interventions	Economic costs of intervention	Effectiveness or economic benefit of intervention
			• *US Clean Air Act:* 30 per cent reduction in annual childhood asthma associated costs in the United States over ten-year period (Trasande and Liu 2011).
Childhood exposure to commercial chemicals	• REACH legislation (European Union).	• Between $3.6 and $6.7 billion over next 30 years (Risk and Policy Analysts Ltd 2003; Pickvance et al. 2005).	• $34 to $68 billion over the next 30 years (adult disease prevention only): (see Risk and Policy Analysts Ltd 2003) and Pickvance et al. 2005).

2003; Pickvance et al. 2005). The economic benefits stream described, however, are for adult disease prevention, especially for those consequences of adult occupational exposures that are likely to be prevented.

Given that data on toxicity of chemical exposures to children have only emerged after extensive diffusion in the environment, it is important to comment that the economic benefits of preventing new toxic exposures through pre-market testing may only be quantifiable by extrapolation from laboratory studies identifying potential toxic consequences. The economic benefits of reducing early life exposures to toxic chemicals in the environment are nonetheless likely to be profound (Table 8.3), given the scope insofar as chemical origins to epidemic childhood conditions are identified in the future, and safer alternatives substituted for those chemicals in the marketplace (Trasande and Liu 2011).

Conclusion

While economic analyses are increasingly appearing in the children's environmental health literature, serious gaps remain that limit cost-effectiveness and cost-benefit analyses for improving policy making (Trasande 2011). For example, updated DALY estimates for conditions increasingly linked to environmental exposures (e.g. childhood cancer, obesity, neurodevelopmental disabilities) would greatly expand the scope of DALY estimates attributable to diseases, and permit examination of DALY gains through interventions to prevent toxic environmental exposures.

Environmental health economics also differs from other, more traditional, areas of public health economics in three crucial respects. First, the existence of large economic externalities (Trasande et al. 2011), in which the agents causing negative health impacts often lie in entirely different sectors of society than those experiencing them, requires a policy perspective that extends well outside of the health care sector (e.g. regulation of electricity producers). Second, because interventions for children's environmental health often are technological in nature (e.g. improved mercury abatement methods in coal plants, engines that can operate without lead additives), static estimates of interventions costs may fail to account for innovation and thus may be overinflated (Ackerman and Heinzerling 2001). Third, complex environmental mediators and long lag times between exposure and disease response in the case of environmental hazards can make traditional risk assessment approaches anachronistic. A great deal of damage can be avoided by shifting the burden of proof from those analyzing the negative health impacts of chemicals to those proposing the introduction of a new, poorly understood chemical. This is, in fact, the primary objective of the European Commission's REACH legislation described above. As a regulation whose full impacts have yet to be seen, REACH should be closely monitored in order to see how efficiently it can achieve its intended objectives.

These distinguishing features of environmental health economics have implications for the way such evidence is amassed and fed into policy. Improved economic analyses of the benefits for improving children's environmental health would be of service for policymakers in prioritizing actions and in formulating economic instruments for correcting aforementioned externalities (OECD 2010). Furthermore, coordinating assessments of children's environmental health risks, as has been done for example with traditional chemicals risk assessments at the OECD (2012a), is necessary for advancing global policy in this area.

The evidence reviewed here suggests large future economic benefits to be gained through relatively modest investments. Because of the particularly large uncertainties involved in estimating the effects of environmental health hazards, it is critical that further research be conducted to better understand, in particular, the long-term health impacts of early-life exposure to chemicals. That said, the policies reviewed here are undoubtedly good buys for giving children healthy environments.

Acknowledgements

We appreciate the thoughtful review and/or contributions from Timothy Taylor, Nathalie Delrue and Emily Barrett.

Notes

1 Environmental hazards can include chemical contaminants in the environment, natural and man-made disasters, pathogens transmitted through the water or via insect vectors, overexposure to the sun, and countless other potential sources of harm in the natural world. Our limitation in scope to chemical contaminants is due both to this book's focus on populations in high- and middle-income countries and to the relatively rich scientific evidence on chemical environmental hazards, their implications for children's health, and interventions to reduce these hazards. Following recent WHO analyses of the health impacts of chemical contaminants (see Prüss-Ustun et al. 2011), we do not address radioactive contaminants, as the exposure pathways for these compounds are quite distinct and deserve a dedicated analysis. We also set aside the study of environmentally mediated pathogens which remain relevant for high- and middle-income countries, and which can disproportionately harm children. These include vector-borne diseases, such as tick-borne encephalitis, Lyme disease, West Nile virus (Githeko et al. 2000) and water-borne pathogens (Griffin et al. 2011). These hazards also deserve dedicated treatment, since the effectiveness of interventions to reduce such pathogens often depends on the ecology of the surrounding environment, which is a specialized topic of study.

2 Economic research on environmental health draws heavily on research in environmental economics, which tends to estimate health impacts using monetary measures, as opposed to DALYs or QALYs, which are more commonly used in health economics. For one explanation of this distinction, see (OECD 2010).

3 This cost figure was obtained by taking the $503 million (US dollars 1983) annualized 1988 cost figure reported by Nichols, inflating it by a factor of 2.08, and then converting it to present value terms using a 3 per cent discount rate. Nichols illustrates that this *ex ante* annualized cost figure was probably overestimated in hindsight. The final figures here have been expressed as 2010 dollars.

References

Ackerman, F. and Heinzerling, L. (2001) Pricing the priceless: Cost–benefit analysis of environmental protection, *University of Pennsylvania Law Review*, 150: 1553–84.

Akinbami, L. J., Moorman, J. E., Garbe, P. L. and Sondik, E. J. (2009) Status of childhood asthma in the United States, 1980–2007, *Pediatrics*, 123: S131–45.

Bearer, C. F. (1995) How are children different from adults?, *Environmental Health Perspectives*, 103: 7.

Bellinger, D. C. (2008) Very low lead exposures and children's neurodevelopment, *Current Opinion in Pediatrics*, 20: 172–7. 10.1097/MOP.0b013e3282f4f97b.

Bierkens, J., Smolders, R., Van Holderbeke, M. and Cornelis, C. (2011) Predicting blood lead levels from current and past environmental data in Europe, *Science of The Total Environment*, 409: 5101–10.

Binns, H. J., Campbell, C., Brown, M. J. and Prevention, ftACoCLP (2007) Interpreting and managing blood lead levels of less than 10 g/dL in children and reducing childhood exposure to lead: Recommendations of the Centers for Disease Control and Prevention Advisory Committee on Childhood Lead Poisoning Prevention, *Pediatrics*, 120: e1285–98.

Bost, L., Primatesta, P., Dong, W. and Poulter, N. (1999) Blood lead and blood pressure: Evidence from the Health Survey for England 1995, *Journal of Human Hypertension*, 13(2): 123–8.

Burtraw, D. and Szambelan, S. J. (2009) *US Emissions Trading Permits for SO₂ and NOₓ*. Dicussion Paper 09-40. Washington, DC: Resources For The Future.

Castranova, V., Ma, J. Y. C., Yang, H. M.et al. (2001) Effect of exposure to diesel exhaust particles on the susceptibility of the lung to infection, *Environmental Health Perspectives*, 109: 609–12.

Demoliou, C. D. and Charalambous, A. (2004) Blood lead levels in preprimary school-age children in Nicosia, Cyprus, and their relationship with leaded soil dust exposure, *Archives of Environmental Health: An International Journal*, 59: 455–61.

Devesa, S. S., Blot, W. J., Stone, B. J., Miller, B. A., Tarone, R. E. and Fraumeni, J. F. (2003) Recent Cancer Trends in the United States, *Journal of the National Cancer Institute*, 87: 175–82.

Dietz, R., Riget, F., Cleemann, M., Aarkrog, A., Johansen, P. and Hansen, J. C. (2000) Comparison of contaminants from different trophic levels and ecosystems, *Science of the Total Environment*, 245: 221–31.

Eliasson, J. (2009) A cost-benefit analysis of the Stockholm congestion charging system, *Transportation Research Part A: Policy and Practice*, 43: 468–80.

EPA (1997) *Mercury Study Report to Congress, Volume I: Executive Summary*. Research Triangle Park, NC: Office of Air Quality Planning and Standards and Office of Research and Development, Environmental Protection Agency EPA-4521R-97-003.

EPA (1998) *Chemical Hazard Data Availability Study: What do we Really Know about the Safety of High Production Volume Chemicals?* Washington, DC: EPA.

EPA (1999) *The Benefits and Costs of the Clean Air Act 1990 to 2010*. Washington, DC: EPA.

EPA (2003) *National Emissions Inventories for Hazardous Air Pollutants, 1999*, version 3, July 2003. Technology Transfer Network (TTN), Clearinghouse for Inventories and Emissions Factors. Available at http://www.epa.gov/ttn/chief [Accessed 18 May 2004].

EPA (2007) *Control of Mercury Emissions from Coal-fired Electric Utility Boilers* (white paper). Research Triangle Park, NC: EPA.

EPA (2010) *Clean Air Mercury Rule* [online]. Available at http://www.epa.gov/air/mercuryrule/basic.html [Accessed September 2014].

EPA (2011) *Regulatory impact analysis for the Final Mercury and Air Toxics Standards.* Research Triangle Park, NC: Office OF Air Quality Planning and Standards, EPA.

EPA (2012a) *The Clean Air Act Amendments of 1990* [online]. Available at http://epa.gov/air/caa/caaa_overview.html [Accessed September 2014].

EPA (2012b) *History of the Clean Air Act* [online]. Available at http://www.epa.gov/air/caa/caa_history.html@a90 [Accessed 18 February 2011].

EPA (2012c) *Summary of the Toxic Substances Control Act* [online]. Available at http://www.epa.gov/lawsregs/laws/tsca.html [Accessed 24 March 2009].

European Commission (2003) *REACH extended impact assessment* [online]. Available at http://ec.europa.eu/enterprise/sectors/chemicals/documents/reach/archives/impact-assessment/ [Accessed 17 January 2012].

Fostier, A. H., Forti, M. C., Guimaraes, J. R. D. et al. (2000) Mercury fluxes in a natural forested Amazonian catchment (Serra do Navio, Amapá State, Brazil), *Science of the Total Environment*, 260: 201–11.

Gauderman, W. J., Avol, E., Gilliland, F. et al. (2004) The effect of air pollution on lung development from 10 to 18 years of age, *New England Journal of Medicine*, 351: 1057–67.

Gilmour, C. C. and Riedel, G. S. (2000) A survey of size-specific mercury concentrations in game fish from Maryland fresh and estuarine waters, *Archives of Environmental Contamination and Toxicology*, 39: 53–9.

Githeko, A. K., Lindsay, S. W., Confalonieri, U. E. and Patz, J. A. (2000) Climate change and vector-borne diseases: A regional analysis, *Bulletin of the World Health Organization*, 78: 1136–47.

Goldman, L., Falk, H., Landrigan, P. J., Balk, S. J., Reigart, J. R. and Etzel, R. A. (2004) Environmental pediatrics and its impact on government health policy, *Pediatrics*, 113: 1146.

Goldman, L. R. and Shannon, M. W. for the American Academy of Pediatrics Committee on Environmental Health (2001) Technical report: Mercury in the environment: Implications for pediatricians, *Pediatrics*, 108: 197–205.

Gould, E. (2009) Childhood lead poisoning: Conservative estimates of the social and economic benefits of lead hazard control, *Environmental Health Perspectives*, 117.

Grandjean, P. and Landrigan, P. J. (2007) Developmental neurotoxicity of industrial chemicals, *The Lancet*, 368: 2167–78.

Griffin, S. M., Chen, I. M., Fout, G. S., Wade, T. J. and Egorov, A. I. (2011) Development of a multiplex microsphere immunoassay for the quantitation of salivary antibody responses to selected waterborne pathogens, *Journal of Immunological Methods*, 364: 83–93.

Grosse, S. D., Matte, T. D., Schwartz, J. and Jackson, R. J. (2002) Economic gains resulting from the reduction in children's exposure to lead in the United States, *Environmental Health Perspectives*, 110: 563–9.

Guimaraes, J. R. D., Ikingura, J. and Akagi, H. (2000) Methyl mercury production and distribution in river water-sediment systems investigated through radiochemical techniques, *Water, Air, & Soil Pollution*, 124: 113–24.

Hedley, A. A., Ogden, C. L., Johnson, C. L., Carroll, M. D., Curtin, L. R. and Flegal, K. M. (2004) Prevalence of overweight and obesity among US children, adolescents, and adults, 1999–2002, *Journal of the American Medical Association*, 291: 2847.

Hill, A. B. (1965) The environment and disease: Association or causation?, *Proceedings of the Royal Society of Medicine*, 58: 295–300.

Jacobs, D. E., Mielke, H. and Pavur, N. (2003) The high cost of improper removal of lead-based paint from housing: A case report, *Environmental Health Perspectives*, 111: 111–85.

Johansson, C., Burman, L. and Forsberg, B. (2009) The effects of congestions tax on air quality and health, *Atmospheric Environment*, 43: 4843–54.

Jones, A. P., Hoffmann, J. W., Smith, D. N., Feeley, T. J. and Murphy, J. T. (2007) DOE/NETL's Phase II Mercury Control Technology Field Testing Program: Preliminary economic analysis of activated carbon injection, *Environmental Science & Technology*, 41: 1365–71.

Karr, C., Lumley, T., Schreuder, A. et al. (2007) Effects of subchronic and chronic exposure to ambient air pollutants on infant bronchiolitis, *American Journal of Epidemiology*, 165: 553–60.

Karr, C. J., Demers, P. A., Koehoorn, M. W., Lencar, C. C., Tamburic, L. and Brauer, M. (2009a) Influence of ambient air pollutant sources on clinical encounters for infant bronchiolitis, *American Journal of Respiratory and Critical Care Medicine*, 180: 995–1001.

Karr, C. J., Rudra, C. B., Miller, K. A. et al. (2009b) Infant exposure to fine particulate matter and traffic and risk of hospitalization for RSV bronchiolitis in a region with lower ambient air pollution, *Environmental Research*, 109: 321–7.

Knox, E. G. (2005) Childhood cancers and atmospheric carcinogens, *British Medical Journal*, 59: 101.

Landrigan, P. J., Trasande, L., Thorpe, L. E. et al. (2006) The National Children's Study: A 21-year prospective study of 100,000 American children, *Pediatrics*, 118: 2173–86.

Lanphear, B. P., Hornung, R., Khoury, J. et al. (2005) Low-level environmental lead exposure and children's intellectual function: An international pooled analysis, *Environmental Health Perspectives*, 113.

Lee, W. J., Cantor, K. P., Berzofsky, J. A., Zahm, S. H. and Blair, A. (2004) Non-Hodgkin's lymphoma among asthmatics exposed to pesticides, *International Journal of Cancer*, 111: 298–302.

Martinez, F. D. (2009) The origins of asthma and chronic obstructive pulmonary disease in early life, *Proceedings of the American Thoracic Society*, 6: 272–7.

Mason, R. P., Reinfelder, J. R. and Morel, F. M. M. (1995) Bioaccumulation of mercury and methylmercury, *Water, Air, & Soil Pollution*, 80: 915–21.

Matasar, M. J., Ritchie, E. K., Consedine, N., Magai, C. and Neugut, A. I. (2006) Incidence rates of acute promyelocytic leukemia among Hispanics, blacks, Asians, and non-Hispanic whites in the United States, *European Journal of Cancer Prevention*, 15: 367.

National Academy of Sciences (2000) *Scientific Frontiers in Developmental Toxicology and Risk Assessment*. Washington, DC: Committee On Developmental Toxicology.

National Heart Lung and Blood Institute (2007) Expert Panel Report 3 (EPR3): Guidelines for the Diagnosis and Management of Asthma. Bethesda, MD: NHLBI. Available at http://www.nhlbi.nih.gov/guidelines/asthma/asthgdln.htm [Accessed 18 February 2011].

National Research Council (1993) *Pesticides in the Diets of Infants and Children*. Washington, DC: National Academy Press.

Neumann, R. M. and Ward, S. M. (1999) Bioaccumulation and biomagnification of mercury in two warmwater fish communities, *Journal of Freshwater Ecology*, 14: 487–98.

Nichols, A. L. (1997) Lead in gasoline, in R. D. Morgenstern (ed.) *Economic Analyses at EPA: Assessing Regulatory Impact*. Washington, DC: RFF Press.

Nriagu, J. O. (1989) A global assessment of natural sources of atmospheric trace metals, *Nature*, 338: 47–9.

Nriagu, J. O. and Pacyna, J. M. (1988) Quantitative assessment of worldwide contamination of air, water and soils by trace metals, *Nature*, 333: 134–9.

OECD (2006) *Ex post Estimates of Costs to Business of EU Environmental Policies*. Paris: OECD.

OECD (2009) *The 2007 OECD List of High Production Volume Chemicals.* Paris: OECD Environment Directorate.

OECD (2010) *Valuation of Environment-Related Health Risks for Children.* Paris: OECD.

OECD (2012a) *eChemPortal* [online]. Available at http://www.echemportal.org [Accessed 14 March 2012].

OECD (2012b) *OECD Environmental Outlook to 2050.* Paris: OECD Environment Directorate/Environment Policy Committee.

Ogden, C. L., Carroll, M. D., Curtin, L. R., Lamb, M. M. and Flegal, K. M. (2010) Prevalence of high body mass index in US children and adolescents, 2007–2008, *Journal of the American Medical Association*, 303: 242–9.

Pacyna, J., Sundseth, K., Pacyna, E. et al. (2008) Socio-economic costs of continuing the status-quo of mercury pollution. Copenhagen: Nordic Council of Ministers. Available at http://norden.diva-portal.org/smash/get/diva2:701754/FULLTEXT01.pdf [Accessed September 2014].

Pacyna, J. M., Sundseth, K., Pacyna, E. G. et al. (2010) An assessment of costs and benefits associated with mercury emission reductions from major anthropogenic sources, *Journal of the Air & Waste Management Association*, 60: 302–15.

Palmer, K., Burtraw, D. and Shih, J.-S. (2007) The benefits and costs of reducing emissions from the electricity sector, *Journal of Environmental Management*, 83(1): 115–30.

Paulozzi, L. J., Erickson, J. D. and Jackson, R. J. (1997) Hypospadias trends in two US surveillance systems, *Pediatrics*, 100: 831–4.

Pichery, C., Bellanger, M., Zmirou-Navier, D., Glorennec, P., Hartemann, P. and Grandjean, P. (2011) Childhood lead exposure in France: Benefit estimation and partial cost-benefit analysis of lead hazard control, *Environmental Health*, 10: 44.

Pickvance, S., Karnon, J., Peters, J. and El-Arifi, K. (2005) *Further Assessment of the Impact of REACH on Occupational Health with a Focus on Skin and Respiratory Diseases.* Brussels: European Trade Union Institute for Research, Education and Health & Safety.

Pino, P., Walter, T., Oyarzun, M., Villegas, R. and Romieu, I. (2004) Fine particulate matter and wheezing illnesses in the first year of life, *Epidemiology*, 15: 702–8.

President's Task Force on Environmental Health Risks and Safety Risks to Children (2000) *Eliminating Childhood Lead Poisoning: A Federal Strategy Targeting Lead Paint Hazards (Report and Appendix).* Washington, DC: US Department of Housing and Urban Development and US Environmental Protection Agency.

Prud'homme, R. and Bocarejo, J. P. (2005) The London congestion charge: A tentative economic appraisal, *Transport Policy*, 12: 279–87.

Prüss-Ustun, A., Vickers, C., Haefliger, P. and Bertollini, R. (2011) Knowns and unknowns on burden of disease due to chemicals: A systematic review, *Environmental Health*, 10: 9.

Rezek, J. P. and Campbell, R. C. (2007) Cost estimates for multiple pollutants: A maximum entropy approach, *Energy Economics*, 29: 503–19.

Rickford, V. (2006) Mercury-free gold mining technologies: Possibilities for adoption in the Guianas, *Journal of Cleaner Production*, 14: 448–54.

Risk and Policy Analysts Ltd (2003) *Assessment of the Impact of the New Chemicals Policy on Occupational Health.* London: European Commision, Environment Directorate-General.

Robison, L. L., Buckley, J. D. and Bunin, G. (1995) Assessment of environmental and genetic factors in the etiology of childhood cancers: The Children's Cancer Group epidemiology program, *Environmental Health Perspectives*, 103: 111.

Ronchetti, R., Zuurbier, M., Jesenak, M. et al. (2006) Children's health and mercury exposure, *Acta Pædiatrica*, 95: 36–44.

Roulet, M., Lucotte, M., Canuel, R. et al. (2000) Increase in mercury contamination recorded in lacustrine sediments following deforestation in the central Amazon, *Chemical Geology*, 165: 243–66.

Roulet, M., Lucotte, M., Farella, N. et al. (1999) Effects of recent human colonization on the presence of mercury in Amazonian ecosystems, *Water, Air, & Soil Pollution*, 112: 297–313.

Rudant, J., Menegaux, F., Leverger, G. et al. (2007) Household exposure to pesticides and risk of childhood hematopoietic malignancies: The ESCALE study (SFCE), *Environmental Health Perspectives*, 115: 1787.

Savitz, D. A. and Feingold, L. (1989) Association of childhood cancer with residential traffic density, *Scandinavian Journal of Work, Environment & Health*, 15: 360–3.

Schechter, C. B. (1999) Re: Brain and other central nervous system cancers: Recent trends in incidence and mortality, *Journal of the National Cancer Institute*, 91: 2050–1.

Schulz, C., Angerer, J., Ewers, U., Heudorf, U. and Wilhelm, M. (2009) Revised and new reference values for environmental pollutants in urine or blood of children in Germany derived from the German Environmental Survey on Children 2003–2006 (GerES IV), *International Journal of Hygiene and Environmental Health*, 212: 637–47.

Sheffield, P., Roy, A., Wong, K. and Trasande, L. (2011) Fine particulate matter pollution linked to respiratory illness in infants and increased hospital costs, *Health Affairs*, 30: 871–8.

Sloss, L. L. (2003) *Trends in Emission Standards*. London: IEA Clean Coal Centre.

Sloss, L. L. (2008) *Economics of Mercury Control*. London: IEA Clean Coal Centre.

Smolders, R., Alimonti, A., Cerna, M. et al. (2010) Availability and comparability of human biomonitoring data across Europe: A case-study on blood-lead levels, *Science of The Total Environment*, 408: 1437–45.

Sundseth, K., Pacyna, J. M., Pacyna, E. G., Munthe, J., Belhaj, M. and Astrom, S. (2010) Economic benefits from decreased mercury emissions: Projections for 2020, *Journal of Cleaner Production*, 18: 386–94.

Taha, T., Kanarek, M. S., Schultz, B. D. and Murphy, A. (1999) Low-cost household paint abatement to reduce children's blood lead levels, *Environmental Research*, 81: 334–8.

Thurlbeck, W. M. (1982) Postnatal human lung growth, *Thorax*, 37: 564–71.

Thurston, G. D., Lippmann, M., Scott, M. B. and Fine, J. M. (1997) Summertime haze air pollution and children with asthma, *American Journal of Respiratory and Critical Care Medicine*, 155: 654–60.

Tonne, C., Beevers, S., Kelly, F. J., Jarup, L., Wilkinson, P. and Armstrong, B. (2010) An approach for estimating the health effects of changes over time in air pollution: An illustration using cardio-respiratory hospital admissions in London, *Occupational and Environmental Medicine*, 67: 422–7.

Trasande, L. (2011) Economics of children's environmental health, *Mount Sinai Journal of Medicine: A Journal of Translational and Personalized Medicine*, 78: 98–106.

Trasande, L., Boscarino, J., Graber, N. et al. (2006) The environment in pediatric practice: A study of New York pediatricians' attitudes, beliefs, and practices towards children's environmental health, *Journal of Urban Health*, 83: 760–72.

Trasande, L., Cronk, C., Durkin, M. et al. (2009) Environment, obesity and the National Children's Study, *Environmental Health Perspectives*, 117: 159–66.

Trasande, L., Landrigan, P. J. and Schechter, C. (2005) Public health and economic consequences of methyl mercury toxicity to the developing brain, *Environmental Health Perspectives*, 113: 590–6.

Trasande, L. and Liu, Y. (2011) Reducing The staggering costs of environmental disease in children, estimated at $76.6 billion in 2008, *Health Affairs*, 30: 863–70.

Trasande, L., Massey, R. I., DiGangi, J., Geiser, K., Olanipekun, A. I. and Gallagher, L. (2011) How developing nations can protect children from hazardous chemical exposures while sustaining economic growth, *Health Affairs*, 30: 2400–9.

Trasande, L. and Thurston, G. D. (2005) The role of air pollution in asthma and other pediatric morbidities, *Journal of Allergy and Clinical Immunology*, 115: 689–99.

Tsai, P. L. and Hatfield, T. H. (2011) Global benefits of phasing out leaded fuel, *Journal of Environmental Health*, 74: 8–15.

UNEP (2011) New draft text for a comprehensive and suitable approach to a global legally binding instrument on mercury. Nairobi: United Nations Environment Programme.

UNEP (2013a) *Global Clean Fuels and Vehicles Database*. Available at http://www.unep. org/cleanfleet_database/home.asp [Accessed September 2014].

UNEP (2013b) *Text of the Minamata Convention on Mercury for Adoption by the Conference of Plenipotentiaries*. Geneva: United Nations Environment Programme.

Ward, M. H., Colt, J. S., Metayer, C. et al. (2009) Residential exposure to polychlorinated biphenyls and organochlorine pesticides and risk of childhood leukemia, *Environmental Health Perspectives*, 117.

WHO (2012) *Global Health Observatory Data Repository*. Available at http://apps.who. int/ghodata/ [Accessed 18 June 2012].

Williams, L. J., Kucik, J. E., Alverson, C. J., Olney, R. S. and Correa, A. (2005) Epidemiology of gastroschisis in metropolitan Atlanta, 1968 through 2000, *Birth Defects Research Part A: Clinical and Molecular Teratology*, 73: 177–83.

Woodcock, J., Edwards, P., Tonne, C. et al. (2009) Public health benefits of strategies to reduce greenhouse-gas emissions: Urban land transport, *The Lancet*, 374: 1930–43.

Yelverton, W. H. (2009) *CUECost Workbook Development Documentation*. Research Triangle Park, NC: EPA.

Yeoh, B., Woolfenden, S., Ridley, G. and Livingston, N. (2012) Household interventions for preventing domestic lead exposure, *Cochrane Database of Systematic Reviews*, 2012.

nine

Preventing road-related injuries

Rob Anderson, David McDaid and A-La Park

Introduction

While much of this volume concentrates on addressing noncommunicable disease, injuries remain a significant contributor to the overall burden of death and disability in Europe. This chapter looks at the economic case for investing in measures to help reduce the risk of injury in one specific arena – that of the road environment. The focus on road injuries is for three main reasons. First, road injuries account for a large proportion of the burden of fatal and disabling unintentional injuries in all European countries. Second, the wide gap in road injury rates and deaths between the 'best performing' and the 'worst performing' countries in the WHO European Region provides a clear indication of how many of these injuries, deaths and disabilities are potentially avoidable by implementing effective strategies. And thirdly, road injuries disproportionately affect vulnerable road users, in particular children and older pedestrians. From an economic perspective, there are externalities associated with road-related injuries which help justify public investment – namely the impacts on pedestrians, vehicle passengers, cyclists and other road users who may inadvertently be harmed through no fault of their own.

The chapter draws on data from a number of published reviews of evidence, including an update to previous reviews of economic evidence for road traffic accident prevention undertaken by the authors. It will also reflect on the main methods used in research on road injury prevention. For instance, in contrast to the evidence from economic evaluations discussed in much of this volume, economic evidence for road safety predominantly uses cost-benefit analysis. But there can be inconsistencies in the use of this evidence, and large differences in the statistical value of a life that have been applied both in cost of injury studies and in cost-benefit analysis. This is set within the context of measurement and evaluation challenges such as the under-reporting of road-related injuries, especially non-fatal injuries.

What do we know about the impact of road traffic collisions in Europe?

Road traffic collisions are a significant public health issue. In the WHO European Region, 120,000 people die each year from road injuries. They are the leading cause of death in children and young adults aged 5 to 29 years, and a further 2.4 million people are estimated to be so seriously injured as to require hospital admission each year. Thirty nine per cent of injuries are to pedestrians, cyclists and motorcycle riders (Zambon et al. 2009). The numbers of deaths in terms of kilometres travelled and per head of the population have generally fallen consistently in most high-income countries in the region, with many of the best performing countries – including Sweden, the Netherlands, Norway and the United Kingdom – having comprehensive multi-sectorial strategies in place.

While marked progress on traffic-related deaths has been made in Europe, including some countries with historically high death rates, progress has been slower in some countries, including the Russian Federation (Figure 9.1). Many of the highest rates for motor vehicle deaths are still to be found in the Commonwealth of Independent States (CIS) member countries. In the Russian Federation alone, in 2008, there were 29,936 road deaths and 270,883 police-reported road injuries (Breen 2010). This can be contrasted with progress in reducing the death rate in the three Baltic states of Estonia, Latvia and Lithuania. However, a lack of standardized data means that less information on trends is available in some low- and middle-income countries in the region, so international comparisons may not be wholly reliable.

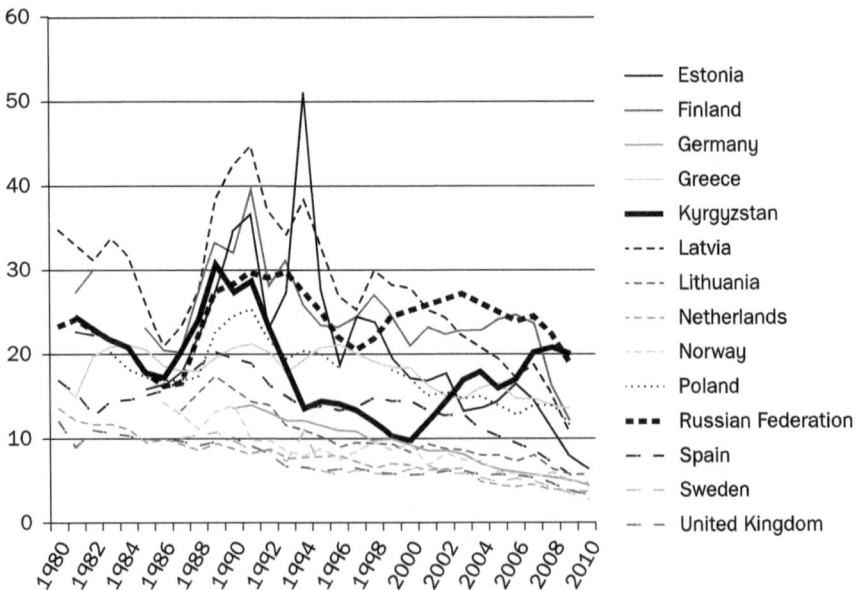

Figure 9.1 Traffic accident deaths (age standardized death rates per 100,000) in selected countries, 1980–2010

Source: WHO Mortality Database 2012.

Even though there has been a 13 per cent reduction in deaths in the Russian Federation between 2004 and 2008 against a 24 per cent increase in traffic (Breen 2010), death rates in crashes on Russian roads are five times as high as those seen in the best performing nations in road safety (e.g. Sweden, the United Kingdom and the Netherlands) (Fig. 9.2). Moreover, the number and types of road safety programmes are generally more limited in the eastern part of Europe, where most of the high deaths rates are to be seen (Hyder and Aggarwal 2009).

Economic impact

The many economic impacts of road traffic accidents have long been recognized. As early as the 1950s this was acknowledged to include the 'pain, fear and suffering imposed by occurrence, or risk of occurrence, of road accidents', as well as 'the more concrete and ascertainable burdens in the form of the net loss of output of goods and services due to death and injury and the expenditure of resources necessary to make good the effects of accidents, e.g. medical expenses, vehicle repairs and costs of administration' (Reynolds 1956).

Standarized death rate (SDR) motor vehicle traffic accidents, all ages per 100000

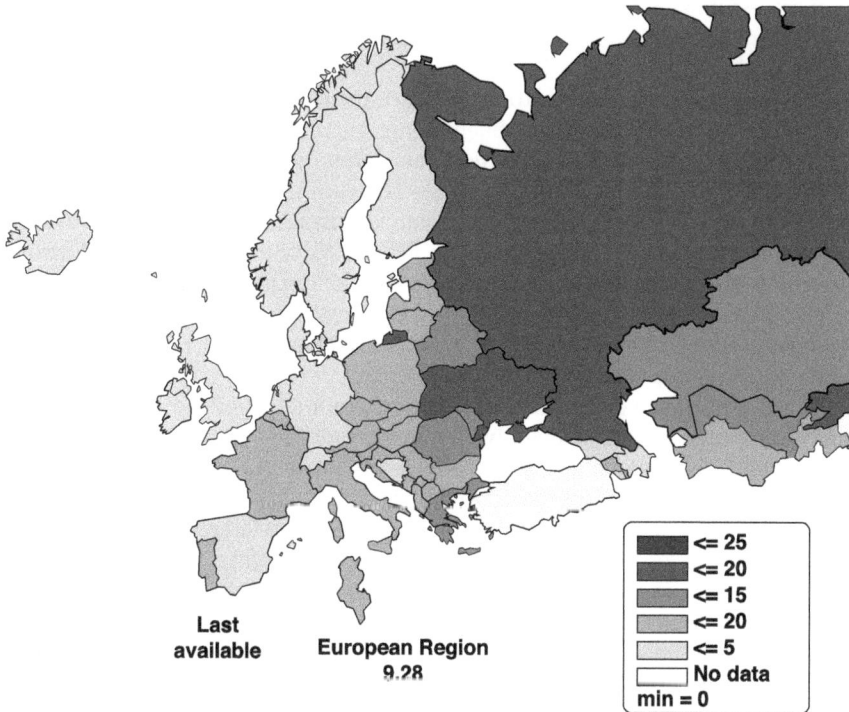

	<= 25
	<= 20
	<= 15
	<= 20
	<= 5
	No data

Last available   European Region 9.28   min = 0

Figure 9.2 Rates of motor vehicle traffic accidents across the WHO European Region (latest available year)

Source: WHO Health For All Database 2013.

A body of literature on the costs of road-related accidents has built up, albeit as in other areas of costing studies, using a variety of methods and assumptions making comparison difficult (Trawen et al. 2002). In addition to the costs falling on the principal parties and economic externalities imposed on innocent victims of crashes, there are further spillover effects on families who may have to provide care and support to those who are injured.

The estimated annual costs, both direct and indirect, of road-related traffic injuries in Europe have been conservatively estimated to be as much as 3 per cent of GDP (Zambon et al. 2009). In 2008, in the Russian Federation, official estimates of these costs were more than $29 billion (RUR 908 billion in 2008 prices) (around US $29 billion) representing over 2 per cent of GDP (Breen 2010). Many estimates of the costs of road traffic accidents as a whole, and for specific modes of transport or target populations in different parts of Europe, have been published (e.g. van Beeck et al. 1997; Lopez et al. 2001; Bastida et al. 2004; Connelly and Supangan 2006; Garcia-Altes and Perez 2007; Veisten et al. 2007; Department of Transport 2010; Garcia-Altes and Puig-Junoy 2011).

What do we know about the effectiveness of interventions?

Having established that there is an economic rationale for public sector investment in road safety, what do we know about the effectiveness of road-safety actions? A complex interaction of vehicles and equipment, as well as human and environmental factors, influence the likelihood of collisions, serious injuries and deaths. There have been numerous reviews and individual studies on the effectiveness of road safety measures, with considerable variation in the quality of evaluations and in the robustness of evidence for different interventions. Table 9.1 illustrates some of these challenges by providing examples of different interventions on actions to prevent crashes and also to prevent injuries when crashes occur based on the results of systematic reviews; in many cases the evidence is equivocal due to study design, but nevertheless promising. Later in this chapter we look at the evidence on the cost-effectiveness of these measures.

We cannot, however, in this brief chapter look at all of these interventions for road-related safety; instead, we focus on some broad areas of intervention. For instance, in one analysis alone, which looked at 132 road safety measures, it was concluded that 59 of these would be potentially effective in a Norwegian context and 62 in a Swedish context (Elvik 2003). The interested reader can be referred to detailed guides on potential measures, together with the emergence of approaches to rank this evidence based on the quality of study design and cost-effectiveness (Elvik et al. 2009a).

Violation of speed limits remains a major problem in many countries. Measures to enforce legislation on speed limits have been evaluated. A review of 35 studies looking at enforcement of speed limits through speed cameras found significantly lower rates of speeding and, again, despite study design limitations, is consistent in reporting a reduction in the rate of injuries and deaths (Wilson et al. 2010). Also, red light cameras that record drivers that 'jump' red lights have been shown in before-and-after controlled studies in the

Table 9.1 Examples of major road safety interventions and their effectiveness

Overall conclusion – in relation to reductions in injuries or crashes	Type of intervention or strategy	
	Pre-crash (crash prevention)	During crashes (preventing injuries in crashes/collisions)
Effective	Traffic light ('red light') cameras.	Wearing bicycle helmets.
	Graduated driver licensing of younger drivers.	Bicycle helmet legislation.
		Booster seats (for 4- to 8-year-olds), including incentives to use booster seats.
	Increasing the minimum legal age for drinking.	Wearing motorcyclist helmets.
		Wearing seat belts.
Potentially effective	Area-wide traffic calming.	
	Speed enforcement cameras.	
	Increased police patrols to reduce alcohol-impaired driving.	
	Media campaigns to reduce alcohol-impaired driving and alcohol-related crashes.	
	Street lighting.	
	Alcohol ignition interlocks.	
Not effective	School-based driver education.[a]	
	Advanced or remedial driver education.	
Don't know – no or limited evidence	Pedestrian safety education for children.	Media campaigns for children to wear bicycle helmets.[b]
	Mandatory vision screening for older drivers.	
	Increasing cyclist and pedestrian visibility.[b]	
	Drug or alcohol screening of occupational drivers.	
	Driving assessment for drivers with dementia.	
	Interventions to modify alcohol consumption in bars/pubs.	

Source: Authors' own

[a] For these interventions, there is some evidence of potential harms or increases in injuries or crashes/collisions.
[b] Although there is evidence of effectiveness for other intermediate outcomes (such as observed wearing of helmets).

United States, Singapore and Australia to be significantly effective in reducing injuries from crashes (Aeron-Thomas and Hess 2005).

Furthermore, a systematic review commissioned by NICE looked at other complementary strategies of speed enforcement (Anderson and Moxham 2010), such as penalty points on drivers' licences, increased fines, as well as media campaigns, alongside other speed enforcement activities. Overall, the review found that while such initiatives can be effective, this is contingent upon broader speed enforcement initiatives and policies present on the same road (e.g. the speed limits, clear signage, physical changes to road layout), regionally (e.g. media campaigns) and nationally (e.g. systems for issuing fines and penalty points).

There is a very heterogeneous mixture of controlled before-and-after studies and multivariate analyses of longitudinal data in diverse countries which shows that rationalized police enforcement of traffic speeds (e.g. targeting 'accident blackspots' or using random surveillance) can reduce injury crashes, car accidents, and collisions, injury collisions, fatalities and speed-related fatalities. Similarly, in other studies, increased levels of police enforcement of traffic speeds reduced injury crashes and all injuries, fatal accidents, and injury accidents. For instance, a study on motorways in the Netherlands showed that increasing the intensity of enforcement – from apprehending 1 in 100 speeding offenders, to 1 in 25, to 1 in 6 – produced statistically significant ($p<0.05$) reductions in mean speed (De Waard and Rooijers 1994).

There are also measures to modify the environment in ways that either physically enforce or subliminally encourage behaviour changes to influence driving. Twenty-two controlled before-and-after studies of various area-wide traffic calming measures, such as road/speed humps, reduced speed zones, changes to road lighting, traffic circulation patterns and road environment have shown that these measures have the potential to reduce injuries and deaths in high-income countries (Bunn et al. 2003). Other promising environmental interventions identified in reviews include improved street lighting (Beyer and Ker 2009).

Legislation and regulation can also influence the likelihood that high-risk individuals are on the roads. For instance, graduated driver licensing programmes which restrict the environments in which young drivers can initially operate, e.g. motorways, have also been shown in a review of studies from the United States, Canada, Australia and New Zealand to be effective (Russell et al. 2011). However, there is insufficient information on the effectiveness of screening older drivers for risk of cognitive impairment and dementia (Martin et al. 2009).

In addition, there are specific measures that can be taken as part of a road safety strategy to reduce the risk of alcohol-related collisions. There is evidence from a systematic review of eight studies of a median 13 per cent decrease in crashes following mass media campaigns (Elder et al. 2004). Specialist 'alcohol ignition interlocks' (which require a clear breathalyser test to start the car) can be effective in reducing repeat drink-driving offences, although these changes are not sustained when locks are removed from vehicles (Willis et al. 2004; Elder et al. 2011). These interlocks have, for instance, been installed in many commercial vehicles in Sweden to help reduce collisions (Magnusson et al. 2011). There remains insufficient evidence on the effectiveness of increased police patrols to identify alcohol impaired drivers in significantly reducing accidents and fatalities, although reviews suggest some beneficial effects (Goss et al. 2008). There is also insufficient information on the effectiveness of employers screening employees who drive for a living for alcohol or drugs (Cashman et al. 2009).

There are, of course, measures targeted at other harmful behaviours that can improve safety on the roads. Driving after drinking alcohol substantially increases the chance of a traffic crash. Restrictions on alcohol consumption discussed by Peter Anderson in this volume highlight a wide range of effective interventions to reduce harmful alcohol consumption. For example, in the United States experiments looking at the impact of raising the minimum legal drinking age to 21 in different states have been associated with a 19 per cent reduction in the risk of road-related fatalities in young adults (Shults et al. 2001), while a reduction in the minimum legal age in New Zealand for purchasing alcohol has been associated with a significant rise in crashes and deaths (Kypri et al. 2006).

There is also evidence that helmets reduce the risk of head injuries and deaths in cyclists and motorcyclists (Thompson et al. 2000; Liu et al. 2008). Mandatory legislation for helmets for children in the United States has also been associated with reduced rates of injury (Macpherson and Spinks 2008), while non-legislative approaches such as community campaigns can increase the use of cycle helmets by children (Owen et al. 2011).

Some ineffective interventions are also highlighted in reviews. These include school-based driver education (Roberts and Kwan 2001), which may actually have adverse effects by reducing the age at which people begin driving, as well as post-licence driver education programmes (Ker et al. 2005). Evaluations of some interventions have looked at immediate changes in behaviours, but do not say anything about long-term impacts on injury such as pedestrian safety education for children (Duperrex et al. 2002). Measures to improve the visibility of cyclists and pedestrians do improve detection by drivers, but no work has been done to look at their impact on accidents (Kwan and Mapstone 2006). No robust trials on vision screening of drivers were found in one recent review (Desapriya et al. 2011).

What do we know about cost-effectiveness?

There is a long-standing literature on the economic impacts of investing in road safety measures with many estimates of different interventions (Elvik 2003). We cannot report all of these economic studies here, but instead highlight findings of some studies illustrating the potential cost-effectiveness of different interventions. In doing so, it is important to remember that most effective road safety strategies involve a combination of measures rather than individual measures in isolation; their cost-effectiveness, in combination, may therefore also be somewhat different. Moreover, many interventions we discuss below depend very much on behaviour modification and compliance with laws and regulations, which may differ substantially across cultures. There will also be issues concerned with infrastructure and the absolute cost of scaling up services. We will return to these issues later in the chapter.

Table 9.2 highlights some of the interventions which have been shown to be cost-effective, largely in high-income country contexts. We focus on actions targeted both at the prevention of collisions and the prevention of injury following collision, in line with the Haddon matrix categorization of actions. It builds on studies identified as part of systematic literature reviews, two focused on child injury prevention on the road (Ashton et al. 2009; Anderson and

Table 9.2 Road safety intervention areas where economic evaluations have been published

Phase		Human	Vehicles and equipment	Environment
Pre-accident	Accident prevention	Police enforcement of laws – e.g. on mobile phones/ alcohol/speeding/ drink-driving/ seat belts, mobile phone use etc. Breathalyser tests. Media campaigns. Screening for dementia in drivers. Automated seat belt reminder systems. Advanced driver training and driving practice. Road safety education. Vision tests for drivers.	Intelligent speed adaptation devices. Regulation of motor vehicle maintenance. Vehicle lighting. Alcohol ignition interlocks.	Speed humps. 20 mph zones. Wide range of road design measures – including 'rumble strips' and other audible measures. Street lighting. Dedicated cycleways. Speed limits. Speed cameras.
Accident	Injury prevention during accident	Use of seat belts/ helmets/restraints etc. Financial incentives/access to loans to buy child-care seats.	Air bags. Seat belts. Rear impact guards. Side protection and other vehicle strengthening actions. Roll-over protectors.	Central reservation barriers on roads. Road shoulder installation.

Source: Authors' own.

Moxham 2010), and two reviews related to the economics of injury prevention for the whole population and children under the age of 15 years (McDaid and Park 2009; McDaid et al. 2009).

Traffic calming measures

Economic analyses point to investment in traffic calming measures being cost-effective, with benefits likely to exceed costs in most circumstances. Schemes in several towns in England which involved measures including road closures, traffic islands, central refuges, additional pedestrian crossings and turning restrictions generated average net first year rates of return (FYRR) on investment between 30 per cent to 40 per cent (Mackie et al. 1990). Drawing on information from a database of more than 4,200 local authority road safety schemes across the United Kingdom, the net FYRR was greater still, being more than 225 per cent for 45 area wide traffic calming schemes and 246 per cent for the 579 schemes to introduce pedestrian crossings and other pedestrian facilities (Gorell and Tootill 2001).

Speed limit zones, sometimes in conjunction with physical measures to enforce slower speed (e.g. chicanes or speed humps), are probably a cost-effective form of injury prevention in many circumstances such as town centres and residential areas. Evidence from one cost-benefit analysis of advisory 20 mph speed limits in Scotland (75 sites, mainly comprising new signage) shows that in the short-term (time horizon 2–3 years; FYRR 48 per cent) benefits are likely to exceed costs (Burns et al. 2001). Again from the United Kingdom, there is good evidence from a cost-benefit analysis of mandatory 20 mph zones in London that shows that in the medium- to long-term (time horizon 5 and 10 years) benefits are likely to exceed costs in between 85 per cent and 47 per cent of schemes, depending on the exact time horizon of the analysis and the prior level of casualties at the location. Across the 144 20 mph zones evaluated, a mean net present value of $32,216 (£19,000 in 2005 prices) was achieved (over 5 years, or $113,605 or £67,000 in 2005 prices over 10 years post-implementation) (Grundy et al. 2008). Two other model-based economic analyses that are based on the same data set have confirmed this finding, and in particular the likely cost-effectiveness in 'high casualty' areas; those with >0.7 casualties per kilometre per year prior to intervention (Peters and Anderson 2012; Steinbach et al. 2012).

Other urban speed management interventions have also been assessed. Positive net benefits of 1.8:1 were observed for investment in roundabouts in Sweden, assuming that benefits last for 20 years (Elvik et al. 2009b). Adopting various structural measures at hazardous road locations has been shown to have net benefit-cost ratios in a Norwegian context ranging from 2:1 for converting four-leg junctions to roundabouts to 19:1 for the removal of roadside obstacles (European Transport Safety Council 2003).

The economic case for investing in a range of road adaptations such as rumble strips (which make a noise when a vehicle comes into contact with them), crash barriers and sealed shoulders to reduce the chances of vehicles coming off a road or crashing into other vehicles, have been assessed. In one example from Australia, the economic benefits of these measures assessed as part of a before-and-after study at 13 different sites had net lifetime benefits of more than $41 million ($A50 million in 2004 prices), as a result of casualty crashes being reduced by 80 per cent (Meuleners et al. 2011). Road safety audits have been used to identify accident blackspots. In Australia, work to make 154 accident blackspots more safe (e.g. through traffic islands, roundabouts etc.) was estimated over a ten-year period to have saved societal costs of more than $43 million ($A50.8 million in 2003 prices) compared with costs of $8.9 million ($A10.4 million in 2003 prices) (Meuleners et al. 2008).

Speed limits

Most recent evaluations have focused on the economic case for automated speed monitoring devices such as cameras and radar guns. In these studies, the benefits of speed enforcement programmes have been found to exceed the costs in the short- to medium-term – especially if placed on road sections of known higher accident risk. This claim is based on three cost-benefit analyses of such schemes (one in British Columbia, Canada; one in the United Kingdom; one in Spain). An early photo radar programme in British Columbia was estimated to produce net benefits to society of about $115 million (C$114 million in 2001 prices), and still produced substantial net savings of $38.4 million (C$38 million in 2001 prices) if only considered from the provincial insurance corporation's perspective (Chen 2005).

Another study for the UK Department for Transport, evaluated the national safety camera programme (PA Consulting and UCL 2005). This study estimated that there would be 4,230 fewer personal injury collisions (any road collision which results in at least one casualty, whether fatal, serious or slight) annually as a result of the safety cameras across all 38 safety camera partnerships. At an estimated value of $105,665 (£61,120 in 2004 prices) per collision avoided (using Department for Transport standard estimates for 2004) this means an annual estimated economic benefit of $446 million (£258 million in 2004 prices). This compares with the total annual cost of the programme of $166 million (£96 million in 2004 prices). Comparing only the revenue costs per collision prevented ($105,665 or £61,120 in 2004 prices) with the corresponding economic benefit per collision due to injuries prevented ($39,163 or £22,653 in 2004 prices) over four years gives a cost-benefit ratio of approximately 2.7:1. Finally, a recent study from Spain of the cost-benefit of a photo radar speed enforcement programme on the inner city motorway in Barcelona, found that the programme produced estimated net benefits of $8.9 million (€6.8 million in 2008 prices) over two years; but with wide variation in this estimate in sensitivity analysis from $7.3 to $30.1 million (€5.6 to €23.1 million in 2008 prices) (Mendivil et al. 2012).

There has also been some analysis in Norway of the potential economic case for better prioritization of police enforcement of traffic regulations, so that more time is allocated to those violations, including speeding, that contribute the most to injuries and fatalities. Better prioritization would reduce the number of fatalities without requiring any additional resources (Elvik et al. 2012). Previous analysis in Norway also indicated that there is scope for increased enforcement (by human resources) of rules on speeding, drinking and driving and seat belt wearing. Trebling resources in Norway for enforcement would generate estimated additional positive net benefits (Elvik 2010). Increased investment in police enforcement measures in Sweden over a 23-year period was observed to have a positive net benefit-cost ratio of 4:1 (Elvik et al. 2009b).

Seat belts

Seat belts are an effective measure in reducing the risk of mortality and serious injury from car accidents; however, their overall rate of effectiveness and cost-effectiveness can be improved through behaviour change to encourage routine use for all journeys (Cummins et al. 2008, 2011). Even in Western Europe, where their use has been mandatory in the EU for 20 years, use may be as low as 70 per cent in some settings (Lie et al. 2008). The use of restraints for rear seat passengers or bus passengers is not mandated to the same extent as for front seat passengers. Recent studies on the cost-effectiveness of seat belts focus on measures to enforce or encourage their use in high-income countries, as their use for front seat passengers as part of road safety policy is so widely accepted.

We have already noted work in Norway suggesting that increasing resources three to fourfold for police enforcement of seat belts would be highly cost-effective (Elvik 2010). In the United States state of Ohio, improved enforcement of seat belt legislation that would increase usage rates from 82 per cent to 92 per cent could avoid an additional $17.9 million per annum ($15.3 million per annum in 2003 prices) in health care costs alone (Conner et al. 2010). In the EU, it has been estimated that the value of benefits of mandating audible seat belt reminders for the front seats of cars in the EU amounts to $85,956 million (€66,043 million in 2000 prices) in 2003, compared with costs of $14,507 (€11,146 million in 2000 prices) (European Transport Safety Council 2003). A cost-benefit analysis in Australia looked at an 'aggressive reminder' system to increase the wearing of seat belts. Benefits outweighed costs 4-to-1 for driver reminders, but when the system was applied to all seating positions, costs exceeded benefits (Fildes et al. 2003).

Work has also been conducted in low- and middle-income countries, albeit outside Europe. In South Africa, a cost-benefit analysis modelled the economic benefits of an enhanced enforcement programme (increased numbers of police), leading to a 16 per cent increase in seat belt use and 9.5 per cent decrease in case severity, and generated a net benefit of $5.42 million (11.6 million Rand in 1998 values) after one year (Harris and Olukoga 2005). A programme of increased enforcement and a public awareness campaign to encourage the wearing of seat belts in one city in China led to an increase in seat belt wearing compared with a nearby control city. The intervention was estimated to be highly cost-effective, at $446 per DALY avoided ($418 in 2006 prices) (Stevenson et al. 2008).

In a recent mathematical modelling study, exploring a wide range of road traffic injury prevention strategies in sub-Saharan Africa and South East Asia, primary enforcement of seat belt use, cost $5,038 per DALY avoided ($Int4,579 in 2005 prices). When combined with other interventions, the average cost per DALY ranged from \$1,514 to \$6,020 (\$Int1,376 to \$Int5,472 in 2005 prices) (Chisholm et al. 2012). In this study, multiple interventions were the most cost-effective – for example, when enforcement of seat belt use was combined with initiatives on enforcement of laws on speed limits, drink driving, and use of motor/bicycle helmets.

Car restraints for children

There is an evidence base supporting the cost-effectiveness of safety restraints in cars for children. Using data on the use of booster seats and other restraints for children aged 0–5 in the US in 1987, the cost per life-year saved was estimated to range from \$32,077 to \$50,649 (\$19,000 to \$30,000 in 1987 prices) (Shew and Dardis 1995). More recently, in Sweden it was estimated that current use of car restraints avoided 6 fatalities, 18 serious injuries and 104 minor injuries in 2005. The costs to families of buying seats was \$25 million (SEK 210 million in 2005 prices), with costs avoided of \$85 million (SEK 711 million in 2005 prices) – a benefit-cost ratio of 3.23:1 (Elvik et al. 2009b). A modelling study also showed very positive return on investment from mandatory legislation on the use of booster seats for children aged 4 to 7 years in most of the United States. Costs avoided, including productivity losses to parents, were almost nine times greater than the \$247 investment (\$200 in 2000 prices) by parents in their purchase and maintenance (Miller et al. 2006).

One of the barriers to using car restraints was found to be high costs associated with the purchase (Owen et al. 2011). A decision-modelling study in the United States looked at the benefits of low-income families receiving funding from Medicare to install car restraints as well as an education campaign. After eight years, from a Medicare perspective, the cost per life-year saved was \$20,229 (\$17,000 in 2002 prices); from a societal perspective the scheme was estimated to be cost saving (Goldstein et al. 2008). Another model-based economic evaluation looked at a scheme for a hospital in Greece to allow new parents to borrow special child seats through a low-cost loan scheme. Compared to no intervention, from a societal perspective the estimated incremental cost per life-year saved was \$4,197 (€3,225 in 2000 prices) (Kedikoglou et al. 2005). Four-fifths of families went on to purchase new child seats as their infants grew.

Use of phones while driving

The use of mobile phones while driving increases the risk of collisions and accidents. Legislation has been introduced in a number of countries to restrict the use of phones by drivers of vehicles, and decision analytic modelling studies have been used to assess the cost-effectiveness of implementing a ban on the use of phones while driving. Early modelling studies suggested that the cost per quality-adjusted life year (QALY) gained through enforcement of regulation was not cost-effective (more than \$300,000) and that it would be better to increase the per-minute cost of calls to reduce their use (Redelmeier and Weinstein 1999; Cohen and Graham 2003). More recently, modelling was used to look at a law banning the use of mobile phones in Alberta, Canada (Sperber et al. 2010). It assumed, unlike previous models, that individuals would be more likely to comply with the law in respect of 'low value' calls only, reducing the adverse impacts of not taking phone calls. They found an 80 per cent chance that the law would be cost saving from a societal perspective with a 94 per cent chance of being less than $41,133 (C$50,000 in 2008 prices) per QALY gained.

Alcohol-impaired driving

Mass media campaigns to reduce the rate of alcohol impaired driving have been shown to generate positive returns on investment due to accidents avoided in studies in the United States and Australia. In the Australian campaign, the monthly costs of the media campaign were $522,506 ($403,174 in 1997 prices) compared with estimated savings from medical costs, productivity losses, pain and suffering, and property damage of over $10 million per month ($8 million in 1997 prices), of which $4.2 million ($3.2 million) was due to medical costs averted (Elder et al. 2004). Similarly, the total six-month costs of media campaigns in two United States cities, Wichita and Kansas City, were $588,376 and $417,306 ($454,000 and $322,000 in 1997 prices) compared to the estimated costs avoided of $4.4 and $4.7 million ($3.4 and $3.6 million in 1997 prices) respectively (Elder et al. 2004). Miller et al. looked at three different approaches to compulsory breath testing in New Zealand, in which a 'standard' intensive campaign was compared with one which also had an enhanced media campaign and another which also made use of 'booze buses'(Miller et al. 2004). All three programmes were estimated to have generated net benefits, with the comprehensive programme having a return of 26:1.

Raising the minimum legal age of drinking from 18 to 21 has been modelled as being more cost-effective than random breath tests or mass media campaigns in Australia, with both better outcomes and reduced costs (Cobiac et al. 2009). Perhaps a more politically feasible alternative with similar cost-effectiveness may be to enforce a zero tolerance blood alcohol level in young drivers to age 21 (Hall et al. 2010).

The scope for alcohol ignition interlocks to be cost-effective is increasing. Alcohol ignition interlocks have been mandated in some commercial vehicles in Sweden with positive societal benefits (Magnusson et al. 2011). Uptake of use of these locks in private cars is more of a challenge, but in Sweden incentives are being used to increase use. A high uptake rate among convicted drivers is encouraged as the alternative is a longer period with a driving licence. A modelling study looking at the use of alcohol ignition interlocks in Australia for all new cars, and not just those of high-risk groups, has also shown this to be cost-effective (Lahausse and Fildes 2009).

Vehicle modifications

The impacts of improved build standards in vehicles have also been examined. For instance, ultraviolet headlights have been shown to increase the visibility of pedestrians and other road users at night. Modelling scenarios on the costs of these lamps and impact on crashes suggests that only modest effectiveness is required for benefits to outweigh costs (Lestina et al. 2002). Data on the potential cost-effectiveness of daytime running lights (lights that come on automatically when the engine is started) was helpful in moving to their mandatory use in all new cars and small vans in the EU from 2011, and in buses and trucks from August 2012. The economic modelling analysis had a benefit-cost ratio of at least 4.4:1, and could reduce deaths (in those countries where it was not already in place) by 2,800 in the EU-15 annually (European Transport Safety Council 2003).

Modest economic benefits have been estimated in studies looking at the use of airbags in cars (Graham et al. 1997; Thompson et al. 2002; Williams et al. 2008), but their cost-effectiveness is much lower than that of the use of seat belts or motorcycle helmets (Kent et al. 2005). One promising technological development concerns Intelligent Speed Adaptation (ISA) systems; these systems can warn drivers about their speed and even prevent vehicles from exceeding speed limits. One recent trial in Australia of an ISA warning system suggests that annual deaths may be reduced by 8 per cent through the use of these systems (New South Wales Centre for Road Safety 2011); exploratory cost-benefit modelling from trials of ISA systems suggests they could avoid 25 per cent of all serious crashes and 30 per cent of all fatal accidents with benefit-cost ratios between 3:1 and 7:1 (Lai et al. 2012). It remains to be seen how and where ISA schemes will be implemented in real-world settings.

Licensing and driver education

Some economic analysis has looked at restrictions on the licensing of new drivers, as well as opportunities for training and education. For instance, in one study in the United States, driving licences placed a midnight to 5am curfew on drivers until the age of 19, or at least six consecutive months without a crash or moving violation, and this was estimated to have a benefit-cost ratio of at least 4:1 even after the costs of enforcement were taken into account (Miller et al. 1998). Work in Sweden making use of information from the national accident database and survey data on the exposure of learner drivers to additional supervized practice from lay drivers reported benefits to outweigh costs by a factor of 30 (Gregersen et al. 2003). Decision modelling of providing all older drivers with speed of cognitive processing interventions designed to maintain or improve functional abilities suggests that this is a less costly way of reducing the risk of collisions in older drivers compared to screening strategies (Viamonte et al. 2006).

Wearing bicycle helmets: legislative and other interventions

Three economic evaluations of legislation about bicycle helmets all compared costs with different measures of effectiveness or societal benefit (e.g. net benefit, cost per life saved, cost per life-year saved, cost per hospitalization prevented, cost per injury avoided) (Hansen and Scuffham 1995; Hatziandreu et al. 1995; Taylor and Scuffham 2002).

There is inconsistent evidence from these studies in New Zealand and the United States that national laws to make the wearing of bicycle helmets compulsory would be cost-effective from a societal perspective. However, from a *public sector* perspective – critically, omitting the cost to individuals or families of purchasing bicycle helmets – the measure is likely to be highly cost-effective. The two New Zealand studies suggested that bicycle helmet laws would be more cost-effective in younger (age 5–12 years) than older children (age 13–18 years), and one of them estimated that costs would probably exceed benefits in older children and adults (again, from a societal perspective) (Hansen and Scuffham 1995; Taylor and Scuffham 2002).

The United States-based study also estimated the cost-effectiveness of community-wide and school-based strategies for promoting the wearing of bicycle helmets, but did not directly compare these strategies with the legislative approach (Hatziandreu et al. 1995). However, when compared with 'no programme' the legislative approach was the most cost-effective of the three strategies (but still with an estimated cost per life-year saved of over $1,207,993 ($900,000 in 1995 prices) – which, from a health care perspective, would not normally be judged as cost-effective).

Very few studies have looked at the economic impact of non-legislative interventions to encourage the wearing of bicycle helmets. This may reflect the limited evidence base on the effectiveness of such interventions. Apart from the Hatziandreu study described above, we found only one other study. This fairly old United States study used a simulation model to look at the potential cost-effectiveness of providing subsidies for bicycle helmets for a hypothetical cohort of 100,000 children aged 5 to 9 years old. Plausible scenarios in terms of the cost of a helmet and a 40 per cent to 50 per cent increase in helmet use would generate net cost savings, if the costs of serious head injuries avoided are included (Thompson et al. 1993).

Wearing motorcycle helmets: legislative interventions

Most European countries have legislation on wearing motorcycle helmets, although helmet wearing behaviour varies. Although they were all conducted before 2000, cost-benefit analyses for mandatory motorcycle helmet laws in the USA have shown positive economic gains. For instance, benefit to cost ratios were 1.33:1 including helmet costs only (Rice et al. 1989), 2.3:1 assuming a 100 per cent compliance rate of wearing a helmet (Muller 1980), and 17:1 (Miller and Levy 2000). Another study from Taiwan also showed a favourable ratio of 4.75:1 when including the cost of a helmet only (Garbacz 1989). In a more recent mathematical modelling study of traffic injury prevention in sub-Saharan Africa and South East Asia, although the per person cost per DALY avoided of wearing motorcycle helmets was $7,353 (Int$6,683 in 2005 prices) in Sub-Saharan Africa, compared to no intervention, and $1,866 (Int$1,696 in 2005 prices) in South East Asia, it was dominated by other more cost-effective interventions in both regions (Chisholm et al. 2012).

The way forward

Enhancing the cost-effectiveness of road safety policies

Road safety has improved tremendously in many European countries in the last 20 years, but there is great variation in the rates of severe injury and death in Europe. Even in the best performing countries in Europe there is scope to improve safety.

The development of any road safety strategy needs to be informed by both evidence on effectiveness and cost-effectiveness. We have indicated that there are reasonable clusters of good quality economic evaluations for some interventions, sometimes in a range of different countries (e.g. speed enforcement devices). For some other aspects of road safety the pattern of economic evidence on preventing road injuries is dogged by a paucity of recent studies and extensive heterogeneity. Much of this heterogeneity relates to the variability in the scale and detailed context of the injury prevention or road safety interventions themselves. This, and the fact that the effectiveness of some interventions is highly context-sensitive, especially those that require behaviour change, means that policymakers need to carefully weigh up the strengths and limitations of existing evidence, factoring in the resources required to scale up effective interventions.

Nonetheless, a number of reviews consistently point to substantial economic benefits of investing in road safety measures, both in high-income country settings and also now in low- or middle-income country contexts. For example, analysis undertaken in the United States found that 19 of 33 road safety measures had net societal benefits (Miller and Levy 2000). An economic evaluation of a range of road safety strategies in New Zealand also concluded that 'safety programmes (particularly those programmes aimed at reducing high-risk behaviour on the road) are producing considerably high returns' (Guria 1999).

Work in Sweden and Norway suggests that if investment in road safety measures over a ten-year period used the many interventions that had been shown to be cost-effective, then around 60 per cent of fatalities would be averted, compared with the existing policies at the time which would have averted only 10–15 per cent of deaths (Elvik 2003). In sub-Saharan Africa and South East Asia, a combination of different road safety interventions has been estimated to have costs per DALY avoided that would be considered cost-effective (Chisholm et al. 2012).

In terms of actions that can be taken, the evidence on effectiveness suggests that the biggest contributions that are made to reducing serious injuries and fatalities are associated with vehicle safety features, police/technological enforcement of traffic regulations and environmental modifications. In the case of the former, the costs to the public purse may be modest as national and international regulations on vehicle standards and commercial competition on the safety features in cars have served to drive up standards, for instance with better structural protection within vehicles, complete air bag systems as standard and seat belt reminder systems in most cars. In Europe, manufacturers also want to achieve '5 star status' as part of the European New Car Assessment Programme (EuroNCAP) which demonstrates that car models have better protection against fatal or serious injury in crashes.

Barriers to implementation of vehicle modifications can be identified; for instance, the conflict between interventions shown to be cost-effective from a societal point of view that may not appear cost-effective from the perspective of the road user (Elvik 2003). This includes some technological features, which have been shown to be cost-effective from a societal perspective, but which would usually have to be paid for as additional extras by private individuals. One such example is the alcohol ignition interlock; there may be a case for public funding of these interlocks for high-risk drivers. Some of the costs of this might be met outside the public sector – for instance, through the mandatory installation of alcohol ignition locks on commercial vehicles. ISA systems also potentially could reduce fatalities greatly and generate favourable cost-benefit ratios, but it is likely to be some time before the technology becomes commonplace, even though its costs have fallen markedly.

In terms of enforcement of traffic laws and regulations, there is a good body of evidence from different countries supporting the use of speed enforcement devices; rational or intensified speed enforcement strategies; the use of seat belts/restraints/booster seats; legislation and enforcement of the wearing of motorcycle helmets and bicycle helmets for children. The way in which existing human resources are used for enforcement can also be examined and potentially redistributed to focus on higher fatality risk behaviours or higher risk locations. There is also ample evidence to support measures particularly targeted at reducing the likelihood of alcohol impaired driving.

There is also an economic case for modifying the road environment. There are numerous economic analyses on a wide range of measures, with encouraging cost-effectiveness for traffic calming measures such as the use of 20 mph/ 30 km ph speed zones, and road adaptations and modifications targeted in accident hotspots, such as the installation of roundabouts and pedestrian islands.

Challenges

Even though we have indicated that there is significant literature on the economic case for road safety interventions, there are some limitations. Some of the heterogeneity in the economic evidence relates to variations in the economic evaluation methods used. In particular, while transport economists usually use cost-benefit analysis to assess 'road safety schemes', health economists evaluating alternative 'interventions to prevent road injuries' will often use cost-effectiveness or cost-utility analysis. Although such cost-effectiveness analyses will generally adopt a broad perspective on costs and benefits, they will generally be less comprehensive, and adhere to different conventions for costing capital investment or valuing productivity losses. In contrast, the analytical conventions of some transport economists, such as estimating costs and benefits for fixed 5- or 10-year time horizons, may also provide an incomplete picture of the costs and benefits of a safety measure over its whole 'effective life'. Whether cost-benefit or cost-effectiveness analyses are used, there is also a lack of consideration of distributional issues in most economic evaluations of road injury prevention programmes, (e.g.

with subgroup analyses being restricted to age-groups, pedestrians vs vehicle occupants, or localities being defined purely in terms of prior casualty rates or urban/rural).

There also seems to be much less economic compared to effectiveness evidence about legislative and regulatory measures, although for seat belts/restraints and child car seats there are a few studies on enforcement strategies and financial incentive/discount schemes to encourage greater use. We could find no economic evaluations of graduated driver licensing for younger drivers, despite a Cochrane systematic review which concluded that this is an effective regulatory intervention for reducing road injuries.

There is a paucity of evaluative and economic evidence generated in the low- and middle-income countries (Hyder and Aggarwal 2009). There are therefore challenges in considering the potential transferability of cost-effective interventions across the European region and beyond. For instance, how effective can legislative and regulatory measures be, and how can resources for enforcement best be distributed?

Another complication is that, despite the useful categorizations of the Haddon Matrix, effective road safety policies will need to combine a range of actions at different levels – vehicle modification, legislative, enforcement, media campaigns, and road design. For example, at a local level there might be 'Safe Routes to Schools' policies (which can incorporate road safety education, road redesign, new pedestrian crossings, and media and curriculum initiatives to foster more active travel to get to school). At a national or regional level, reducing injuries from speeding probably results from the combined effects of targeted road redesign, rational setting of speed-limits, and effective automated and non-automated enforcement on different types of road – perhaps in the context of national road safety targets (Chisholm et al. 2012). Such multi-component and cumulative strategies are typically harder to rigorously evaluate. Will some interventions reduce the effectiveness or cost-effectiveness of others? Quite possibly. To date, there has been very little research on appropriate methods for determining the combined effectiveness of road safety measures (Elvik 2009) or indeed their cost-effectiveness.

References

Aeron-Thomas, A. S. and Hess, S. (2005) Red-light cameras for the prevention of road traffic crashes, *Cochrane Database of Systematic Reviews*, CD003862.

Anderson, R. and Moxham, T. (2010) *Preventing Unintentional Injuries in Children: Systematic Review to Provide an Overview of Published Economic Evaluations of Relevant Legislation Regulations, Standards and/or their Enforcement or Promotion by Mass Media.* Report for NICE Programme Development Group. Exeter: PenTAG, University of Exeter.

Ashton, K., Moxham, T., Frier, J., Rogers, G., Garside, R. and Anderson, R. (2009) *Interventions to Prevent Unintentional Injury to Children on the Road – Report 1: Systematic Reviews of Effectiveness and Cost-effectiveness of Road and Street Design-based Interventions aimed at Reducing Unintentional Injuries in Children.* Report for NICE Public Health Interventions Advisory Committee. Exeter: PenTAG, University of Exeter.

Bastida, J. L., Aguilar, P. S. and Gonzalez, B. D. (2004) The economic costs of traffic accidents in Spain, *Journal of Trauma*, 56: 883–8; discussion 888–9.

Beyer, F. R. and Ker, K. (2009) Street lighting for preventing road traffic injuries, *Cochrane Database of Systematic Reviews*, CD004728.

Breen, J. (2010) *Road Safety Performance: National Peer Review: Russian Federation. 2010 Update*. Paris: International Transport Forum, OECD.

Bunn, F., Collier, T., Frost, C., Ker, K., Roberts, I. and Wentz, R. (2003) Area-wide traffic calming for preventing traffic related injuries, *Cochrane Database of Systematic Reviews*, CD003110.

Burns, A., Johnstone, N. and Macdonald, N. (2001) *20 mph Speed Reduction Initiative*. Edinburgh: Scottish Executive Central Research Unit.

Cashman, C. M., Ruotsalainen, J. H., Greiner, B. A., Beirne, P. V. and Verbeek, J. H. (2009) Alcohol and drug screening of occupational drivers for preventing injury, *Cochrane Database of Systematic Reviews*, CD006566.

Chen, G. (2005) Safety and economic impacts of photo radar program, *Traffic Injury Prevention*, 6.

Chisholm, D., Naci, H., Hyder, A. A., Tran, N. T. and Peden, M. (2012) Cost effectiveness of strategies to combat road traffic injuries in sub-Saharan Africa and South East Asia: mathematical modelling study, *British Medical Journal*, 344.

Cobiac, L., Vos, T., Doran, C. and Wallace, A. (2009) Cost-effectiveness of interventions to prevent alcohol-related disease and injury in Australia, *Addiction*, 104: 1646–55.

Cohen, J. T. and Graham, J. D. (2003) A revised economic analysis of restrictions on the use of cell phones while driving, *Risk Analysis*, 23: 5–17.

Connelly, L. B. and Supangan, R. (2006) The economic costs of road traffic crashes: Australia, states and territories, *Accident Analysis & Prevention*, 38: 1087–93.

Conner, K. A., Xiang, H. and Smith, G. A. (2010) The impact of a standard enforcement safety belt law on fatalities and hospital charges in Ohio, *Journal of Safety Research*, 41: 17–23.

Cummins, J. S., Koval, K. J., Cantu, R. V. and Spratt, K. F. (2008) Risk of injury associated with the use of seat belts and air bags in motor vehicle crashes, *Bulletin of the NYU Hospital for Joint Diseases*, 66: 290–6.

Cummins, J. S., Koval, K. J., Cantu, R. V. and Spratt, K. F. (2011) Do seat belts and air bags reduce mortality and injury severity after car accidents?, *American Journal of Orthopedics (Belle Mead NJ)*, 40: E26–9.

Department of Transport (2010) *A Valuation of Road Accidents and Casualties in Great Britain in 2010*. London: Department of Transport.

Desapriya, E., Wijeratne, H., Subzwari, S. et al. (2011) Vision screening of older drivers for preventing road traffic injuries and fatalities, *Cochrane Database of Systematic Reviews*, CD006252.

De Waard, D. and Rooijers, T. (1994) An experimental study to evaluate the effectiveness of different methods and intensities of law enforcement on driving speed on motorways, *Accident Analysis & Prevention*, 26(6): 751–65.

Duperrex, O., Roberts, I. and Bunn, F. (2002) Safety education of pedestrians for injury prevention, *Cochrane Database of Systematic Reviews*, CD001531.

Elder, R. W., Shults, R. A., Sleet, D. A., Nichols, J. L., Thompson, R. S. and Rajab, W. (2004) Effectiveness of mass media campaigns for reducing drinking and driving and alcohol-involved crashes: A systematic review, *American Journal of Preventive Medicine*, 27: 57–65.

Elder, R. W., Voas, R., Beirness, D. et al. (2011) Effectiveness of ignition interlocks for preventing alcohol-impaired driving and alcohol-related crashes: A Community Guide systematic review, *American Journal of Preventive Medicine*, 40: 362–76.

Elvik, R. (2003) How would setting policy priorities according to cost-benefit analyses affect the provision of road safety?, *Accident Analysis & Prevention*, 35: 557–70.

Elvik, R. (2009) An exploratory analysis of models for estimating the combined effects of road safety measures, *Accident Analysis & Prevention*, 41: 876–80.

Elvik, R. (2010) *Utviklingen i oppdagelsesrisiko for trafikkforseelser*. Rapport 1059. Oslo: Transportökonomisk institutt.

Elvik, R., Hoye, A., Vaa, T. and Sorenson, M. (eds.) (2009a) *Handbook of Road Safety Measures*, 2nd edn. Bingley: Emerald Group.

Elvik, R., Kolbenstvedt, M., Elvebakk, B., Hervik, A. and Braein, L. (2009b) Costs and benefits to Sweden of Swedish road safety research, *Accident Analysis & Prevention*, 41: 387–92.

Elvik, R., Sogge, C. V., Lager, L. et al. (2012) Assessing the efficiency of priorities for traffic law enforcement in Norway, *Accident Analysis & Prevention*, 47: 146–52.

European Transport Safety Council (2003) *Cost Effective EU Transport Safety Measures*. Brussels: European Transport Safety Council.

Fildes, B., Fitzharris, M., Koppel, S., Vulcan, P. and Brooks, C. (2003) Benefits of seat belt reminder systems, *Annual Proceedings of the Association for the Advancement of Automotive Medicine*, 47: 253–66.

Garbacz, C. (1989) Traffic fatalities in Taiwan, *Journal of Transport Economics and Policy*, 23: 317–27.

Garcia-Altes, A. and Perez, K. (2007) The economic cost of road traffic crashes in an urban setting, *Injury Prevention*, 13: 65–8.

Garcia-Altes, A. and Puig-Junoy, J. (2011) What is the social cost of injured people in traffic collisions? An assessment for Catalonia, *Journal of Trauma*, 70: 744–50.

Goldstein, J. A., Winston, F. K., Kallan, M. J., Branas, C. C. and Schwartz, J. S. (2008) Medicaid-based child restraint system disbursement and education and the vaccines for children program: Comparative cost-effectiveness, *Ambulatory Pediatrics*, 8: 58–65.

Gorell, R. S. J. and Tootill, W. (2001) *Monitoring Local Authority Road Safety Schemes using MOLASSES*. Wokingham: Transport Research Laboratory.

Goss, C. W., Van Bramer, L. D., Gliner, J. A., Porter, T. R., Roberts, I. G. and Diguiseppi, C. (2008) Increased police patrols for preventing alcohol-impaired driving, *Cochrane Database of Systematic Reviews*, CD005242.

Graham, J. D., Thompson, K. M., Goldie, S. J., Segui-Gomez, M. and Weinstein, M. C. (1997) The cost-effectiveness of air bags by seating position, *Journal of the American Medical Association*, 278: 1418–25.

Gregersen, N. P., Nyberg, A. and Berg, H. Y. (2003) Accident involvement among learner drivers – an analysis of the consequences of supervised practice, *Accident Analysis & Prevention*, 35: 725–30.

Grundy, C., Steinbach, R., Edwards, P., Wilkinson, P. and Green, J. (2008) *20 mph Zones and Road Safety in London: A Report to the London Road Safety Unit*. London: London Road Safety Unit.

Guria, J. (1999) An economic evaluation of incremental resources to road safety programmes in New Zealand, *Accident Analysis & Prevention*, 31: 91–9.

Hall, W. D., Wallace, A. L., Cobiac, L. J., Doran, C. M. and Vos, T. (2010) How can we reduce alcohol-related road crash deaths among young Australians?, *Medical Journal of Australia*, 192: 464–6.

Hansen, P. and Scuffham, P. A. (1995) The cost-effectiveness of compulsory bicycle helmets in New Zealand, *Australian Journal of Public Health*, 19: 450–4.

Harris, G. T. and Olukoga, I. A. (2005) A cost benefit analysis of an enhanced seat belt enforcement program in South Africa, *Injury Prevention*, 11: 102–5.

Hatziandreu, E. J., Sacks, J. J., Brown, R., Taylor, W. R., Rosenberg, M. L. and Graham, J. D. (1995) The cost effectiveness of three programs to increase use of bicycle helmets among children, *Public Health Reports*, 110: 251–9.

Hyder, A. A. and Aggarwal, A. (2009) The increasing burden of injuries in Eastern Europe and Eurasia: Making the case for safety investments, *Health Policy*, 89: 1–13.

Kedikoglou, S., Belechri, M., Dedoukou, X. et al. (2005) A maternity hospital-based infant car-restraint loan scheme: Public health and economic evaluation of an intervention for the reduction of road traffic injuries, *Scandinavian Journal of Public Health*, 33: 42–9.

Kent, R., Viano, D. C. and Crandall, J. (2005) The field performance of frontal air bags: A review of the literature, *Traffic Injury Prevention*, 6: 1–23.

Ker, K., Roberts, I., Collier, T., Beyer, F., Bunn, F. and Frost, C. (2005) Post-licence driver education for the prevention of road traffic crashes: A systematic review of randomised controlled trials, *Accident Analysis & Prevention*, 37: 305–13.

Kwan, I. and Mapstone, J. (2006) Interventions for increasing pedestrian and cyclist visibility for the prevention of death and injuries, *Cochrane Database of Systematic Reviews*, CD003438.

Kypri, K., Voas, R. B., Langley, J. D. et al. (2006) Minimum purchasing age for alcohol and traffic crash injuries among 15- to 19-year-olds in New Zealand, *American Journal of Public Health*, 96: 126–31.

Lahausse, J. A. and Fildes, B. N. (2009) Cost–benefit analysis of an alcohol ignition interlock for installation in all newly registered vehicles, *Traffic Injury Prevention*, 10: 528–37.

Lai, F., Carsten, O. and Tate, F. (2012) How much benefit does Intelligent Speed Adaptation deliver: An analysis of its potential contribution to safety and environment, *Accident Analysis & Prevention*, 48: 63–72.

Lestina, D., Miller, T., Langston, E., Knoblauch, R. and Nitzburg, M. (2002) Benefits and costs of ultraviolet fluorescent lighting, *Traffic Injury Prevention*, 3: 209–15.

Lie, A., Krafft, M., Kullgren, A. and Tingvall, C. (2008) Intelligent seat belt reminders – do they change driver seat belt use in Europe?, *Traffic Injury Prevention*, 9: 446–9.

Liu, B. C., Ivers, R., Norton, R., Boufous, S., Blows, S. and Lo, S. K. (2008) Helmets for preventing injury in motorcycle riders, *Cochrane Database of Systematic Reviews*, CD004333.

Lopez, J., Serrano, P., Duque, B. and Artiles, J. (2001) [Socio-economic costs of road traffic accidents in the Canary Islands, Spain, in 1997] [Spanish], *Gac Sanit*, 15: 414–22.

Mackie, A., Ward, H. and Walker, R. (1990) *Urban Safety Project, 3: Overall Evaluation of Area-wide Schemes*. Crowthorne: Transport and Road Research Laboratory.

Macpherson, A. and Spinks, A. (2008) Bicycle helmet legislation for the uptake of helmet use and prevention of head injuries, *Cochrane Database of Systematic Reviews*, CD005401.

Magnusson, P., Jakobsson, L. and Hultman, S. (2011) Alcohol interlock systems in Sweden: 10 years of systematic work, *American Journal of Preventive Medicine*, 40: 378–9.

Martin, A. J., Marottoli, R. and O'Neill, D. (2009) Driving assessment for maintaining mobility and safety in drivers with dementia, *Cochrane Database of Systematic Reviews*, CD006222.

McDaid, D. and Park, A. (2009) *A Systematic Review of the Economic Costs and Consequences of Road Traffic Safety Interventions*. Report prepared for EU APOLLO project on Best Practice in Injury Prevention. London: PSSRU.

McDaid, D., Park, A., Anderson, R., Liu, Z. and Moxham, T. (2009) *Current Practice and Innovative Approaches to Prevent Childhood Unintentional Injuries: An Overview and Synthesis of International Comparative Analyses and surveys of Injury Prevention Policies, Legislation and Other Activities.* Report prepared for Child Injury Prevention Programme Development Group. London: NICE.

Mendivil, J., Garcia-Altes, A., Perez, K., Mari-Dell'Olmo, M. and Tobias, A. (2012) Speed cameras in an urban setting: A cost-benefit analysis, *Injury Prevention*, 18: 75–80.

Meuleners, L. B., Hendrie, D. and Lee, A. H. (2011) Effectiveness of sealed shoulders and audible edge lines in Western Australia, *Traffic Injury Prevention*, 12: 201–5.

Meuleners, L. B., Hendrie, D., Lee, A. H. and Legge, M. (2008) Effectiveness of the black spot programs in Western Australia, *Accident Analysis & Prevention*, 40: 1211–16.

Miller, T., Blewden, M. and Zhang, J. F. (2004) Cost savings from a sustained compulsory breath testing and media campaign in New Zealand, *Accident Analysis & Prevention*, 36: 783–94.

Miller, T. R., Lestina, D. C. and Spicer, R. S. (1998) Highway crash costs in the United States by driver age, blood alcohol level, victim age, and restraint use, *Accident Analysis & Prevention*, 30: 137–50.

Miller, T. R. and Levy, D. T. (2000) Cost–outcome analysis in injury prevention and control: Eighty-four recent estimates for the United States, *Med Care*, 38: 562–82.

Miller, T. R., Zaloshnja, E. and Hendrie, D. (2006) Cost–outcome analysis of booster seats for auto occupants aged 4 to 7 years, *Pediatrics*, 118: 1994–8.

Muller, A. (1980) Evaluation of the costs and benefits of motorcycle helmet laws, *American Journal of Public Health*, 70(6): 586–92.

New South Wales Centre for Road Safety (2011) *Results of the New South Wales Intelligent Speed Adaptation (ISA) trial.* Wollongong: Roads & Traffic Authority of New South Wales. Available at http://roadsafety.transport.nsw.gov.au/downloads/isa_trial/rta_isa_trial_factsheet_final.pdf [Accessed September 2014].

Owen, R., Kendrick, D., Mulvaney, C., Coleman, T. and Royal, S. (2011) Non-legislative interventions for the promotion of cycle helmet wearing by children, *Cochrane Database of Systematic Reviews*, 9.

PA Consulting and UCL (2005) *The National Safety Camera Programme: Four-year Evaluation Report.* London: PA Consulting.

Peters, J. L. and Anderson, R. (2012) The cost-effectiveness of mandatory 20 mph zones for the prevention of injuries, *Journal of Public Health (Oxford)*.

Redelmeier, D. A. and Weinstein, M. C. (1999) Cost-effectiveness of regulations against using a cellular telephone while driving, *Medical Decision Making*, 19: 1–8.

Reynolds, D. J. (1956) The cost of road accidents, *Journal of the Royal Statistical Society*, 119: 393–408.

Rice, D. P., Mackenzie, E. J., Jones, A. S. et al. (1989) Cost of injury in the United States: A report to congress. Atlanta, GA: Centers for Disease Control and Prevention.

Roberts, I. and Kwan, I. (2001) School based driver education for the prevention of traffic crashes, *Cochrane Database of Systematic Reviews*, CD003201.

Russell, K. F., Vandermeer, B. and Hartling, L. (2011) Graduated driver licensing for reducing motor vehicle crashes among young drivers (Review), *The Cochrane Library*, Issue 10.

Shew, R. and Dardis, R. (1995) An economic analysis of child restraints, *Journal of Consumer Policy*, 18: 417–35.

Shults, R. A., Elder, R. W., Sleet, D. A. et al. (2001) Reviews of evidence regarding interventions to reduce alcohol-impaired driving, *American Journal of Preventive Medicine*, 21: 66–88.

Sperber, D., Shiell, A. and Fyie, K. (2010) The cost-effectiveness of a law banning the use of cellular phones by drivers, *Health Economics*, 19: 1212–25.

Steinbach, R., Cairns, J., Grundy, C. and Edwards, P. (2012) Cost benefit analysis of 20 mph zones in London, *Injury Prevention*; doi:10.1136/injuryprev-2012-040347.

Stevenson, M., Yu, J., Hendrie, D. et al. (2008) Reducing the burden of road traffic injury: Translating high-income country interventions to middle-income and low-income countries, *Injury Prevention*, 14: 284–9.

Taylor, M. and Scuffham, P. (2002) New Zealand bicycle helmet law – do the costs outweigh the benefits?, *Injury Prevention*, 8: 317–20.

Thompson, D. C., Rivara, F. P. and Thompson, R. (2000) Helmets for preventing head and facial injuries in bicyclists, *Cochrane Database of Systematic Reviews*, CD001855.

Thompson, K. M., Segui-Gomez, M. and Graham, J. D. (2002) Validating benefit and cost estimates: The case of airbag regulation, *Risk Analysis*, 22: 803–11.

Thompson, R. S., Thompson, D. C., Rivara, F. P. and Salazar, A. A. (1993) Cost-effectiveness analysis of bicycle helmet subsidies in a defined population, *Pediatrics*, 91: 902–7.

Trawen, A., Maraste, P. and Persson, U. (2002) International comparison of costs of a fatal casualty of road accidents in 1990 and 1999, *Accident Analysis & Prevention*, 34: 323–32.

van Beeck, E. F., van Roijen, L. and Mackenbach, J. P. (1997) Medical costs and economic production losses due to injuries in the Netherlands, *Journal of Trauma*, 42: 1116–23.

Veisten, K., Saelensminde, K., Alvaer, K. et al. (2007) Total costs of bicycle injuries in Norway: Correcting injury figures and indicating data needs, *Accident Analysis & Prevention*, 39: 1162–9.

Viamonte, S. M., Ball, K. K. and Kilgore, M. (2006) A cost-benefit analysis of risk-reduction strategies targeted at older drivers, *Traffic Injury Prevention*, 7: 352–9.

Williams, R. F., Fabian, T. C., Fischer, P. E., Zarzaur, B. L., Magnotti, L. J. and Croce, M. A. (2008) Impact of airbags on a Level I trauma center: Injury patterns, infectious morbidity, and hospital costs, *Journal of the American College of Surgeons*, 206: 962–8; discussion 968–9.

Willis, C., Lybrand, S. and Bellamy, N. (2004) Alcohol ignition interlock programmes for reducing drink driving recidivism, *Cochrane Database of Systematic Reviews*, CD004168.

Wilson, C., Willis, C., Hendrikz, J. K., Le Brocque, R. and Bellamy, N. (2010) Speed cameras for the prevention of road traffic injuries and deaths, *Cochrane Database of Systematic Reviews*, CD004607.

World Health Organization (2013) *European Health For All Database*. Copenhagen: World Health Organization [Accessed December 2013].

World Health Organization (2014) WHO Mortality Database. Geneva: World Health Organization.

Zambon, F., Sethi, D. and Racioppi, F. (2009) *European Status Report on Road Safety: Towards Safer Roads and Healthier Transport Choices*. Copenhagen: WHO Regional Office for Europe.

chapter ten

Protecting mental health, preventing depression

Filip Smit, Pim Cuijpers,
Ionela Petrea and David McDaid

Introduction

Poor mental health can have long lasting impacts across the life course. From an economic perspective, externalities associated with poor mental health help justify public investment in mental health promotion. They include the adverse impacts on family members who may have to provide care and support, an increased risk of avoidable physical health problems, reduced opportunities in all aspects of life for young people, including reduced participation in the workforce and reduced career opportunities when at work.

What is clear is that current psychological and pharmaceutical treatments can only reduce poor mental health to a limited extent. For instance, one modelling study in Australia estimated that even if all people living with depression received evidence-based treatment, only about 34 per cent of the disease burden of major depression could be averted (Andrews et al. 2004). When adjusted to the actual availability of evidence-based treatment within the current health system, this percentage decreases to 16 per cent. Another modelling study, stratified for each of the WHO regions, shows similar findings for European countries (Chisholm et al. 2004).

These findings suggest that preventive interventions could play a key role in decreasing the disease burden currently not averted by treatments alone (Cuijpers 2003; Smit et al. 2006a). Another reason for a focus on looking at the economic case for preventing depression in particular, is the improved understanding of the processes involved in its aetiology. In the past 15 years, knowledge has increased considerably on identifying target groups for prevention, underlying risk factors, and the effectiveness of preventive interventions

A greater focus on prevention could potentially help to alleviate disease burden, bring additional benefits, and stem subsequent avoidable health care uptake and productivity losses. We therefore need to know how effective and cost-effective are actions to promote mental health and prevent the onset of mental health problems. Are such investments a better use of scarce resources than investment in treating mental health problems when they arise in the population?

This chapter aims to bring together this evidence base, looking at actions across the life course and in different settings. It focuses on relatively simple, feasible interventions that are potentially scalable. Much of the material is taken from a database of the clinical trial literature at the Department of Clinical Psychology at the VU University, Amsterdam (www.psychotherapyrcts.org) in addition to published reviews on the economics of mental health promotion (Zechmeister et al. 2008; Knapp et al. 2011b; McDaid and Park 2011; Mihalopoulos et al. 2011, 2012). In terms of economic evidence we have sought to identify both empirical studies conducted alongside trials and economic modelling studies making use of data from trials. A broad range of interventions are available, many of which can be delivered on a face-to-face basis or through self-help materials, as well as using new electronic media.

What do we know about the impacts of depression?

Depressive disorder is characterized by an abnormal depressed mood (dysphoria) or a loss of pleasure (anhedonia). The prognosis is often very unfavourable. This blunted effect is present most of the day for at least two weeks and, on average, lasts for six months; in 15–20 per cent of the cases it lasts longer than two years (Spijker et al. 2002). One study suggested an 85 per cent probability after recovery of a new episode occurring within five years (Mueller et al. 1999), but other studies usually put the recurrence rates somewhat lower (Vos et al. 2004).

The resulting lack of motivation can be quite crippling. In addition, there are other depressive symptoms causing marked functional impairment, such as sleep disturbance (insomnia or hypersomnia), lack of energy, poor concentration, a lack or increase in appetite and inappropriate feelings of self-reproach. Compulsively contemplating death and suicide is often symptomatic for depression and makes suicide a real risk. About 60 per cent of all suicides occur in people who are depressed (Marquet et al. 2005), and all-cause mortality rates are higher by a factor of 1.65 in people with depression (Cuijpers and Smit 2002; de Hert et al. 2011). It is therefore perhaps not surprising that people with depression make more frequent use of health services and stay absent from their work more often, which has significant economic ramifications (Smit et al. 2004).

The high influx of new and recurrent cases – in the Netherlands 47 per cent of all people with a depressive disorder experienced the first onset or a recurrence of the disorder in the past 12 months – also emphasizes the economic importance of tackling depression. The potential for prevention is even more pronounced in the relatively healthy working population, where a formidable 71 per cent of the costs due to common mental disorders, most notably depression, can be attributed to new cases – indicating that there is a good business case for prevention in work settings (Adema et al. in preparation).

Globally, major depressive disorders are the second leading cause of years lived with disability (Vos et al. 2012). They affect about 150 million people worldwide at any moment in time, including about 33.4 million people in the WHO European Region. The costs are substantial, with costs for major depression in 30 European countries estimated to be $108 billion (€92 billion in 2010), while costs for all anxiety disorders accounted for a further $87 billion (€74 billion in 2010) (Olesen et al. 2012).

What do we know about the economic case for promoting mental health and preventing depression in school settings?

The consequences of poor mental health and behavioural problems in childhood can reverberate well into adulthood, with many personal, social and economic consequences such as reduced rates of employment, poorer career trajectories and greater likelihoods of contact with social welfare and criminal justice systems (Fergusson et al. 2005; Knapp et al. 2011a; McDaid et al. 2014; Suhrcke and Kenkel this volume). With an estimated prevalence of up to 2.5 per cent in children and up to 8.3 per cent in adolescents, depression is a frequent condition associated with poor psychosocial and academic outcomes and an increased risk for other mental disorders (Birmaher et al. 1996). Furthermore, clinically relevant depressive symptoms that do not meet criteria for major depressive disorders are found in up to 30 per cent of adolescents (Ryan 2005). These, in turn, increase risks of future mental health problems. From a public health perspective, actions within the school setting can therefore be particularly helpful in both promoting better mental health and emotional well-being and preventing the early onset of depression, given that school is an ideal place to reach large numbers of the target group in a logistically convenient way.

Mental health promotion

In terms of promoting emotional health and well-being in school, a review of reviews of evidence in schools uncovered 52 systematic reviews and meta-analyses (Weare and Nind 2011). The interventions identified had a wide range of beneficial effects on children, families and communities and on a range of mental health, social, emotional and educational outcomes. Effect sizes associated with most interventions were generally small to moderate in statistical terms, but large in terms of real-world impacts. However, the effects associated with interventions were variable and their effectiveness could not always be relied on. The characteristics of more effective interventions included: teaching skills, focusing on positive mental health; balancing universal and targeted approaches; starting early with the youngest children and continuing with older ones; operating for a lengthy period of time and embedding work within a multi-modal/whole-school approach which included such features as changes to the curriculum including teaching skills and linking with academic learning, improving school ethos, teacher education, liaison with parents, parenting education, community involvement and coordinated work with outside agencies. Interventions were only effective if they were completely and accurately implemented: this applied particularly to whole-school interventions, which could be ineffective if not implemented with clarity, intensity and fidelity.

There is also a small body of literature on the cost-effectiveness of some of these interventions, including parenting and teacher support programmes in particular (McDaid and Park 2011; Mihalopoulos et al. 2011). The more robust evidence tends to focus on children already identified as being at risk of emotional health problems, rather than for the population as a whole. For example, an evaluation of one parenting programme, the Webster-Stratton Incredible Years (IY) parenting programme in Wales, while finding the intervention to be cost-effective for all 3–5-year-old children at risk of conduct disorder, suggested that the intervention would be most cost-effective for children with the highest risk of developing conduct disorder (Edwards et al. 2007). Analysis from a trial looking at 3–8-year-old children in the United States also suggests that combining the parenting component of IY with child-based training and teacher training, even though more expensive, can be more cost-effective (Foster 2010). In an Australian context, another programme delivered to all children, with stepped care actions targeted at children with behavioural problems and their parents, known as Triple-P, has been modelled to be cost-effective in most circumstances (Mihalopoulos et al. 2011).

Prevention of depression

Many studies have also examined the possibilities of specifically preventing depression in the school setting. A recent systematic review (Corrieri et al. 2013) identified 24 trials in schools of interventions to prevent depression, of which 18 were delivered universally to all children. Sixteen of these 24 studies reported significant lower levels of depression in their intervention groups, although the clinical size of these effect differences was very small, with immediate post-intervention mean effect sizes of –0.14 on the (Children's Depression Inventory) CDI scale for universal interventions and –0.08 for indicated interventions. Small-scale effects persisted in the long-term for universal (–0.05) and indicated (–0.13) interventions.

There is also some limited evidence that some of these school-based interventions can be cost-effective. An economic modelling study assessed the incremental cost-effectiveness of after-school screening and subsequent psychological intervention against use of the regular health curriculum in Australian teenagers (aged 11–17 years) manifesting elevated depressive symptom levels at school (Mihalopoulos et al. 2012). From a health system perspective, the intervention had an incremental cost-effectiveness ratio of $4,622 (AUD 5,400 in 2003) per DALY averted, with just 2 per cent of simulated ratios falling above a $42,797 (AUD 50,000 in 2003) per DALY value-for-money threshold. Results appeared robust to model assumptions. At the same time, acceptability issues, particularly to intervention providers, including schools and mental health professionals, would need to be considered before any large-scale implementation.

Another preventive intervention targeted at-risk group teenagers (13–18 years) who had parents with depressive disorder (Lynch et al. 2005). Teenagers had depressive symptoms, but did not yet meet diagnostic criteria. Those in the intervention group (n = 49) were offered a 15-session cognitive behavioural intervention, in addition to usual care, compared with controls (n = 45) offered usual care alone. From a societal perspective the incremental cost per QALY gained was $11,463 ($9,275 in 2000). This remained robust under various sensitivity analyses, suggesting that the intervention would be cost-effective in most high-income country settings.

What do we know about the economic case for prevention of post-partum depression?

New mothers are another important target group for action. About one in every seven new mothers is affected by post-partum (also known as post-natal) depression (Wisner et al. 2006) resulting in an overall prevalence rate of 13 per cent (O'Hara and Swain 1996). It has the same characteristics as other depressive disorders, except that it occurs within four weeks post-partum (Elliott et al. 2000) and is the most frequent form of maternal morbidity following delivery (Stocky and Lynch 2000). Untreated, it often remits spontaneously after four to six months, but can last longer in some cases, causing prolonged and significant distress (Cooper and Murray 1998).

In addition to health problems and the increased risk of hospitalization (Dennis 2004), it can increase the risk of marital stress and divorce (Holden 1991), child abuse and neglect (Buist 1998), and maternal suicide and infanticide (Sit et al. 2006). Although not well explored, there is some evidence that depression in new mothers may also be correlated with an increased risk of post-partum depression in fathers (Paulson and Bazemore 2010).

Post-partum depression can have serious consequences for the children of affected mothers, in the short term and long term (Murray and Cooper 2004). The negative effects of maternal depression on children include an increased risk of impaired mental and motor development, difficult temperament, poor self-regulation, low self-esteem, long-term behavioural problems, as well as impact on cognitive skills and language development (Beck 1999; Wisner et al. 2006; Feldman et al. 2009).

Effectiveness evidence

In England, the National Institute for Health and Care Excellence (NICE) recommends screening for post-partum depression as part of routine care, and the use of psychosocial interventions and psychological therapy for women depending on the severity of depressive symptoms. Potentially, prevention of post-partum depression could be implemented relatively easy, because most new mothers are regularly in contact with health care services following a new birth.

A considerable number of studies have looked at preventing post-partum depression. Many have used cognitive behavioural interventions (Hagan et al. 2004; Muñoz et al. 2007), although other studies have used psycho-educational interventions (Elliott et al. 2000) and interpersonal psychotherapy (Zlotnick et al. 2006). There is some evidence from the United Kingdom that universal prevention of post-partum depression is feasible and effective in reducing the risk of depression onset (Brugha et al. 2011). In this United Kingdom study, all mothers and their children received individual care after childbirth from a specialist health visitor (community nurse). This contact offered an opportunity to screen mothers for depression risk and to offer 'at risk' women a brief intervention using cognitive behavioural and person-centred approaches. Nurses also received training in systematic assessment of depressive symptoms and psychologically informed approaches to health care. After six months, the odds of post-partum depression were lower by a factor of 0.71 in the intervention group, compared to the usual care group (p = 0.031), representing a risk reduction of 29 per cent.

Economic evidence

There is also evidence that universal actions to prevent post-partum depression can be cost-effective. One randomized trial in England again looked at the use of health visitors to identify depression and then to deliver either cognitive behavioural or person-centred approach psychological interventions to at risk mothers (Morrell et al. 2009). There were mean gains of 0.003 QALYs in the intervention group compared to usual care, with lower costs to the health care system. While the study was too small to generate and show a statistically significant difference, sensitivity analysis indicated that there was a 90 per cent probability of the intervention being cost-effective from a health system perspective.

Another study of a preventive intervention targeted at women at high risk of developing post-partum depression also suggested this may be cost-effective (Petrou et al. 2006); over 18 months, women in the intervention group receiving counselling and support had a non-significant lower number of months with depression at an additional cost of $81 (£43 in 2000) per month. The study was limited by not being able to look at cost per QALY gained, but reported a 71 per cent probability of being cost-effective if decision-makers were willing to spend up to $1,895 (£1,000 in 2000) per month to prevent post-partum depression.

More recently, an economic modelling analysis compared the universal health visitor delivered approach with a targeted approach where individuals were identified as being at risk while in hospital (Bauer et al. 2011). The universal intervention appeared cost-effective with an incremental cost per QALY gained per annum of $6,667 (£4,500 in 2010); the intervention would be even more cost-effective if the benefits were to last beyond one year. It should also be noted that other potential economic benefits have not been considered, such as benefits to the child (and siblings) and the father of improved mental health in mothers.

What do we know about mental health promotion and prevention of depression in the workplace?

Typically, at least two-thirds of the costs of common mental health problems, including depression and anxiety disorders, are for lost productivity. This may be due to poor performance while at work, sick leave or early retirement on the grounds of poor mental health, as well as exclusion from the workplace due to discrimination linked to an individual's mental health status. Overall, data from the European Labour Force Survey 2007 ad hoc module on accidents at work and work-related health problems indicate that stress, depression and anxiety problems were the third most common group of serious health problems reported by employees in a 12-month period. The impacts of poor mental health in a workplace also go beyond individual workers: for those working in teams, ill health and sickness absence may lead to an increased workload and potential risk for work-related stress in other team members.

Substantial costs arize for employers when their employees stay absent from work (absenteeism) or are less productive while at work (presenteeism) due to depressive disorder. For example, it is estimated that depression in employees is associated with a loss of 27.3 workdays per annum in Great Britain, equivalent to an average of $11,918 (£7,230 in 2005/6) per employee with depression (McCrone et al. 2008). In the Netherlands, an even more sobering picture emerges: depression in employees is associated with a loss of 35.3 workdays per year. Projected to the Dutch workforce, this would amount to $280 million (€242 million in 2008) in every 1 million employees (De Graaf et al. 2011).

Effective evidence

A number of reviews have looked at evaluations of the effectiveness of interventions delivered in the workplace to promote better mental health and well-being (Kuoppala et al. 2008; Corbiere et al. 2009; Martin et al. 2009). Actions can be implemented at both an organizational level within the workplace, and targeted at specific individuals. National guidelines on mental health promotion at work recently published by NICE in England include better line-management training, opportunities for career progression, flexible working arrangements, better employer-employee communication and workplace stress audits (National Institute for Health and Clinical Excellence 2009). Much of the organizational level actions do not lend themselves easily to randomized trial evaluation, and evidence supporting their effectiveness comes from other research designs.

Actions targeted at individuals can include modifying workloads, providing cognitive behavioural therapy, relaxation and meditation training, time-management training, exercise programmes, journalling, biofeedback and goal setting. These have been the subject of randomized controlled trials, albeit mostly in a United States context (Corbiere et al. 2009). However, it is reasonable to assume that meta-analytic evidence across a variety of populations can be projected on the working population. A clear challenge is the extent to which the workplace itself is a place either both for the identification of those at risk, and/or a setting where these preventive interventions can be delivered.

Economic evidence

At an organizational level, potential economic benefits have been reported from investment in stress and well-being audits, better integration of occupational and primary health care systems, and an extension in flexible working hours arrangements (Foresight Mental Capital and Well-being Project 2008). There is also some workplace-specific evidence on the economic benefits of mental health promoting actions targeted at individuals. These data are largely from a United States context where employers have a direct incentive to protect the health of their employees, although a number of studies are now being conducted in Europe (McDaid and Park 2011).

Potentially, interventions that can prevent depression and anxiety can be cost-saving from a business perspective. Drawing on effectiveness data from a multinational study focused on the mental health of 'white collar' employees, the cost-effectiveness of a work-based preventive intervention for depression and anxiety for a hypothetical cohort of 500 employees in England was estimated (McDaid et al. 2011). It was assumed that the company would bear the full costs of the intervention in which all employees are screened for depression risk and two-thirds of employees are subsequently offered six sessions of face-to-face cognitive behavioural therapy. Total intervention costs of \$30,766 (£20,767 in 2010) are more than compensated for by pay-offs gained through reduced absenteeism (valued at \$34,083 or £23,006 in 2010) and presenteeism (\$44,519 or £30,050 in 2010), before any benefits through avoided health care and social care costs are included (\$15,633 or £10,552 in 2010). However, a research challenge is to firstly replicate the effectiveness study in different workplace settings, such as those where staff turnover is high and skill requirements low, and then look at potential cost-effectiveness.

What do we know about mental health promotion and the prevention of depression in older age?

Sixteen per cent of older people may have depression and related disorders; rates can be as high as 30 per cent in medical and long-term care facilities. Potentially the prevention of such depression, particularly among high-risk groups such as the bereaved, might help avoid significant costs to families and health and social care systems (Smit et al. 2006b). It also creates challenges for economies seeking to encourage more employees to continue working later in life. There are opportunities to engage older people in preventive interventions, because many older people are seen by their general practitioner on a regular basis and are in frequent contact with other health services for treatment of chronic physical illnesses. Moreover, residential homes and nursing homes provide a setting where it is logistically easy to reach many older people at risk of becoming depressed. Finally, the older population segment is the fastest growing group of new internet users, which is increasing the scope for wide-scale provision of preventive interventions via the web.

Effectiveness evidence

It is difficult to determine whether interventions targeted at the population in general to prevent depression are effective because of the large sample sizes required to determine a statistically significant effect. There is also evidence that actions targeted at high-risk groups for depression can be effective (Cuijpers et al. 2011). This can include social support programmes to tackle issues such as social isolation, as well as different modes of psychological and pharmacological therapies. A recent meta-analysis of 30 studies with psychosocial interventions to prevent depression in older people reported a small but statistical effect – this being most pronounced for the use of social activities (Forsman et al. 2011).

Problem-solving therapy can also be used (Rovner and Casten 2008). This approach helps people to identify a problem that has an adverse impact on their lives and can, in principle, be solved. They are then taught how to systematically tackle and solve the problem and regain control. When targeted at older people with older neo-vascular macular degeneration it significantly reduced their risk of developing depression, compared to those receiving care as usual. After two months, only 11.6 per cent of people in the prevention group had developed a depressive disorder, compared to 23.2 per cent in the control group (p<0.05). This difference, however, was not significant after six months, with the authors suggesting the need for booster therapy sessions.

Preventive interventions targeting older stroke patients can also help reduce the incidence of depression (Robinson et al. 2008). Over a 12-month intervention period, 22 per cent of people receiving placebo developed depression, compared with rates of 8.5 per cent in those who were prescribed a precautionary antidepressant (escitalopram) and 12 per cent in those receiving problem-solving therapy. Some general health promoting interventions, such as participation in regular group exercise classes, can have a protective influence on mental health; this may be due to the social interaction that such group classes provide (Forsman, Schierenbeck and Wahlbeck 2011).

A study carried out in the Netherlands tested the effect of a stepped-care programme to prevent depression and anxiety among older people with sub-threshold depressive symptoms identified in primary care (van't Veer-Tazelaar et al. 2009). Stepped-care encompassed: (i) watchful waiting, (ii) guided self-help, (iii) problem-solving, and (iv) referral to general practitioner for further evaluation and treatment, when required. The intervention was successful in reducing the incidence of anxiety or depressive disorders by 50 per cent, with effects maintained over 12 months (van't Veer-Tazelaar et al. 2011). Another controlled trial of this approach, adapted for people living in residential care homes, had similar success in reducing the incidence of depression, but did not impact on anxiety disorders, which appeared to be unaffected by the intervention (Dozeman et al. 2012).

Economic evidence

The economic evidence on promoting better mental health and avoiding depression in older people has been reviewed (McDaid and Park 2011). Participation in group-based activities potentially may be cost-effective. Regular participation in exercise classes by older people was associated with better mental health at a cost per QALY gained of $15,174 (€17 172 in 2004) from a health system perspective (Munro et al. 2004). This is likely to have been due to social engagement rather than the exercise. In Finland, a trial of psychosocial group therapy for older people identified to be lonely was also reported to lead to significant improvements in psychological well-being, with a net mean reduction in health care costs per participant of $972 (€943 in 2009) (Pitkala et al. 2009).

The stepped-care approach we have highlighted for the prevention of depression in older people identified as being at risk through primary care in the Netherlands has been shown to be more cost-effective than routine primary care. A modelling analysis based on the trial data reported an incremental cost of $5,162 (€4,367 in 2007) for a depression-free year (van't Veer-Tazelaar et al. 2010). The intervention had a 57 per cent likelihood of being more cost-effective than routine primary care at a willingness to pay ceiling of $5,910 (€5,000 in 2007) for a depression-free year.

What do we know about the economic case for investing in e-health to deliver effective interventions to prevent depression?

The increasing evidence base on the effectiveness of interventions to prevent depression that we have highlighted is encouraging. However, the impact of prevention on population health remains unimpressive if few people make use of preventive interventions. Low-threshold interventions that are highly scalable, such as interventions offered over the internet or via mobile devices, may offer one innovative solution, because people can then access preventive interventions at times they find convenient, with privacy, in a setting of their choosing and without fear of labelling and being stigmatized.

The potential can be seen by looking at the evidence on their role in treating depression. There is good evidence from several meta-analyses that new forms of intervention delivery can be effective for the treatment of people with depression and anxiety problems, especially when these interventions are supported by a limited amount of contact with a face-to-face support (Spek et al. 2007; Andersson and Cuijpers 2009).

Computer-delivered cognitive behavioural therapy (CBT) has been shown in a meta-analysis of five trials to be equally effective to face-to-face delivered CBT (Andrews et al. 2010). The equivalence (or non-inferiority) of e-health vis-à-vis face-to-face interventions is an important 'take home' message, because there is a widespread, but mistaken, belief that e-health interventions cannot be as good as face-to-face interventions.

A minimally supported web-based intervention for depressive and anxiety symptoms and for stress, making use of problem-solving therapy, has also been evaluated (van Straten et al. 2008). We noted that this approach can be effective in preventing depression in people with physical health problems when delivered on a face-to-face basis. In this Dutch trial, the intervention was delivered largely to people who had major depression at baseline, although those with mild depressive symptoms were eligible for inclusion. It nonetheless indicated that web-based problem-solving therapy was effective in reducing depression

While there is an ever-increasing evidence base on e-health interventions to treat depression, anxiety and related disorders, the evidence on the effectiveness of these delivery mechanisms, specifically targeted at the prevention of depression and related disorders, is less well developed. In one meta-analysis of internet-delivered interventions for depression, only 2 of 12 studies focused on the prevention of depression; unlike interventions for the treatment of depression no significant difference in effect from control interventions was reported (Spek et al. 2007).

Economic evidence

Given our knowledge on the effectiveness of prevention interventions and the delivery of these interventions through the internet or other mobile technologies, it is clear they carry the promise of being even more cost-effective, because the per-user costs of offering the intervention can drop significantly when more people make use of these intervention delivery mechanisms. Thus, when prevention of depression is considered at a general population level, then it might be a good idea to opt for e-health, or at least to offer a mix of face-to-face interventions and e-health interventions.

As with effectiveness evidence, to date, most studies have focused on e-health delivered treatment interventions, with less focus on prevention. Several studies have already indicated that internet-delivered interventions for the treatment of anxiety and depressive disorders can be cost-effective. One trial of computer delivered CBT in the United Kingdom was shown to generate more depression free days, whilst the costs of CBT were more than covered by a reduction in other health service costs and absenteeism from work. A highly cost-effective cost per QALY gained of $2,369 (£1,250 in 2000) was reported (McCrone et al. 2004).

The cost-effectiveness of both web-based CBT and problem-solving therapy for depressive symptoms, compared to usual care in the Netherlands, has been assessed. In this study, two e-health interventions were compared with usual care (Warmerdam et al. 2010). At a willingness-to-pay level of $35,460 (€30,000 in 2007) for gaining one QALY, there is a 52 per cent probability that CBT and a 61 per cent likelihood that problem-solving therapy can be regarded as cost-effective. There was no substantial difference between CBT and problem-solving therapy.

Modelling investment in depression prevention at a national level

The evidence suggests that e-health is likely to be a cost-effective mode of delivery of psychological interventions. We have noted that most of the evidence to date focused on treatment rather than prevention. We have used a Markov simulation model to evaluate the cost-effectiveness of standard care for depression in the Dutch care system without prevention, compared with a health care system augmented with prevention. Under the alternative (augmented) scenario it was assumed that the Coping with Depression course (Lewinsohn et al. 1984) was either offered as group-based face-to-face intervention, or as a web-based self-help intervention (Colour your Life).

Table 10.1 Population-level cost-effectiveness for two prevention scenarios versus a base-case scenario without prevention: health care perspective over five years

Scenario	Prevention mix: Face-to-Face/e-health		Costs in $ millions (€ millions in 2010)	DALYs averted	Costs per DALY in $ (€ in 2010)	Savings per DALY in $ (€in 2010)
0 (base-case)	0%	0%	1,272 (1,109)	80,328	15834 (13,807)	(–)
1 (face-to-face)	10%	0%	1,281 (1,117)	94,229	14266 (12,440)	900 (785)
2 (e-health)	0%	10%	1,278 (1,114)	93,215	14060 (12,260)	1,576 (1,374)

The epidemiology of depressive disorder was modelled using data from the Netherlands Mental Health Survey and Incidence Study, while data on depression-related excess mortality were obtained from the literature (Cuijpers and Smit 2002). Effectiveness data were taken from meta-analyses of randomized trial literature, and costs and effectiveness then estimated for a five-year period for a population of ten million adults between 18–65 years.

The 'prevention mix' for three scenarios is presented in Table 10.1. There is a base-case scenario (scenario 0) with no preventive interventions. In scenario 1, 10 per cent of people with sub-clinical levels of depressive symptoms receive preventive face-to-face interventions. In scenario 2, 10 per cent of this target group have preventive actions delivered through e-health. The remainder of the table shows the impact of these prevention mixes on health care expenditures and health gains measuring as disability-adjusted life-years averted in a population of 10 million adults.

The results indicate that e-health delivered interventions are less expensive than traditional face-to-face services, although a greater number of DALYs are averted using face-to-face services. 'Costs per DALY averted' indicate that prevention helps to reduce the overall costs per DALY averted in the whole Dutch health care system – that is, in the preventive and curative sector combined, with the greatest level of savings realized through the delivery of e-health interventions.

These findings have two important implications. First, that prevention of depression – either on a face-to-face or e-health basis – can be a cost-effective way of improving population health. As we noted earlier, a mental health promotion and prevention strategy will involve a combination of both types of approaches. Second, by implementing prevention, one can either generate the same amount of population health gains for a smaller health care budget or, conversely, generate more health gains with the same budget.

Conclusions

It is clear that poor mental health has a major impact on quality of life, lessens productivity in the workplace, and is an obstacle to fulfilment of social and familial roles. The corollary is that depressive disorders have become a major cause of disability worldwide, and are projected to become the single leading cause of disease burden in the high-income countries by the year 2030 (Mathers and Loncar 2006).

Mental disorders affect both resource rich and resource poor countries across the WHO European Region. In 2007, the economic costs of all depressive disorders amounted to $151.5 billion (€136.3 billion in 2007) in the European Economic Area. The bulk of these costs stem from lesser productivity $120 billion (€99.3 billion in 2007) and the remaining $44.9 billion (€37.0 billion in 2007) (27.5 per cent) fell on the health care system (McDaid et al. 2008). Poor mental health impacts on population mental capital (i.e. people's cognitive, emotional and social-skills resources required for social and professional role functioning) which are vital to the economic outputs of any country. There is also a vicious cycle between poverty and poor mental health.

The need to promote mental health and prevent mental disorders

Even the most well-endowed health care systems in high-income countries can only avert some of the burden of poor mental health through treatments (Andrews et al. 2004; Chisholm et al. 2004). Low coverage, poor adherence rates and the use of treatments that are not always evidence-based all play a debilitating role in the effectiveness of current mental health care systems. Investment in the promotion of mental well-being to reduce the risk of becoming vulnerable to poor mental health, and strategies to protect the mental health of the population who are at risk of developing mental health problems, should be critical elements of any mental health strategy.

Not only do common mental health problems such as depression and anxiety disorders have a high incidence rate, they also can have high rates of recurrence, causing large numbers of people to look for help, not once, but multiple times during the course of their life. Prevention can both help to reduce the influx of new cases and the risk of recurrence in those who have recovered from past problems. The economic case for investing in a wide range of mental health promotion and prevention interventions is encouraging, given the many adverse impacts that can be avoided both within and external to the health system.

A key issue in the cost-effectiveness of any public health intervention is the extent to which multiple doses of an action are required; encouraging initial and repeat uptake of interventions can be challenging (McDaid and Needle 2009). Evidence from meta-analyses show that some actions to prevent depression can be offered as a 'one shot' intervention (Cuijpers et al. 2008; Muñoz et al. 2010). The numbers needed to prevent one case of depression typically ranges between eight and ten, an effect size that compares favourably with established preventative interventions elsewhere in medicine – e.g. number needed to treat over one hundred when treating hypertension to prevent cardiovascular disease (Thompson et al. 2011). Moreover, offering preventive interventions in a stepped-care format is successful in reducing incidence by 50 per cent (van't Veer-Tazelaar et al. 2009; Dozeman et al. 2012) and this effect is maintained over two years (van't Veer-Tazelaar et al. 2011).

Economic evidence also indicates that depression prevention in adults is potentially cost-effective (Zechmeister et al. 2008), especially when offered in a self-help format (either bibliotherapy or internet-based) with minimal guidance from a therapist (Smit et al. 2006b; Warmerdam et al. 2010; Mihalopoulos et al. 2011) and may even be cost-saving from a societal perspective when the cost offsets due to changes in productivity are accounted for (van den Berg et al. 2011). Preventive e-health interventions also have much potential to become cost-effective as they do not rely on scarce resources such as therapists' time, but instead promote self-management and are highly scalable, thus bringing down marginal costs a significant way (Kaltenthaler et al. 2006; Warmerdam et al. 2010).

We have also highlighted actions across the life course. Actions in childhood to both promote emotional well-being and address behavioural problems that increase the risk of mental health problems in adulthood can be cost-effective (McDaid and Park 2011; Mihalopoulos et al. 2012; McDaid et al. 2014). Health visitor-led identification of new mothers at risk of post-partum depression, coupled with subsequent therapy also appears cost-effective (Bauer et al. 2011). There is a small but growing literature on actions at work (McDaid and Park 2011) and we have also highlighted actions for later life.

There are nonetheless areas where the evidence base requires strengthening. There is still little on the long-term benefits of better psychological well-being – does this, for instance, protect against a future risk of mental health problems? When it comes to the prevention of depression, the current evidence-base supports such action; but any action needs to be based on good business judgement and sensitivity to local conditions, including size of enterprise and the availability of occupational health services.

Evidence on the delivery through e-health mechanisms of interventions specifically targeted at prevention of depression and related disorders needs to be increased. There also remain differences in access to and trust in the internet for health information across Europe (McDaid and Park 2010), while factors such as speed of connections and quality of mobile phone networks also need to be factored into implementation considerations.

Finally, there is still a dearth of information on the effectiveness of actions in many countries in the WHO European Region, with most evidence generated in Western Europe, North America and Australasia. This evidence base needs to be strengthened. Considering the diversity across WHO European countries, the studies in our review are best interpreted as illustrative showcases. Acknowledging that public health strategies that work well in one country may not offer the best solutions in another country, our findings need to be interpreted within the context of these limitations and with some caution.

References

Adema, D., en Have, M., De Graaf, R., Cuijpers, P., Weehuizen, R. and Smit, F. (in preparation) *Economic Costs of Common Mental Disorders in the Working Population: Towards a Business Case for Prevention.*

Andersson, G. and Cuijpers, P. (2009) Internet-based and other computerized psychological treatments for adult depression: A meta-analysis, *Cognitive Behaviour Therapy*, 38: 196–205.

Andrews, G., Cuijpers, P., Craske, M. G., McEvoy, P. and Titov, N. (2010) Computer therapy for the anxiety and depressive disorders is effective, acceptable and practical health care: A meta-analysis, *PLoS One*, 5: e13196.

Andrews, G., Issakidis, C., Sanderson, K., Corry, J. and Lapsley, H. (2004) Utilising survey data to inform public policy: Comparison of the cost-effectiveness of treatment of ten mental disorders, *British Journal of Psychiatry*, 184: 526–33.

Bauer, A., Knapp, M. and McDaid, D. (2011) Health visiting and reducing post-natal depression, in M. Knapp, D. McDaid and M. Parsonage (eds.) *Mental Health Promotion and Mental Illness Prevention: The Economic Case*. London: Department of Health.

Beck, C. T. (1999) Maternal depression and child behaviour problems: A meta-analysis, *Journal of Advanced Nursing*, 29: 623–9.

Birmaher, B., Ryan, N. D., Williamson, D. E. et al. (1996) Childhood and adolescent depression: A review of the past 10 years. Part I, *Journal of the American Academy of Child and Adolescent Psychiatry*, 35: 1427–39.

Brugha, T. S., Morrell, C. J., Slade, P. and Walters, S. J. (2011) Universal prevention of depression in women postnatally: Cluster randomized trial evidence in primary care, *Psychological Medicine*, 41: 739–48.

Buist, A. (1998) Childhood abuse, parenting and postpartum depression, *Australian and New Zealand Journal of Psychiatry*, 32: 479–87.

Chisholm, D., Sanderson, K., Ayuso-Mateos, J. L. and Saxena, S. (2004) Reducing the global burden of depression: Population-level analysis of intervention cost-effectiveness in 14 world regions, *British Journal of Psychiatry*, 184: 393–403.

Cooper, P. and Murray, L. (1998) Fortnightly review: Postnatal depression, *British Medical Journal*, 316: 1884–6.

Corbiere, M., Shen, J., Rouleau, M. and Dewa, C. S. (2009) A systematic review of preventive interventions regarding mental health issues in organizations, *Work*, 33: 81–116.

Corrieri, S., Heider, D., Conrad, I., Blume, A., Konig, H. H. and Riedel-Heller, S. G. (2013) School-based prevention programs for depression and anxiety in adolescence: A systematic review, *Health Promotion International*. doi: 10.1093/heapro/dat001.

Cuijpers, P. (2003) Examining the effects of prevention programs on the incidence of new cases of mental disorders: The lack of statistical power, *American Journal of Psychiatry*, 160: 1385–91.

Cuijpers, P. and Smit, F. (2002) Excess mortality in depression: A meta-analysis of community studies, *Journal of Affective Disorders*, 72: 227–36.

Cuijpers, P., Smit, F., Lebowitz, B. and Beekman, A. (2011) Prevention of mental disorders in late life, in M. Abou-Saleh, C. Katona and A. Kumar (eds) *Principles and Practice of Geriatric Psychiatry*. Chichester: Wiley.

Cuijpers, P., van Straten, A., Smit, F., Mihalopoulos, C. and Beekman, A. (2008) Preventing the onset of depressive disorders: A meta-analytic review of psychological interventions, *American Journal of Psychiatry*, 165: 1272–80.

De Graaf, R., Tuithof, M., Van Dorsselaer, S. and Ten Have, M. (2011) *Verzuim door psychische en somatische aandoeningen bij werkenden: Resultaten van NEMSIS-2 [Absenteeism caused by Mental and Physical Illnesses in Employees: Results from NEMESIS-2]*. Utrecht: Trimbos Institute.

de Hert, M., Correll, C. U., Bobes, J. et al. (2011) Physical illness in patients with severe mental disorders. I. Prevalence, impact of medications and disparities in health care, *World Psychiatry*, 10: 52–77.

Dennis, C. L. (2004) Treatment of postpartum depression, part 2: A critical review of nonbiological interventions, *Journal of Clinical Psychiatry*, 65: 1252–65.

Dozeman, E., van Marwijk, H. W., van Schaik, D. J. et al. (2012) Contradictory effects for prevention of depression and anxiety in residents in homes for the elderly: A pragmatic randomized controlled trial, *International Psychogeriatrics*, 24: 1242–51.

Edwards, R. T., Ceilleachair, A., Bywater, T., Hughes, D. A. and Hutchings, J. (2007) Parenting programme for parents of children at risk of developing conduct disorder: Cost effectiveness analysis, *British Medical Journal*, 334: 682.

Elliott, S. A., Leverton, T. J., Sanjack, M. et al. (2000) Promoting mental health after childbirth: A controlled trial of primary prevention of postnatal depression, *British Journal of Clinical Psychology*, 39(Pt 3): 223–41.

Feldman, R., Granat, A., Pariente, C., Kanety, H., Kuint, J. and Gilboa-Schechtman, E. (2009) Maternal depression and anxiety across the postpartum year and infant social engagement, fear regulation, and stress reactivity, *Journal of the American Academy of Child and Adolescent Psychiatry*, 48: 919–27.

Fergusson, D. M., Horwood, L. J. and Ridder, E. M. (2005) Show me the child at seven: The consequences of conduct problems in childhood for psychosocial functioning in adulthood, *Journal of Child Psychology and Psychiatry*, 46: 837–49.

Foresight Mental Capital and Well-being Project (2008) *Final Project Report*. London: Government Science Office.

Forsman, A. K., Schierenbeck, I. and Wahlbeck, K. (2011) Psychosocial interventions for the prevention of depression in older adults: Systematic review and meta-analysis, *Journal of Aging and Health*, 23: 387–416.

Foster, E. M. (2010) Costs and effectiveness of the fast track intervention for antisocial behavior, *Journal of Mental Health Policy and Economics*, 13: 101–19.

Hagan, R., Evans, S. F. and Pope, S. (2004) Preventing postnatal depression in mothers of very preterm infants: A randomised controlled trial, *BJOG: An International Journal of Obstetrics & Gynaecology*, 111: 641–7.

Holden, J. M. (1991) Postnatal depression: Its nature, effects, and identification using the Edinburgh Postnatal Depression scale, *Birth*, 18: 211–21.

Kaltenthaler, E., Brazier, J., De Nigris, E. et al. (2006) Computerised cognitive behaviour therapy for depression and anxiety update: A systematic review and economic evaluation, *Health Technology Assessment*, 10, iii: xi–xiv, 1–168.

Knapp, M., King, D., Healey, A. and Thomas, C. (2011a) Economic outcomes in adulthood and their associations with antisocial conduct, attention deficit and anxiety problems in childhood, *Journal of Mental Health Policy and Economics*, 14: 137–47.

Knapp, M., McDaid, D. and Parsonage, M. (eds) (2011b) *Mental Health Promotion and Mental Disorder Prevention: The Economic Case*. London: Department of Health.

Kuoppala, J., Lamminpaa, A. and Husman, P. (2008) Work health promotion, job well-being, and sickness absences – a systematic review and meta-analysis, *Journal of Occupational and Environmental Medicine*, 50: 1216–27.

Lewinsohn, P. M., Antonuccio, D. O., Breckenridge, J. S. and Teri, L. (1984) *The Coping with Depression course*. Eugene, OR: Castalia.

Lynch, F. L., Hornbrook, M., Clarke, G. N. et al. (2005) Cost-effectiveness of an intervention to prevent depression in at-risk teens, *Archives of General Psychiatry*, 62: 1241–8.

Marquet, R. L., Bartelds, A. I., Kerkhof, A. J., Schellevis, F. G. and van der Zee, J. (2005) The epidemiology of suicide and attempted suicide in Dutch General Practice 1983–2003, *BMC Family Practice*, 6: 45.

Martin, A., Sanderson, K., Scott, J. and Brough, P. (2009) Promoting mental health in small–medium enterprises: An evaluation of the 'Business in Mind' program, *BMC Public Health*, 9: 239.

Mathers, C. D. and Loncar, D. (2006) Projections of global mortality and burden of disease from 2002 to 2030, *PLoS Medicine*, 3: e442.

McCrone, P., Dhanasiri, S., Patel, A., Knapp, M. and Lawton-Smith, S. (2008) *Paying the Price: The Costs of Mental Health Care in England to 2026*. London: King's Fund.

McCrone, P., Knapp, M., Proudfoot, J. et al. (2004) Cost-effectiveness of computerised cognitive-behavioural therapy for anxiety and depression in primary care: Randomised controlled trial, *British Journal of Psychiatry*, 185: 55–62.

McDaid, D., King, D., Park, A.-L. and Parsonage, M. (2011) Promoting well-being in the workplace, in M. Knapp, D. McDaid and M. Parsonage (eds) *Mental Health Promotion and Mental Illness Prevention: The Economic Case*. London: Department of Health.

McDaid, D. and Needle, J. (2009) What use has been made of economic evaluation in public health? A systematic review of the literature, in Z. Morris and S. Dawson (eds) *The Future of Health: Burdens, Challenges and Opportunities*. Basingstoke: Palgrave McMillan.

McDaid, D. and Park, A.-L. (2010) *Online Health: Untangling the Web*. London: BUPA.

McDaid, D. and Park, A.-L. (2011) Investing in mental health and well-being: Findings from the DataPrev project, *Health Promotion International*, 26(Suppl. 1): i108–39.

McDaid, D., Park, A.-L., Currie, C. and Zanotti, C. (2014) Investing in the well-being of young people: Making the economic case, in D. McDaid and C. L. Cooper (eds) *Well-being: A Complete Reference Guide. Volume 6: Economics and Well-being* Oxford: Wiley: Blackwell.

McDaid, D., Zeichmeister, I., Kilian, R., Medeiros, H., Knapp, M. and Kennelly, B. (2008) *Making the Economic Case for the Promotion of Mental Well-being and the Prevention of Mental Health Problems*. London: London School of Economics and Political Science.

Mihalopoulos, C., Vos, T., Pirkis, J. and Carter, R. (2011) The economic analysis of prevention in mental health programs, *Annual Review of Clinical Psychology*, 7: 169–201.

Mihalopoulos, C., Vos, T., Pirkis, J. and Carter, R. (2012) The population cost-effectiveness of interventions designed to prevent childhood depression, *Pediatrics*, 129: e723–30.

Morrell, C. J., Warner, R., Slade, P. et al. (2009) Psychological interventions for postnatal depression: Cluster randomised trial and economic evaluation. The PoNDER trial, *Health Technology Assessment*, 13, iii–iv: xi–xiii, 1–153.

Mueller, T. I., Leon, A. C., Keller, M. B. et al. (1999) Recurrence after recovery from major depressive disorder during 15 years of observational follow-up, *American Journal of Psychiatry*, 156: 1000–6.

Muñoz, R. F., Cuijpers, P., Smit, F., Barrera, A. Z. and Leykin, Y. (2010) Prevention of major depression, *Annual Review of Clinical Psychology*, 6: 181–212.

Muñoz, R., Le, H., Ippen, C. et al. (2007) Prevention of postpartum depression in low-income women: Development of the Mamas y Bebes/Mothers and Babies course, *Cognitive Behavior Practice*, 14: 70–83.

Munro, J. F., Nicholl, J. P., Brazier, J. E., Davey, R. and Cochrane, T. (2004) Cost effectiveness of a community based exercise programme in over 65 year olds: Cluster randomised trial, *Journal of Epidemiology and Community Health*, 58: 1004–10.

Murray, L. and Cooper, P. (2004) The impact of postpartum depression on child development, in I. Goodyer (ed.) *Aetiological Mechanisms in Developmental Psychopathology*. Oxford: Oxford University Press.

National Institute for Health and Clinical Excellence (2009) *Workplace Interventions that are Effective for Promoting Mental Well-being: Synopsis of the Evidence of Effectiveness and Cost-effectiveness*. London: NICE.

O'Hara, M. and Swain, A. (1996) Rates and risk of postpartum depression: A meta-analysis, *International Review of Psychiatry*, 8: 37–54.

Olesen, J., Gustavsson, A., Svensson, M., Wittchen, H. U. and Jonsson, B. (2012) The economic cost of brain disorders in Europe, *European Journal of Neurology*, 19: 155–62.

Paulson, J. F. and Bazemore, S. D. (2010) Prenatal and postpartum depression in fathers and its association with maternal depression: A meta-analysis, *Journal of the American Medical Association*, 303: 1961–9.

Petrou, S., Cooper, P., Murray, L. and Davidson, L. L. (2006) Cost-effectiveness of a preventive counseling and support package for postnatal depression, *International Journal of Technology Assessment in Health Care*, 22: 443–53.

Pitkala, K. H., Routasalo, P., Kautiainen, H. and Tilvis, R. S. (2009) Effects of psychosocial group rehabilitation on health, use of health care services, and mortality of older persons suffering from loneliness: A randomized, controlled trial, *Journals of Gerontology, A: Biological Sciences & Medical Sciences*, 64: 792–800.

Robinson, R. G., Jorge, R. E., Moser, D. J. et al. (2008) Escitalopram and problem-solving therapy for prevention of poststroke depression: A randomized controlled trial, *Journal of the American Medical Association*, 299: 2391–400.

Rovner, B. W. and Casten, R. J. (2008) Preventing late-life depression in age-related macular degeneration, *American Journal of Geriatric Psychiatry*, 16: 454–9.

Ryan, N. D. (2005) Treatment of depression in children and adolescents, *The Lancet*, 366: 933–40.

Sit, D., Rothschild, A. J. and Wisner, K. L. (2006) A review of postpartum psychosis, *Journal of Womens Health (Larchmt)*, 15: 352–68.

Smit, F., Beekman, A., Cuijpers, P., de Graaf, R. and Vollebergh, W. (2004) Selecting key variables for depression prevention: Results from a population-based prospective epidemiological study, *Journal of Affective Disorders*, 81: 241–9.

Smit, F., Cuijpers, P., Oostenbrink, J., Batelaan, N., de Graaf, R. and Beekman, A. (2006a) Costs of nine common mental disorders: Implications for curative and preventive psychiatry, *Journal of Mental Health Policy and Economics*, 9: 193–200.

Smit, F., Ederveen, A., Cuijpers, P., Deeg, D. and Beekman, A. (2006b) Opportunities for cost-effective prevention of late-life depression: An epidemiological approach, *Archives of General Psychiatry*, 63: 290–6.

Spek, V., Cuijpers, P., Nyklicek, I., Riper, H., Keyzer, J. and Pop, V. (2007) Internet-based cognitive behaviour therapy for symptoms of depression and anxiety: A meta-analysis, *Psychological Medicine*, 37: 319–28.

Spijker, J., de Graaf, R., Bijl, R. V., Beekman, A. T., Ormel, J. and Nolen, W. A. (2002) Duration of major depressive episodes in the general population: Results from the Netherlands Mental Health Survey and Incidence Study (NEMESIS), *British Journal of Psychiatry*, 181: 208–13.

Stocky, A. and Lynch, J. (2000) Acute psychiatric disturbance in pregnancy and the puerperium, *Baillieres Best Practice & Research: Clinical Obstetrics & Gynaecology*, 14: 73–87.

Thompson, A. M., Hu, T., Eshelbrenner, C. L., Reynolds, K., He, J. and Bazzano, L. A. (2011) Antihypertensive treatment and secondary prevention of cardiovascular disease events among persons without hypertension: A meta-analysis, *Journal of the American Medical Association*, 305: 913–22.

van den Berg, M., Smit, F., Vos, T. and van Baal, P. H. (2011) Cost-effectiveness of opportunistic screening and minimal contact psychotherapy to prevent depression in primary care patients, *PLoS One*, 6: e22884.

van Straten, A., Cuijpers, P. and Smits, N. (2008) Effectiveness of a web-based self-help intervention for symptoms of depression, anxiety, and stress: Randomized controlled trial, *Journal of Medical Internet Research*, 10: e7.

van't Veer-Tazelaar, P., Smit, F., van Hout, H. et al. (2010) Cost-effectiveness of a stepped care intervention to prevent depression and anxiety in late life: Randomised trial, *British Journal of Psychiatry*, 196: 319–25.

van't Veer-Tazelaar, P. J., van Marwijk, H. W., van Oppen, P. et al. (2009) Stepped-care prevention of anxiety and depression in late life: A randomized controlled trial, *Archives of General Psychiatry*, 66: 297–304.

van't Veer-Tazelaar, P. J., van Marwijk, H. W., van Oppen, P. et al. (2011) Prevention of late-life anxiety and depression has sustained effects over 24 months: A pragmatic randomized trial, *American Journal of Geriatric Psychiatry*, 19: 230–9.

Vos, T., Flaxman, A. D., Naghavi, M. et al. (2012) Years lived with disability (YLDs) for 1160 sequelae of 289 diseases and injuries 1990–2010: A systematic analysis for the Global Burden of Disease Study 2010, *The Lancet*, 380: 2163–96.

Vos, T., Haby, M. M., Barendregt, J. J., Kruijshaar, M., Corry, J. and Andrews, G. (2004) The burden of major depression avoidable by longer-term treatment strategies, *Archives of General Psychiatry*, 61: 1097–103.

Warmerdam, L., Smit, F., van Straten, A., Riper, H. and Cuijpers, P. (2010) Cost-utility and cost-effectiveness of internet-based treatment for adults with depressive symptoms: Randomized trial, *Journal of Medical Internet Research*, 12: e53.

Weare, K. and Nind, M. (2011) Mental health promotion and problem prevention in schools: What does the evidence say?, *Health Promotion International*, 26(Suppl. 1): i29–69.

Wisner, K. L., Chambers, C. and Sit, D. K. (2006) Postpartum depression: A major public health problem, *Journal of the American Medical Association*, 296: 2616–8.

Zechmeister, I., Kilian, R. and McDaid, D. (2008) Is it worth investing in mental health promotion and prevention of mental illness? A systematic review of the evidence from economic evaluations, *BMC Public Health*, 8: 20.

Zlotnick, C., Miller, I. W., Pearlstein, T., Howard, M. and Sweeney, P. (2006) A preventive intervention for pregnant women on public assistance at risk for postpartum depression, *American Journal of Psychiatry*, 163: 1443–5.

Part III

Broader perspectives on the economics of health promotion and disease prevention

chapter eleven

Social determinants of health: early childhood development and education

Marc Suhrcke and Don Kenkel

Introduction

The Commission on Social Determinants of Health (CSDH) and the English Marmot Review have strongly argued for investing in a range of social determinants of health (SDH) on the grounds of social justice. In this chapter we look at social determinants from an economic perspective. In particular, we examine the economic evidence, in the form of 'value for money', to support the case for SDH investments.

Since we cannot cover all possible social determinants, we select two areas that undoubtedly fall under the SDH domain: investments in early childhood development (ECD), and primary and secondary education. Both of these areas have been strongly recommended. The CSDH places special emphasis on investments during early childhood, from prenatal development to eight years of age. At the same time, the CSDH also calls for 'quality, compulsory primary and secondary education'. Another reason we chose to examine ECD and education is that they are two examples with sufficient evidence to support some conclusions about their value for money. For other important examples of social determinants, for example social capital, there is great hope but little current economic evidence on value for money.

Why are early childhood development and education policies justified?

Before turning to what we know about the effectiveness and possibly cost-effectiveness of ECD and education interventions there is a need – from an economic perspective – to consider what might be the fundamental justification for public policy in these areas. Basic economic principles suggest two types of justifications: economic efficiency and equity.

Public policy can improve economic efficiency when there are market failures that keep resources from being allocated to their most highly valued use. Or, in the terminology of welfare economics, market failures result in inefficient resource allocation and lead to sub-optimal levels of societal welfare. Market failures relevant to the case for ECD interventions include: information failures – parents may not adequately gauge the benefits of formal early childcare; and imperfections in capital markets – i.e. the cost of childcare might, in the short run, be greater than the immediate returns from employment, and thus some parents cannot borrow to finance current childcare costs by themselves. Similar market failures related to parents' information and access to capital markets remain relevant to the case for primary and secondary education policies. Additional market failures might arise because the decisions about primary, and especially secondary education, are made by school children themselves. Oreopoulos (2007) estimates that high school dropouts in the United States, Canada, and the United Kingdom 'missed out on an opportunity to increase lifetime spending by more than 10%', as well as missing out on potential gains in life expectancy and reduced unemployment. He suggests that dropouts might be myopic and focus too much on the immediate costs of schooling, while heavily discounting future benefits. The idea that myopia leads to sub-optimal decisions about staying in school is another example of a market failure that can be corrected, for example, by compulsory schooling policies.

The equity-based justification for ECD and education interventions relates to the idea of achieving 'equality of opportunity' in society. For instance, ECD interventions in the childcare market may be required to help children to get an equal starting point in life, regardless of household economic status. Given limited resources of low-income families, and given the potential long-term educational impact of early investment, a prioritization of early investment – particularly among families from lower socioeconomic groups – might help improve equity in a wide range of socioeconomic and health outcomes. Improving primary and secondary school quality and/or requiring compulsory schooling have similar potential to reduce disparities in socioeconomic and health outcomes.

Hence, there are at least in principle good reasons to justify ECD and education interventions as a public policy to correct for existing market failures and/or to redress inequities. This justification, however, is not sufficient to complete the economic argument, as what is needed in addition is the evidence that (1) something can be done to improve ECD and education outcomes and (2) what could be done (ideally) is also providing acceptable value for money (the criterion for which may be defined in different ways).

Early childhood development

While the importance of ECD may appear highly plausible and intuitive to many, it is only after the accumulation of scientific evidence during the last quarter century or so that ECD has been given greater attention as a medium of potential intervention (Dodge 2004). Although, in theory, ECD intervention is more a concept than a specific programme (Guralnick 1998; Shonkoff and Meisels 2000), in practice, ECD interventions generally involve coordinated, multidisciplinary provision of health, educational and social services to families with pre-school children (Gray and Francis 2007). In general, the aim of such interventions is to promote children's health, as well as their physical, social and cognitive development (Guralnick 1997; Shonkoff and Meisels 2000; Zigler et al. 2002). In a comprehensive review of all ECD interventions implemented, Karoly et al. (2005) found that early intervention programmes usually do not follow specific strategies/approaches, but rather tend to follow a combination of strategies or approaches to achieve their aims – a feature that does not facilitate their evaluation. Therefore, ECD interventions vary according to a number of aspects, ranging from the outcomes targeted for improvement, to the people and ages targeted, to the type of services provided (see Table 11.1 for a tabulation of the various dimensions ECD programmes may take).

Ample research on ECD has shown that virtually every aspect of early human development (physical, cognitive, socio-emotional) is highly sensitive to external influences in early childhood and has lifelong effects (Shonkoff and Phillips 2000). To the extent that health inequalities have their origins in early life, ECD interventions might at least in principle also be a key tool for tackling the roots of health inequality. ECD has also received significant support from leading economists, perhaps most notably from nobel laureate James Heckman, who argued that investment in early childhood would be one of the most powerful investments a country can make, with returns over the lifecourse many times the amount of the original investment (Heckman 2000).

Over the last quarter century, many ECD interventions have been implemented in various settings and contexts and with different aims. The first large-scale ECD intervention programme, Head Start, was established in the United States in 1965. Since then, a large number of ECD intervention programmes have been performed globally, most of them in developed countries, such as Australia, Canada, France, the United Kingdom, and the United States (OECD 2006). A number of these programmes have undergone extensive evaluations with regard to their effectiveness in achieving their aims, whether these aims were related to education, behaviour, health, or economics. Hence, evidence is now available from which some cautious conclusions can be drawn on the effectiveness of such programmes in achieving the various outcomes which they set out to improve, as well as whether they may represent an economically worthwhile intervention policy. Here we review the evidence on the effectiveness of ECD programmes, as well as on the relevant evidence for their 'value for money'.[1]

Are ECD interventions effective in achieving their desired outcomes? Evidence from high-income countries

Although many ECD interventions have taken place over the last quarter century, only a few have been systematically evaluated. A review on the effectiveness of ECD interventions performed globally showed that, although 108 national and international interventions with some type of published evaluation data were identified, only 32 were child focused and had a sufficient evaluation component, and only 12 reported evaluations of effects on a number of child outcomes (Wise et al. 2005). Another review, on the effectiveness of

Table 11.1 Key dimensions of early childhood development intervention programmes

Dimension	Examples
Outcomes targeted for improvement	Pregnancy outcomes (parent) Cognitive (child) Socio-emotional (child) Behavioural (child) Health (parent or child) Economic (parent or child) Parent education (e.g. literacy) Parenting skills
Target person(s)	Child Parent Child–parent dyad Other carer Family unit
Targeting criteria	Child or family characteristics (minority or immigrant status, single-parent family, mother's age, first-time parents) Low-socioeconomic status or low-income families Child health problems (e.g. low birthweight) Child cognitive problems (e.g. low IQ) Child behavioural problems Child assessed as high risk (e.g. developmental delay) Parental problems (e.g. substance abuse, low education, psychological, divorce, child abuse or neglect) Relationship or social problems (parent-child, child-peers, child-adults, parent-parent) Universal
Age of focal child	Prenatal to age 8, for shorter or longer age spans
Location of services	Home Non-home (childcare centre, school, medical setting)
Services offered	Educational (e.g. pre-school, parenting education) Family supports (e.g. links to social services) Health- or nutrition- related Job-related Therapeutic Facility related (e.g. affordable leisure facilities, 'child-friendly' facilities) Monetary benefits (e.g. tax breaks)
Intensity of intervention	Starting age to ending age Hours per week Weeks per year
Individualized attention	Individuals Small or large group
Programme reach	Nationwide Regionwide Citywide Single setting

Source: Adapted from Karoly et al. 2005

ECD interventions implemented and evaluated in the United States, identified 20 programmes that had reported effects on child outcomes (Karoly et al. 2005).

In the high-income-country context, evaluated ECD interventions took place almost entirely in the United States, with the only exceptions being specific programmes in Canada and Australia. Apart from the aforementioned United Kingdom-based studies, no other relevant evidence appears to exist with findings in developed European countries. If such existed, their findings could be more directly extrapolated to the United Kingdom context and avoid the United States bias (Wise et al. 2005).

Considering that the aim of most ECD interventions is to enhance ECD outcomes, it is no surprise that the barometer of success of these programmes is whether the children had improved developmental outcomes compared to their comparison group counterparts. Hence, most outcomes measured during childhood related to the child's cognitive and socio-emotional/behavioural development. Other types of outcomes, especially those relating to health, were not given a similar emphasis, as only eight out of 20 evaluations reported effects on health outcomes (Karoly et al. 2005).

Overall, evaluations of ECD interventions showed statistically significant benefits in at least 70 per cent of the programmes (Karoly et al. 2005). Although evaluations focused on developmental outcomes, when health or other outcomes were included in the evaluation, positive effects were identified. Table 11.2 presents the type of outcomes that were measured and the benefits that were identified at a statistically significant level. Only a few studies reported effect sizes relating to the outcomes measured, indicating that although immediate and short-term effects were noticeable, the effects were often small to moderate (Wise et al. 2005).

Of the 20 ECD interventions reported in the 2005 Karoly et al. review, only five had undergone some form of systematic evaluation in the longer term, i.e. following the participating children into adulthood. Results indicate that the benefits accrued by the study participants were maintained over the longer term as the children transitioned to adulthood. This effect was reported to be the case in the various domains evaluated in adulthood, such as educational attainment, employment and earnings, and criminal behaviour. Effect sizes reported in long-term evaluations are somewhat larger than those reported during childhood, ranging from 0.2 to 0.5 (Karoly et al. 2005). Brooks-Gunn (2003) notes that even a small effect size retained at primary school-aged follow-up is impressive, and an effect retained throughout childhood and until adulthood is even more so. It must be noted that no study to date has evaluated effects on outcomes directly relevant to health (let alone health inequality) over such a long period.

The beneficial impact of some ECD interventions has been shown to fade somewhat in the long term in some domains, such as school test scores. Studies that have explored this phenomenon explain that ECD intervention participants, coming from disadvantaged backgrounds, attend schools of significantly lower quality than their counterparts who did not participate. Hence, no matter how beneficial the intervention was initially, such benefits are structurally undermined when the children are subsequently exposed to systematically lower quality schooling (Lee 1995). This indicates the necessity

Table 11.2 Benefits of early childhood development interventions delivered in the United States to children and adults

Type of ECD Intervention	Positive impacts of ECD interventions performed in the United States						
	Health	Child maltreatment	Behavioural/ emotional	Cognitive/ achievement	Crime	Education	Employment and earnings
Child outcomes							
Visiting the home or parent education	Emergency room visits Hospitalizations Reflexes Weight gain Child health rating Injuries	Child abuse/ maltreatment	Positive behaviours Developmental delay Behaviour problems Social competence	Achievement test scores Mental indices Vocabulary Developmental level	Arrests	(not measured)	(not measured)
Home visiting or parent education combined with early childhood education	Child health rating Teen pregnancy Immunizations Other positive health behaviours	Child abuse	Positive behaviours Behaviour problems Social competence	Achievement test scores IQ	Arrests Delinquency	Grades (girls) Attendance (girls) Teacher ratings (girls) Special education Grade retention	(not measured)
Early childhood education only	(not measured)	(not measured)	(not measured)	Achievement test scores	(not measured)	(not measured)	(not measured)

Adult outcomes

Visiting the home or parent education combined with early childhood education	(not measured)	(not measured)	(not measured)	Arrests	Years of completed schooling	Employment/ skilled employment
				Charged with crime	High school graduation	Earnings
				Time in prison/ jail	College attendance	Income

Source: Adapted from Karoly et al 2005.

of continuity of support required for the benefits of ECD interventions to be maintained until adulthood and when the participant enters the labour market.

Since the vast majority of the ECD interventions included in both reviews have had targets, e.g. focused on high-risk children and/or children from low-income families, one may suggest that the positive effects of these interventions are essentially reducing the inequality gap between the deprived and the affluent. Since very few ECD interventions have been carried out with universal coverage, the current evidence base does not allow any solid conclusions as to whether universal interventions are more or less effective than targeted ones. On the other hand, some evidence on this issue may be derived from a meta-analysis of 34 pre-school prevention programmes in the United States, which found that programmes serving predominantly African–American children demonstrated substantially larger benefits than non-targeted programmes (a three times larger positive impact on cognitive and parent-family outcomes) (Nelson et al. 2003). Future research on ECD interventions will hopefully address this fundamental issue.

Because ECD interventions vary greatly in terms of their strategy/approach, populations targeted and resources/services available, it is very difficult to isolate specific characteristics/types of interventions which may be more effective than others. Considering the very limited evidence base available, several features of ECD interventions have been suggested to be associated with better outcomes for the participants:

1. Programmes are more successful when they have smaller child-to-staff ratios (Karoly et al. 2005; Reynolds and Temple 2008).
2. Programmes with better-trained caregivers/teachers appear to be more effective (Karoly et al. 2005; Reynolds and Temple 2008).
3. More intensive and comprehensive programmes that meet the different needs of children are associated with better outcomes (Berlin et al. 1998; MacLeod and Nelson 2000; Nelson et al. 2003; Karoly et al. 2005; Reynolds and Temple 2008).

It is apparent that all three features rely on substantial increases in the cost of an ECD intervention, hence, it will be an empirical question whether the extra cost is more than compensated by extra benefits, and would thereby represent good value for money. The following sub-section looks more closely at the evidence on value for money of ECD interventions.

Are ECD Interventions good value for money?

Since social and economic policy decisions are made under resource constraints, the value of public investments must be judged, at least in part, in terms of economic efficiency; that is, in terms of value for money (Heckman 2000). In deciding how funds should be allocated, one needs to know not only what is most effective, but also which choice brings the greatest benefits (appropriately defined) for a given set of resources.

In the case of ECD interventions, the long-term economic impact would ideally be determined by comparing the society-wide benefits to the costs accrued. Benefits to society would include the benefits to the programme recipient and family, as well as broader benefits to society (Wise et al. 2005).

Because of the large differences in the methodologies adopted by studies aiming to evaluate the economic impact of ECD interventions, it is difficult to compare results across interventions. Nevertheless, these studies do provide indications regarding whether ECD interventions generate benefits in the long-term which outweigh the costs.

A number of reviews have investigated the long-term costs and benefits of ECD programmes (see Aos et al. 2004; Karoly et al. 2005; Wise et al. 2005; Penn et al. 2006; Wolfe and Tefft 2007; Reynolds and Temple 2008; Watson and Tully 2008). The returns to society for each dollar invested varied considerably, from $1.26 to $17.07, but, overall, indicated the potential for efficient ECD interventions to provide benefits to society substantially larger than the resources invested in programme delivery. The limited evidence available indicates that the internal rates of return (the interest rate received for an investment consisting of payments and revenue that occur at regular periods) are high enough to suggest that ECD interventions are worthwhile investments. A benefit-cost analysis of four United States-based ECD interventions found that, even when adjusted for inflation, internal rates of return from these interventions, ranged from 7 per cent to 20 per cent (Burr and Grunewald 2006). Rolnick and Grunewald (2003) focused on the rates of return of ECD interventions, arguing that such rates are high when placed next to other spending by governments made in the name of economic development, such as subsidies and preferential tax treatment for private businesses, and yet ECD interventions are rarely considered as an economic development measure. The authors argue that with such high rates of return, ECD interventions should also be portrayed as economic development initiatives.

The positive net benefits that the ECD interventions accrued were found to be irrespective of per-child costs, suggesting that large per-child investments may not be the most efficient. Overall, evaluations with a longer-term follow-up were associated with the largest benefit-cost ratios, because they could include measurements at older ages of outcomes which more conveniently translated into monetary benefits, such as educational attainment, earnings, and criminal behaviour (Karoly et al. 2005). This finding indicates that the benefit-cost estimates from the various economic evaluations of ECD interventions are very likely to be underestimated, since not all benefits could be translated into monetary values. For example, had juvenile justice savings not been included in the cost-benefit evaluations, the rate of return for certain programmes would be substantially lower (Penn et al. 2006). These studies' conclusions may not apply to the context of all European countries, as certain aspects of the criminal system in the United States, such as incarceration rates, are different from other industrialized countries. For example, the United States has higher incarceration rates than other countries (International Centre for Prison Studies 2005). This difference would inflate savings if the intervention had an impact on criminal activity. Penn et al. (2006) state that the fixation in the United States literature on early intervention as a means of crime reduction is partly a reflection of the very high costs of crime in that country.

Economic evaluations did not analyse all the potential positive effects that an intervention may have. For example, economic evaluations failed to include health outcomes in their estimations of the benefits, and no study monetized health outcomes in order to provide a valuation of health itself. Therefore, the limited number of evaluations which included health outcomes, focused only on cost-savings (such as savings from reduced emergency room visits during childhood, or public health care savings due to a reduced incidence of smoking and substance abuse). Instead, economic evaluations focused largely on savings generated in the areas of educational attainment, earnings, crime and delinquency, or from reduced expenses in child welfare and social welfare programmes (Karoly et al. 2005). The reason for omitting the inclusion of health measures in such cost-benefit evaluations may be due to the fact that such outcomes are more difficult to monetize in comparison to other outcomes (e.g. income), although this may also be due to other methodological reasons (see Kenkel 2009 for an analysis of the issue of incorporating health benefits in cost-benefit evaluations of ECD interventions). In addition, many of the outcomes affected by ECD interventions can generate spillover benefits which may take a monetary value (for a comprehensive list of potential quantifiable effects, including spillover effects from ECD interventions see Karoly et al. 2005; Meadows 2007). Additional benefits have been shown to accrue to younger siblings of ECD intervention participants (Garces et al. 2002) and may also positively affect the participants' offspring, as improved outcomes for participating children could very likely result in improved parenting towards their own children (Wolfe and Haveman 2002). Also, considering that many of the benefits of ECD interventions accrue over the long-term, certain returns to investment can only be detected after at least 15–20 years post-intervention (Burr and Grunewald 2006), suggesting that a long-term follow up is necessary in order to detect the complete returns to the initial ECD intervention investment.

An important finding arising from the economic evaluations is that the economic returns from investing in ECD intervention programmes are larger when the programmes follow a more targeted approach. This can be observed within ECD interventions, as a United States-based intervention showed that the returns for each dollar invested were five times higher for the high-risk population than for the lower-risk population (Burr and Grunewald 2006). Analyses from other studies support this finding, suggesting that the returns from a universal pre-school programme would be less than those from programmes that target a more disadvantaged population (Belfield 2004; Karoly and Bigelow 2005; Burr and Grunewald 2006). Karoly et al. (2005) suggest that these findings indicate that it is not reasonable to expect the returns from a programme serving a specific disadvantaged population to apply when the same programme serves a different population.

Other key features observed of ECD interventions with a better cost-effectiveness potential are to involve children as participants, to focus on enhancing parenting efficacy, and to be intensive in nature (Wise et al. 2005). On the issue of programme intensity, other studies have shown different results, as a United States-based intervention indicated that benefit-cost ratios decline with increased programme intensity (Reynolds et al. 2002). On the other hand, with the limited data available it is impossible to draw precise conclusions regarding the minimum amounts of programme intensity necessary to achieve substantial returns or the optimal intensity required to achieve the highest benefit-cost ratio (Karoly et al. 2005). In addition, limited evidence exists suggesting that increased cost-efficiency may be achieved through increased investment on aspects of programmes that reach the child directly. Findings from the US Head Start intervention indicate that, even when holding per capita expenditure constant, regional programmes that devoted higher shares of their budgets to child-specific expenditures resulted in better outcomes for the children (Currie and Neidell 2007).

Cost-effectiveness has also been shown to vary by age of entry into an ECD intervention. A recent review of the cost-effectiveness of pre-school interventions on children aged from three up to nine showed that interventions at age three to four are substantially more cost-effective than those at age five and older, or even compared to interventions which took place prenatally (Reynolds and Temple 2008) (Figure 11.1). It must be noted that such findings must be treated with caution as, given the large differences in costs and saving components included in these estimations, it is difficult to compare results across interventions. Research into the cost-effectiveness of ECD programmes such as Sure Start in the United Kingdom, with infancy as the age of entry, is needed to elucidate how such interventions would compare, in terms of returns to investment, to those starting during pre-school.

In judging the above comparisons, it is of course important to bear in mind some significant methodological challenges associated with cost-benefit evaluations of ECD interventions, all of which may affect estimates of net programme benefits and benefit-cost ratios: differences in evaluation methodologies, follow-up periods, methods used for discounting returns, and benefits/beneficiaries included (for a comprehensive discussion of ECD intervention cost-benefit methodology, see Karoly et al. (2005) and Wise et al.

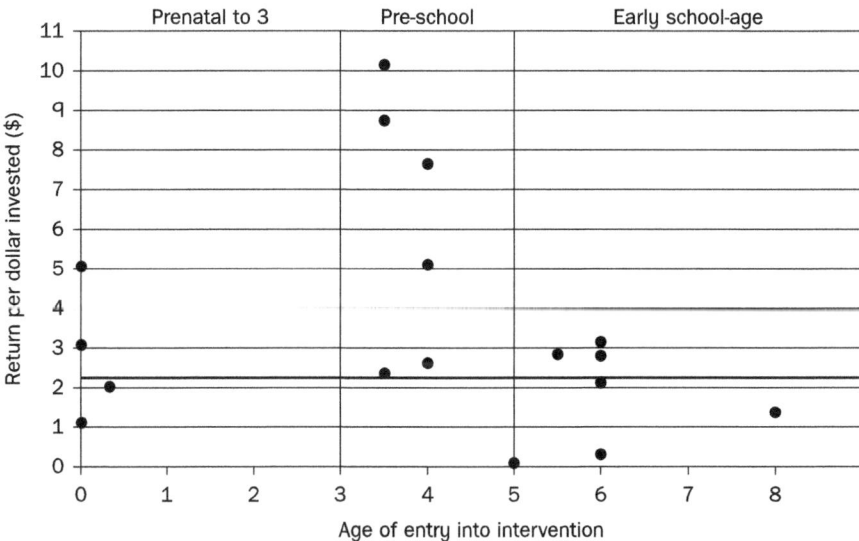

Figure 11.1 Return per dollar invested by age of entry into intervention

Source: Reynolds and Temple (2008)

(2005)). Given the large differences among methodologies, it is difficult to draw solid conclusions regarding comparisons between studies. That said, it is likely that the existing economic evaluations of ECD interventions have tended to understate the return of investment, as the scope followed by all the evaluations was a narrow one at best. From a health perspective, it is particularly important to point out that health outcomes (in monetized form) have been largely neglected from long-term cost-benefit evaluations of ECD interventions.

Education

Now, turning to the role of education, a long line of empirical research in economics has established the labour market returns to investments in education: people with more schooling enjoy higher lifetime earnings (Card 2001). Health economists have extended this line of research to consider whether investments in education also pay off in the form of better health. In this section we begin by reviewing the empirical evidence on the potential health benefits of public policies that broadly increase education. Typical examples are the reforms that have been implemented in many countries to increase the number of years of compulsory schooling. Other examples include public sector investments in school infrastructure and the supply of teachers to expand access to schooling. These broad educational policies typically lead to increases in years of completed schooling and increases in graduation rates at the primary, secondary, and post-secondary levels. We review estimates of whether increases in the years of completed schooling translate into improvements in health. We then discuss evidence on these investments' value for money.

As with ECD, the idea that education can improve health probably seems intuitive to many. In fact, in a variety of data sets there are strong positive statistical associations between more education and better health. In a study of middle-aged and older men and women in eight Western European countries, Huisman et al. (2005) found that the age-adjusted mortality rate for people with upper-secondary and post-secondary education is about 20 to 25 percent lower than for those with less education. Education can improve health through a number of pathways. First, because education increases lifetime earnings, people with more education have more flexibility and financial resources to protect themselves from threats to their health and to deal with health problems when they arise. Second, people with more education also have more 'health knowledge resources'. School health and science classes provide information about specific diseases. General literacy and scientific training may also help people learn, process, and respond to new advances in scientific understanding of disease processes. Health knowledge helps people prevent disease through healthier lifestyle choices about smoking, weight, and exercise (Kenkel 1991; Cutler and Lleras-Muney 2010). Education and health knowledge may also help people when they are ill – for example, through better self-management of complex medical treatment regimens (Goldman and Smith 2002).

Despite the plausibility of the pathways from education to health, there are also good reasons to question whether the strong statistical associations are convincing evidence of a causal link where more education yields improvements in health. First, there might be reverse causality, where poor health prevents children, adolescents, and young adults from completing as much education (Eide and Showalter 2011). Second, both education and health might be driven by a 'hidden' third factor or factors. For example, people who are more future-oriented and who have a greater sense of self-efficacy might be more likely to invest in education and in lifestyles that pay off in better health. To the extent they would have made the health investments even without more education, part of the statistical association between education and health is not causal.

Sorting out the extent to which the statistical associations between education and health reflect causation is a very challenging social science research problem. In cases like the ECD programmes discussed above, randomized experiments can be used to evaluate the effectiveness of an intervention in achieving its desired outcome. Randomized experiments are practical for the evaluation of specific educational practices and narrow policy changes, such as reducing class size (Krueger 1999). However, randomized experiments are generally impractical for evaluating the broader question of whether an additional year of education causes a reduction in mortality rates or other health improvement. Instead, economists and other social scientists analyse observational data, where differences in education are not randomly assigned but result from people's choices.

Using observational data, one approach economists have taken to explore causality relies on findings from natural quasi-experiments that help isolate the causal effect of education on health. In a typical example, a country's schooling reform creates the natural experiment. For example, in the United Kingdom the change in 1947 in compulsory schooling ages led to large increases in the years of completed schooling for the affected cohort, compared to previous cohorts. Economists exploit the resulting 'regression discontinuity' to estimate the impact of the increase of years of completed schooling on health outcomes (Clark and Royer 2013). Compulsory schooling laws and other educational policies and interventions also serve as 'instrumental variables' to isolate the causal effect of schooling on health outcomes (e.g. Lleras-Muney 2005). Meeting the methodological challenges of the quasi-experimental approach is an active area of econometric research (Angrist and Pischke 2009).

For the purposes of this chapter, an important advantage of quasi-experimental research on the link between education and health is that the results are directly relevant for policy evaluation. These research studies use a standardized measure of different education policies and examine the health benefits per additional year of completed education.[2] After summarizing that evidence, we provide evidence on the economic value of those health benefits and the value for money invested in education.

Are investments in education good for health? Evidence from high-income countries

Grossman (2006), Eide and Showalter (2011), Lochner (2011) and Mazumder (2011) provide comprehensive reviews of the economic research on the health benefits of education. The research literature is broad and growing. Although much of the evidence comes from the United States, the research provides estimates for a number of different countries, and for different populations (e.g. age groups and gender) within countries. The studies use several econometric techniques, although all the studies discussed below follow the general quasi-experimental approach. Most of the studies measure education in terms of years of completed schooling, although some use measures of educational attainment like high school graduation. Finally, the studies examine a range of health outcomes, including mortality rates, self-reported health, disability, and health behaviours including cigarette smoking and obesity. Lochner (2011, Table 2.7) lists 39 recent estimates of the benefits of education across these different health outcomes.

Table 11.3 summarizes five recent estimates of the effects of an additional year of education on mortality rates. The estimates range widely. In a United States study, Lleras-Muney (2005) estimates that an extra year of education substantially reduces mortality, but Mazumder's (2008) re-analysis of those data casts doubt on this finding. Studies using data from France, the Netherlands, and the United Kingdom find more modest effects, and several of the estimated effects are not statistically significantly different from zero.

Across the 39 estimates he reviews, Lochner (2011: 242) suggests that: 'education appears to have a weaker effect on mortality, self-reported health, and physical health in Europe than in the United States'. Lochner (2011) goes on to point out that 'although it is tempting to speculate . . . we are far from understanding' the observed differences in the health benefits of education across countries. This is an important direction for future research. Lochner's review also suggests that there is evidence that education reduces smoking, but in many studies education appears to have negligible effects on obesity. Future research that sheds more light on the different links between education and

Table 11.3 Effects of years of education on health and mortality (from selected studies)

Study	Country	Outcome Details	Effect as % of average
Albouy and Lequien (2009)	France	37-year mortality rate	Ages 15–42: –18.6% Ages 45–82: –15.8%
Clark and Royer (2013)	United Kingdom	Probablity of dying between ages 45 and 69	Women: 2.7% Men: 5.4%
Lleras-Muney (2005, 2006)	United States	10-year mortality rates	–59.4%
Mazumder (2008)	United States	10-year mortality rates	2.8%
van Kippersluis et al. (2011)	Netherlands	Probability of dying between ages 81 and 89	–6.0%

Source: Adapted from Lochner (2011, Table 2.7)

Note: The estimates by Lleras-Muney and van Kippersluis et al. are statistically significantly different from zero at conventional confidence levels.

different health outcomes would also be useful. In addition, Eide and Showalter (2011) suggest that a promising direction for future research is to move beyond measuring education by years of completed schooling, to examine how the quality of education affects health.

Are investments in education good value for money?

The economic case for investing in education because of the health benefits can be made at several levels. One place to start is to build on the well-established findings in labour economics that investing in education increases lifetime earnings and leads to better jobs and lower unemployment (e.g. Card 2001). These returns suggest that from either an individual or societal perspective, the evidence clearly establishes that investments in education are good value for money. In this light, evidence that education also improves health simply strengthens an already strong case for investing in education.

To provide more guidance for difficult policy trade-offs, it is necessary to go further and try to quantify the case that investing in education to improve health is good value for money. Lochner (2011) provides a useful framework and illustrative calculations of the value of the reduced mortality risks from more education. Economic evaluations of health and safety interventions use a standard approach to place a monetary value on mortality risk reductions, usually summarized as the value of a statistical life. Lochner uses a simple framework to combine estimates of the value of a statistical life with an estimate of the mortality benefits of schooling. Based on the range of estimates similar to what is shown in Table 11.3, Lochner (2011) concludes that a reasonable ballpark estimate is that the value of the mortality risk reduction due to an additional year of education is in the order of $1,530 to $2,550 ($1,500 to $2,500 in 2008 prices) per year. From the perspective of investing in the education of a 17-year-old, this flow of benefits begins 28 years in the future and continues for 35 years through age 80. Using a standard discount rate of 3 per cent, the discounted present value of this stream of benefits is in the order of $14,789–$24,478 ($14,500–$24,000 in 2008 prices). This calculation neglects the value of mortality risk reductions before the age of 35, which are probably small because young adults face very low mortality risk. It also neglects the value of mortality risk reductions past the age of 80, which is more problematic because van Kippersluis et al. (2011) estimate that education reduces mortality risks for people aged 80 to 89. However, at standard discount rates the value of these mortality risk reductions will be heavily discounted because they accrue almost 60 years in the future.[3]

Lochner's calculation of the value of education also focuses on the value of the mortality risk reduction, and neglects the value of reductions in morbidity that will improve quality of life. In a meta-analysis, Furnee et al. (2008) summarize estimates of the effect of education on health-related quality of life, using the metric of quality-adjusted life-years (QALYs). Their meta-analysis concludes that an additional year of schooling yields 0.036 QALYs.[4] A standard estimate of the monetary value of a QALY is around $100,000. This suggests that adding the value of the quality of life benefits increases the estimated value of the health returns to schooling by $3,600, in addition to the mortality risk reduction worth between $14,500 and $24,000.

The illustrative calculations above suggest that, as a ballpark estimate, an additional year of education yields health benefits worth around $23,000 per student in discounted present value. Whether this investment is good value for money depends upon the relevant cost-basis. A narrow cost-basis considers only the government's budgetary costs of educating more students. This can be termed 'the education minister's perspective'. Following Krueger and Whitmore (2000), a reasonable assumption is that the incremental budgetary cost is approximately equal to the average educational expenditures per student, which in the US were about $13,000 in 2008–9 (Snyder and Dillow 2012). From the education minister's perspective, then, the health benefits from a year of education appear to be good value for money, returning over $1.75 in health benefits for every $1 invested.

However, it is standard to supplement analyses from narrower perspectives with a cost-effectiveness analysis from the societal perspective (Gold et al. 1996). The societal perspective implies that the cost-basis should be much broader than the government's budgetary costs. In the context of education interventions, Dhaliwal et al. (2012) argue in favour of the assumption that 'the policymaker cares not just about their own budgetary costs, but also about the costs that a particular programme will impose on the beneficiaries'. From the perspective of an adolescent who remains in school for an additional year, the most significant costs are likely to be the opportunity costs of foregoing earnings from full-time employment. At the current federal minimum wage of $7.25 an hour, the opportunity cost of foregoing a full-time (40 hours per week for 50 weeks) minimum wage job for a year is $14,500. When these opportunity costs are added to the budgetary cost of an additional year of education, the value for money falls to less than $1 returned for every $1 invested. It should be kept in mind that these are just the health returns; taking into account the financial returns as well means that investments in education are very good value for money.

In addition to the education minister's perspective and the broad societal perspective, cost-effectiveness analysis can be conducted from various other perspectives. Because we are considering the health benefits from investing in education, another natural approach is to adopt what can be termed 'the health minister's perspective' and consider the implications for health expenditures.[5] While it seems intuitive that improvements in health reduce health care expenditures, this is not necessarily the case. To the extent education increases life expectancy, health care expenditures over a longer life can exceed health care expenditures over a shorter, albeit unhealthier, life. The evidence base is not yet sufficient to provide estimates of the impact of investments in education on total health care expenditures.

The illustrative calculations provide ballpark estimates of the value for money from investing in education, and also highlight the importance of the perspective adopted. A large and well-established body of studies uses a systematic framework to complete economic evaluations of education and training programmes (Boardman et al. 2011). The framework uses the broad societal perspective, and considers not only the cost of the education programme and the student's opportunity costs, but also the implications for tax payments, use of transfer programmes such as welfare payments, and so on. In principle, it is straightforward to extend the illustrative calculations along these lines to provide a more complete economic evaluation of investing in education to improve health. In practice, the economic evaluation would require detailed analysis tailored to the circumstances of the specific education investment under consideration.

Conclusions

In this chapter we have reviewed and discussed two areas of potential social determinants of health – ECD and education – from an economic perspective. Most existing economic evaluations demonstrate good – sometimes very good – value for money for ECD interventions, despite the fact that most such studies did not even incorporate the health benefits in their cost-benefit calculations, thereby likely understating its true return on investment. Yet the term ECD is an umbrella for a wide range of likely very heterogeneous programmes, and upon closer scrutiny, the existing economic evaluations differ considerably in the way they have conceptualized and measured the relevant cost and benefit components. What also remains hard to say is what the optimal or most cost-effective ECD programme should look like, even though a number of factors have been suggested to be associated with improved outcomes, such as better trained staff and a child-focused approach. It is also important to emphasize that there is a strong bias in the ECD evaluation work towards the United States, and a scarcity of European evidence. With the socioeconomic and political contexts differing widely between the United States and Europe – as well as within Europe – the extent to which the predominantly United States evidence is transferrable to other countries may be limited. Evidently, more evaluations of the effectiveness and cost-effectiveness of ECD interventions in Europe are required.

The economic evidence for the financial returns from investments in education is well-established. The added value of the health benefits of education further strengthens the overall case. When considering just the health returns to education, the question of good value for money hinges on the perspective taken when considering costs. From a perspective that considers the narrow cost-basis of government budgets, illustrative calculations suggest good value for money, but this might not hold for broader perspectives. As with ECD interventions, given the heterogeneity of education interventions and differences across time and between countries, more research is required before more specific and definitive conclusions can be drawn.

Notes

1   For more details and background on ECDs and their potential importance for health, see e.g. the extensive work of the Commission on Social Determinants (CSDH) on this subject (see Maggi et al. 2005; ECDKN 2007; CSDH 2008).

2   More technically, the econometric results provide estimates of local average treatment effects. Because the 1947 United Kingdom school reform affected a large fraction

of the entire population, Oreopoulos (2006) argues that in this case econometric analysis provides an estimate close to the average treatment effect for the entire population. In contrast, Lleras-Muney's (2005) results provide estimates of the local average treatment effect for the more select group in the population that responded to the compulsory schooling laws studied. Although results like Lleras-Muney's cannot be extrapolated to the entire population, they remain directly relevant to evaluate similar policy interventions that affect similarly select population sub-groups.

3   More controversially, it has been suggested that the value of statistical life estimates from working age individuals over-estimate the value of risk reductions at older ages, because willingness to pay for mortality risk reductions declines with age.

4   Unlike the studies reviewed by Lochner, and included in Table 11.3, the sample of studies in the meta-analysis by Furnee et al. is not limited to studies based on a strong quasi-experimental research design. As discussed above, the statistical associations in these studies do not necessarily reflect causation, so this estimate probably overestimates the causal effect education has on quality of life. In a more recent study, Golberstein et al. (2011) take into account both quantity and quality of life and estimate that an additional year of education is associated with 0.20–0.38 additional QALYs over a 23-year payoff period. Although Golberstein et al. do not use the stronger quasi-experimental designs, their study attempts to control for important sources of upward bias in the relationship between education and health. In this light, the relatively small QALY return from the meta-analysis by Furnee et al. might be a reasonable first approximation to the QALY benefits, until additional research is completed.

5   Instead of the health minister, this is perhaps more accurately the perspective of a minister with a broader policy portfolio who is considering the possible trade-off of higher educational expenditures for reduced health care expenditures.

References

Albouy, V. and Lequien, L. (2009) Does Compulsory Education Lower Mortality?, *Journal of Health Economics*, 28: 155–68.

Angrist, J. D. and Pischke, J.-S. (2009) *Mostly Harmless Econometrics: An Empiricist's Companion*. Princeton and Oxford: Princeton University Press.

Aos, S., Lieb, R., Mayfield, J., Miller, M. and Pennucci, A. (2004) *Benefits and Costs of Prevention and Early Intervention Programmes for Youth*. Olympia: Washington State Institute for Public Policy.

Belfield, C. R. (2004) *Investing in Early Childhood Education in Ohio: An Economic Appraisal*. Washington, DC: Renewing Our Schools, Securing Our Future: A National Task Force on Public Education.

Berlin, L. J., O'Neal, C. R. and Brooks-Gunn, J. (1998) What makes early intervention programmes work? The programme, its participants, and their interaction, *Zero to Three*, 18: 4–15.

Boardman, A. E., Greenberg, D. H., Vining, A. R. and Weimer, D. L. (2011) *Cost–Benefit Analysis*. Upper Saddle River, NJ: Prentice Hall.

Brooks-Gunn, J. (2003) Do you believe in magic? What we can expect from early childhood intervention programmes, *Social Policy Report*, 17(1): 3–14.

Burr, J. and Grunewald, R. (2006) *Lessons Learned: A review of Early Childhood Development Studies*. Minneapolis, MN: Federal Reserve Bank of Minneapolis.

Card, D. (2001) Estimating the return to schooling: Progress on some persistent econometric problems, *Econometrica*, 69: 127–60.

Clark, D. and Royer, H. (2013) The effect of education on adult mortality and health: Evidence from Britain, *American Economic Review*, 103(6): 2087–120

CSDH (Commission on Social Determinants of Health) (2008) *CSDH Final Report: Closing the Gap in a Generation: Health Equity through Action on the Social Determinants of Health*. Geneva: World Health Organization.

Currie, J. and Neidell, M. (2007) Getting inside the 'black box' of Head Start quality: What matters and what doesn't?, *Economics of Education Review*, 26: 83–99.

Cutler, D. M. and Lleras-Muney, A. (2010) The education gradient in old age disability, in D. Wise (ed.) *Research Findings in the Economics of Aging*. Cambridge, MA: NBER, pp. 101–22.

Dhaliwal, I., Duflo, E., Glennerster, R. and Tulloch, C. (2012) *Comparative Cost-Effectiveness Analysis to Inform Policy in Developing Countries: A General Framework with Applications for Education*. Working paper. Boston: Abdul Lantif Jameel Poverty Action Lab (J-PAL), MIT.

Dodge, D. (2004) Human capital, early childhood development and economic growth, in R.E. Tremblay, R.G. Barr and R. DeV. Peters (eds) *Encyclopedia on Early Childhood Development* [online]. Montreal: Centre of Excellence for Early Childhood Development.

ECDKN (Early Child Development Knowledge Network) (2007) *Early Child Development: A Powerful Equalizer*, Final report of the Early Childhood Development Knowledge Network of the Commission on Social Determinants of Health. Geneva: World Health Organization.

Eide, E. R. and Showalter, M. H. (2011) Estimating the relation between health and education: What do we know and what do we need to know?, *Economics of Education Review*, 30: 778–91.

Furnee, C. A., Wim Groot, W. and van den Brink, H. M. (2008) The health effects of education: A meta-analysis, *European Journal of Public Health*, 18(4): 417–21.

Garces, E., Thomas, D. and Currie, J. (2002) Longer-term effects of Head Start, *American Economic Review*, 92: 999–1012.

Golberstein, E., Hirth, R. A. and Lantz, P. M. (2011) Estimating the education–health relationship: A cost-utility approach, *B.E. Journal of Economic Analysis & Policy*, 11(3): 1–27.

Gold, M. R., Siegel, J. E., Russell, L. B. and Weinstein, M. C. (1996) *Cost-Effectiveness in Health and Medicine*. Oxford: Oxford University Press.

Goldman, D. P. and Smith, J. P. (2002) Can patient self-management help explain the SES health gradient?, *Proceedings of the National Academy of Science*, 99(16): 10929–34.

Gray, R. and Francis, E. (2007) The implications of US experiences with early childhood interventions for the UK Sure Start Programme, *Child: Care, Health and Development*, 33(6): 655–63.

Grossman, M. (2006) Education and nonmarket outcomes, in E. Hanushek and F. Welch (eds) *Handbook of the Economics of Education*, Volume 1. Amsterdam: North-Holland, an imprint of Elsevier Science, pp. 577–633.

Guralnick, M. J. (1997) *The Effectiveness of Early Intervention*. Baltimore, MD: Brookes.

Guralnick, M. J. (1998) The effectiveness of early intervention for vulnerable children: A developmental perspective, *American Journal of Mental Retardation*, 102: 319–45.

Heckman, J. J. (2000) Policies to foster human capital, *Research in Economics*, 54: 3–56.

Huisman, M., Kunst, A., Bopp, M. et al. (2005) Educational inequalities in cause-specific mortality in middle-aged and older men and women in eight western European populations, *The Lancet*, 365(9458): 493–500.

International Centre for Prison Studies (2005) *World Prison Report*. London: Kings College.

Karoly, L. A. and Bigelow, J. H. (2005) *The Economics of Investing in Universal Preschool Education in California*. Santa Monica, CA: RAND Corporation.

Karoly, L. A., Kilburn, M. R. and Cannon, J. S. (2005) *Early Childhood Intervention: Proven Results, Future Promise*. Santa Monica, CA: RAND Corporation.

Kenkel, D. (1991) Health behaviour, health knowledge and schooling, *Journal of Political Economy*, 99(2): 287–305.

Kenkel, D. (2009) *Valuation in Health Economics*. Prepared for Panel 5: Valuation of Outcomes and Resources/Costs, Workshop on Strengthening Benefit–Cost Methodology for the Evaluation of Early Childhood Interventions, National Research Council/Institute of Medicine Board on Children, Youth and Families. Washington, DC, 4–5 March.

Krueger, A. B. (1999) Experimental estimates of education production functions, *Quarterly Journal of Economics*, 115(2): 497–532.

Krueger, A. B. and Whitmore, D. M. (2000) *The Effect of Attending a Small-Class in the Early Grades on College-Test Taking and Middle School Test Results: Evidence from Project Star*. NBER Working Paper 7656. Cambridge, MA: NBER.

Lee, V. E. (1995) Where do Head Start attendees end up? One reason why preschool effects fade out, *Educational Evaluation and Policy Analysis*, 17: 62–82.

Lleras-Muney, A. (2005) The relationship between education and adult mortality in the United States, *Review of Economic Studies*, 72(1): 189–221.

Lleras-Muney, A. (2006) Erratum: The relationship between education and adult mortality in the United States, *Review of Economic Studies*, 73(3): 847.

Lochner, L. (2011) Nonproduction benefits of education: Crime, health, and good citizenship, in E. A. Hanushek, S. Machin and L. Woessmann (eds) *Handbook of the Economics of Education*, Volume 4. Amsterdam: Elsevier, pp. 183–282.

MacLeod, J. and Nelson, G. (2000) Programmes for the promotion of family wellness and the prevention of child maltreatment: A meta-analytic review, *Child Abuse and Neglect*, 24: 1127–49.

Maggi, S., Irwin, L. G., Siddiqi, A., Poureslami, I., Hertzman, E. and Hertzman, C. (2005) *Analytic and Strategic Review Paper: International Perspectives on Early Child Development*. Geneva: The World Health Organization's Commission on the Social Determinants of Health.

Mazumder, B. (2008) Does education improve health? A reexamination of the evidence from compulsory schooling laws, *Economic Perspective*, 2–16.

Mazumder, B. (2011) The effects of education on health and mortality. Unpublished manuscript. Denmark: Nordic Economic Policy Review.

Meadows, P. (2007) The costs and benefits of Sure Start local programmes, in J. Belsky, J. Barnes and E. Melhuish (eds) *The National Evaluation of Sure Start: Does Area-Based Early Intervention Work?* Bristol: Policy Press, pp. 113–30.

Nelson, G., Westhues, A. and MacLeod, J. (2003) A meta-analysis of longitudinal research on preschool prevention programmes for children, *Prevention and Treatment*, 6(1); doi: 10.1037/1522-3736.6.1.631a.

OECD (Organisation for Economic Co-operation and Development) (2006) *Starting Strong II: Early Childhood Education and Care*. Paris: OECD.

Oreopoulos, P. (2006) Estimating average and local average treatment effects of education when compulsory schooling laws really matter, *American Economic Review*, 96(1): 152–75.

Oreopoulos, P. (2007) Do dropouts drop out too soon? Wealth, health, and happiness from compulsory schooling, *Journal of Public Economics*, 2213–29.

Penn, H., Burton, V., Lloyd, E., Potter, S., Sayeed, Z. and Mugford, M. (2006) *What is Known about the Long-term Economic Impact of Centre-based Early Childhood Interventions?* Technical report. Research Evidence in Education Library. London: EPPI, Social Science Research Unit, Institute of Education, University of London.

Reynolds, A. J. and Temple, J. A. (2008) Cost-effective early childhood development programmes from preschool to third grade, *Annual Review of Clinical Psychology*, 4: 109–39.

Reynolds, A. J., Temple, J. A., Robertson, D. L. and Mann, E. A. (2002) Age 21 cost-benefit analysis of the Title I Chicago Child–Parent Centers, *Educational Evaluation Policy Analysis*, 24: 267–303.

Rolnick, A. and Grunewald, R. (2003) Early childhood development = economic development (Editorial), *Fedgazette* (a publication of the Federal Reserve Bank of Minneapolis, MN), March. Available at http://www.minneapolisfed.org/publications_papers/pub_display.cfm?id=1839 [Accessed 24 June 2009].

Shonkoff, J. P. and Meisels, S. J. (eds) (2000) *Handbook of Early Childhood Intervention*, 2nd edn. New York: Cambridge University Press.

Shonkoff, J. and Phillips, D. (eds) (2000) *From Neurons to Neighbourhoods: The Science of Early Childhood Development*. Washington, DC: National Academy Press.

Snyder, T. D and Dillow, S. A. (2012) *Digest of Education Statistics 2011*. Washington, DC: National Center for Education Statistics, Institute of Education Sciences, US Department of Education.

Van Kippersluis, H., O'Donnell, O. and van Doorslaer, E. (2011) Long-run returns to education: Does schooling lead to an extended old age?, *Journal of Human Resources*, 46(4): 695–721.

Watson, J. and Tully, L. (2008) *Prevention and Early Intervention Update: Trends in Recent Research*. Sydney: Centre for Parenting & Research, New South Wales Department of Community Services.

Wise, S., da Silva, L., Webster, E. and Sanson, A. (2005) *The Efficacy of Early Childhood Interventions: A Report Prepared for the Australian Government Department of Family and Community Services*. Melbourne: Australian Institute of Family Studies.

Wolfe, B. L. and Haveman, R. H. (2002) Social and nonmarket benefits from education in an advanced economy, in Y. K. Kodrzycki (ed.) *Education in the 21st Century: Meeting the Challenges of a Changing World*. Conference Series No. 47. Boston, MA: Federal Reserve Bank of Boston, pp. 97–131.

Wolfe, B. and Tefft, N. (2007) *Child Interventions that May Lead to Increased Economic Growth*. Early Childhood Research Collaborative Discussion Paper 111. Madison, WI: University of Wisconsin-Madison.

Zigler, E. F., Finn-Stevenson, M. and Hall, N. W. (2002) *The First Three Years and Beyond*. New Haven, CT: Yale University Press.

chapter twelve

Health promotion, disease prevention and health inequalities

Cristina Hernández-Quevedo and Helen Weatherly

Introduction

Discussions of equity and fairness often take a central role in policy debates. Health inequality is a key policy challenge worldwide, and is an important indicator of health care systems' performance. Underlying the focus on health inequalities are ethical considerations, such as the role of stewardship which places obligations on governments to enable conditions in which everyone can lead a healthy life (Nuffield Council on Bioethics 2007), and libertarian paternalism or nudge theory whereby choices are presented in such a way as to increase the likelihood that people will make choices which will lead to a healthier life (McColl 2009). Policy debates include the finance and delivery of health care, the responsiveness of the system to population needs, the distribution of health across different groups of the population and, more broadly, the economic and social conditions in which people live. Policies to enhance equity in health and health care provision include those implemented within the health care system directly, but also extend to sectors of the wider economy with impacts on health.

A particular feature of many prevention programmes is a concern with health inequalities. Prevention programmes aim to improve or maintain the health of individuals who are susceptible to disease, and to treat those who have a disease by preventing repeat events or worsening of the disease. These activities may be targeted at population sub-groups, including at-risk individuals, or across whole communities, as well as at providers both within and outside the health care sector. A range of prevention interventions exist, including clinical interventions (e.g. screening), the impact of which tend to be evaluated using the randomized controlled trial (RCT) gold standard approach to assessing effectiveness, and the use of educational, financial, regulatory and legislative tools where it is relatively difficult to undertake RCTs. Some programmes seek to promote positive behaviour change such as diet and exercise to improve health and reduce obesity and overweight, whereas others do not require that individuals engage in health enhancing behaviour, for example water fluoridation. Consideration of the different characteristics of prevention programmes is useful when exploring their impact on health inequalities and the analytic methods used for assessment.

To evaluate the impact of prevention programmes on health inequalities, it is necessary to define and measure health inequality. The WHO Commission on Social Determinants of Health has produced a guide to measuring equity in health. The guide focuses on the poor health of the poor, the social gradient in health within countries, and the existence of health inequities between countries (CSDH WHO 2008). Evidence suggests that systematic disparities in health exist, with risk factors for ill health and chronic conditions tending to be concentrated among disadvantaged groups of the population (Hernández-Quevedo et al. 2006, 2010; Costa-Font et al. 2011). Hernández-Quevedo et al. (2010) examined socioeconomic inequalities in 20 (of the 27) EU countries, from 2005–7, and found health limitations disproportionately concentrated among the worse off. Over this period, inequalities in health limitations increased or remained stable in most countries except Sweden and Italy, where they decreased slightly. Table 12.1 reports a range of approaches that have been implemented in these countries to tackle inequalities in health and to promote equity in health care systems.

Table 12.1 Examples of approaches to tackle health inequality among EU member states

Approaches	*EU country*
Legislative commitments: laws with specific references to health inequalities.	**Greece, Germany**
General goals: evidence of commitment to reduce health inequalities; no quantitative targets.	
• Focus on ethnic differences.	**Hungary**
• Prevent premature births, low birth weight and reduction of related negative health effects. Aim to achieve through improvements in nutrition for pregnant women living in poverty.	**Poland**
• Acknowledge role of social disadvantage as a determinant of poor health.	**Italy**
• Focus on reducing inequalities in health in marginalized groups (drug misusers and immigrants).	**Italy**
• Reduce avoidable mortality and morbidity.	**France**
• Reduce health disparities between regions.	**France**
• No national targets. Policies at a regional or local level.	**Spain (e.g. Basque country health plan)**

Quantitative health inequalities targets

• **First group:** follow targets specified by European Regional Office of WHO (*Health 21*).	**Czech Republic, Latvia, Lithuania**
• **Second group:** one or two quantitative targets.	**The Netherlands, Finland**
• **Third group:** wider range of quantitative targets.	**Ireland, United Kingdom**

Source: Adapted by author from Dahlgren and Whitehead (2006)

Factors such as education, income and job status are shown to have a substantial effect on the health of individuals (Mackenbach 2006; CSDH WHO 2008; Hernández-Quevedo et al. 2006, 2008, 2010). The evidence suggests that there are also large disparities in the health within countries where there are large differences in the health status of people belonging to different groups. There is a considerable body of health economic research on vertical inequity in the financing of health care, which is concerned with whether or not those on higher incomes pay proportionally more (progressive) or proportionally less (regressive) of their income towards health care. Although health care is free at the point of delivery in many European health care systems, consumption goods with public health (dis)benefits are often purchased in the market place. Prevention programmes, such as taxes on products like cigarettes and high-fat food, tend to be regressive as lower socioeconomic groups are more likely to engage in unhealthy behaviours, including tobacco use, physical inactivity and poor diet (Pampel et al. 2010), compared to higher socioeconomic groups.

To date, little research has been undertaken to evaluate the impact of prevention programmes on inequalities in health and equity in health care (Van Doorslaer and Van Ourti 2011), with few econometric studies (Le Grand 1987; Wagstaff and Van Doorslaer 2004) and even fewer cost-effectiveness studies (Sassi et al. 2001; Weatherly et al. 2009). The majority of the research has focused on social determinants of health outcomes, and examples are provided in Table 12.2. This literature has shown that health is related to socioeconomic factors and the organization of society (Marmot and Wilkinson 1999), including the influence of social class (Kelleher et al. 2003), self-reported education (Silventoinen et al. 2005) and disposable household income (Nummela et al. 2007), current income, wealth, knowledge and environmental effects (Costa-Font and Hernández-Quevedo 2012), all of which may vary across an individual's life cycle. To associate differences in health outcomes with any of these factors, it is necessary to be able to group the outcome measures by any of the socioeconomic variables being examined.

Methods

An assessment of the impact of prevention programmes on health inequalities remains crucial. A core objective of prevention programmes is to reduce health inequality; but, is this objective achieved in practice? Review of the published literature is useful to explore whether there is evidence to demonstrate that these programmes reduce health inequalities. It is also worth considering whether

Table 12.2 Examples of research on social determinants of health in Europe

Source of inequality	Country-specific evidence	Reference
Education-related inequalities in self-assessed health	Austria, Denmark, Italy, the Netherlands, Norway, Spain, United Kingdom, West Germany	Kunst et al. (2005)
Education-related inequalities in chronic diseases	Belgium, Denmark, Finland, France, Italy, the Netherlands, Spain, United Kingdom	Dalstra et al. (2005)
Education and material deprivation as important determinants of self-assessed health	Russia, Estonia, Lithuania, Latvia, Hungary, Czech Republic	Bobak et al. (2000)
Education-related inequalities in health generally stable over time (1994–2004)	Estonia, Latvia, Lithuania, Finland	Helasoja et al. (2006)
Income-related inequalities in health	Belgium, Denmark, Finland, France, the Netherlands, Norway, United Kingdom	Mackenbach et al. (2005)
Income-related inequalities in health limitations	Austria, Belgium, Denmark, England, Finland, France, Germany, Greece, Ireland, Italy, Luxembourg, the Netherlands, Portugal, Spain, United Kingdom	Hernández-Quevedo et al. (2006)

Source: Authors' compilation

analytic methods are available and utilized to assess the impact of prevention programmes on health inequalities. Empirical questions for evaluation include whether prevention programmes can reduce the gap in health inequalities in the population, whether some prevention programmes are more effective in reducing health inequalities than others, and at whom health equality promoting programmes should be directed.

The aim of this chapter is to inform policymakers about some of the prevention programmes that have been implemented to reduce health inequalities, their rationale, and their effectiveness in reducing health inequalities. It provides an overview of the health inequality implications of implementing prevention programmes and some of the issues encountered in striving to achieve this goal. This chapter reviews the evidence on the impact of prevention programmes on health inequalities in: (1) obesity, physical activity and nutrition, (2) smoking and (3) screening, immunization and health check-ups. These domains have been considered, given that the evidence base in these areas is sizeable relative to other areas of public health. The review includes evaluations of prevention programmes from around the world and is illustrative, rather than comprehensive. It is likely that some findings will be context-specific, so the results reported may require adaptation to ensure transferability to other settings. The chapter does not offer a critical appraisal of the evaluation methods applied in the different studies: almost all public health interventions are implemented without being tested experimentally, and this poses challenges for obtaining unbiased estimates of effect.

Prevention programmes

Obesity, physical activity and nutrition

'Fat taxes' are levied on food stuffs that are considered unhealthy if eaten to excess, e.g. high-fat foods, high-calorie foods, or foods with low macronutrient content. The aim is to reduce consumption of these foods through direct price increases to the consumer and indirectly through encouraging manufacturers to reduce the unhealthy content of foods produced. As a secondary benefit, revenues generated by a fat tax could be invested in additional prevention programmes, such as increasing awareness among the general public about dietary health risks (Clark and Levedahl 2006).

The cost-effectiveness of food taxes has been assessed in a small number of modelling studies, all of which find taxes to have favourable cost-effectiveness ratios (see Chapter 7). These taxes also run the risk of being regressive. Where the tax is passed on to the consumer in the form of a price increase and consumption levels remain constant, fat taxes are regressive: on purchasing the foodstuff, those on lower incomes pay a greater proportion of their income on the good as a result of the tax, than those on higher incomes.

Evidence from a study on macronutrient intake by Leicester and Windmeijer (2004) suggests that those on lower incomes tend to spend a greater proportion of their income on food, and on unhealthy foods, so, all else being equal, a fat tax would impact more on the budget of lower income compared to higher income households. Based on data from the 2000 UK National Food Survey, Leicester and Windmeijer (2004) found that a flat tax targeting fat, sodium and cholesterol would be regressive, with an effective tax rate of 0.7 per cent for the poorest consumers – that is, the very poorest 2 per cent of the population would spend 0.7 per cent of their total income on the fat tax. By comparison, those at median income would only spend 0.25 per cent of their total income, and the wealthiest households as little as 0.1 per cent of their total income. Similar patterns were seen by Tiffin and Arnoult (2011), who estimated the effect of increasing the price of fatty foods by 1 per cent for every percent of saturated fats contained. The effectiveness of the policy in improving diet-related health in relation to heart conditions, cancers and chronic disease was higher in the high managerial group, followed by the low managerial group, and least effective in the workers. These differences arose primarily due to the higher existing levels of risk within lower socioeconomic groups; absolute changes in risk were broadly similar across groups. Another study, which investigated a tax on fat content in dairy products, found this tax to be highly regressive, falling mostly on older people and the poor (Chouinard et al. 2007).

Fat taxes may also penalize the person making that choice, in relation to price. There is some evidence to suggest that the cost per calorie of energy-dense, nutrition-poor food items, such as sugar, is much lower than for healthier food items such as vegetables and lean meats (Cash and Lacanilao 2007). Assuming that meeting basic energy needs is more important than meeting other (healthier) nutritional needs, the difference in food energy prices suggests that there is considerable price pressure to buy energy-dense, nutrition-poor foods, for the lowest-income consumers. Hence, raising the prices of those foods that provide food energy at the lowest cost is likely to be very regressive. Another argument posed is that fat taxes are not only regressive but also unfair, penalizing those who include unhealthy foods in their diet in moderation in an otherwize healthy diet (Cash et al. 2005).

Taxes that are imposed on behaviours disproportionately concentrated in the poor, however, will not automatically be regressive as the demand for the taxed item may also decline with income. This has raised the question of whether taxes might be designed that focus on those whose (unhealthy) behaviours are most sensitive to price (elastic) (Cawley and Ruhm 2012).

'Thin subsidies', also known as price subsidies, have also been applied to healthy foods to encourage consumption of a healthier diet by increasing their affordability. Using epidemiological evidence and simulation methods, Cash et al. (2005) explored the health potential of subsidizing fruit and vegetables, and the effectiveness of this on reducing heart disease and stroke. For the United States, they estimated that a 1 per cent reduction in the price of these foods might be associated with almost 10,000 prevented cases of coronary heart disease and ischemic strokes. They concluded that a thin subsidy could be an effective way to provide health benefits, especially to disadvantaged consumers. There is evidence to suggest that policies designed to make a healthy diet more affordable may be most effective among those with lower socioeconomic status, as measured by social class or household income (Darmon et al. 2002; Cash et al. 2005). A few studies that conducted experiments exploring the impact of reducing the price of fruit and vegetables on specific groups, e.g. university and high school students, found that this might be an effective way of increasing sales of these items (Jeffery et al. 1994; French et al. 1997).

Although there is some evidence to support the use of thin subsidies in reducing health inequalities, there is also some evidence to suggest subsidies might benefit higher income consumers more. Where there are disproportionately greater benefits among this group of the population, health inequality may increase, even though average population health may also increase. Tiffin and Arnoult (2011) examined the impact on nutrient intake of a tax on saturated fat combined with a subsidy on fruit and vegetables. Based on United Kingdom household data from the expenditure and food survey for 2005–6, they found that the subsidy brought consumption of fruit and vegetables in line with dietary recommendations, but the tax was insufficient to bring about a large enough change to achieve this goal for fat intake. Gustavsen and Rickertsen (2004) distinguished households with high and low consumption of vegetables. High-consuming households were more sensitive to vegetable price, and therefore more likely to alter their behaviour than low-consuming households. Use of income support to improve buying power for vegetables, as well as removal of a vegetables' value-added tax (VAT) at point of consumption, did not have an effect over the consumption of vegetables for low-consuming households; but health information did have a positive impact, and was also less costly.

Physical activity programmes have been used to reduce obesity and improve health. An example of a community-based physical activity intervention is 10,000 Steps Rockhampton, in Australia (Eakin et al. 2007). The multi-component intervention utilized several strategies, including a media campaign, engaging general practitioners and other health professionals in promoting physical activity, worksite physical activity promotion, and collaboration with local government on environmental supports such as signage and walking trails, as well as pedometer use. Pedometer use differed significantly by age group, education level, household income and physical activity. In particular, pedometer use was concentrated among the employed and educated, women, older people and obese people, suggesting some aspects of health inequality may increase.

As reported by Avenell et al. (2004), the addition of certain drugs to diet appears beneficial for the treatment of adults with obesity. Exercise and/or behaviour therapy appear to improve weight loss when added to diet. Low-fat diets with exercise, with or without behaviour therapy, are associated with the prevention of type 2 diabetes and hypertension. This intervention is especially effective in high-risk individuals, particularly in those with co-morbidities, cardiovascular risk factors or obesity. However, findings varied by sex: women with obesity-related illnesses who had intentional weight loss enjoyed a reduced risk of death, cardiovascular disease (CVD) death, and cancer and diabetes-related death; men with general illness who were intentionally losing weight had a reduction in the risk of diabetes-related death, but no effect was found on CVD mortality, while cancer mortality increased (Avenell et al. 2004).

Food labelling has been used to promote healthy eating – for example, the better choice label in Finland, the pyramid label in the Netherlands, and the traffic light label in the United Kingdom (Nordström and Thunström 2009). Very limited information on the cost-effectiveness of these schemes is available (see Chapter 7). There is some research which highlights the potential role of food labelling in tackling health inequalities. In the United Kingdom in 2009, the effectiveness of three front-of-pack labelling schemes was assessed: monochrome schemes, providing information on the percentage of guideline daily amount (GDA); traffic light colour-coded schemes, indicating nutrient levels; and schemes providing a traffic light colour code and percentage of GDA. The report found that the most effective label combined use of the words 'high, medium and low', traffic light colours and percentage of GDA, together with levels of nutrients in a portion of the product. Those with lower education levels were more likely to better understand these combined labels (Stockley et al. 2009).

Food regulation and agreements between the government and the food industry have been used in some countries to reduce consumption of unhealthy foodstuffs. Modelling studies also suggest a reduction in salt in processed foods would be cost-effective (see Chapter 7). In the United Kingdom, in 2003, a strategy was implemented to reduce population salt intake. This involved voluntary agreements by the food industry to reduce salt content in processed foods, improving food labelling, and public awareness campaigns to change personal behaviour such as reducing salt added to food when cooking. This strategy was strengthened in 2006, with a national target to reduce population salt intake to 6 g per day by 2010, which was then delayed until 2012. Millet et al. (2012) evaluated the impact of this strategy on salt intake in England. The national salt reduction strategy was associated with a significant but small reduction in salt intake across the population, with salt intake remaining high for younger people, men, ethnic minorities and lower social class groups, and therefore it is uncertain that the strategy was effective in reducing health inequality.

Food fortification has also been used to improve health. There is a considerable evidence base from the United States from the 1990s on the effectiveness of a population-wide intervention to fortify cereals with folic acid. Absolute social differences in blood folate levels were subsequently reduced by 67 per cent (Dowd and Aiello 2008). However, the evidence base, more generally, is not unambiguous. For example, recent food safety concerns in Denmark led to legislation in 2004 to restrict foods fortified with extra vitamins or minerals, and banning of some products, including some cereals and yeast extract products. The WHO states that limitations to food fortification might include equity issues about the right to choose to consume fortified products or not, the potential for insufficient demand for the fortified product, increased production costs that may be passed on to the consumer, and the potential that the fortified products will still not be a solution to nutrient deficiencies among low-income populations who may not be able to afford the new products, and children who may not be able to consume adequate amounts (WHO/FAO 2006).

Smoking

Regulation and taxation polices are used widely across the WHO European Region. The benefits of regulation and taxation in reducing smoking are not conclusive within the economics literature. Some early simulation studies, based on United States and United Kingdom data, suggested potential increases in tobacco smoking in some European countries, and a very small reduction in other member states following tax harmonization in the EU (Trigg and Bosanquet 1992; Bosanquet 1995). More recent studies suggest that raizing the price of cigarettes through taxation is the most cost-effective taxation policy (see Chapter 4). An analysis of Canadian data examined whether regulation and taxation were effective in inducing smokers to quit smoking (Lanoie and Leclair 1998). It was found that the total demand for cigarettes was responsive to taxes, but not regulation. However, in those who smoked, demand was responsive to regulation, but not to taxes. Some studies suggest that revenue generated through cigarette taxes exceeds the estimated financial external costs of smoking, which include future costs incurred by smokers, such as higher insurance costs, as well as costs imposed on society such as passive smoking costs, passive smoking insurance costs, and non-residential fire deaths (Viscusi 1994). Several United Kingdom and United States studies have shown that increased cigarette taxes would reduce observed differences in smoking among socioeconomic groups (Townsend et al. 1994; Farrelly et al. 1998) as individuals from the highest social class were less price responsive (at least in the United Kingdom) (Townsend et al. 1994), and those with less education were more price responsive than more educated individuals (Chaloupka 1991).

Regulation on anti-smoking, combined with taxation, has proved more successful than taxation alone. Some research has been undertaken to evaluate the impact of smoking bans on smoking. Following the introduction of legislation in 2006 to prohibit smoking in enclosed public places in Scotland, hospital admissions for heart attack and acute coronary syndrome fell substantially, with a 14 per cent reduction in smokers and a 21 per cent fall in non smokers. The drop was uniform across social groups, suggesting improved average health of the population, constant relative health inequality, and a reduction in absolute health inequality. Regulatory policies, particularly those including increases in cigarette price, are also associated with a reduction in tobacco use of a similar magnitude across socioeconomic groups (Schaap et al. 2008). This suggests that, in the many countries where smoking rates are higher in poorer groups, the absolute benefit will be greater than in affluent groups. Indeed, men and women in lower socioeconomic groups appear more responsive to uniform increases in cigarette price than affluent groups (Townsend et al. 1994; Main et al. 2008). In 2007, England introduced similar legislation banning public smoking. Jones et al. (2011) have developed a theoretical model of smoking exploring an individual's life cycle addiction, and cigarette consumption with and without a public smoking ban. Based on the model, the ban affects individuals differently according to their age, gender, and previous level of cigarette consumption. Using longitudinal data for Scotland and England from the British Household Panel Survey (BHPS), the model predicts that smoking bans have no impact on overall smoking prevalence. However, there was some evidence of a reduction in the level of cigarette consumption in particular groups, especially among male heavy smokers, female moderate and heavy smokers, and young people.

Public information policies have also been implemented to reduce smoking. While provision of new information may impact on consumer behaviour, there may be marked socioeconomic inequalities in their uptake. For example, the release of the first Surgeon General's Report on smoking and health in 1964 was followed by a 5 per cent decrease in smoking in the United States; however, this was more pronounced among educated mothers as they were more likely to reduce their smoking, with a subsequent increase of their newborn's health (Aizer and Stroud 2010). Some research has shown that warning labels on cigarette packs and anti-smoking advertisements significantly cut tobacco use (Chaloupka and Warner 2000); however, again, there is evidence that the reduction in total use was greater among more highly educated individuals (Grossman 2000).

Clinical interventions and services are available to help reduce smoking and they are typically available to all, usually being delivered on a one-to-one basis. There is some evidence to support the cost-effectiveness of smoking cessation services (Parrott et al. 1998; WHO 2003); however, there is a concern that uptake is higher and that effectiveness is greater among more advantaged individuals, thus increasing relative health inequality (Low et al. 2007). Affluent smokers tend to receive more help, and are more likely to quit (Browning et al. 2008; Bauld et al. 2007). Increasing quit rates in more affluent smokers were also recently reported in Inter99, the Danish trial of primary prevention in general practice (Jakobsen 2009). Similar inequalities have also been reported in workplace smoking interventions (Browning et al. 2008).

Screening, immunization and check-ups

Childhood immunization programmes are offered routinely in many jurisdictions, but differences in immunization uptake across the population persist. A range of social, demographic, maternal and infant-related factors have been identified as barriers to full immunization (Peckham et al. 1989; Samad et al. 2006). Within the United Kingdom, for example, the evidence shows that the following groups of children and young people are at risk of not being fully immunized: those who have missed previous vaccinations, whether as a result of parental intent or otherwise; looked after children; children with physical or learning difficulties; children of teenage or lone parents; children not registered with a general practitioner (GP); younger children from large families; children who are hospitalized; minority ethnic groups; and vulnerable children, such as those whose families are travellers, asylum seekers or homeless (Peckham et al. 1989; Hill et al. 2003; Department of Health 2005; Samad et al. 2006). These characteristics may be correlated with belonging to a household at the bottom of the income distribution.

Differences in uptake of the **influenza vaccine** have been found in the United Kingdom. Since the late 1960s, influenza vaccination has been recommended for patients of all ages from selected high-risk groups, including older people with underlying medical conditions, as well as those living in long-stay residential homes where the spread of influenza is likely to be rapid. In 1998, influenza vaccination was recommended for all people aged 75 years and over, regardless of predisposing risk conditions. In 2000, this policy was extended to include all persons aged 65 years and over. The risk group categories in people aged under 65 years has been expanded over time in an attempt to reduce the morbidity from influenza in these groups. Studies have been conducted in the United Kingdom and Europe looking at the uptake of the influenza vaccine among older people, and in the high-risk groups (American Diabetes Association 2004; Breeze et al. 2004; Joseph et al. 2005; Jiménez-García et al. 2006). Monthly data on vaccination uptake showed that Department of Health target rates were met, but also showed that there was considerable variation in uptake at local levels (Nichol 2003). Local differences in vaccination uptake may arise due to factors including socioeconomic deprivation, ethnicity and rurality. Breeze et al. (2004) found that, between 1997 and 2000, uptake of the influenza immunization in 73 British GP practices was lower among women, people aged 85 years and over compared to people aged under 80, and those in the most deprived areas, compared to the least deprived.

A more recent United Kingdom study (Coupland et al. 2007) examined trends in uptake of influenza immunization by sex, deprivation, rurality, ethnicity of area of residence and risk group. Based on the QRESEARCH database, using patients of all ages between 1999 and 2005, a marked increase (59.5 per cent) in the overall population uptake of influenza vaccine was found over the 6-year period, including a 62.5 per cent increase in uptake in people aged 65 years and over, with 70 per cent vaccinated in 2004 to 2005. Over this period, however, only 29 per cent of all patients in a clinical risk group aged less than 65 were vaccinated. Overall, men, and patients from deprived areas and areas with a higher proportion of non-white residents, had lower vaccination rates. There was little effect of rurality on vaccination rates. This work suggests more emphasis should be placed on the identification and immunization of younger high-risk groups.

Von Wagner et al. (2009) assessed **faecal occult blood test (FOBT)** participation in relation to neighbourhood socioeconomic characteristics in the London area over the first 30 months of the national roll-out of the Bowel Cancer Screening Programme (BCSP). Data were based on test kit return rates for 401,197 individuals aged 60–69, resident in 808 postcode sectors, who were sent FOBT kits between October 2006 and January 2009. Socioeconomic deprivation was measured using the Townsend Material Deprivation Index, which is based on four area-level indicators from the Census: levels of unemployment among those who are economically active, owner-occupancy, car ownership, and home overcrowding. Higher Townsend scores indicate greater deprivation. They showed a strong socioeconomic status (SES) differential in uptake of the FOBT-based BCSP in London. Residents in the most affluent areas were significantly more likely to return the test kits than those in slightly less, but still relatively affluent areas, and this pattern continued linearly through the quintiles of deprivation. In particular, uptake in the most affluent quintile was 50 per cent higher than in the most deprived quintile, showing as much of a gradient as was seen in the early days of the breast or cervical screening programmes (Majeed et al. 1995; Baker and Middleton 2003). Some potential areas to implement policies to reduce inequalities in the uptake of FOBT are linked to overcoming severe difficulties in health literacy identified within the lowest SES group, the perceived value of early detection of cancer (fatalism), which has shown a graded association with SES (Wardle et al. 2004), as well as the 'disgust' response, with some evidence showing a social gradient (Rozin et al. 2000). At WHO European Region level, some evidence also shows that **dental check-ups** are utilized more by women and the most educated. A possible explanation given for this was the greater personal initiative shown by these people (Eurobarometer 2007). At the same time, individuals aged 55 years and older are more likely to take an eye test, while more men than women take an annual hearing test.

Wide variation has been found in national rates of **X-rays, ultrasound and scans**, with a high take-up of heart check-ups in the Baltic countries, higher rates of scans, tests and check-ups among older respondents, with testing for women increasing with levels of education and being consistently lower among unemployed women than their employed counterparts (Eurobarometer 2007). Inequalities have also been reported in the **screening and detection of cancer, as well as for CVD**. For instance, women who choose to attend the National Health Service (NHS) Breast Screening Programme come more from affluent areas (Banks et al. 2002).

Inequalities in anti-hypertensive therapy have been also reported. A study by Ashworth and Millett (2008) suggested that social and ethnic disparities in the **detection and management of hypertension** have persisted in the United Kingdom, despite major investment in quality improvement initiatives, including pay for performance. In Germany, the CVD prevention study compared three strategies involving advice from professionals and media. After seven years, hypercholesterolemia improved only in upper social groups, thereby increasing the gap between the health of rich and poor (Helmert et al. 1995).

Discussion

Central to most, if not all, prevention programmes is the aim of reducing health inequality. This might involve targeting disadvantaged individuals to improve their health relative to more advantaged individuals, or through delivering programmes to all to raise the health of all, including those who are most disadvantaged. Based on the literature that is included in this review, gains in health equality are likely to be largest where prevention programmes are targeted at disadvantaged communities and individuals, and for those interventions that do not require behaviour change on the part of the recipient. Targeting may require redesign of current prevention programme initiatives, so that programme benefits are spread more evenly between different social groups. Some prevention programmes, once implemented, do not rely on individuals to engage with the programme in order to reap the benefits. For the large majority of prevention programmes, however, to improve health it is essential that people first access and then take up the programmes. Across the general population, access and take up tends to be lowest in more disadvantaged groups. Prevention programmes that only require a one-off behaviour change on the part of the recipient, such as colorectal screening, are more likely to be effective than those that require sustained behaviour change, such as exercise or quit smoking programme. In the case of the latter, they are likely to be most effective in those recipients who continue to engage with a programme and, again, this is most likely to happen in more advantaged groups. Where this is so, it is likely that such prevention programmes will increase socioeconomic health inequality, even if total population health may increase; hence, the relevance of targeting care at disadvantaged groups.

Policymakers should be cautious in designing and implementing prevention programmes to ensure that they do not increase health inequalities or discriminate among groups of the population by demographic (e.g. age, gender, ethnicity) and/or socioeconomic variables (e.g. income, education). There is a high degree of uncertainty associated with the effectiveness of prevention programmes in reducing health inequality as a result of differential access and uptake between social groups; however, once taken up, and once behaviour changes are instilled, prevention programmes may be effective in reducing health inequality, especially when risks of disease are higher in lower socioeconomic groups as they may have more to gain from taking up the intervention. In many areas of prevention, there is little or no evaluation available as yet, and where there is, findings may be context-specific and not straightforward to generalize to other settings. Most prevention programmes require that changes in behaviour take place, but behavioural change is not easy to instigate or sustain, and cultural norms and organizational structures may hamper behaviour change. To build on the existing evidence base in prevention, greater availability of information systems for measuring and assessing the often long-term impact of the prevention programmes on health inequalities is required. This would contribute to the careful design of prevention programmes, reducing the likelihood of unintended negative consequences.

While health inequality is a central objective of prevention programmes, there is relatively little evaluation to assess the effectiveness of prevention programmes and the impact of these programmes on health inequality. This is particularly the case in terms of assessing the *cost-effectiveness* of prevention programmes, where there is almost no explicit evaluation of health equity (Cookson et al. 2009). As improvement in health inequalities is of such importance within the public health arena, identifying and monitoring the impact of prevention programmes on health inequalities remains essential. As argued by Suhrcke and Cookson (2012), economic evaluations could provide some insight into the 'equity-efficiency trade-off' associated with different policies, 'providing policymakers a clearer, more balanced, and more evidence informed understanding about the nature, size and importance of any policy trade-offs' (Suhrcke and Cookson 2012).

Several approaches have been suggested to explicitly evaluate equity within the economic evaluation of prevention programmes, including narrative review of background information on equity, health inequality impact assessment, and the analysis of the opportunity cost of equity and equity weighting of health outcomes (Cookson et al. 2009; McDaid and Sassi 2010). However, in practice, distributional effects have been almost entirely neglected in existing economic evaluations (Sassi et al. 2001; Weatherly et al. 2009). The evidence summarized here suggests that continuous, ongoing evaluation of prevention programmes is required to review their impact on health inequalities, to monitor for possible unintended consequences, and to take action to mitigate unintended consequences, including possible redesign of programmes, such as targeting programmes at disadvantaged sections of the community.

References

Aizer, A. and Stroud, L. (2010) *Education, Knowledge and the Evolution of Disparities in Health*. NBER Working Paper No. 15840. Cambridge, MA: NBER.

American Diabetes Association (2004) Influenza and pneumococcal immunisation in diabetes, *Diabetes Care*, 27: S111.

Ashworth, M. and Millet, C. (2008) Quality improvement in UK primary care: The role of financial incentives, *Journal of Ambulatory Care Management*, 31: 220–5.

Avenell, A., Broom, J., Brown, T. J. et al. (2004) Systematic review of the long-term effects and economic consequences for obesity and implications for health improvement, *Health Technology Assessment*, 8(21): iii–iv, 1–182.

Baker, D. and Middleton, E. (2003) Cervical screening and health inequality in England in the 1990s, *Journal of Epidemiology and Community Health*, 57: 417–23.

Banks, E., Beral, V., Cameron, R. et al. (2002) Comparison of various characteristics of women who do and do not attend for breast cancer screening, *Breast Cancer Research*, 4: R1.

Bauld, L., Judge, K. and Platt, S. (2007) Assessing the impact of smoking cessation services on reducing health inequalities in England, *Tobacco Control*, 16: 400–4.

Bobak, M., Pikhart, H., Rose, R., Hertzman, C. and Marmot, M. (2000) Socioeconomic factors, material inequalities, and perceived control in self-rated health: Cross-sectional data from seven post-communist countries, *Social Science & Medicine*, 51(9): 1343–50.

Bosanquet, N. (1995) Have higher taxes reduced the European smoking rate?, in: K. Slama (ed.) *Tobacco and Health: Proceedings from the 9th World Conference on Tobacco and Health*. New York: Plenum Press, pp. 213–16.

Breeze, E., Mangtani, P., Fletcher, A. E., Price, G. M., Kovats, S. and Roberts, J. (2004) Trends in influenza vaccination uptake among people aged over 74 years 1997–2000: Survey of 73 general practices in Britain, *BMC Family Practice*, 5: 8.

Browning, K. K., Ferketich, A. K., Salsberry, P. J. and Wewers, M. E. (2008) Socioeconomic disparity in provider-delivered assistance to quit smoking, *Nicotine Tobacco Research*, 10: 55–61.

Cash, S. B. and Lacanilao, R. D. (2007) *Calorie Prices*. Research Fact Sheet. Edmonton, Alberta: Department of Rural Economy, University of Alberta.

Cash, S., Sunding, D. L. and Zilberman, D. (2005) Fat taxes and thin subsidies: Prices, diet and health outcomes, *Acta Agriculturae Scandinavica*, Section C – Food Economics, 2(3/4): 167–74.

Cawley, J. and Ruhm, C. J. (2012) The economics of risky health behaviours, in M. V. Pauly, T. G. Mcguire and P. P. Barros (eds) *Handbook of Health Economics*, Volume 2. New York: Elsevier BV, pp. 95–199.

Chaloupka, F. J. (1991) Rational addictive behaviour and cigarette smoking, *Journal of Political Economy*, 99(4): 722–42.

Chaloupka, F. J. and Warner, K. E. (2000) The economics of smoking, in A. J. Culyer and J. P. Newhouse (eds.) *Handbook of Health Economics*. Philadelphia, PA: Elsevier Inc., pp. 1539–627.

Chouinard, H. H., Davis, D. E., LaFrance, J. T. and Perloff, J. M. (2007) Fat taxes: Big money for small change, *Forum for Health Economics and Policy*, 10(2): 1–30. Available at http://www.bepress.com/fhep/10/2/2 [Accessed September 2014].

Clark, J. S. and Levedahl, J. W. (2006) Will fat taxes cause Americans to become fatter? Some evidence from US meats. Paper contributed at the International Association of Agricultural Economists Conference, Gold Coast, Australia, August.

Commission on the Social Determinants of Health, World Health Organization (CSDH WHO) (2008) *Closing the Gap in a Generation: Health Equity through Action on the Social Determinants of Health*. Final report on the Commission on the Social Determinants of Health. Geneva: World Health Organization.

Cookson, R., Drummond, M. and Weatherly, H. (2009) Explicit incorporation of equity considerations into economic evaluation of public health interventions, *Health Economics Policy and Law*, 4(2): 231–45.

Costa-Font, J. and Hernández-Quevedo, C. (2012) Measuring inequalities in health: What do we know? What do we need to know?, *Health Policy*, 106(2): 195–206.

Costa-Font, J., Hernández-Quevedo, C. and Jimenez Rubio, D. (2011) *Should we be Concerned about Income Inequalities in Unhealthy Life Styles?* IEF Working Paper. Madrid: Instituto de Estudios Fiscales.

Coupland, C., Harcourt, S., Vinogradova, Y. et al. (2007) Inequalities in uptake of influenza vaccine by deprivation and risk group: Time trends analysis, *Vaccine*, 25: 7363–71.

Dahlgren, G. and Whitehead, M. (2006) *European Strategies for Tackling Social Inequities in Health: Levelling up*, Part 2. Copenhagen: WHO Regional Office for Europe.

Dalstra, J. A., Kunst, A. E., Borrell, C. et al. (2005) Socioeconomic differences in the prevalence of common chronic diseases: An overview of eight European countries, *International Journal of Epidemiology*, 34(2): 316–26.

Darmon, N., Ferguson, E. L. and Briend, A. (2002) A cost constraint alone has adverse effects on food selection and nutrient density: An analysis of human diets by linear programming, *Journal of Nutrition*, 132(12): 3764–71.

Department of Health (2005) *Vaccination Services: Reducing Inequalities in Uptake*. London: Department of Health.

Dowd, J. B. and Aiello, A. E. (2008) Did national folic acid fortification reduce socioeconomic and racial disparities in folate status in the US?, *International Journal of Epidemiology*, 37: 1059–66.

Eakin, E. G., Mummery, K., Reeves, M. M. et al. (2007) Correlates of pedometer use: Results from a community-based physical activity intervention trial (10,000 Steps Rockhampton), *International Journal of Behavioral Nutrition and Physical Activity*, 4: 31.

Eurobarometer (2007) *Special Eurobarometer: Health in the European Union*. Luxembourg: European Commission.

Farrelly, M. C. and Bray, J. W., Office on Smoking and Health (1998) Response to increases in cigarette prices by race/ethnicity, income and age groups – United States, 1976–1993, *Morbidity and Mortality Weekly Report*, 47(29): 605–9.

French, S. A., Jeffery, R. W., Story, M., Hannan, P. and Snyder, P. (1997) A pricing strategy to promote low-fat snack choices through vending machines, *American Journal of Public Health*, 87: 849–51.

Grossman, M. (2000) The human capital model, in A. J. Culyer and J. P. Newhouse (eds) *Handbook of Health Economics*, Volume 1A. New York: Elsevier, pp. 347–408.

Gustavsen, G. W. and Rickertsen, K. (2004) For whom reduced prices count: A censored quantile regression analysis of vegetable demand. Amercian Agricultural Economics Association's annual meetings (August 1–4), Denver, CO.

Helasoja, V., Lahelma, E., Prättälä, R. et al. (2006) Trends in the magnitude of educational inequalities in health in Estonia, Latvia, Lithuania and Finland during 1994–2004, *Public Health*, 120(9): 841–53.

Helmert, U., Shea, S. and Maschwesky-Schneider, U. (1995) Social class and cardiovascular disease risk factor changes in West Germany 1984–1991, *European Journal of Public Health*, 5: 103–8.

Hernández-Quevedo, C., Jones, A. M. López-Nicolás, A. and Rice, N. (2006) Socioeconomic inequalities in health: A longitudinal analysis of the European Community Household Panel, *Social Science and Medicine*, 63: 1246–61.

Hernández-Quevedo, C., Jones, A. M. and Rice, N. (2008) Persistence in health limitations: A European comparative analysis, *Journal of Health Economics*, 27(6): 1472–88.

Hernández-Quevedo, C., Masseria, C. and Moissalos, E. (2010) *Analysing the Socioeconomic Determinants of Health in Europe: New Evidence from EU-SILC*. Luxembourg: European Commission.

Hill, C. M., Mather, M. and Goddard, J. (2003) Cross-sectional survey of meningococcal C immunisation in children looked after by local authorities and those living at home, *British Medical Journal*, 326: 364–5.

Jakobsen, M. (2009) Cardiovascular disease prevention: INTER99. PHD dissertation, University of Copenhagen.

Jeffery, R. W., French, S. A., Raether, C. and Baxter, J. E. (1994) An environmental intervention to increase fruit and salad purchases in a cafeteria, *Preventive Medicine*, 23(6): 788–92.

Jiménez-García, R., Hernández-Barrera, V., Carrasco Garrido, P., del Pozo, S. V.-F. and de Miguel, A. G. (2006) Influenza vaccination among cardiovascular disease sufferers in Spain: Related factors and trends, 1993–2003, *Vaccine*, 24(23): 5073–82.

Jones, A. J., Laporte, A., Rice, N. and Zucchelli, E. (2011) *A Model of the Impact of Smoking Bans on Smoking with Evidence from Bans in England and Scotland*. HEDG Working Paper 05/11. York: The University of York.

Joseph, C., Goddard, N. and Gelb, D. (2005) Influenza vaccine uptake and distribution in England and Wales using data from the General Practice Research Database, 1989/90–2003/04, *Journal of Public Health*, 27(4): 371–7.

Kelleher, C. C., Friel, S., Nic Gabhainn, S. and Tay, J. B. (2003) Socio-demographic predictors of self-rated health in the Republic of Ireland: Findings from the National Survey on Lifestyle, Attitudes and Nutrition, SLAN, *Social Science & Medicine*, 57(3): 477–86.

Kunst, A. E., Bos, V., Lahelma, E. et al. (2005) Trends in socioeconomic inequalities in self-assessed health in 10 European countries, *International Journal of Epidemiology*, 34(2): 295–305.

Lanoie, P. and Leclair, P. (1998) Taxation or regulation: Looking for a good anti-smoking policy, *Economic Letters*, 58: 85–9.

Le Grand, J. (1987) Inequalities in health: Some international comparisons, *European Economic Review*, 31: 182–91.

Leicester, A. and Windmeijer, F. (2004) *The Fat Tax: Economic Incentives to Reduce Obesity*. Briefing Note No.49. London: Institute for Fiscal Studies.

Low, A., Unsworth, L. and Miller, I. (2007) Avoiding the danger that stop smoking services may exacerbate health inequalities: Building equity into performance assessment, *BMC Public Health*, 7: 198.

Mackenbach, J. P. (2006) *Health Inequalities: Europe in Profile*. London: Department of Health.

Mackenbach, J. P., Martikainen, P., Looman, C. W. N. et al. (2005) The shape of the relationship between income and self-assessed health: An international study, *International Journal of Epidemiology*, 34(2): 286–93.

Main, C., Thomas, S., Ogilvie, D. et al. (2008) Population tobacco control interventions and their effects on social inequalities in smoking: Placing an equity lens on existing systematic reviews, *BMC Public Health*, 8: 178.

Majeed, F. A., Cook, D. G., Given-Wilson, R., Vecchi, P. and Poloniecki, J. (1995) Do general practitioners influence the uptake of breast cancer screening?, *Journal of Medical Screening*, 2: 119–24.

Marmot, M. G. and Wilkinson, R. (1999) *Social Determinants of Health*. Oxford: Oxford University Press.

McColl, K. (2009) Betting on health, British Medical Journal, 338: 1173–5.

McDaid, D. and Sassi, F. (2010) Equity, efficiency and research synthesis, in I. Shemilt, M. Mugford, L. Vale, K. Marsh and C. Donaldson (eds) *Evidence-based Decisions and Economics: Health Care, Social Welfare, Education and Criminal Justice*. Oxford: Wiley, BMJ Books, pp. 67–78.

Millett, C., Laverty, A. A., Stylianou, N., Bibbins-Doming, K. and Pape, U. J. (2012) Impacts of a national strategy to reduce population salt intake in England: Serial cross sectional study, PLoS One, 7(1): e29836.

Nichol, K. L. (2003) The efficacy, effectiveness and cost-effectiveness of inactivated influenza virus vaccines, *Vaccine*, 21: 1769–75.

Nordström, J. and Thunström, L. (2009) The impact of tax reforms designed to encourage healthier grain consumption, *Journal of Health Economics*, 28: 622–34.

Nuffield Council on Bioethics (2007) *Public health: Ethical issues*. London: Nuffield Council on Bioethics.

Nummela, O., Sulander, T., Heinonen, H. and Uutela, A. (2007) Self-rated health and indicators of SES among the ageing in three types of communities, *Scandinavian Journal of Public Health*, 35: 39–47.

Pampel, F. C., Kreuger, P. M. and Denney, J. T. (2010) Socioeconomic disparities in health behaviours, *Annual Review of Sociology*, 36: 347–70.

Parrott, S., Godfrey, C., Raw, M., West, R. and McNeill, A. (1998) Guidance for commissioners on the cost-effectiveness of smoking cessation interventions, *Thorax*, 53 (Suppl. 5, part 2): S1–38.

Peckham, C., Bedford, H., Seturia, Y. et al. (1989) *The Peckham Report – National Immunisation Study: Factors Influencing Immunisation Uptake in Childhood*. London: Action Research for the Crippled Child.

Rozin, P., Haidt, J. and McCauley, C. R. (2000) Disgust, in M. J. Lewis and J. M. Haviland-Jones (eds) *Handbook of Emotions*. New York: Guildford Press, pp. 637–53.

Samad, L., Tate, A. R., Dezateux, C. et al. (2006) Differences in risk factors for partial and no immunisation in the first year of life: Prospective cohort study, *British Medical Journal*, 332: 1312–13.

Sassi, F., Archard, L. and Le Grand, J. (2001) Equity and the economic evaluation of healthcare, *Health Technology Assessment*, 5(3): 1–138.

Schaap, M. M., Kunst, A. E., Leinsalu, M. et al. (2008) Effect of nation-wide tobacco control policies on smoking cessation in high and low educated groups in 18 European countries, *Tobacco Control*, 17: 248–55.

Silventoinen, K., Pankow, J., Jousilahti, P., Hu, G. and Tuomilehto, J. (2005) Educational inequalities in the metabolic syndrome and coronary heart disease among middle-aged men and women, *International Journal of Epidemiology*, 34(2): 327–34.

Stockley, R., Jordan, E., Hunter, A. and BMRB Qualitative (2009) *Citizens' Forums on Food: Front of Pack (FoP) Nutrition Labelling*. Report commissioned by Food Standards Agency. London: FSA.

Suhrcke, M. and Cookson, R. (2012) *Using Economic Evidence to Support the Case for Action to Tackle Health Inequality*. Economics Task Group Background paper. London: Economics Task Group.

Tiffin, R. and Arnoult, M. (2011) The public health impacts of a fat tax, *European Journal of Clinical Nutrition*, 65(4): 427–33.

Townsend, J., Roderick, P. and Cooper, J. (1994) Cigarette smoking by socioeconomic group, sex and age: Effects of price, income and health publicity, *British Medical Journal*, 309: 923–7.

Trigg, A. B. and Bosanquet, N. (1992) Tax harmonization and the reduction of European smoking rates, *Journal of Health Economics*, 11(3): 329–46.

Van Doorslaer, E. and Van Ourti, T. (2011) Measurement of inequality and inequity in health and health care, in S. Glied, and P. C. Smith (eds) *Oxford Handbook of Health Economics*. Oxford: Oxford University Press, pp. 837–69.

Viscusi, W. K. (1994) Cigarette taxation and the social consequences of smoking, in J. M. Poterba (ed.) *Tax Policy and the Economy*, vol. 9. Cambridge, MA: MIT Press, pp. 51–102.

Von Wagner, C., Good, A., Wright, D., et al. (2009) Inequalities in colorectal cancer screening participation in the first round of the national screening programme in England, *British Journal of Cancer*, 101: S60–3.

Wagstaff, A. and Van Doorslaer, E. (2004) Overall versus socioeconomic health inequality: A measurement framework and two empirical illustrations, *Health Economics*, 13(3): 297–301.

Wardle, J., McCaffery, K., Nadel, M. and Atkin, W. (2004) Socioeconomic differences in cancer screening participation: Comparing cognitive and psychosocial explanations, *Social Science and Medicine*, 59: 249–61.

Weatherly, H., Drummond, M., Claxton, K. et al. (2009) Methods for assessing the cost-effectiveness of public health interventions: Key challenges and recommendations, *Health Policy*, 93: 85–92.

World Health Organization (WHO) (2003) *Which are the Most Effective and Cost-effective Interventions for Tobacco Control?* Copenhagen: Health Evidence Network, World Health Organisation Regional Office for Europe.

World Health Organization (WHO) and Food and Agricultural Organization of the UN (FAO) (2000) *Guidelines on Food Fortification with Micronutrients*, eds L. Allen, B. de Benoist, O. Dary and R. Hurrell. Geneva: WHO and FAO.

Part IV

Translating evidence into policy

chapter thirteen

Evidence into policy: the case of public health

Michael P. Kelly and Natalie Bartle

Introduction

This chapter considers some of the ways that evidence on effectiveness and cost-effectiveness has been translated into effective policies and actions at local, national and international levels, using public health evidence to illustrate the arguments. There is considerable discussion in the literature about this (Nutley et al. 2007; Orton et al. 2011; Liverani et al. 2013). However, most policy is not based on evidence in the way that the natural and social sciences understand that term, and the relationship between evidence and policy is neither simple nor linear. In democracies, policy arises from a mixture of political or ideological preference, narrow sectional interest, administrative imperative, political expediency, necessity, reforming zeal, and sometimes science and evidence. Therefore judgements about success are seldom simple because it rather depends on your viewpoint as to whether a policy is regarded as successful, or for whom.

Mostly, dispassionate evaluation, before or after the introduction of policy, is relatively rare. A cogent argument can be made that the obvious alternative would be to base policy on evidence to a greater degree than is usually the case. This is not a new idea. Royal Commissions used evidence to reach judgements, and these have sometimes influenced policy, especially before major reform, as in the case of the Fulton Committee report on the British Civil Service (1968) and the Redcliffe-Maud Royal Commission report on local government in England (1969). The current UK Parliamentary Select Committee system is also based on the use of evidence. However, in general, scientific evidence has an attenuated link with policy.

Evidence-based medicine

One area where there has been a determined effort to use evidence to guide decision-making has been in medicine, particularly in respect of the introduction of new drugs; but there have also been some efforts to improve the health of the public (Greenhalgh 2001; Egger et al. 2001; Kelly et al. 2010). The approach is known as evidence-based medicine. It uses the demonstrable effectiveness *and* cost-effectiveness of the innovation, be it a new drug or some other initiative, as the basis for decision-making (Drummond et al. 2005). Evidence-based medicine depends on a number of things. The first is a reliable method to assess effectiveness. This is the randomized controlled trial. Using the trial, it is possible to assess what works, and with what degree of effect. The second is a method to determine cost-effectiveness. As discussed earlier in Chapter 3 of this volume, there are several different methods of economic evaluation that can be used to assess the merits of the economic case for investing in any action to improve health. The cornerstone of this in many high-income countries is the use of cost-utility analysis, where outcomes are measured in terms of quality of life (Kelly et al. 2005). This allows the assessment of whether something which is effective – demonstrated by the randomized controlled trial (RCT) – is cost-effective, and therefore something on which budget holders should spend their limited resources.

The third is summing the results of multiple trials. Results of a single trial may mislead. It may have had biases which were unnoticed by researchers, it may have been conducted sub-optimally, or it may be the result of chance, and it may show nothing more than early trial bias whereby initial results outperform subsequent ones in terms of magnitude of effect. So, where possible, the accumulated results of trials looking at the same intervention are examined, the principle being that the more trial results that can be brought together, the less the likelihood that biases could conceal the true result. This is made easier by the existence of computerized databases of scientific published papers which can be rapidly searched for all trials seeking to answer the same question. Powerful search engines can interrogate computerized databases quickly and easily. The Cochrane Collaboration is a worldwide network of systematic reviewers generating reviews of particular clinical treatments, according to these principles (Chalmers 1993; Chandler and Hopewell 2013). A fourth is to ensure that resource and cost data are appropriate to the local context. Uncertainty on cost-effectiveness increases the likelihood of making a sub-optimal policy decision. Poor decisions are not without consequence; at best, opportunities to improve health are missed, but in the worst case there may be detrimental impacts (McDaid 2014). Economic modelling techniques can be used to look at the importance of any uncertainty in estimates of resource use, cost to deliver an intervention, and any comparators. This is particularly important when evidence on the effectiveness of any intervention is drawn from trials undertaken in multiple countries with very different socio-economic circumstances and health systems.

The tools of evidence-based medicine can be translated to other fields, and indeed, there has been much interest in this. There is now a considerable literature assessing the applicability of the method, the problems associated with it, and the difficulty of applying it to areas beyond clinical medicine (Dixon-Woods et al. 2005; Petticrew and Roberts 2006; Egan et al. 2009; Kelly and Moore 2010). One area where it has been applied is public health. There follow a number of case examples of the kinds of issues which arise in the application of these evidence-based principles, or otherwise, in public health.

The failure of the evidence: the attempt to tackle health inequalities in Britain

One of the areas where evidence has been pressed into service has been finding ways to reduce health inequalities. There is plentiful evidence, and political will has been generously predisposed, at least in recent years, to finding solutions. In Great Britain, the story of the evidence-based approach to health inequalities, and the failure to implement it, begins with the publication of the Black Report in 1980 (Townsend et al. 1992; Macintyre 1997). This report summarized data about differential life expectancy between social classes in England. The data showed that the death rate among men in social class five was about two and a half times higher than in social class one. These data were already in the public domain and very well known to epidemiologists and sociologists interested in patterns of inequalities in British society. However, known or not, the Black Report created a furore when it was published, not so much for what it said, but by the way the report was mishandled by the government of the day who, having inherited a report commissioned by the previous government, probably unwittingly, gave the impression that they were trying to suppress its findings (Kelly 2006).

Although in scientific terms the Black Report said nothing new, its influence was profound; health inequalities were hip and radically controversial. In the years that followed, further data were accumulated. This showed, unequivocally, the differences in life expectancy across social groups (Blane et al. 1990; Townsend et al. 1992; Marmot and Wilkinson 2005; Sacker et al. 2005) However, what the burgeoning literature on health inequities did not do was provide guidance about what might be done to remedy the situation (Millward et al. 2003). Indeed, by the time that the New Labour government came into office in 1997, there were very many excellent descriptions of the problem, sometimes in extraordinarily complex and arcane detail, and a political determination to do something about it. But the evidence said little or nothing about how to change the situation beyond very general arguments about increasing public expenditure or redistributing wealth.

There is little doubt that the New Labour administration was committed politically to the idea of doing something to tackle health inequalities, and there began a long series of initiatives and interventions to deal with the problem. The fact was, there was precious little in the evidence armoury to help them, in spite of the fact that the evidence of the problem was very extensive. So, in part, it was the case that there was evidence – but it was the wrong evidence; it described the problem, but said little about effective interventions (Millward et al. 2003).

That said though, there had been a serious attempt to identify effective interventions. As part of a new national NHS Research and Development Strategy, a new body called the Health Development Agency that would lead the evidence-based assault on improving public health and reducing health inequalities was outlined. The underlying idea here was to try to apply insights from evidence-based medicine to evidence-based public health. The Health Development Agency was, in fact, the new name for the old Health Education Authority, and so it had considerable staff and resources to tackle this problem. The Health

Development Agency was given the remit to populate the public health evidence base. The Agency developed methodological and empirical resources to support an evidence-based approach to tackling health inequalities (Graham and Kelly 2004). Between 2000 and 2005, the organization produced a range of reports and reviews which constituted the first attempt to systematically map the evidence base for public health in the United Kingdom. It examined a number of areas, including interventions to promote the duration of breastfeeding, housing interventions for health, the prevention and reduction of alcohol abuse, youth suicide prevention, and the promotion of physical activity in adults. This was done primarily through the device of evidence synthesis produced summaries on what was then known in these arenas (Kelly 2006). This was a significant achievement, not least because, in the worlds of public health and health promotion, there was initially a good deal of scepticism about the application of the principles of evidence-based medicine to complex public health and behavioural problems (Speller et al. 1997). Alongside these evidence summaries, a number of methodological and conceptual briefing papers on topics, including the role of economic evaluation (Kelly et al. 2005), were published.

The Agency transferred into the National Institute for Clinical Excellence (NICE) in 2005 (at which point it became the National Institute for Health and Clinical Excellence,[1] but still known as NICE), and its remit broadened to producing guidance, not just evidence (Littlejohns and Kelly 2005). This was a very important and positive development, because NICE produced not just evidence, but guidance, to the NHS and other sectors about health improvement, including reducing health inequalities and now, very explicitly, using the evidence-based medicine platform, including assessment of cost-effectiveness, to do so.

However ultimately, even though NICE has produced public health evidence and guidance of the very highest scientific quality, it has not been used as extensively as it might, at least directly in policy or policies about health inequalities. So, while NICE produced evidence-based guidance at the same time, a range of non-evidence-based policy options were also pursued by the New Labour administration. Numerous pilots were rolled out around the country, and a whole unit existed inside the Department of Health to work with and lead on these various initiatives. Many of these initiatives were claimed to be evidence based, and indeed some may have had some evidence to support them, but they were not based on the sound and tried and tested evidence accumulation and synthesis of the Cochrane approach, nor the methods used by the Health Development Agency, and then by NICE. And worse, few of these initiatives were ever systematically evaluated in ways that might provide learning or evidence for the future (House of Commons Health Select Committee 2009). By the time New Labour left office, health inequalities were greater than when they had entered it, leading one not unsympathetic observer to question whether health inequities were ever likely to be amenable to the evidence-based approach at all, or indeed any kind of intervention (Mackenbach 2010). Of course, the riposte to this is actually we don't know, because the opportunity to find the answer was squandered on pilots, initiatives and activities which added nothing to the evidence base, and where the evidence base was developed and effective interventions identified, they were not implemented universally across the system. At local level, NICE's public health guidance has changed practice; but the opportunity to give them traction by mandating actions in the practice of organizations working outside the health care system to apply only those practices that were evidence based and cost-effective was lost.

A failure to understand the evidence or the lowest common denominator politics

Another interesting example of the relation between policy and evidence comes from the World Health Organization. In 2005, WHO established the Commission on the Social Determinants of Health (Solar and Irwin 2010). Nine Knowledge Networks were established around the world to support the Commission. This was a very explicit attempt to find the evidence to explain the origins of health inequalities and to learn from the evidence-based medicine approach. For WHO, this was a very important departure. It was quite different to any previous WHO public health initiative such as the Alma Ata Declaration (WHO 1978), the Ottawa Charter on Health Promotion (WHO 1986) and the Adelaide and Jakarta Declarations (WHO 1988; WHO 1997). Previous WHO initiatives were mixtures of aspiration, political commitment, high-sounding rhetoric, and some evidence mostly describing the background epidemiology of noncommunicable disease. The WHO Commission on the Social Determinants of Health put evidence centre stage, and a considerable effort went into the assembly of evidence to explain the workings of the social determinants and to develop policies on the basis of the evidence (Bonnefoy et al. 2007).

   Certainly the project was politically very visible globally (CSDH 2008). Sir Michael Marmot, who chaired the Commission, became one of the most high-profile figures in public health in the world, and the importance of the social determinants of health as a political mantra has passed into the common parlance of the political classes (HM Government 2010). Scientifically, the huge amount of evidence which was drawn together by the nine knowledge networks was very considerable and something which no other report or commission had done previously. The number of academic spin-offs from the original work has been great (Blas et al. 2008) and, in England, and then Europe, Sir Michael Marmot was asked to lead similar investigations.

   But the question of the degree to which the findings have been implemented remains uncertain. Towards the end of 2011, a high-level meeting to consider the social determinants of health was held in Rio de Janeiro (WHO 2012), and despite considerable razzmatazz the fundamental political messages that the social determinants are the product of particular forms of economic arrangements, and that to tackle the determinants requires political changes to those political and economic structures, have not been universally greeted with enthusiasm; indeed many, including Sir Michael himself, have questioned the degree to which the arguments have gone past lowest denominator politics within the corridors of power in the WHO. But there is a still more fundamental problem scientifically. The scientific fact is that the social determinants approach to the explanation of health inequities is a social explanation; it sees the origins of the problem residing in structures and systems. These structures, political actors find quite difficult to manipulate, no matter how sincere they are in their desire to eliminate inequities in health. This was very well illustrated in the day of the launch of the Commission in London in 2007, when delegates assembled from around the world to celebrate the completion of the Commission's work and the publication of its Report. There was very high-level political support, with the conference graced by a Prime Minister, and two Secretaries of State from the United Kingdom government, as well a host of political figures and politicians from around the world. However, the moment the politicians tried to articulate their understanding of the social determinants of health inequalities it was clear that their pronouncements were limited to notions of lifestyle and behaviour change, an individualistic and reductionist approach to explanation, rather than a socioeconomic or political explanation. One might argue that it was the political speech writers or advisors who did not equip their ministers with the right linguistic tools. But the reality is that few speak the language of the social determinants with any facility or scientific understanding of the evidence before them. And while the policy implications of the Report are obvious, and indeed are spelled out in some detail in the Report itself (CSDH 2008), presently, at least in Britain, public policy shows no sign of moving in that direction. So the argument is won, the evidence collected, but the facility to do anything about it remains very limited indeed.

Taking a risk on the basis of incomplete evidence

So here we have a number of examples of where there is a high-level commitment to an evidence-based approach, with various structures and agencies in place to deliver, but little penetration. On the other hand, there are some remarkable examples where evidence has become the basis for policy, to the great benefit of the population. Invariably this has happened where politicians have not been afraid to court unpopularity to force through measures which were politically very risky, even though the evidence base was very clear. Two examples are instructive. In 1966, in the USA, the Grand Rapids study of the relationship between blood alcohol levels and impaired driving performance was published (Allsop 1966). The evidence strongly suggested that road traffic fatalities and non-fatal casualties would be greatly reduced if people drank less alcohol before driving. The data were reviewed by scientists at the Road Transport Research Laboratory in the United Kingdom. They concluded that the evidence was clear, and an approach to road accident reduction by compelling people not to drink was born in the United Kingdom – the breathalyser backed up by the force of law. It took several years, during which time the evidence did not change, but eventually Barbara Castle, the then Minister of Transport, took the decision to support the introduction of the breathalyser. The resultant decline in deaths and serious injuries must be considered a major public health triumph.

The second example is that of the response to HIV/AIDS in the 1980s. The evidence that was available at the time made clear that there was an epidemic to be dealt with. The minister responsible, Norman Fowler, decided on the basis of the advice from the Chief Medical Officer, Donald Acheson, to go with the difficult choice, and authorized an unprecedentedly frank and hard-hitting campaign supporting safer sexual practices. It went into territory about sex where mainstream media at that time seldom ventured. Along with the campaign, a range of measures were put in place, resources deployed, and partnerships with third-sector groups with links to the gay communities were established. Of course, this was not the decision of one minister, and the Chief Medical Officer, and teams of public health professionals worked hard, in concert with the English Health Education Authority and the Scottish Health Education Group, to alert the population to the potential problem. Remember that, at that time, there was no treatment available, death was the only outcome, and all that was in the armoury of possible protection was condom use, safer sexual practices, and discouraging the use of shared injecting equipment. And most of all, it shouldn't be forgotten that this all took place under a government which was intent on rolling back the state, of liberating the populace from state interference, and espousing family values. It would no doubt have been easy not to engage in the public health actions which were enacted and to try to ignore the problem. Fortunately, this is not what happened. The politicians on the basis of the best available evidence and advice took the difficult and ultimately right decision to tackle the problem head on with whatever was available by means of defence.

Examples of evidence into practice: NICE and public health

Since 2005, NICE has had a public health role and has operated with very complex public health problems, with evidence which is of variable quality and on topics which are quintessentially difficult. NICE has had to turn its attention to the best ways to bring about health-related behaviour change, preventing the misuse of alcohol, increasing rates of physical activity, preventing obesity, preventing drug misuse, preventing teenage conceptions, increasing the uptake of vaccinations, and improving provision for looked-after children. These topics relate to public health problems which, other than at the margins, governments have found difficult to deal with. The epidemics of noncommunicable diseases associated with smoking, overeating, drinking too much and not taking any physical activity originate in the ways people live their lives. So, in one sense, the solutions are obvious – people should change their behaviour. But, as governments all eventually discover, getting people to change is very tricky. The problems attached to poor provision for looked-after children – one of the most marginalized groups in society – are well documented. Finding organizational and managerial solutions has proved to be surprisingly elusive (National Institute for Health and Care Excellence 2010a).

Since 2005, NICE has produced guidance on cost-effective actions that can improve health or prevent disease, not only for the NHS, but also for bodies like local authorities, whose actions have always impinged on the health of the public. Indeed, since 2013, they have been given responsibility for much of public health in England. These recommendations do not offer policy solutions, but within a broad policy framework provide clear practical recommendations about the actions which are known to be effective and are good value for money. The idea behind this approach draws directly from the evidence-based medicine paradigm. NICE's method involves finding the best available evidence relating to a well-defined problem, and applying the evidence or the implications that flow from the evidence and putting them into practice. Between 2005 and the spring of 2014, some 52 different publications have provided evidence-based solutions.

This turns out to be a good illustration of the intricacies attaching to the evidence chain. Leaving aside all the technical problems associated with assembling and interrogating the evidence, once the recommendations are made, even when seen to be highly cost-effective, the path to implementation is littered with pitfalls. First, although there will always have been good policy reasons why ministers chose to ask NICE to produce the guidance – and there will have been extensive discussion and interaction with stakeholders and agreement that there is a good need for the guidance – it doesn't follow that those working on the ground share the policymakers' views or understanding of the need. So, sometimes the response in the field has been that they don't need the guidance because they are already doing a good job. On occasions there have been some interesting *volte faces*, where guidance has initially been attacked and then subsequently adopted as policy (National Institute for Health and Care Excellence 2010b).

There has been another vexing problem too, which has been where the guidance indicated that best practice is rare and that, notwithstanding professional claims to the contrary, that practice at the coal face is sub-optimal, and that overall, through a few simple changes to practice, things could be greatly improved for clients and patients (National Institute for Health and Care Excellence 2007a). Here, the resistance comes from professional vested interests and sheer institutional inertia.

Implications

So what conclusions can be drawn from these examples? Despite a strong rhetoric about evidence espoused by many, the reality of the way that evidence gets into policy is varied, is patchy, and in many ways a matter of chance. It is certainly the case that evidence into policy involves politics as much as it involves the evidence and, not surprisingly, political scientists have been able to describe the processes involved in some detail.

One of the most important ideas they have brought to the table is that of the implementation chain (Exworthy et al. 2002). They draw attention to the fact that there are a number of distinct links in a chain from the evidence to the policy, and to its implementation, and that if one link in the chain is weak or broken then the policy will not reach ultimate implementation and have its desired effects. The process is described as non-linear and iterative, and the message is that there is not some quick fix in getting from the evidence to the policy. Ogilvie et al. argue that the linear translational medicine pathway described in the Cooksey Report on United Kingdom health research funding, for example, has limitations for public health research, and a wider, more inclusive framework needs to be considered to reflect the complexity of the public health environment (Ogilvie et al. 2009). They used a case study from NICE on physical activity and the environment to illustrate this point, emphasizing the importance of using a broader range of evidence, including on the environmental correlates of physical activity and striving for interdisciplinary consensus.

Colby et al., from the Robert Wood Johnson Foundation (RWJF), USA, developed a model for translating research for policymakers (Colby et al. 2008). The model comprises of 'Synthesis Products' – a 20-page synthesis report and 4-page policy brief – that are 'easy to use', and relevant to the policy context. Lessons learned from the RWJF Synthesis Project include creating incentives for the practice of synthesizing research evidence, greater transparency in the evidence-weighing process, involving policymakers throughout the research process, and timely release of the products to coincide with policy 'windows'. Gold has also developed a framework showing how research may get applied in policymaking through ten pathways with a series of intermediate activities and feedback loops, which can determine how messages are communicated and used in the policy process (Gold 2009).

Undoubtedly, timescales are important. Policy decisions are of the moment. Politicians and policymakers have to respond to events, and politicians like to give the appearance of being in control of events. They also work on time horizons in which the most important imperative is the next election or the next hostile editorial in the newspapers. In this regard, it is important to remember that when the first papers appeared linking smoking to lung cancer (Doll and Hill 1950) not only was this not a political priority, it scarcely registered as an issue at all. It took more than ten years, and the accumulation of more and more evidence pointing in the direction of the unequivocal nature of the link, before it really registered as a political issue with government in the United Kingdom with the publication of the report on Smoking and Health in 1962 (Royal College of Physicians 1962) and the Report of the Advisory Committee to the Surgeon General in the United States (1964). And even then the evidence was disputed. The tobacco industry mounted a long campaign to protect its interests, and all sorts of other organizations weighed into the fray. Piece by piece, however, the evidence was assembled, and very gradually public and political opinion moved in line with the evidence with the kinds of action that eventually led to the ban on smoking in the workplace and in public places in England in 2007. Yet, to the very last minute, political nerve nearly failed. The then Secretary of State for Health, John Reid, wanted to seriously diminish the force of legislation. It was only when he was replaced by Patricia Hewitt that the legislation emerged with full force. In the end, the policy followed the evidence, but arguably the evidence suggested that bans on advertising, on smoking in public places, on restrictions to children, and on mass education were known by the early 1960s. It was not until the new century that practical politics followed.

In the case of tobacco, the evidence as it accumulated all pointed in the same direction, and the case eventually became compelling. But the 60-year time horizon that it took not only meant that many people died who need not have done, but that it demonstrates the very different timelines that politicians and scientists work to. So evidence sometimes has a slow burn; it accumulates over a period of time and takes an age to seep into the consciousness of other scientists, long before it gets to policymakers. The communication process in science is of course itself, not instantaneous. New findings do not always find favour with colleagues, especially if they are a challenge to the current orthodoxy. On the other hand, there sometimes comes a moment when evidence which has been around a long time is needed, then and there, and can slip easily into use. In one example, an economic perspective was also employed to help aid in implementation of a smoking ban in the workplace. NICE guidance, in 2007, on effective workplace smoking cessations reached out to employers during the process of guideline development by demonstrating that there would be economic benefits to business from improvements in productivity due to the eventual end of smoking breaks (National Institute for Health and Care Excellence 2007b).

Evidence into policy and practice is not just a matter of the dispassionate evaluation of new findings, the weight of which displaces old ideas; nor is it the slow and inevitable march of progress. There are a series of social processes which operate and which mediate the journey from evidence to policy. We have already mentioned the prolonged rearguard action of the tobacco industry to the findings about the dangers of tobacco smoke. This is an illustration of the fact that particular vested, sometimes commercial, interests may actively seek to refute, suppress, conceal or disparage research findings because they damage their particular interests. Other well-known examples include the asbestos industry's suppression in the USA by censorship of the scientific press of evidence relating to the dangers of industrial exposure to asbestos fibres (Greenberg 1999, 2003). Certain parts of the food industry opposed the United Kingdom Food Standards Agency's development of a nutrient profiling tool for use by advertising regulators to prevent the showing of television advertisements with sugary and fatty snacks and foods to children (Food Standards Agency 2009). Submissions of evidence by the alcohol industry to a Scottish government consultation, it has been argued, included unsubstantiated claims on the adverse effects of policies that industry opposed, while advocating their favoured policies without providing supporting evidence (McCambridge et al. 2013). The advertising industry have contested recommendations by NICE about the control of alcohol advertising. The food industry has also been very good over the years at introducing spurious and confusing evidence into the public arena relating to salt, fat and sugar, deliberately to confuse what in nutritional terms are very clear messages about a healthy diet.

Of course, given the legitimate commercial interests of manufacturers, it should surprise no one that this is what happens in a free society. It is in these arenas that scientists have to be aware of the slow-burn effect of their evidence. In the end, the claim that there was no link between tobacco and lung cancer was shown to be utterly false. The lethal nature of industrial exposure to asbestos was verified beyond doubt. Interestingly, the industries in question then shifted the locus of their operations away from countries like the United Kingdom and the United States with their prohibitions, regulations and controls, to do their business in the developing world.

Conclusions

Academic commentators have offered a variety of suggestions to turn evidence into policy. Blendon and Steelfisher have argued that to have an impact on health care policy more effectively, researchers need to understand the politics of health policy decision-making (Blendon and Steelfisher 2009). For this to happen, the latter needs to be studied and made available to researchers. The problem is that this process defies easy description, but ways of systematically increasing the use of research evidence in policy decisions have been suggested (Jewell and Bero 2008). On the basis of American experience, and from the perspective of 28 State Legislators and Administrators, Jewell and Bero suggested evidence-based skills training for policymakers and emphasize the importance of partnerships between policymakers and researchers, the creation of research-focused working groups and advisory committees, and the inclusion of the economic impact, societal costs and benefits, in compelling policy accounts.

Increasing policy responsibilities and decreasing budgets are described as hindering policymakers in identifying, evaluating and using research. Oxman and colleagues have developed SUPPORT tools that can be used to support evidence-informed health policymaking, identifying needs for research evidence, finding and assessing evidence, and then using evidence in decisions across different settings (Oxman et al. 2009). The emphasis is on 'support' as the tools are designed to aid the use of the best research evidence available at the time. Contandriopoulos and colleagues have advised on how best to design and implement a knowledge exchange intervention in the absence of any context-independent evidence pertaining to a specific strategy (Contandriopoulos et al. 2010). Their findings indicate that collective knowledge exchange and use are embedded in organizational, policy and institutional contexts. As such, any intervention needs to take account of levels of polarization, the cost-sharing equilibrium and channels of communication.

These suggestions provide us with a framework for action. In the absence of any one strategy, the emphasis is on preparedness; equipping researchers and policymakers with the skills and resources to infiltrate each other's realm of interest for the benefit of the wider population. This is the critical point. Without collaborative working, evidence into policy will be hindered, which has implications for people's health and well-being. This is a real problem with real consequences, and Chapter 14 in this volume looks at how economic arguments have been used to influence stakeholders in multiple sectors and encourage them to work on an intersectoral basis.

The process of implementation can be enhanced by taking simple steps. These steps, taken together, can be referred to as an implementation chain. The stronger the chain, the more likely policy will reach implementation and have its desired effects. It is best understood as a non-linear process; time-to-completion, if at all, is context specific and depends ultimately on the individuals involved. The role of the individual must not be understated in this process. Without the courage and determination of political visionaries the achievements in public health that we have described would not have been possible. Speaking the language of the visionaries is important. Non-dialogue between researchers and policymakers will not work; their *willingness* for evidence-based policy will prevail.

Note

1 Subsequently, in April 2013, following a further expansion of the role of NICE to also cover social care, the name of the institution changed to the National Institute for Health and Care Excellence. The acronym remains the same.

References

Advisory Committee to the Surgeon General of the Public Health Service (1964) *Smoking and Health: Report of the Advisory Committee to the Surgeon General of the Public Health Service*. Washington, DC: Public Health Service, US Department of Health, Education and Welfare.

Allsop, R. E. (1966) *Alcohol and Road Accidents: A Discussion of the Grand Rapids Study*. RRL Report no. 6. Harmondsworth: Road Research Laboratory, Ministry of Transport.

Blane, D., Smith, G. D. and Bartley, M. (1990) Social class differences in years of potential life lost: Size, trends, and principal causes, *British Medical Journal*, 301: 429–32.

Blas, E., Gilson, L., Kelly, M. P. et al. (2008) Addressing social determinants of health inequities: What can the state and civil society do?, *The Lancet*, 372: 1684–9.

Blendon, R. J. and Steelfisher, G. K. (2009) Commentary: Understanding the underlying politics of health care policy decision making, *Health Services Research*, 44: 1137–43.

Bonnefoy, J., Morgan, A., Kelly, M. P. et al. (2007) *Constructing the Evidence Base on the Social Determinants of Health: A Guide*. Report to the World Health Organization Commission on the Social Determinants of Health, from Measurement and Evidence Knowledge Network. Concepcion: Universidad del Desarrollo, Chile and National Institute for Health and Care Excellence.

Chalmers, I. (1993) The Cochrane collaboration: Preparing, maintaining, and disseminating systematic reviews of the effects of health care, *Annals of the New York Academy of Sciences*, 703: 156–63; discussion 163–5.

Chandler, J. and Hopewell, S. (2013) Cochrane methods – twenty years experience in developing systematic review methods, *Systematic Reviews*, 2: 76.

Colby, D. C., Quinn, B. C., Williams, C. H., Bilheimer, L. T. and Goodell, S. (2008) Research glut and information famine: Making research evidence more useful for policymakers, *Health Affairs (Millwood)*, 27: 1177–82.

Contandriopoulos, D., Lemire, M., Denis, J. L. and Tremblay, E. (2010) Knowledge exchange processes in organizations and policy arenas: A narrative systematic review of the literature, *Milbank Quarterly*, 88: 444–83.

CSDH (2008) *Closing the Gap in a Generation: Health Equity Through Action on the Social Determinants of Health*. Final Report of the Commission on Social Determinants of Health. Geneva: World Health Organization.

Dixon-Woods, M., Agarwal, S., Jones, D., Young, B. and Sutton, A. (2005) Synthesising qualitative and quantitative evidence: A review of possible methods, *Journal of Health Services Research & Policy*, 10: 45–53.

Doll, R. and Hill, A. B. (1950) Smoking and carcinoma of the lung: Preliminary report, *British Medical Journal*, 2: 739–48.

Drummond, M. F., Schulpher, M., Torrance, G. W., O'Brien, B. J. and Stoddart, G. (2005) *Methods for the Economic Evaluation of Health Care Programmes*. Oxford and New York: Oxford University Press.

Egan, M., Bambra, C., Petticrew, M. and Whitehead, M. (2009) Reviewing evidence on complex social interventions: Appraising implementation in systematic reviews of the health effects of organisational-level workplace interventions, *Journal of Epidemiology & Community Health*, 63: 4–11.

Egger, M., Davey Smith, G. and Altman, B. G. (2001) *Systematic Reviews in Health Care: Meta-Analysis in Context*. London: BMJ Books.

Exworthy, M., Berney, L. and Powell, M. (2002) How great expectations in Westminster may be dashed locally: The local implementation of national policy on health inequalities, *Policy and Politics*, 30: 79–96.

Food Standards Agency (2009) *Review of the Agency's Nutrition Profiling Model*. London: FSA.

Fulton Committee (1968) *The Civil Service: Vol 1: Report of the Committee 1966–68 (Fulton Report)*. London: HMSO.

Gold, M. (2009) Pathways to the use of health services research in policy, *Health Services Research*, 44: 1111–36.

Graham, H. and Kelly, M. P. (2004) *Health Inequalities: Concepts, Frameworks and Policy*. Briefing paper. London: Health Development Agency.

Greenberg, M. (1999) A study of lung cancer mortality in asbestos workers: Doll, 1955, *American Journal of Industrial Medicine*, 36: 331–47.

Greenberg, M. (2003) Biological effects of asbestos: New York Academy of Sciences 1964, *American Journal of Industrial Medicine*, 43: 543–52.

Greenhalgh, T. (2001) *How to Read a Paper: The Basics of Evidence Based Medicine*. London: BMJ Books.

HM Government (2010) *Healthy Lives, Healthy People: Our Strategy for Public Health in England*. London: HMSO.

House of Commons Health Select Committee (2009) *Health inequalities: Third Report*. London: House of Commons.

Jewell, C. J. and Bero, L. A. (2008) 'Developing good taste in evidence': Facilitators of and hindrances to evidence-informed health policymaking in state government, *Milbank Q*, 86: 177–208.

Kelly, M., Morgan, A., Ellis, S., Younger, T., Huntley, J. and Swann, C. (2010) Evidence based public health: A review of the experience of the National Institute of Health and Clinical Excellence (NICE) of developing public health guidance in England, *Social Science & Medicine*, 71: 1056–62.

Kelly, M. P. (2006) The development of an evidence based approach to tackling health inequalities in England, in A. Killoran, C. Swann and M. P. Kelly (eds) *Public Health Evidence: Tackling Health Inequalities*. Oxford: Oxford University Press.

Kelly, M. P., McDaid, D., Ludbrook, A. and Powell, J. (2005) *Economic Appraisal of Public Health Interventions*. Briefing paper. London: Health Development Agency.

Kelly, M. P. and Moore, T. A. (2010) *Making a Difference: Using the NICE Public Health Guidance and Embedding Evaluation*. London: IDEA.

Littlejohns, P. and Kelly, M. (2005) The changing face of NICE: The same but different, *The Lancet*, 366: 791–4.

Liverani, M., Hawkins, B. and Parkhurst, J. O. (2013) Political and institutional influences on the use of evidence in public health policy: A systematic review, *PLoS One*, 8: e77404.

Macintyre, S. (1997) The Black Report and beyond: What are the issues?, *Social Science & Medicine*, 44: 723–45.

Mackenbach, J. P. (2010) Has the English strategy to reduce health inequalities failed?, *Social Science & Medicine*, 71: 1249–53; discussion 1254–8.

Marmot, M. and Wilkinson, R. (eds) (2005) *Social Determinants of Health*, 2nd edn. Oxford: Oxford University Press.

McCambridge, J., Hawkins, B. and Holden, C. (2013) Industry use of evidence to influence alcohol policy: A case study of submissions to the 2008 Scottish government consultation, *PLoS Med*, 10: e1001431.

McDaid, D. (2014) Economic modelling for global mental health, in G. Thornicroft and V. Patel (eds) *Global Mental Health Trials*. Oxford: Oxford University Press.

Millward, L., Kelly, M. P. and Nutbeam, D. (2003) *Public Health Intervention Research – the Evidence*. London: Health Development Agency.

National Institute for Health and Care Excellence (2007a) *Behaviour Change: The Principles for Effective Interventions*. NICE public health guidance 6. London: NICE.

National Institute for Health and Care Excellence (2007b) *Workplace Interventions to Promote Smoking Cessation*. NICE public health guidance 5. London: NICE.

National Institute for Health and Care Excellence (2010a) *Looked-after Children and Young People*. NICE public health guidance 28. London: NICE.

National Institute for Health and Care Excellence (2010b) *Weight Management Before, During and After Pregnancy*. NICE public health guidance 27. London: NICE.

Nutley, S. M., Walter, I. and Davies, H. T. O. (eds) (2007) *Using Evidence: How Research can Inform Public Services*. Bristol: Policy Press.

Ogilvie, D., Craig, P., Griffin, S., Macintyre, S. and Wareham, N. J. (2009) A translational framework for public health research, *BMC Public Health*, 9: 116.

Orton, L., Lloyd-Williams, F., Taylor-Robinson, D., O'Flaherty, M. and Capewell, S. (2011) The use of research evidence in public health decision making processes: Systematic review, *PLoS One*, 6: e21704.

Oxman, A. D., Lavis, J. N., Lewin, S. and Fretheim, A. (2009) SUPPORT Tools for evidence-informed health policymaking (STP) 1: What is evidence-informed policymaking?, *Health Research Policy and Systems*, 7(Suppl. 1): S1.

Petticrew, M. and Roberts, H. (2006) *Systematic Reviews in the Social Sciences: A Practical Guide*. Oxford: Blackwell Publishing.

Redcliffe-Maud Royal Commission (1969) *Royal Commission on Local Government in England (Redcliffe-Maud Report)*. London HMSO.

Royal College of Physicians (1962) *Smoking and Health*. London: Pitman Medical Publishing Limited.

Sacker, A., Clarke, P., Wiggins, R. D. and Bartley, M. (2005) Social dynamics of health inequalities: A growth curve analysis of aging and self assessed health in the British household panel survey 1991–2001, *Journal of Epidemiology & Community Health*, 59: 495–501.

Solar, O. and Irwin, A. (2010) *A Conceptual Framework for Action on the Social Determinants of Health*. Geneva: World Health Organization.

Speller, V., Learmonth, A. and Harrison, D. (1997) The search for evidence of effective health promotion, *British Medical Journal*, 315: 361–3.

Townsend, P. B., Whitehead, M. and Davidson, N. (1992) *Inequalities in Health: The Black Report and the Health Divide*. London: Penguin Books Ltd.

World Health Organization (WHO) (1978) *Declaration of Alma-Ata International Conference on Primary Health Care, Alma-Ata, USSR, 6–12 September 1978*. Geneva: World Health Organization.

World Health Organization (WHO) (1986) *The Ottawa Charter on Health Promotion*. Geneva: World Health Organization.

World Health Organization (WHO) (1988) *Adelaide Recommendations on Healthy Public Policy*. Geneva: World Health Organization.

World Health Organization (WHO) (1997) *Jakarta Declaration on Leading Health Promotion into the 21st Century*. Geneva: World Health Organization.

World Health Organization (WHO) (2012) *World Conference on Social Determinants of Health: Meeting Report, Rio de Janeiro, Brazil, 19–21 October 2011*. Geneva: World Health Organization.

chapter fourteen

Making an economic case for intersectoral action

David McDaid and Matthias Wismar

The need for an intersectoral approach

Previous chapters have highlighted the profound social and economic consequences of poor health and well-being. Much of this is avoidable, and the volume has highlighted a diverse set of actions that can be cost-effective in promoting health and preventing the onset of disease. There is also an increased focus now on looking for major initiatives to tackle health inequalities and promote better health, with a shift away from a focus largely on changing individual lifestyles and behaviours and improving access to medical care, towards greater attention being placed on addressing the social determinants of health such as education, levels of income, and the quality of the social environments in which people live and work (Commission on Social Determinants of Health 2008; Braveman et al. 2011). In Europe, the World Health Organization's new European Health Policy, *Health 2020*, emphasizes building on a whole-of-government and a whole-of-society approach to health, with implications for developing new roles not only for the Ministry of Health but also for actors beyond government, including providers, stakeholders and citizens (WHO 2012). In Norway, the Public Health Act 2012 made health promotion and public health a formal whole-of-government responsibility; in public health work, municipalities must involve all sectors for the promotion of public health – not just the health sector.

Many ministries will shape many of the determinants of health, often inadvertently, through their policies and programmes (Wismar et al. 2006, 2013). Actions will therefore need to be implemented outside the health system in many different settings, such as schools, workplaces and leisure environments. This will often mean relying not only on non-health sector stakeholders for financial support, but also for effective management, administration and coordination for many health-promoting actions. Many critical areas of policy will lie far outside the control of health systems, such as transport safety, environmental and urban planning, business regulation and fiscal policy.

Of course, this is not new – the importance of intersectoral actions and shared responsibility for health has long been recognized by those working in the area of health promotion (WHO 1986). Lifestyles, social and community networks, living and working conditions and general socioeconomic, cultural and environmental conditions are all multifaceted determinants of health which cannot easily be tackled by direct ministry of health action, or be attributed to a single policy or sectoral activity outside the health sector (Dahlgren and Whitehead 1991). Intersectoral collaboration may also be necessary to attain important health promotion objectives such as local community participation, which facilitates community and individual-level capacity building and empowerment, making it more likely that programme goals and methods are adapted to local conditions, which in turn increases the chance of sustainability and programme effectiveness (Johansson et al. 2009).

Yet, while the importance of a holistic intersectoral approach to health has long been known, little attention has been placed on how economics can be used to help achieve this objective. As Chapter 13 has highlighted, there are already challenges in translating robust evidence-based messages on cost-effective health promotion and disease prevention measures to actions, even when responsibility rests solely with a ministry of health. When moving beyond the health sector, these challenges are exacerbated. As will be described, the different departmental fiefdoms and budgetary silos in place in many countries can make intersectoral working difficult at best, and nigh on impossible at worst.

While examples of intersectoral cooperation can be found, for instance, examples can be seen in the transport sector where the importance of reducing serious injuries and fatalities on the roads is a major policy objective of many ministries of transport (Stead 2008), health promotion and disease prevention are unlikely to feature prominently as key goals for most government departments and non-health sector budget holders. Too often, there is a lack of any strong incentives and shared objectives on health promotion. Moreover, the long time to payoff of many health promotion and public health initiatives, requiring complex actions and funding across different sectors, further makes them vulnerable to cancellation when budgets are tight. A lack of strong incentives for intersectoral collaboration may therefore mean that society ends up with an economically inefficient sub-optimal allocation of resources as opportunities to realize substantial health, non-health and cross-sectoral economic benefits may thus be missed (Audit Commission 2007).

One of the reasons opportunities are missed is because of a lack of knowledge of the full impacts of health promotion and disease prevention measures among policymakers within, and external to, the health sector. It was the nineteenth-century American education reformer, Horace Mann, who stated that 'every addition to true knowledge is an addition to human power' (Mann 1845). There has been a lack of focus on methods of knowledge exchange between those who produce evidence-based information and potential budget-holders that may fund implementation. One academic has described a 'phantom zone' occupied by a public health community that can produce evidence on effective actions, but is rarely listened to, and is generally powerless to influence policy and practice (Raphael 2009). The process of exchanging knowledge between knowledge producers, policymakers and practitioners across the different sectors that influence health, is far from straightforward; institutional structures and political conditions will also have an impact.

This chapter therefore looks at different ways to facilitate the implementation of effective health-promoting actions outside the health sector. It first looks at some of the barriers to action before focusing on how economic evidence has been used to appeal to different stakeholders. It also considers different economic levers that can be pulled to encourage intersectoral working. In doing this, it also draws on work from political and implementation science to look at how institutional arrangements and ways of communication can help or hinder in advancing health promotion and disease prevention in the economy as a whole.

What do we know about barriers to intersectoral investment in health promotion and disease prevention?

It is important to better understand the barriers to the implementation of health-promoting actions outside the health sector, and the potential role to be played by economic evidence if more effective implementation is to be achieved. A number of studies have reported on some of the theoretical and practical challenges in working across sectors for health promotion and disease prevention (Mannheimer et al. 2007; Public Health Agency of Canada 2007; Stead 2008; Storm et al. 2011; Hunter and Perkins 2012; McQueen et al. 2012; Taylor-Robinson et al. 2012; Hendriks et al. 2013; Kranzler et al. 2013).

Box 14.1 lists some of the key barriers to implementation, and will probably be familiar to many readers. These include issues such as poor communication and trust between stakeholders acting as an impediment to partnership working. The lack of clear, well-defined aims and objectives of any partnership across sectors is often highlighted. For cost-effective health promotion and disease prevention actions that need to be delivered outside the health sector to be translated into well-implemented policies, it is important to foster good relationships between a diverse set of policymakers and service providers at international, national, local and regional levels. Having key individuals – either from these sectors, or from central government – who can advocate for health promotion may help, but such champions are often hard to find.

At national and local levels, while there may be rhetoric on the importance of health in all policies there may be little in the way of institutional structures and communication mechanisms, such as cabinet sub-committees on public health or targets in all policies for health promotion to encourage action. Another perennial challenge is the short-term horizons many politicians have. Many health promoting actions take years to have an impact; thus, they may not register positively with the electorate.

Frequent reforms to the organization of health care systems may also mean that any existing partnerships between health and other sectors may continually be in jeopardy. Fragmented decision-making structures for public policy also hinder opportunities for implementation of health-promoting actions; responsibility for some key health-influencing sectors, such as education, may be devolved down to regions or municipalities, making it more difficult to have a consistent approach to health promotion in schools across a country. The public health community and public health institutional structures need to engage with many policymakers and service deliverers, but may have limited capacity to undertake this level of activity without charging a fee to other sectors for advice. This may mean that there is a lack of expert guidance and support from the public health sector for the development of health-promotion programmes.

> **Box 14.1** Barriers to the cross-sectoral implementation of health-promotion measures

---

- Poor communication and trust across different sectors.
- Poor communication between different governmental stakeholders.
- Lack of well-defined aims and objectives for partnership working.
- Lack of champions for health promotion.
- Short-term policy perspectives and political cycles.
- Fragmented decision-making structures.
- Lack of flexibility in budgets and funding mechanisms.
- Lack of incentives and rewards for non-health sectors from investing in health promotion.
- Poor communication of the broader socioeconomic costs and benefits of health promotion.
- Disruption to established partnerships across sectors due to constant health system reforms.
- Lack of guidance and support for implementation outside the health sector.
- Lack of targets related to health in policy goals outside the health sector.

Economic barriers to intersectoral implementation

Box 14.1 includes some barriers which are inherently economic in nature, revolving around the scope and use of economic evidence, as well as on the level of flexibility in the way health-promotion activities can be funded across multiple sectors. These issues appear to have been less well discussed in much of the literature on intersectoral implementation. This also may reflect capacity issues, or a more limited engagement of the health economics community with the public health community. We look briefly at each of these issues in turn.

A lack of focus on the full socioeconomic costs and benefits of investing in health

The public health community can be its own worst enemy when it comes to promoting the case for cross-sectoral public health actions. Take, for example, the case of school-based mental health-promotion programmes. While a strong evidence-based case can be made for investment in many programmes, analysis of economic benefits is often restricted to impacts on the health of children, rather than a fuller range of impacts to society. There may be little or no discussion with budget holders about the education-related benefits of better child mental health. Yet education budget holders will, for example, be interested in the impacts of any investment on average examination grade scores, levels of truancy, or classroom disruption in schools. They may be much more interested in the impact of any initiative on the rate of teacher absenteeism or turnover because of stress, rather than the health impacts on pupils.

Equally, ministries of business or local governments may have reservations about the commercial impacts of some health-promotion activities, such as measures to restrict smoking or drinking. Alcohol control policy is illustrative of this point. The causal links between the social determinants of alcohol consumption and health imply many different actions to influence alcohol control policy. Most of these actions will fall to ministries responsible for taxes, retail, transport, education, economic development, criminal justice and social welfare. These ministries may seek different objectives: they want to stimulate economic activity, enhance mobility or provide security. Having evidence on the economic impacts of public health measures may be critical, given the vocal lobbies from commercial interests seeking to downplay specific interventions, and dissuade governments from taking health-promoting action (see Chapter 13).

This has been the case with measures to ban smoking in workplaces and its impact on the alcohol trade. The tobacco industry has argued that these bans have had a disproportionate adverse impact on trade in bars and pubs. It is important, therefore, to be able to point to what is now a consistent evidence base from a number of countries that, contrary to industry submissions, such smoking bans do not have a major impact on overall revenue in the bar and pub sector. Analysis of the impact on pub sales in Ireland following the introduction of legislation on smoke-free workplaces in 2004 reported a negligible overall impact on revenues, while at the same time compliance rates with the legislation have continued to be high, helping to promote better health (Cornelsen and Normand 2012, 2013). This is also consistent with findings in the state of Tasmania in Australia where no long-term impact on sales turnover was observed (Lal and Siahpush 2009), while in Washington State in the USA revenue levels in bars following the introduction of legislation were actually greater than anticipated (Boles et al. 2010).

Thus, when making an economic case for health-promoting activities which need to be delivered outside the health sector, it is important for evaluations to look at costs and benefits beyond health. When public health professionals, health economists and others are making a case for investment it will be important to speak the language of the other sectors, highlighting any non-health benefits that are demonstrated. Jargon can be unhelpful and serve to reinforce barriers between different constituencies. It will also be important to transparently flag up any adverse impacts to other sectors of investment in health promotion in a credible way, so as to counter early arguments from those who are opposed to action. Investing in a full-impact assessment, and not just an assessment of the impact of a policy on health, is one way this can be done at national or supranational level (Davenport et al. 2006).

A lack of flexibility in funding

A major obstacle to the implementation of effective health-promoting interventions is the lack of flexibility in funding arrangements between different governmental departments. Multiple short-term funding streams, often with tight restrictions on how funding can be used, subject to different financial incentives and cost-containment concerns, can act as major impediments to investment in health promotion. At both national and local governmental levels, separate funding streams are inevitably more likely to mean that policies may concentrate on achieving internal departmental goals and policy targets, rather than broader cross-sectoral aims.

Any predominance of vertical policymaking structures and funding silos means that, unchallenged, many health concerns that potentially could be addressed more efficiently through actions outside the health care system remain unimplemented (Timpka, Nordqvist and Lindqvist 2009). Any reluctance to invest outside a non-health sector's core activities may be even more pronounced in times of constrained economic circumstances, when all public services are under heightened pressure to demonstrate their efficiency and added value.

For example, education budget holders are usually more interested in improving education outcomes than improving health outcomes. They may be reluctant to spend their limited budgets on activities such as school-based anti-obesity or mental health-promotion programmes which are ostensibly seen as health activities. The agriculture sector may be more focused on the issue of food security, rather than on investing in measures to reduce the level of sugar in foods, while labour ministries may prefer to focus on reducing the rate of unemployment and improving economic competitiveness, rather than having to invest in extensive health-promotion activities at work.

How can we overcome barriers to implementation?

Having briefly described some of the barriers to implementation, potential ways to increase the chances of successfully implementing health promotion and disease prevention actions outside the health sector are now described. The main focus here is on how to better make and convey economic arguments, as well as looking at ways to overcome some of the challenges posed by budgetary silos.

Targeting messages to policymakers and stakeholders in health and other sectors

No discussion on overcoming barriers can begin without looking at levels of understanding and awareness on health issues. The public health community has often not been particularly effective in generating a sustained awareness of the importance of health-promotion messages, particularly those messages that concentrate on the social determinants of health (Raphael et al. 2008). It is important that there is awareness both in ministries of health, and in other sectors of evidence based health-promoting interventions. Ministries of health may be minded to contribute technical expertise and support in funding actions outside the health sector if they believe there is a strong case for action. Yet awareness of the health and economic consequences of policies developed and implemented outside the health sector may be limited. Surveys of civil servants in Canada and New Zealand reported a lack of knowledge, despite the publication of major policy documents on the socioeconomic determinants of ill health and the promotion of population health (Lavis et al. 2003; Gauld et al. 2006).

Intersectoral strategies and opportunities for policy change

Many different methods can be used for getting these messages to policymakers, which go beyond the scope of this chapter, and detailed descriptions of approaches are available (Oxman et al. 2009). The most effective mechanisms usually include regular face-to-face dialogue, between policymakers and so-called 'knowledge brokers', who act as intermediaries familiar with both the research and policymaking environments. These knowledge brokers, if politically savvy, may be in a better position to help build coalitions and partnerships and achieve a health-promotion goal. Short documents and social media located materials that have been prepared in the language of policymaking and/or making use of visual imagery, such as infographics, can be of some help in informing discussions between different stakeholders.

This process of knowledge exchange will be iterative and involve ongoing dialogue; it will not usually create opportunities that lead to immediate changes in policy and practice, but rather lead to incremental change over time. However, there will be some opportunities for rapid intersectoral action, perhaps in response to public or political pressure on some immediate health crisis. Examples of these issues may include public concern over the safety of foods, the aftermath of chemical and other environmental disasters, and public concern about access to firearms after a multiple homicide.

Four strategies for knowledge exchange between health and other sectors have been identified (Ollila 2011). One strategy focuses purely on ensuring that other ministries and sectors adopt policies and interventions consistent with the objectives of the ministry of health. This approach may well be weak, as intersectoral strategies require some form of co-operation or coalition building to work. A second strategy addresses this issue; it looks for mutual benefits to sectors to help in adoption, and may prioritize those areas of health policy where quick 'win wins' can be achieved. This is an area where we will see that economic evidence can play an important role. A third strategy focuses on cooperation, where the health sector provides information to help other ministries achieve their aims; having flexible funding arrangements can help here. A final defensive strategy seeks to minimize the harms to health in the policies of other sectors; this again could flag up some of the economic costs and consequences of policies.

Making a cross-sectoral economic argument for investment

If well conveyed to different stakeholders, economic arguments can help overcome some of the barriers to implementation of health-promoting actions in all sectors. One qualitative analysis on partnership working for public health in England concluded that arguments based on economic evidence were particularly effective, and that some actions in the field of transportation had failed to get a buy-in from all sectors because they did not sufficiently cover all health and non-health areas of economic benefit (Taylor-Robinson et al. 2012).

A good starting point in making an economic case is to point out that there are economic consequences of not taking action to protect health. For instance, at a Europe-wide level, the WHO Tallinn Charter clearly stated that investment in health promotion and health care are an investment in better future health, and that there is an association between health and wealth (WHO 2008). Although not a mandatory requirement, assessments of public health interventions undertaken in England by the National Institute for Health and Care Excellence (NICE) often report economic cost and benefits that go beyond health.

This does not mean that the only incentive stakeholders will respond to is a reduction in costs; they may also gain other welfare benefits from investing in a health-promoting programme. Analysis of two programmes in Sweden – one on a community-based scheme to reduce the risk of falls in older people, and the other a health-promotion campaign to promote healthy lifestyles and reduce the risk of diabetes – found that most stakeholders that contributed to the implementation costs over the programme did not save money (Johansson and Tillgren 2011). They may, though, have considered other benefits: for instance, community development and the fostering of social capital, to be of importance. There may also have been other benefits as a result of healthier lifestyles, such as greater participation in sports, which may be important to some stakeholders. Nonetheless, identifying as many costs and benefits to different sectors as possible can be a good starting point for discussions on intersectoral collaboration.

One example of this is analysis of the economic impact to business of actions to promote mental health workplaces (National Institute for Health and Care Excellence 2009). There is a growing recognition in the business community of the benefits to business of better workplace health promotion, not just because of analysis from NICE, but also because of analysis conducted by a number of other organizations and groups. This included work done as part of the United Kingdom government's Foresight review on Mental Capital and Well-being, which demonstrated economic returns through better health as a result of more flexible working arrangements and better risk assessment training for line managers (Foresight Mental Capital and Well-being Project 2008; McDaid and Park 2014). Economic arguments, using the cost-benefit analysis methodology, have also been used successfully to argue for investment for transport safety and environmental protection (see Chapter 9) (Elvik et al. 2009, 2012). Economic modelling has also been used to look at costs that may be avoided by health care systems as a result of an increase in rates of walking and cycling in the population; potentially, these avoidable costs are substantial if effective ways of encouraging more 'active travel' – for instance, through city planning – can be developed (Jarrett et al. 2012).

Evaluation of road safety partnership schemes in the United Kingdom found an overall favourable rate of return on investment of around 190 per cent (Department for Transport 2009). The business case for these schemes took account of cost offsets for different sectors, such as reduced costs to the health care system as a result of decreased road casualties. The economic impacts on the environment of the promotion of cycling and walking to different sectors have also been considered (Kahlmeier et al. 2011).

Economic arguments have also been applied to the area of early years interventions for children. Chapter 11 in this volume described the strength of the evidence base on interventions targeted at improving the health and well-being of young children (see Chapter 11). Arguments about the economic return on investment have played a significant role, helping to act as a catalyst for continued long-term implementation of services like nurse home visiting programmes for new mothers in the United States (McDaid and Park 2011), as well as parenting programmes and actions targeted at promoting social and emotional learning for young children in North America, Europe and Australasia (McDaid and Park 2011; Mihalopoulos et al. 2012; Stevens 2014). These interventions have the potential not only for better health, but also to generate economic gains to the economy, arising not just from a reduction in the use of specialist health care services, but also reductions in the need for specialist social and foster care services and contacts with the juvenile criminal justice system (Kilian et al. 2010; McDaid and Park 2011; McDaid et al. 2014) (see Chapter 11). Such economic arguments can make a difference. They have been prominent in achieving a consensus between all three major political parties in England in endorsing and committing to continued investment of resources in early years interventions (Allen 2011).

Example: tailoring an economic argument for education sector budget holders

So how can an economic argument be tailored to be relevant to a specific sector such as education? One thing is to ensure that outcomes of direct interest to the education sector are among data that will be collected as part of any health economic evaluation of a health-promoting intervention. So, when looking at the merits of an emotional resilience programme, this might mean collecting data on outcomes such as classroom disruption, teacher sickness leave, use of special educational need services and performance in academic tests, in addition to measures of mental and physical well-being. Equally, when synthesizing evidence from previously conducted studies, it will be important to extract data on comparable outcomes of relevance to the education sector. If the intervention has a positive effect on health and well-being, this message might be persuasively reinforced by complementary positive improvements in outcomes of direct interest to the education sector.

One example of this is an evaluation of the long-term effects of a universal, comprehensive, community-based mental health promotion and behavioural problem prevention project for children aged 0–4 and 4–8 years, and their families, living in three disadvantaged communities in Ontario, Canada – the Better Beginnings, Better Futures (BBBF) project (Peters et al. 2010). The research programme and intervention has been funded by three different ministries in Ontario: Ministry of Community and Social Services, Ministry of Health, and Ministry of Education and Training.

This has so far monitored changes in a broad range of outcomes at one, four and seven years after programme participation in comparison with control school populations. Importantly, in addition to looking at social, emotional and behavioural outcomes for children and their parents, the evaluation has also considered a number of outcomes related to school performance. Levels of current academic achievement have been measured in terms of each child's relative position in their class and in their performance on a standardized maths test. The long-term economic costs and benefits of the programme have also been considered, including the costs of special educational services and any need to repeat a year of school. The evaluation has also assessed outcomes related to criminal justice, community cohesiveness and social services.

This evaluation reported a number of significant improvements in health outcomes and also in educational outcomes (Peters et al. 2010); moreover, children in the intervention group were less likely to need to repeat school years or to use special educational needs services compared with their control school counterparts. The overall economic analysis demonstrated that the programme had net benefits of $3,777 (United States dollars in 2010 prices) per family. Two-thirds of all costs avoided were in the educational sector, due largely to the reduction in the need for special education services, with a reduction in the need for social services to pay social welfare benefits. Costs to the health system actually increased modestly due to greater contact with health services. Overall, these benefits were considered to be conservative as any eventual benefits of achieving higher levels of qualification at school leaving age will only be possible to calculate after the children have finished their schooling. This data will eventually be available to policymakers as the study will follow participants for 25 years. Nonetheless, this analysis already can be very persuasive to budget holders in the education sector as they can see that a programme to improve emotional well-being in school has substantial benefits to the education sector.

The potential benefits of economic modelling

Demonstrating a range of benefits across sectors may also potentially lead to funds being received from unexpected quarters. A recent example of this can be seen in one local authority in England where the police and crime commissioner has decided to use his budget to help support parenting and child mental health programmes in schools. A key reason for policing funds being used in this way in schools has been the development of an economic case showing the long-term benefits of improved mental health on the future levels of violence in the community. The local economic case model was developed, adapting information from an economic model created for the Department of Health in England (Knapp et al. 2011).

Similarly, there may also be scope for developing simulation models that can estimate the impacts of investment in health projects and the costs and benefits to different stakeholders, as has been illustrated by modelling work on health-promotion activities of four European cities (Whitfield et al. 2013). For such models to be of use, however, there will need to be significant inputs from the local public health community and other stakeholders to adapt any generic model to a local context.

Budgetary transfers to share risks and rewards of investment

While non-health sector budget holders may be persuaded to take action on the basis of sector-specific benefits that they can gain, there will be cases when there may be few sector-specific benefits of a health-promotion intervention delivered outside of the health sector. In this case compensatory financial mechanisms might be considered so that any cost offsets for all sectors are distributed between different budget holders (McDaid et al. 2008). In this way all sectors share in the potential rewards of investment. Equally, they may also all agree to share some of the costs of implementation. Contracts between budget holders and service providers across different sectors can also build in shared risks and rewards.

Reforming institutional structures

Successful implementation of cost-effective population health interventions will also be influenced by the institutional structures and governance arrangements in countries. Having a ministry specifically focused on health promotion in all sectors would be one way to overcome some of the challenges of facilitating implementation across sectors. It could be given powers to work with different sectors. With a dedicated budget for non-health sector health-promoting activities, the approach might be used to ensure adequate funding for specific health-related activities, particularly more upstream population-wide measures to tackle some of the socioeconomic risk factors for poor health. It might also help in ensuring that consideration is given to impacts on health in the development of policy in all sectors, and help foster partnerships with other stakeholders.

There have, however, been very few attempts to set up such structures. The risks with this approach may be the challenge of coordinating activities with a ministry of health; public health might become more marginalized from mainstream health care policy. One rare example was the relatively short-lived Ministry of Health Promotion in Ontario, Canada, established in 2005 and merged into the Ministry of Health and Long-Term Care in 2011. This was entirely separate from the provincial Ministry of Health.

One more modest alternative may be to ensure that a health ministry has specific governance structures for population health. This might include having specific ministerial posts for public health as found, for example, in England

and Scotland. Another option might be a cross-departmental mechanism to coordinate activities, perhaps coordinated by the finance ministry or the office of the prime minister or president. Such an effort was coordinated in Denmark, by the then Ministry of the Interior and Health, involving then other ministries, to develop mid-term national public health policy in the earlier part of the millennium (Government of Denmark 2002).

Activities may also be coordinated at a local level. Area-based partnerships may be attractive because they allow for local involvement and ownership, which in turn can help facilitate cooperation and implementation. Examples of cooperation for health promotion across sectors can be found in several countries, such as the establishment of Health and Well-being Boards at local authority level in England to help local authorities who hold budgets for public health collaborate with local clinical commissioning groups that are responsible for funding most health care services in the same locality. The Healthy Cities network within the WHO European Region, which now includes more than 90 cities and towns from 30 countries, provides further examples of local area partnerships. It also highlights the powerful role that can be played by some city and municipal governments that have responsibility and a budget for many areas of health promotion. Moreover, being branded as a WHO Healthy City may help raise the profile and credibility with local policymakers and other stakeholders (Lipp et al. 2013).

Targets, monitoring and evaluation

Joint targets on health across government departments might help with implementation of intersectoral policies. Negative publicity from failing to achieve targets may serve as a powerful incentive for action, but evaluation of the impact of targets remains limited. They are only likely to make a difference if they are concrete enough to be measured and realistic enough to be achieved within a specific time frame. Setting targets requires an understanding of potential mutual benefits, as well as differences in organizational culture and structures between sectors.

Delegated finance

Delegated financing may be one way to reduce the risk of having insufficient resources for action. This is an intersectoral governance structure that pools monies outside the ministry of health and therefore allows for input from sources outside of the government. Examples include health-promotion foundations operational in Switzerland, Austria, Australia and Thailand. Some of the active foundations are co-financed from tax revenues, sin taxes on alcohol and tobacco as in Thailand, or health insurance contributions, they can operate as matching-fund financing projects to a certain percentage. While there can be a risk that they will duplicate some activities implemented in ministries, these foundations have in fact been shown to raise the amount of health-promotion spending (Schang et al. 2011; Schang and Lin 2012).

Shared funding for health promotion and disease prevention

Another approach to encourage intersectoral collaboration may be to modify financial incentives and structures so as to tear down the budgetary silos that hamper partnership working. There are different ways in which this has been undertaken. Looking at the case of school-based health promotion, one simple option to incentivize implementation may be to transfer some of the responsibility and budgets for child health to the education sector.

Another option is to have some form of joint funding across sectors (Advisory Group on the Review of the Centre 2001; Audit Commission and Healthcare Commission 2007; Audit Commission 2008). Any pooling of funds may also help reduce administration and transaction costs, generating economies of scale through pooling of staff, resources and purchasing power, while facilitating more rapid decision-making (Weatherly et al. 2010).

There are a number of different ways in which financial resources can be shared across sectors (Box 14.2) (McDaid 2012). All of these will involve cooperation between two or more government departments and/or tiers of government, in order to help achieve one or more shared goals. They can range from fully integrated budgets for the provision of a service or policy objective, to loose agreements between sectors to align resources for common goals, while maintaining separate accountability for the use of funds. A very limited approach might be to have jointly funded posts to help coordinate intersectoral policies.

Agreements on joint budgeting can be mandatory or voluntary in nature and operate at a national, regional and/or local level. They may be accompanied by legislation and regulatory instruments. There may be detailed legal agreements between sectors on how budgeting mechanisms will work. These could, for example, include identification of any host partner, clarity on functions, agreed aims and outcomes and the levels of financial contributions, as well as relevant accountability issues. Such agreements may also deal with the ownership of common premises and equipment, as well as how any surpluses or liabilities are dealt with. The temporal nature of joint budgeting arrangements also varies – they can be time-limited, short-term initiatives, particularly when receiving grant funding from central government, or envisaged as a longer-term, more permanent organizational change.

Box 14.2 Different approaches to joint budgeting

Budget alignment: Budgets may be aligned rather than actually joined together. For instance, a health commissioner can manage both a health budget and a separate local authority budget to meet an agreed set of health-promotion aims.

Dedicated joint funds: Departments may contribute a set level of resources to a single joint fund to be spent on agreed projects or delivery of specific services. This may often be a time-limited activity. There is usually some flexibility in how funds within the budget can be spent.

Joint-post funding: There may be an agreement to jointly fund a post where an individual is responsible for services and/or attaining objectives relevant to both departments. Theoretically this can help ensure cooperation and avoid duplication of effort.

Fully integrated budgets: Budgets across sectors might become fully integrated, with resources and the workforce fully coming together. One partner typically acts as the 'host' to undertake the other's functions and to manage all staff. To date, this has largely been restricted to partnerships between health and social care organizations, or for the provision of services for people with mental health needs; there have been few initiatives in the field of health promotion.

Policy-orientated funding: Central or local government may set objectives that cut across ministerial and budget boundaries and the budget system. Money may be allocated to specific policy areas, such as the health of the nation, rather than to specific departments.

Source: McDaid 2012

Examples of joint budgeting and discussion in policy documents in the health sphere can be identified in a number of countries, including Australia, Canada, England, Italy, the Netherlands and Sweden, but most of these have focused on providing care and support (McDaid et al. 2007). Initiatives have often been set up with the explicit aim of overcoming the fragmentation in funding and service provision that has hindered the development of seamless care pathways. There has been much less emphasis on health promotion and disease prevention in these initiatives, although in England, Scotland and Wales, road safety initiatives have also brought together partners from the health, transport, child and safety sectors (Audit Commission 2007). In the Netherlands, joint budgets have been used for research and policy activities in connection with the national action programme on environment and health, funded by ministries of environment and health (Stead 2008).

In New Zealand, there has been a drive to encourage more partnership arrangements for public health, with funding arrangements being one way of achieving this (Advisory Group on the Review of the Centre 2001). Legislation in response to recommendations from a major report on the workings of the public sector allowed for better integration and flexibility in cross-sectoral funding between government departments to encourage 'clustering projects', bringing together relevant government agencies to pool budgets and resources (Public Health Advisory Committee 2004). For instance, the Healthy Eating, Healthy Action (HEHA) Initiatives Fund allowed for partnership arrangements and some dedicated budgets and commitments for matched funding between local district health boards, agencies for nutrition action and non-governmental organizations, the fitness and food industry and Sport and Recreation New Zealand. The aim was to promote improved nutrition, physical activity and a healthy weight for all New Zealanders (Ministry of Health 2008). Another example is that of the town of Swindon in England, where £28 million in health and social care funds were pooled for children's services, at a set-up cost of

£10,000. Involving three separate agreements and phasing in integration, moving first from aligned to pooled budgets, there were improvements both in rates of obesity and youth employment or training participation rates in the year after the scheme was launched (Willis 2011).

Factors aiding in the implementation and sustainability of shared funding arrangements

A number of factors that can aid in the implementation of joint budgets have been identified (McDaid 2012). It is clear that the process must begin by carefully defining health and other policy issues that may benefit from joint budgeting, considering what actors and stakeholders need to be involved and understanding their priorities and goals. At national and local levels finance ministries and departments have an important role to play in quantifying and disseminating information on the costs and benefits of better intersectoral working (Audit Commission 2007). Even when agreement in principle has been reached between partners that some form of joint budgeting is worth pursuing, it is important to determine how current patterns of funding operate in different sectors and clarify what institutional and legal structures are in place, in order to consider what joint budgeting arrangements may work best. Establishing clear outcomes on what should be achieved is a prerequisite to looking at issues around budget and risk sharing. Legal and regulatory frameworks ideally should have sufficient flexibility to allow maximum discretion in how pooled funds are used. Ideally, they should allow funds to be used for any reasonable purpose rather than being earmarked; a single accountability structure looking at actions of the joint planning team as a whole, rather than separate accountability structures for each sector, can also help promote transparency and flexibility in how funds are used.

Partners also need to perceive any pooling of resources and structures as being in their own interests, adding value to what they can achieve in isolation. Health stakeholders also need to be able to converse in the language of potential partner sectors; too often stakeholders from the health sector do not look at the consequences of health promotion for their partners. As Stead (2008) notes in respect of partnerships between transport, the environment and health sectors, 'there is the impression that [the health sector] is not so very interested in transport or environmental matters and more concerned with medical infrastructure (hospitals), equipment or consumables (medicines)'. Stakeholder willingness to participate may be enhanced by highlighting non-health benefits – for example, a reduction in delays due to accidents as a result of safer roads.

Once mechanisms are in place, sustained efforts will probably be needed to develop good cross-cultural working relationships to help realize the potential benefits that may come from the elimination of duplication of effort and reorganization of working practices (Ovretveit et al. 2010). The reality is that it can take time to build up trust between partners with very different languages and perspectives, even when all partners are financially contributing to the budget. Involving team members from all sectors in determining the culture and values operating within an integrated health team has been considered important in establishing clear identity and purpose in successful initiatives (Willis 2011). There may also be a need for training in common skills and competences for all individuals, in addition to preserving their key skills and expertise.

Physically co-locating staff from different sectors in the same office so that they can start to build up face-to-face working relationships and start thinking of themselves as part of a common team can also help. Employing facilitators at the start of a partnership can help in fostering trust and dealing with disagreements (Norman and Axelsson 2007). Transparency and access to information from different financial systems is also important. Employing a dedicated individual, funded through the joint budget, to help coordinate efforts across sectors can also be important for those forms of joint budget that stop short of the full integration of funding and services. Finally, and regardless of the model of joint budgeting used, potentially there may be a place for performance-related financial and non-financial rewards linked to achievement of joint policy goals. The establishment of a common set of performance and outcome indicators that include success in establishing joint budgeting initiatives, or in the proportion of budgets that are pooled for health-promoting actions, would be a prerequisite to this (Schwedler 2008; Audit Commission 2009).

Conclusions

Previous chapters have highlighted the profound social and economic consequences of poor health and well-being. Much of this is avoidable, and the volume has highlighted a diverse set of actions that can be cost-effective in promoting health and preventing the onset of disease. While intersectoral action is fundamental to promoting health and preventing disease, it's implementation is challenging. This chapter has collated information on many different barriers, recognizing that too often actions fail to be implemented.

While many of the challenges to intersectoral working involve issues such as trust between stakeholders in different sectors, different political climates and organizational structures, there are a number of barriers which are inherently economic in nature. These include a failure to flag up the economic benefits to non-health sectors of investing in health-promoting interventions – too often the public health community focuses solely on health impacts alone. We have highlighted the role that can be played by better presenting an economic case, taking on board issues of concern to all sectors. This can act as one catalyst for intersectoral action. The issue of separate funding structures between different sectors is one key barrier to intersectoral action. It is a barrier that perhaps has not received as much attention as some of the organizational and political issues, but it is fundamental. There is a growing literature on potential ways to tear down silos between budgets, with different forms of shared financing on either a voluntary or mandatory basis being possible. Where well implemented, measures to bring budgets together can help embed health impacts in all policies. In the longer term, if such initiatives and partnerships are sustained, then a common working culture can be established, reducing potential distrust and misunderstandings between partners.

Without intersectoral actions, society's approach to health promotion and disease prevention will be sub-optimal – resources will not be allocated in the best possible way. A multi-faceted approach to encouraging intersectoral action is required, and economic evidence and theory has a role to play. This is not easy, and much still needs to be evaluated and understood. Going forward it will be critical to learn from different experiences in encouraging intersectoral actions so that approaches can be tailored to take account of different political climates and cultures, infrastructure and resources.

References

Advisory Group on the Review of the Centre (2001) *Report of the Advisory Group on the Review of the Centre*. Wellington: State Services Commission.

Allen, G. (2011) *Early Intervention: The Next Steps. An independent report to Her Majesty's Government*. London: HM Government.

Audit Commission (2007) *Changing Lanes: Evolving Roles in Road Safety*. London: Audit Commission.

Audit Commission (2008) *Clarifying Joint Financing Arrangements: A Briefing Paper for Health Bodies and Local Authorities*. London: Audit Commission.

Audit Commission (2009) *Means to an End: Joint Financing across Health and Social Care*. London: Audit Commission.

Audit Commission and Healthcare Commission (2007) *Better Safe than Sorry: Preventing Unintentional Injury to Children*. London: Audit Commission.

Boles, M., Dilley, J., Maher, J. E., Boysun, M. J. and Reid, T. (2010) Smoke-free law associated with higher-than-expected taxable retail sales for bars and taverns in Washington State, *Preventing Chronic Disease*, 7: A79.

Braveman, P. A., Egerter, S. A. and Mockenhaupt, R. E. (2011) Broadening the focus: The need to address the social determinants of health, *American Journal of Preventive Medicine*, 40: S4–18.

Commission on Social Determinants of Health (2008) *Closing the Gap in a Generation: Health Equity Through Action on the Social Determinants of Health: Final Report of the Commission on Social Determinants of Health*. Geneva: World Health Organization.

Cornelsen, L. and Normand, C. (2012) Impact of the smoking ban on the volume of bar sales in Ireland: Evidence from time series analysis, *Health Economics*, 21: 551–61.

Cornelsen, L. and Normand, C. (2013) Impact of the Irish smoking ban on sales in bars using a large business-level data set from 1999 to 2007, *Tobacco Control*; doi:10.1136/tobaccocontrol-2013-051145.

Dahlgren, G. and Whitehead, M. (1991) *Policies and Strategies to Promote Social Equity in Health*. Stockholm: Institute for Future Studies.

Davenport, C., Mathers, J. and Parry, J. (2006) Use of health impact assessment in incorporating health considerations in decision-making, *Journal of Epidemiology & Community Health*, 60: 196–201.

Department for Transport (2009) *Review of the Road Safety Partnership Grant Scheme*. London: Department for Transport.

Elvik, R., Kolbenstvedt, M., Elvebakk, B., Hervik, A. and Braein, L. (2009) Costs and benefits to Sweden of Swedish road safety research, *Accident Analysis & Prevention*, 41: 387–92.

Elvik, R., Sogge, C. V., Lager, L. et al. (2012) Assessing the efficiency of priorities for traffic law enforcement in Norway, *Accident Analysis & Prevention*, 47: 146–52.

Foresight Mental Capital and Well-being Project (2008) *Final Project Report*. London: The Government Office for Science.

Gauld, R., Bloomfield, A., Kiro, C., Lavis, J. and Ross, S. (2006) Conceptions and uses of public health ideas by New Zealand government policymakers: Report on a five-agency survey, *Public Health*, 120: 283–9.

Government of Denmark (2002) *Healthy Throughout Life: The Targets and Strategies for Public Health Policy of the Government of Denmark, 2002–2010*. Copenhagen: Government of Denmark.

Hendriks, A. M., Kremers, S. P., Gubbels, J. S., Raat, H., de Vries, N. K. and Jansen, M. W. (2013) Towards health in all policies for childhood obesity prevention, *Journal of Obesity*, 2013: 632540.

Hunter, D. and Perkins, N. (2012) Partnership working in public health: The implications for governance of a systems approach, *Journal of Health Services Research & Policy*, 17(Suppl. 2): 45–52.

Jarrett, J., Woodcock, J., Griffiths, U. K. et al. (2012) Effect of increasing active travel in urban England and Wales on costs to the National Health Service, *The Lancet*, 379: 2198–205.

Johansson, P. M., Eriksson, L. S., Sadigh, S., Rehnberg, C. and Tillgren, P. E. (2009) Participation, resource mobilization and financial incentives in community-based health promotion: An economic evaluation perspective from Sweden, *Health Promotion International*, 24: 177–84.

Johansson, P. and Tillgren, P. (2011) Financing intersectoral health promotion programmes: Some reasons why collaborators are collaborating as indicated by cost-effectiveness analyses, *Scandinavian Journal of Public Health*, 39: 26–32.

Kahlmeier, S., Cavill, N., Dinsdale, H. et al. (2011) *Health Economic Assessment Tools (HEAT) for Walking and for Cycling: Methodology and User Guide: Economic Assessment of Transport Infrastructure and Policies*. Copenhagen: WHO Regional Office for Europe.

Kilian, R., Losert, C., Park, A., Knapp, M. and McDaid, D. (2010) Cost-effectiveness analysis in child and adolescent mental problems: An updated review of literature, *International Journal of Mental Health Promotion*, 12(4): 45–57.

Knapp, M., McDaid, D. and Parsonage, M. (eds) (2011) *Mental Health Promotion and Mental Disorder Prevention: The Economic Case*. London: Department of Health.

Kranzler, Y., Davidovich, N., Fleischman, Y., Grotto, I., Moran, D. S. and Weinstein, R. (2013) A health in all policies approach to promote active, healthy lifestyle in Israel, *Israel Journal of Health Policy Research*, 2: 16.

Lal, A. and Siahpush, M. (2009) The effect of smoke-free policies on revenue in bars in Tasmania, Australia, *Tobacco Control*, 18: 405–8.

Lavis, J. N., Ross, S. E., Stoddart, G. L., Hohenadel, J. M., McLeod, C. B. and Evans, R. G. (2003) Do Canadian civil servants care about the health of populations?, *American Journal of Public Health*, 93: 658–63.

Lipp, A., Winters, T. and de Leeuw, E. (2013) Evaluation of partnership working in cities in phase IV of the WHO Healthy Cities Network, *Journal of Urban Health*, 90(Suppl. 1): 37–51.

Mann, H. (1845) *Lectures on Education*. Boston: Fowle & Capen.

Mannheimer, L. N., Lehto, J. and Ostlin, P. (2007) Window of opportunity for intersectoral health policy in Sweden – open, half-open or half-shut?, *Health Promotion International*, 22: 307–15.

McDaid, D. (2012) Joint budgeting: Can it facilitate intersectoral action?, in D. McQueen, M. Wismar, V. Lin, C. Jones and M. Davies (eds) *Intersectoral Governance for Health in all Policies: Structure, Actions and Experiences*. Copenhagen World Health Organization, pp. 111–28.

McDaid, D., Drummond, M. and Suhrcke, M. (2008) *How can European Health Systems support Investment in and Implementation of Population Health Strategies?* Copenhagen: Health Evidence Network, World Health Organization.

McDaid, D., Oliveira, M., Jurczak, K. and Knapp, M. (2007) Moving beyond the mental health care system: An exploration of the interfaces between health and non-health sectors, *Journal of Mental Health*, 16: 181–94.

McDaid, D. and Park, A. L. (2011) Investing in mental health and well-being: Findings from the DataPrev project, *Health Promotion International*, 26(Suppl. 1): i108–39.

McDaid, D. and Park, A.-L. (2014) Investing in well-being in the workplace: More than just a business case, in D. McDaid and C. L. Cooper (eds) *Well-being: A Complete Reference Guide. Volume 5: Economics of Well-being*. Oxford: John Wiley, pp. 215–28.

McDaid, D., Park, A. L., Currie, C. and Zanotti, C. (2014) Investing in the well-being of young people: Making the economic case, in D. McDaid and C. L. Cooper (eds) *Well-being: A Complete Reference Guide. Volume 5: Economics of Well-being*. Oxford: John Wiley, pp. 181–214.

McQueen, D., Wismar, M., Lin, V., Jones, C. and Davies, M. (eds) (2012) *Intersectoral Governance for Health in all Policies: Structure, Actions and Experiences*. Copenhagen: World Health Organization.

Mihalopoulos, C., Vos, T., Pirkis, J. and Carter, R. (2012) The population cost-effectiveness of interventions designed to prevent childhood depression, *Pediatrics*, 129: e723–30.

Ministry of Health (2008) *Healthy Eating – Healthy Action Oranga Kai – Oranga Pumau: Progress on Implementing the HEHA Strategy 2008*. Wellington: Ministry of Health.

National Institute for Health and Care Excellence (2009) *Promoting Mental Well-being at Work*. NICE public health guidance 22. London: NICE.

Norman, C. and Axelsson, R. (2007) Co-operation as a strategy for provision of welfare services – a study of a rehabilitation project in Sweden, *European Journal of Public Health*, 17: 532–6.

Ollila, E. (2011) Health in All Policies: From rhetoric to action, *Scandinavian Journal of Public Health*, 39: 11–18.

Ovretveit, J., Hansson, J. and Brommels, M. (2010) An integrated health and social care organization in Sweden: Creation and structure of a unique local public health and social care system, *Health Policy*, 97: 113–21.

Oxman, A. D., Lavis, J. N., Lewin, S. and Fretheim, A. (2009) SUPPORT Tools for evidence-informed health Policymaking (STP) 1: What is evidence-informed policymaking?, *Health Research Policy and Systems*, 7(Suppl. 1): S1.

Peters, R. D., Bradshaw, A. J., Petrunka, K. et al. (2010) The Better Beginnings, Better Futures Project: Findings from Grade 3 to Grade 9, *Monographs of the Society for Research in Child Development*, 75: 1–176.

Public Health Advisory Committee (2004) *The Health of People and Communities: A Way Forward: Public Policy and the Economic Determinants of Health*. Wellington: Ministry of Health.

Public Health Agency of Canada (2007) *Crossing Sectors – Experiences in Intersectoral Action, Public Policy and Health*. Ottawa: Public Health Agency of Canada.

Raphael, D. (2009) Escaping from the Phantom Zone: Social determinants of health, public health units and public policy in Canada, *Health Promotion International*, 24: 193–8.

Raphael, D., Curry-Stevens, A. and Bryant, T. (2008) Barriers to addressing the social determinants of health: Insights from the Canadian experience, *Health Policy*, 88: 222–35.

Schang, L., Czabanowska, K. M. and Lin, V. (2011) Securing funds for health promotion: Lessons from health promotion foundations based on experiences from Austria, Australia, Germany, Hungary and Switzerland, *Health Promotion International*, 27(2): 295–305.

Schang, L. and Lin, V. (2012) Delegated financing, in D. McQueen, M. Wismar, V. Lin, C. Jones and M. Davies (eds) *Intersectoral Governance for Health in all Policies:*

Structure, Actions and Experiences. Copenhagen: World Health Organization, pp. 129–46.

Schwedler, H.-U. (2008) *Working Together for Sustainable and Healthy Transport: Guidance on Supportive Institutional Conditions for Policy Integration of Transport, Health and Environment.* Geneva: United Nations Economic Commission for Europe.

Stead, D. (2008) Institutional aspects of integrating transport, environment and health policies, *Transport Policy*, 15: 139–48.

Stevens, M. (2014) The cost-effectiveness of UK parenting programmes for preventing children's behaviour problems – a review of the evidence, *Child and Family Social Work*, 19(1): 109–18.

Storm, I., Aarts, M. J., Harting, J. and Schuit, A. J. (2011) Opportunities to reduce health inequalities by 'Health in All Policies' in the Netherlands: An explorative study on the national level, *Health Policy*, 103: 130–40.

Taylor-Robinson, D. C., Lloyd-Williams, F., Orton, L., Moonan, M., O'Flaherty, M. and Capewell, S. (2012) Barriers to partnership working in public health: A qualitative study, *PLoS One*, 7: e29536.

Timpka, T., Nordqvist, C. and Lindqvist, K. (2009) Infrastructural requirements for local implementation of safety policies: The discordance between top-down and bottom-up systems of action, *BMC Health Services Research*, 9: 45.

Weatherly, H., Mason, A. and Goddard, M. (2010) *Financial Integration across Health and Social Care: Evidence Review.* Edinburgh: Scottish Government.

Whitfield, M., Machaczek, K. and Green, G. (2013) Developing a model to estimate the potential impact of municipal investment on city health, *Journal of Urban Health*, 90(Suppl. 1): 62–73.

Willis, B. (2011) Integrated care and pooled budgets help council improve children's social care services, *Community Care*, published on 18 February.

Wismar, M., Lahtinen, E., Ståhl, T., Ollila, E. and Leppo, K. (2006) Introduction, in T. Ståhl, M. Wismar, E. Ollila, E. Lahtinen and K. Leppo (eds) *Health in all Policies: Prospects and Potentials.* Helsinki: Ministry of Social Affairs and Health, pp. xvii–xxx.

Wismar, M., McQueen, D., Lin, V., Jones, C. M. and Davies, M. (2013) Rethinking the politics and implementation of health in all policies, *Israel Journal of Health Policy Research*, 2: 17.

World Health Organization (WHO) (1986) *Ottawa Charter for Health Promotion.* Ottawa: World Health Organization.

World Health Organization (WHO) (2008) *The Tallinn Charter: Health Systems for Health and Wealth.* Tallinn: World Health Organization Regional Office for Europe.

World Health Organization (WHO) (2012) *Health 2020: A European Policy Framework Supporting Action across Government and Society for Health and Well-being.* Copenhagen: World Health Organization Regional Office for Europe.

chapter fifteen

The economics of health promotion and disease prevention: the way forward

Sherry Merkur, David McDaid and Franco Sassi

At a time when public resources continue to be constrained, the role of economic evaluation in health promotion and disease prevention is an important consideration for policymakers to ensure that they are spending public money wisely. Helping people to achieve healthier lifestyles through effective policy action is imperative, particularly when markets fail. Market inefficiencies in these areas include, but are not limited to, externalities (when one's health-related behaviours entail costs that are borne by others), and information challenges (when sound reliable information is limited or inaccessible). These inefficiencies mean that we cannot leave health promotion to markets alone.

Other research has shed light on behavioural failures which can be important in understanding people's decision-making capabilities, the effects of influence, and inconsistencies in their preferences overtime. However, directly working to correct these types of failures may interfere with individual choice and be less acceptable to the public (see Chapter 1). Despite this, government intervention may be justified when health-related behaviours are addictive or habit-forming, and interventions may help to improve health and prevent disease.

This concluding chapter seeks to synthesize the evidence to make the economic case for investing upstream – that is, prior to the onset of noncommunicable diseases, and before health care services are required. It summarizes some of the most efficient health promotion and disease prevention policies for each of the major risk factors, discusses gaps in the evidence, highlights assumptions and potential limitations of the study, and presents trends in the use of cost-effective interventions. Finally, it looks at the economics of health promotion and disease prevention in the future, and proposes an agenda for future research.

Summary of the evidence

This book has brought to light actions that can be supported by sound economic analyses to limit the risks produced by tobacco smoking, alcohol consumption, unhealthy diet, childhood exposure to environmental hazards and road-related injuries, and to promote physical activity and mental health. It has gone further to look at some of the social determinants of health by discussing the benefits of improved early childhood development and education. It also discussed the impact of these prevention programmes on health inequalities, the challenges of policy implementation, and the importance of intersectoral actions. The main messages of each chapter are captured in the evidence statements presented in the tables in the Policy Summary document online (Merkur et al. 2013: 48–72). Below, we have summarized some of the most important findings of the study by looking at important interventions and policy actions aimed at combating the major risk factors.

In the topic areas presented below, which focus on health-promoting interventions, it is necessary to recognize that we are not usually talking about interventions in isolation, but packages of actions – this can be seen most clearly in the smoking, alcohol, diet, and physical activity chapters, but applies more generally. The marginal benefits of expanded packages of actions often would still be considered cost-effective.

Tobacco smoking

The most cost-effective single tobacco control policy has been identified as raising taxes. The most cost-effective health care intervention to tackle smoking includes brief opportunistic advice from a general practitioner, along with telephone or self-help material. Pregnant women provide a particularly important group where low-cost smoking cessation interventions would be cost saving. An effective area towards raising awareness and changing attitudes, particularly in emerging economies, is the use of mass media campaigns, but these are often neglected. Other actions, such as labelling, smoking restrictions in public places and full advertising bans, often generate savings in health care expenditures which offset implementation costs. Importantly, the most effective means of reducing youth smoking is to reduce adult smoking via the mechanism of price increases, smoke-free policies, and of good, well-directed multimedia programmes.

Alcohol

Economic efficiency can be improved in the alcohol market when the negative externalities due to alcohol consumption can be reduced and where the socially optimum level of alcohol is sold and consumed in society. The three most cost-effective alcohol policies for reducing alcohol-related harm, and ones which correct some of alcohol's market failures, are price increases, restrictions on availability, and bans on advertising. Impediments to implementing effective policy in this area include failure to regulate the alcohol industry and to engage it in reducing harm in any meaningful way.

Physical inactivity

There is a strong economic case for investing in the promotion of physical activity. This is a leading contributor to good health, but more than one-third of Europeans are not sufficiently active. Mass media campaigns have been shown to have a positive, moderate effect on the increase of physical activity in targeted populations with a good cost-effectiveness ratio, and could even be cost saving. Brief primary care interventions to encourage physical activity, despite the higher cost, have been shown to be cost-effective. Some school-based interventions, particularly those that combine actions on physical activity and diet, seem to be more efficient than interventions on a single domain. Community-based interventions focussing on walking in particular (using pedometers) have been shown to be effective as well as cost-effective in the short term.

Unhealthy diets

When looking at policy actions to address unhealthy diets, taxes on foods high in salt, sugar, fat, and on junk food, are consistently cost saving and have a favourable health impact at the population level; both effectiveness and distributional impact of taxes appear to be enhanced by coupling them with subsidies targeting healthy foods or disadvantaged consumers. When designing interventions, one must be mindful of the challenge of product substitution when tax is used as an instrument, as consumers may switch to products that are also not healthy (as discussed later on). Policies aimed at the market environment for food choices, including making fruit and vegetables more available in schools, were found to have positive though modest effects on dietary intake and were cost-effective. Product reformulation policies (i.e. reducing salt in processed foods) were found to be cost saving or cost-effective, but the economic evidence on other efforts (e.g. to reduce trans-fat content) is very limited. The economic evidence on information campaigns is mixed, though food labelling schemes (especially mandatory ones) were found to perform better in terms of cost-effectiveness.

Environmental hazards for children

Because children are uniquely vulnerable to many common exposures in the environment, tackling environmental pollutants can help to protect children's health. Abating mercury emissions by burning less or cleaner coal at power plants, or by capturing mercury during combustion, can reduce mercury hazards where the forecast health benefit is four times the cost. Similarly, lead decontamination in homes provides benefits in terms of avoided cost of illness. Positive health impacts have also been shown from reducing outdoor air pollution from, for example, ozone and fine particulate matter, with efforts including congestion-charging schemes. In line with the objectives of the European Commission's REACH (Regulation on Registration, Evaluation, Authorisation and Restriction of Chemicals) legislation, lots of damage can be avoided by shifting the burden of proof towards those proposing the introduction of a new, poorly understood chemical, and away from those analysing the negative health impacts of chemicals.

Road-related injuries

Cost-effective road safety policies have the potential to reduce injuries and deaths caused by road traffic accidents. Many interventions in this area are not only cost-effective, but likely to be cost saving from a societal perspective. These include road environmental modifications (i.e. traffic-calming measures, speed limit zones), police/technological enforcement of traffic regulations, investment in vehicle safety features and special targeted actions for high-risk drivers. This is also an area where there is substantial information available on the impact of legislative interventions. Furthermore, there is scope to work with industry to enhance safety standards of vehicles, and technological changes can be phased in over time.

Mental health

In an effort to protect mental health and prevent depression, there are cost-effective actions that are relatively simple, feasible and potentially scalable, across the life course and in different settings. For younger children at risk of developing conduct disorders, interventions targeting parents, parents and children – as well as those including parents – child-based training and teacher training, can be cost-effective, particularly when taking account of the well-document lifetime adverse impacts of poor mental health developing in childhood. Interventions to prevent depression in at-risk adolescents through after-school screening, and subsequent psychological intervention, would be cost-effective. New mothers at risk of post-natal depression (as identified by health visitors), coupled with subsequent therapy, appears cost-effective. Workplace interventions that can prevent depression and anxiety can be cost saving from a business perspective for white-collar employment; this area provides another example of the importance of working outside the governmental sector to promote health. There are potentially cost-effective actions for older people, from regular participation in group-based activities to tackle risks, to mental health and well-being that arise from isolation and loneliness, and stepped care approaches for older people at risk of depression (as identified in the primary care setting). Depression prevention in adults, which can be made accessible through self-help formats, that in some cases can be delivered through new technologies, reaching hard-to-reach populations such as young men, is potentially cost-effective, and may be cost saving when accounting for productivity losses averted.

Social determinants

When working to improve the social determinants of health, the economic returns from investing in early childhood development intervention programmes are larger when the programmes follow a more targeted approach (e.g. high-risk or disadvantaged populations), involve children as participants, focus on enhancing parenting efficacy, and have better trained staff. But both targeted and universally delivered early childhood development interventions can demonstrate good value for money, despite the likelihood of underestimation of benefits due to the omission of health benefits in many cost-benefit calculations. The economic evidence for the financial returns from investments in education is well-established, and the added value of the health benefits of education further strengthens the overall case. The economic case for investing in early years interventions has been strengthened by evidence from numerous birth cohort studies that there are long-term consequences of adverse health in childhood – not just poor health, but poor educational outcomes, employment and career prospects, difficulties in personal relationships, and more risk of contact with criminal justice systems. This is an example of how long-term monitoring systems can help inform the evidence base for health promotion and disease prevention.

Measurement considerations

There are some key considerations for policymakers and others when considering and interpreting the evidence provided by economic evaluations in health promotion and disease prevention. First, to account for the way that intervention outcomes are measured – in natural units, utilities or monetary values, depending on the type of economic evaluation technique used. Utility measures like quality-adjusted life-years (QALYs) and disability-adjusted life-years (DALYs) are the most commonly used generic outcome measures.

There are also challenges in the way in which evidence of effectiveness can be determined. For many complex interventions it may be difficult to conduct randomized controlled trials, and other forms of study design have to be used. They may have greater risks of bias in their internal validity, but may be more helpful in terms of external validity, especially where issues such as cultural sensitivity and appropriateness are considered – the cost-effectiveness of interventions for health promotion and disease prevention will often be heavily influenced by rates of uptake and continued participation. Modelling studies, which synthesize costs and benefits from a number of studies, are also widely used. They can be helpful in assessing the potential long-term economic benefits of investment, and can also be adjusted to take account of uncertainty – for instance, in respect of levels of effectiveness and uptake rates. These types of studies can also be used to model the long time horizons by using intermediate outcomes, e.g. stopping smoking or changing a risky behaviour. Taking a long-term perspective is necessary in many cases because, with interventions, the largest health gain is to be expected when a healthy lifestyle is adapted early on (possibly in childhood) and maintained throughout adulthood.

Moreover, it is useful to consider differences in the cost-effectiveness and equity implications of interventions between several population subgroups, because public health interventions have a high potential to reduce socioeconomic health inequalities, but can in some circumstances widen health inequalities depending on which population groups actually make use of an intervention.

Specific gaps in the evidence

The evidence presented in this book has relied on published articles and larger studies; where systematic reviews have been undertaken on a policy or intervention, these have been presented. Gaps in the evidence remain, and the evidence on many interventions is equivocal.

This book has focused on interventions for the prevention of chronic noncommunicable diseases (NCDs), and certain types of injuries. Less attention has been devoted to prevention efforts within the health care system, such as screening programmes or pharmacological prevention, and this book has not covered the prevention of infectious diseases. There are systematic reviews of evidence and studies on the cost-effectiveness of screening procedures, vaccinations and other interventions available from the National Institute of Health and Care Excellence and the Centers for Disease Control and Prevention.

There is also potential for using behavioural science to design interventions that could be more acceptable to users and/or may steer them to make a choice to engage in health promoting behaviour. There is emerging evidence on the potential of 'nudging' interventions, although this area is still in its infancy. Hollands et al. (2013) argue that the limitations of the evidence base for altering environments to induce behavioural change – so-called choice architecture – goes beyond a lack of evidence to an absence of definitions and concepts of what this actually means to public health interventions. The Behavioural Insights Team in England, which has worked on applying behavioural science principles to government policy, has promoted a Parliamentary Select Committee review to find that 'non-regulatory measures used in isolation, including "nudges", are less likely to be effective. Effective policies often use a range of interventions.' (UK Select Committee 2011). They also cautioned that the preference of government for non-regulatory interventions has prompted officials to 'exclude consideration of regulatory measures when thinking about behaviour change' (UK Select Committee 2011).

With regards to gaps in the evidence, in the literature on alcohol there remains insufficient evidence on the effectiveness of school-based interventions and mass media campaigns. There is a gap in the physical activity literature around community-based interventions with regards to walking. Future research could study the potential cost-effectiveness around walking groups and remote mediated interventions. Also, for children, mixed evidence remains on the cost-effectiveness of walking buses. Another area where the cost-effectiveness evidence is inconsistent is related to road traffic accidents, specifically national compulsory bicycle helmet laws. More studies could be undertaken in this area, as from a public sector perspective (where the private cost of purchasing helmets is omitted) the measure is likely to be highly cost-effective. Nevertheless, when considering cycling from a physical activity perspective, there is good evidence that a comprehensive set of infrastructures can lead to increases in cycling in a population.

Crucial gaps are also still present in the cost-effectiveness of potential policy options for combating unhealthy diets. Future research in this area could aim to examine the architecture of food choices and restricting junk food in schools. Effectiveness evidence needs to be gathered on supply-side changes triggered by government regulation and policies, as well as on agricultural and food-chain incentives. Another important area for research could examine the broader effects of interventions on people's overall preferences and dietary habits, rather than specific foods or nutrients.

Serious gaps remain in the children's environmental-health literature. Towards reducing outdoor air pollution, schemes for low-emission zone requirements need to be assessed for potential health and economic benefits. Future research could focus on combating the large uncertainties that remain in estimating the effects of environmental health hazards and improving our understanding of the long-term health impacts of early-life exposure to chemicals. Furthermore, additional coordination of assessments of children's environmental health risks, beyond traditional chemicals risks, is necessary for advancing global policy in this area.

Future work will also need to consider the lack of evidence on social determinants and the poor evidence of equity. New technologies may offer some potential to test the evidence on effectiveness and equity. For example, work on virtual (but real) supermarkets using computer software is being used to study food choice in a randomized controlled trial in New Zealand.

There is a high concentration of evidence in a small number of countries, as seen in the evidence tables (these can be found in the Policy Summary document available online: Merkur et al. 2013: 48–72). This presents challenges when considering the appropriateness of actions in different countries or settings. For instance, there is very little evidence from most countries in the east of the European Region. This may have many causes, including capacity issues, issues of priority, publication of early work in languages that are inaccessible to researchers abroad, etc.

Study assumptions and limitations

In order to conduct rigorous economic evaluations, good evidence must be available. Some economic evaluations make up for gaps in the effectiveness evidence by making assumptions and extrapolations. The specific methodological assumptions and techniques involved in cost-effectiveness analyses can have significant implications. The main assumptions include the value of health and life, the appropriate discount rate, the selected end point, as well as taking the economic perspective rather than other ethical considerations, such as fairness and distributive justice. Even where evidence is available, it can suffer from a lack of generalizability and reliance on relatively weak investigation approaches.

One of the key challenges for effectively utilizing economic evaluation to assess public health interventions is the length of the causal chain between interventions and outcomes. Rather than wait for the long time horizon to pass between intervention and health outcome, researchers have to use intermediate outcomes or risk factors – which have a shorter time horizon – to calculate expected outcomes or long-term effects using a modelling approach. The challenges with modelling are that many assumptions have to be made, including about the long-term effects of a policy. For example, when considering a school-based intervention it is necessary to make an assumption about what percentage of children will retain in the long term the health-related information that is taught (i.e. to not smoke) or the behavioural change that is introduced (i.e. to eat more fruit and vegetables). Although some studies use intermediate outcomes, the key challenge remains to effectively map clinical disease pathways to improve the validity of modelling approaches in all relevant areas for public health intervention.

Next, it is difficult to predict what individuals will consume as substitutes, e.g. for a fat tax on soft drinks, individuals may consume another beverage that falls outside the tax, but has a comparable amount of sugar. Another example of substitution is the German alcopop tax, which simply switched consumption of spirits-based mixed beverages to beer-based mixed beverages. Since individuals make substitutions that may cause interventions to have unintended consequences, policies must be designed carefully to avoid undesirable substitution effects. Moreover, the food industry, for instance, is continuously innovating, creating new complex foods that may serve as substitutes in the future; the alcohol and tobacco industries continue to make substitution products as well, thus relevant regulations may need to increase in scope to catch these new substitutes.

There are many challenges to communicating health-promotion messages effectively. For instance, vested interests have actively worked against research findings that damage their particular interests. In Chapter 13, examples are provided for the tobacco industry, asbestos industry and others about how commercial interests can use weak but well-resourced arguments to challenge good evidence regarding health promotion. Therefore, it is important to effectively communicate the evidence to counter this – for example, by providing information using language that is accessible and easily understood by the public.

For some policy actions which have been shown to have positive economic gains, and for which there is already legislation implemented in most European countries – for example, motorcycle helmet legislation – the behaviour may continue to vary due to cultural norms. Furthermore, to combat mental health problems in the target group of new mothers, a preventative intervention for women at high risk of developing post-partum depression would require an understanding and recognition of early risk factors, along with the availability of relevant health professionals to reach this group. These examples show that, even where there is a strong case for careful investment in action, any intervention needs to be sensitive to local conditions, culture, infrastructure and resources. The importance of context in any evaluation, whether analysing effectiveness or cost-effectiveness, must not be overlooked.

In particular, when examining programmes to tackle the social determinant of health, it is difficult to compare results across interventions. This has to do with the intensity of interventions, different ages of participants in early childhood interventions, and given the large differences in costs and saving components included in the estimations. Also, when analysing early childhood development interventions from a health perspective, economic evaluations have scarcely taken account of the health benefits; thus the full return on investment may actually be higher than what is suggested by current studies.

In areas where there is a scarcity of evaluative and economic evidence generated in low- and middle-income countries (for example on road safety), this raises challenges in the potential transferability of cost-effective interventions across the European region. There are also areas where the majority of evidence comes from other regions. For example, there is a strong American bias on the evaluation of early childhood development interventions, as well as a scarcity of European evidence on the long-term effects of these programmes. Furthermore, more evidence is needed on cost-effective interventions in low- and middle-income countries.

Even when the above obstacles are understood and potentially overcome, simply identifying that there is an economic case for action, or even to identify cost-effective interventions, is just the start. The implementation of actions faces many challenges. Cross-sectoral working is vital, as many of the costs – as well as some benefits – fall outside the health sector and under the responsibility of other government ministers, i.e. education, environment, finance, transport and even agriculture. In areas where effective policies will need to combine a range of actions at different levels, e.g. in tackling tobacco smoking, alcohol consumption or improving road safety, there remains a need to further develop methods to estimate the effectiveness and cost-effectiveness of different packages of interventions that could be included in a national policy involving other government ministries beyond the health minister.

Trends in cost-effective interventions

Most countries are putting efforts into improving health education and information. However, the evidence in this book has suggested that these measures alone are not sufficient, nor are they always cost-effective. More stringent measures, such as regulation of advertising or fiscal measures, are more intrusive on individual choices and more likely to generate conflict among relevant stakeholders, but are also likely to weigh less on public finances and to produce health returns more promptly.

Fiscal measures, such as taxation, are effective for increasing the prices of tobacco and alcohol towards reducing consumption. Advertising bans are also effective at reducing consumption levels, but these must be full bans. Nevertheless, fiscal measures are complex to design and enforce; their impact may be unpredictable; and they can bear more heavily on low-income groups than on those with higher incomes. Despite this latter point though, it can be argued that the low-income groups stand to gain the most from these interventions in terms of increased health outcomes. For example, food taxes are likely to be regressive, although the less well off also benefit disproportionately from their effects.

Having different government ministries working together with the ministry of health is an important consideration, as many of the interventions discussed in the book are often delivered outside the health care system, using resources from different areas of government spending. Although there may be discussion in various levels of government on the importance of health in all policies, there may be little in the way of institutional structures and communication mechanisms to encourage action. Chapter 14 provides a long list of barriers to the cross-sectoral implementation of health-promotion measures. However, some methods have been proposed to promote intersectoral work, including presenting the economic benefits to non-health sectors of investing in health-promoting interventions; tearing down silos between budgets, with different forms of shared financing on either a voluntary or mandatory basis; and bringing budgets together can help embed health impacts in all policies. These methods require trust, and approaches need to be tailored to account for different political climates and cultures, infrastructure and resources.

The economics of health promotion in the future

The ideas and evidence explored in this book provide a valuable starting point for action, but also bring forward a research agenda for the future. Ongoing work in the areas already discussed will allow policymakers to consider a broader range of actions in the future. By undertaking research in the areas listed below, decision-makers will gain greater insights and better knowledge for the full range of outcomes those interventions may produce.

Areas for future work in the various areas include:

- Creating consistent monitoring systems of epidemiological data will help to understand differences in disease burden between countries.
- Monitoring different policy efforts in risk factor areas between countries could help researchers explain some of the differences in lifestyle factors.
- Undertaking research into national policies which include the important elements of multiple, coherent, long-lasting and large-scale strategies.
- Bettering our understanding of how to facilitate closer cooperation between all the relevant actors in different government ministries.
- Improving methods of engagement and voluntary participation by industry towards health-promoting efforts particularly related to tobacco, alcohol and food.
- For mental health, collecting evidence on different workplace settings – for example, where staff turnover is high and skill requirements low – would help strengthen the case for companies to invest. Also, improving our understanding of the links between mental and physical health to make a more holistic argument for prevention.
- Expanding research on early childhood development to other parts of the European Region. Previously, much of the evidence had come from the United States, but there are now many European studies underway to assess a variety of interventions in a European context, especially in the United Kingdom, the Netherlands and the Nordic countries.

- Understanding the long-term benefits of better psychological well-being, and understanding whether better well-being is actually going to be a protective factor for health at a future point in time.

Reducing the risk of chronic diseases and injury through interventions aimed at modifying lifestyle risk factors is possible and cost-effective, and potentially could reduce health inequalities within countries. However, turning the tide of chronic health problems that have assumed epidemic proportions during the course of the twentieth century requires fundamental changes in the social norms that regulate individual and collective behaviours. Such changes can only be triggered by wide-ranging prevention strategies addressing multiple determinants of health across social groups. The challenge now is to look at ways in which the evidence may be used to translate evidence-based knowledge into routine everyday practice across all of the WHO European Region.

References

Hollands, G., Shemilt, I., Marteau, T. et al. (2013) Altering micro-environments to change population health behaviour: Towards an evidence base for choice architecture interventions, *BMC Public Health*, 13: 1218. doi: 10.1186/1471-2458-13-1218.

Merkur, S., Sassi, F. and McDaid, D. (2013) *Promoting Health, Preventing Disease: Is there an Economic Case?* Policy summary 6. Copenhagen: WHO Regional Office for Europe. Available at http://www.euro.who.int/__data/assets/pdf_file/0004/235966/e96956.pdf?ua=1 [Accessed September 2014].

UK Select Committee (2011) *Science and Technology Committee – Second Report: Behaviour Change*. London: British Parliament. Available at http://www.publications.parliament.uk/pa/ld201012/ldselect/ldsctech/179/17902.htm [Accessed 30 April 2014].

Index

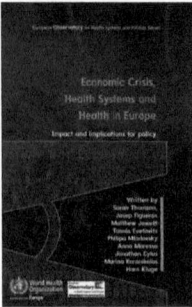

Economic Crisis, Health Systems and Health in Europe
Impact and implications for policy

Sarah Thomson et al

ISBN: 978-0-335-26400-1 (Paperback)
eBook: 978-0-335-26401-8
2015

Economic Crisis, Health Systems and Health in Europe looks at how health systems in Europe reacted to pressure created by the financial and economic crisis that began in 2008. The book is essential reading for anyone who wants to understand the choices available to policy-makers - and the implications of failing to protect health and health-system performance.

Key features include:

- Analysis of health system responses to the crisis in three policy areas
- Identification of policies most likely to sustain the performance of health systems facing financial pressure
- Explores the political economy of implementing reforms in a crisis

www.openup.co.uk

OPEN UNIVERSITY PRESS
McGraw - Hill Education